Business and the State in International Relations

T0382818

Interventions • Theory and Contemporary Politics

Stephen Eric Bronner, Series Editor

Business and the State in International Relations,
edited by Ronald W. Cox

Education, Democracy, and Public Knowledge,
Elizabeth A. Kelly

*Unequal Struggle: Class, Gender, Race, and Power
in the U.S. Congress,* John C. Berg

The Revision of Psychoanalysis, Erich Fromm

*Corporate Society: Class, Property, and Contemporary
Capitalism,* John McDermott

Television and the Crisis of Democracy, Douglas Kellner

FORTHCOMING

Technical Fouls: Democracy and Technical Change,
John Kurt Jacobson

*Crises and Transitions: A Critique of the
International Economic Order,* David Ruccio,
Stephen Resnick, and Richard D. Wolff

Business and the State in International Relations

EDITED BY

Ronald W. Cox

Routledge
Taylor & Francis Group

LONDON AND NEW YORK

First published 1996 by Westview Press

Published 2018 by Routledge
52 Vanderbilt Avenue, New York, NY 10017
2 Park Square, Milton Park, Abingdon, Oxon OX14 4RN

Routledge is an imprint of the Taylor & Francis Group, an informa business

Copyright © 1996 Taylor & Francis

A CIP catalog record for this book is available from the Library of Congress.
ISBN 13: 978-0-367-01740-8 (hbk)
ISBN 13: 978-0-367-16727-1 (pbk)

Contents

Acronyms

ABC	American Broadcasting Company
ACDA	Arms Control and Disarmament Agency
AFL-CIO	American Federation of Labor and Congress of Industrial Organizations
AMD	Advanced Micro Devices
ASC	American Security Council
CBI	Caribbean Basin Initiative
CBS	Columbia Broadcasting System
CCAA	Caribbean/Central American Action
CDM	Coalition for a Democratic Majority
CED	Committee for Economic Development
CEO	chief executive officer
CIA	Central Intelligence Agency
CPD	Committee of the Present Danger
DFI	direct foreign investment
ECAT	Emergency Committee on American Trade
EIA	Electronics Industry Association
EPROM	erasable programmable read-only memory
FDI	foreign direct investment
GATT	General Agreement on Tariffs and Trade
GDP	gross domestic product
GOP	Grand Old Party
IMF	International Monetary Fund
MFN	most-favored nation
MIC	military-industrial complex
MITI	Ministry of International Trade and Industry (Japan)
MNC	multinational corporation
MPSSL	Maritime Protection Services of Sierra Leone
NAFTA	North American Free Trade Agreement
NAM	National Association of Manufacturers
NATO	North Atlantic Treaty Organization
NBC	National Broadcasting Company
NMTBA	National Machine Tool Builders Association

NSC	National Security Council
NSIC	National Strategy Information Center
OEP	Office of Emergency Planning
OPEC	Organization of Petroleum Exporting Countries
PAC	political action committee
PAN	Partido Accion Nacional (right-wing Mexican group)
PEER	"Public Economy Emergency Regulations"
PMDB	Partido Movimento Democratico Brasileiro (Brazilian opposition party)
SALT	Strategic Arms Limitation Talks
SIA	Semiconductor Industry Association
SSI	Specialist Services International
UN	United Nations
USTR	United States Trade Representative
VER	voluntary export restraint
WAF	West African Fisheries

Foreword: "Serious Business"

In scholarship, unlike finance, events only rarely furnish irrevocable proof of comprehensive bankruptcy. In 1989, however, the Berlin Wall abruptly crumbled, leaving a whole generation of lavishly subsidized Western analysts in a position strikingly reminiscent of that of the fictional Wizard of Oz. Since then, one subfield after another of political science and international relations has experienced predictive failures of almost equally wrenching magnitude. Instead of trying to take over the world, or even catch up with the United States, the Soviet Union disintegrated in a cloud of rescheduled debts. So did the "Evil Empire's" eastern satellites.

The famously unchanging Japanese party system (the so-called 1955 system) suddenly broke into pieces, as police moved in on the gold hoard amassed by the single most powerful leader of the long-dominant Liberal Democratic Party, and the party itself committed binary fission. No less inconveniently for the neoclassical economists who dominate the U.S. policy debate, the Japanese trade surplus with the United States, which was supposed to disappear, kept growing.

In Italy, magistrates finally ventured where social scientists had never dared to tread: They brought to light a gigantic system of payoffs and political corruption involving the country's major political parties and the best-known businesses. In France, a series of mysterious deaths (including one in the Elysee Palace itself) and court investigations revealed a dense network of financial ties stretching between major business and political figures—an arrangement that looks far more like Italy's (or that of the prewar Third Republic) than anyone would ever have guessed from reading postwar academic literature.

Equally surprising from an academic standpoint were events in Spain. Former top officials of the Spanish Central Bank, high-ranking business figures, and parts of the police and security services have all been implicated in a series of scandals that now seems likely to bring down the government. In the United States, a well-known election analyst published a study debunking *The Myth of the Independent Voter* virtually on the eve of an election in which a billionaire achieved one of the best showings by a third-party candidate in the country's history. And after a congressional election that broke all records for total (on-the-record) public spending, journalists and citizens are beginning to ask why academic analysts of Latin America failed to foresee the debacle of the Mexican peso crisis.

Events such as these make weather forecasting look like an exact science. Such performance threatens the good name of empirical social science; and, in the long run, it could discredit the whole enterprise. Thus the publication of books such as this one should be readily welcomed. Political science— indeed, all the social sciences—desperately needs to pay far more attention to the world economy. As do the various essays in this book, it needs to investigate in a nondogmatic fashion how industrial structure, financial variables, and related factors help shape political outcomes in the real world. Is it too much to hope that in an era in which even the Soviet Politburo eventually warmed to "new thinking," comparative politics and international relations can also acknowledge that the cold war is over and centrally address the kinds of questions so challengingly tackled by the essays in this book?

Thomas Ferguson

Introduction: Bringing Business Back In—The Business Conflict Theory of International Relations
ౌ
Ronald W. Cox

A group of scholars in international and comparative politics has argued that state officials act autonomously in the formulation and implementation of policy. Often dubbed the "statist" or "realist" tradition, this school of thought contends that state bureaucracies are able to advance their own agendas against the competing demands of societal interest groups. The dominance of the statist paradigm has meant that the power and influence of business groups has often been minimized or ignored in the study of international politics.[1]

Each author in this volume provides a theoretical and empirical contribution to an alternative paradigm in international politics, which is labeled the "business conflict" model. This model represents a challenge to the realist paradigm by focusing on the importance of business-state alliances in determining policy outcomes. Contributors argue that business interests have been central players in international politics and often work with government officials in the development of policy options. The power of business is articulated through the interaction of three entities within the international system: the nation-state, the multinational corporation, and domestic firms. It is argued that firms' policy preferences are related to their sectoral position within the world economy and that policy differences among business groups are reflected in policy disputes at the level of the nation-state.[2] In addition, attention is focused on how business conflict is mediated through state institutions in the formulation of foreign policy and trade policy.

This volume concentrates on two central actors in international politics: multinational corporations and the U.S. state. It is proffered here that business groups maximize power by working with powerful state bureaucracies in formulating and implementing foreign policy. The U.S. state is an especially appropriate level of analysis, since its military and foreign policy bureaucracies allow it to carry out a wide range of policies that have a major impact upon the world system. The multinational corporation is important because of its sophisticated hierarchical structure and vast political and economic resources that allow it to be influential in a wide variety of settings, either vis-à-vis the U.S. state or a less-developed state in need of investment.

The relationship among U.S.-based multinational corporations, the U.S. state, and domestic U.S. business firms is important for the development of the business conflict model. Contrary to the dominant opinion within international relations literature, the multinational corporation (MNC) often relies on institutional connections with powerful state elites to further its agenda. The MNC should not be viewed as a "floating" international actor with no ties to domestic nation-states. Instead, multinational firms depend on their home-based corporate headquarters to develop both economic and political strategies to promote investment and trade abroad. The extent to which MNCs are successful depends on the depth of their institutional ties to political elites in the United States. and elsewhere, and on the resistance to their policies by domestic societal actors, including domestic business firms and labor interests.

Furthermore, both multinational and domestic business firms rely on powerful states such as the United States to pursue foreign policy agendas consistent with their interests. Debates over U.S. foreign policy involve competition between interest blocs that include government bureaucracies and their allies in the business world. In the United States, the State Department often solicits the advice of business groups such as the Business Roundtable, the Business Advisory Council, the Council on Foreign Relations, and the National Foreign Trade Council, to name a few. In the area of U.S. trade policy, these business groups typically advance the agenda of corporations and policymakers who favor free trade policies. Conversely, regional trade associations, local chambers of commerce, and, in some cases, labor unions concentrate on their institutional ties to local congressional districts in order to advance a protectionist agenda supported by less competitive domestic firms. In this fashion, the federal political structure of the United States mediates and conditions the influence of multinational and domestic business firms in the area of U.S. trade policy. As Cox and Stant point out in their contributions to this volume, recent U.S. trade policies, such as Super 301, the North American Free Trade Agreement (NAFTA), and the Caribbean Basin Initiative (CBI), have been influenced by competition between interest blocs of policymakers and business elites.

This insight is especially important in explaining U.S. foreign policy in the post–cold war period, when statist paradigms predict important shifts in policymaking as a result of the demise of the Soviet threat. For statist theorists, U.S. foreign policy and, to a large extent, trade policy were driven by geostrategic competition between the United States and the Soviet Union. In contrast, this volume argues that U.S. policies cannot be explained adequately by anticommunism. Instead, business groups were often able to influence the adoption of policies designed to counter the Soviet threat, and they are likely to remain influential in the post–cold war period. Anticommunism may have provided the overriding rationale for U.S. policy during the cold war, but it cannot explain why some policies were chosen over others. This explanation requires attention to the relationship between business interests and state policymakers.

Business Conflict and Sectoral Interests

Most of the contributors to this study focus on attempting to understand the nature of political divisions among organized business interests and on how those divisions impact upon policymaking. In the areas of U.S. trade and foreign policy, business groups often adopt different political positions depending on their sectoral position in the domestic and global economies. Sectoral position refers to the productive characteristics of business firms, such as their relative stake in international investments, whether or not such investments are labor-intensive or capital-intensive, and the location of such investments on a regional and a global scale. The extent to which firms are directly interested in international politics, including U.S. trade and foreign policy questions, usually hinges on how their particular sectoral position is affected by policy decisions.

In a study of business interests and the Vietnam War, Erik Devereux argues that business firms took opposing positions on the war based mainly on how the war was affecting (or was perceived to be affecting) their sectoral economic interests. Devereux traces the ideological expression of business conflict through the pages of competing U.S. newspapers, based on the premise that newspaper editorials on the Vietnam War tended to coincide with the views of blocs of investors linked to individual publications.

In a sophisticated theoretical elaboration, Devereux provides convincing evidence that capital-intensive investors, especially commercial and investment banking, real estate, and home construction industries, came to oppose the war because increased military spending was contributing to spiraling inflation and deepening balance-of-payments deficits. These investors, which Devereux labels "liberal internationalists," did not gain increased profits from increased military spending. Rather, they were concerned that spending on the Vietnam War was "crowding out" the potential for lucrative investments elsewhere in the less developed world while creating potentially disastrous macroeconomic imbalances within the U.S. economy. These investors, as Devereux notes, were well positioned ideologically and organizationally to generate opposition to U.S. escalation in Vietnam.

Other blocs of investors supported a continuation of the war and, in some cases, an expansion of U.S. involvement. Firms with the most direct ties to military contracts and with a stake in basic manufacturing industries, such as steel, rubber, and textiles, favored a continued escalation of military spending. These firms, described by Devereux as "conservative Republicans," benefited from increased military spending and saw the war as a way to maintain increased production and sales in the midst of macroeconomic problems. Rather than end the war, which was preferred by their capital-intensive opponents, these firms wanted to continue the war and reduce the level of Great Society domestic spending, which was seen as the leading inflationary threat.

In a related chapter, David Gibbs explores the industrial firms and bureaucratic actors comprising the military-industrial complex. Like Devereux, Gibbs argues that business firms are divided in their policy preferences, with firms engaged in military or military-related production tending to support an aggressive U.S. foreign policy buttressed by increased military spending. Just as many of these firms supported increased military spending necessary to sustain the Vietnam War, they also supported increased military expenditures to contain the Soviet Union at the height of the second cold war of the late 1970s. Gibbs argues that military contractors combined with the Defense Department, military personnel, and intelligence organizations to form powerful lobbies that influenced U.S. foreign policymaking toward Afghanistan from 1979 through the 1980s.

Following Gibbs, Amy Ansell contends that the military-industrial complex was part of a broad coalition of firms and ideologues that promoted a "right turn" in U.S. foreign policy during the late 1970s and early 1980s. Ansell argues that business groups were influential in promoting dramatic increases in military spending during the last two years of the Carter administration and throughout the Reagan presidency. Affected by an international economic environment of increased competitive pressures and declining profit rates, various sectors of the business community shifted to the right by the late 1970s and advocated increased military spending and a more interventionist U.S. foreign policy. Ansell claims that business groups were more likely to advocate these policies if they had labor-intensive foreign investments, faced threats to their investments from insurgent movements in the Third World, were part of the military-industrial complex, and were ideologically oriented to the far right.

In addition to sectoral divisions over U.S. foreign policy, firms have split along sectoral lines in their relative commitment to free trade. William Stant identifies a liberal-internationalist historic bloc of U.S. firms and policymakers committed to free trade in the post–World War II period. Stant identifies capital-intensive manufacturers, international oil companies, mineral-extractive industries, investment bankers, and internationally oriented commercial bankers as the core of this coalition, which achieved its peak influence in the 1960s. By the 1970s, this coalition had fallen apart as a result of defections by firms facing declining profit rates and intensified international competition. In an elegant theoretical model, Stant locates the disintegration of this coalition within a "trade-political cycle," whereby multinational firms faced with high import competition and low trade dependence have been most likely to break away from the free trade coalition.

In a similar analysis, Ronald Cox posits that a diverse coalition of multinational firms have come together to promote regional trade agreements that depart from the multilateralism of the General Agreement on Tariffs and Trade (GATT). Cox argues that U.S.-based multinationals in the auto and electronics industries have promoted trade agreements that institutionalize discrimination against foreign firms who are late entrants to the North American and Caribbean Basin markets. These multinationals have sought restrictive regional content laws in order to deflect competition from Japanese and European firms for the U.S. market. As foreign direct investors, they view NAFTA and CBI as protective measures taken against vigorous foreign competition. Other U.S. firms, more competitive in global markets and favoring the multilateralism of GATT, have supported regional trade agreements as a "second-best" alternative to a renewed multilateralism. At the same time, these interests are opposed by nationalist firms who have joined with labor bureaucracies to oppose NAFTA.

In a third analysis of sectoral pressures in U.S. trade policy, Jerri-Lynn Scofield argues that a coalition of business groups in the 1960s pressured the State Department to increase cooperation with the Soviet Union in order to open trade opportunities. A key factor in the successful mobilization of this coalition was the Soviet Union's switch in its commodity pricing policy, that resulted in new trade opportunities for U.S. oil and commodity producers. Oil companies joined agricultural producers, capital equipment manufacturers, automobile producers, and computer manufacturers to form a powerful lobby that contributed to the pressures for détente in the late 1960s and early 1970s.

Finally, the economic and political context of the 1980s saw a weakening of state structures in Africa; this enhanced the power and privileges of business groups, especially of multinational corporations, allied with political elites. In the extreme case of West Africa, as William Reno points out, state structures have virtually collapsed, only to be replaced by a loose set of alliances between rival military strongmen and multinational corporations. At the very time statist theorists were "bringing the state back in," the importance of private actors in formulating state policies was actually increasing in Africa and elsewhere in the less-developed world.

In the case of Latin America, Jeffry Frieden shows how the debt crisis affected the political behavior of domestic business groups. According to

Frieden, business interests with fixed assets were especially burdened by the debt crisis and sought, on the one hand, to pressure various Latin American states to protect their investments; on the other hand, the response of liquid asset-holders to the debt crisis was to diversify their investments internationally to avoid the effects of currency depreciation and economic slowdown that faced Latin American countries. The result in Latin America has been a clash between business interests based on their sectoral position and their ability to strategically respond to the effects of the debt crisis.

In the final section of the volume, Greg Nowell compares and contrasts the business conflict approach (which he calls "neopluralist theory") to other international relations theories. Following Nowell, Dan Skidmore-Hess contrasts the business conflict approach with neo-Marxian theories of the state. Both authors argue that the business conflict model represents important advances over traditional and radical approaches to state theory.

The Political Implications of the Business Conflict Model

The insights of this volume suggest that business conflict has played an important role in affecting political outcomes in U.S. foreign policies. In addition, the international circumstances facing less-developed countries have strengthened business relative to other social actors. We argue that the business conflict model is more relevant to understanding international politics since the 1970s based on a number of specific developments, all of which are important for understanding the enhanced political power of business organizations. First, the increased competition within the world economy has resulted in a process of corporate restructuring that is international in scope. Such restructuring entails efforts by multinational corporations to reduce their costs by introducing new technologies that decrease the unit costs of production, by laying off workers, and by pressuring states to reduce regulations and social welfare programs that interfere with profit maximization.

In the U.S., such restructuring has resulted in a proliferation of business lobbying organizations committed to furthering government policies that weaken labor organizations. Corporate think tanks created in the mid-1970s have demanded a rollback in government spending on a range of regulatory and social programs that were advanced in the 1960s and early 1970s. In addition, there have been numerous instances of corporations using the threat of plant shutdowns or relocation within the United States and abroad to win greater bargaining power vis-à-vis organized labor. For corporations that are relatively labor-intensive, this has meant a shift to low-wage locations or nonunion environments. A classic example is the case of U.S. electronics, automobile, and textile industries in Mexico, where relocation has involved an effort to increase bargaining leverage with Mexican workers in nonunion settings. The result has been a steady decline in Mexican wages in U.S.-owned assembly plants.

On the one hand, there is clearly business conflict over a range of issues from U.S. trade policy to intervention, as this volume documents. On the other hand, many corporations have undertaken an aggressive strategy toward labor both in the United States and abroad, coupled with pressure on the state to reduce social costs (i.e., taxes and regulation) that impact upon profit margins. Statist theorists would expect states to be able to maintain their autonomy in this climate, given the fact that state actors still have impressive bureaucracies and large budgets that give them a stake in perpetuating their interests. As evidenced, however, even when states were better able to cope with business pressure during the relatively prosperous period of the 1960s, they still forged relations with business to advance particular policies. Now, because of increased business lobbying networks, the increasingly competitive international economic climate, and mounting pressure on states to reduce their regulatory apparatus, business groups are better positioned to influence policy. This book argues that these recent developments make the business conflict model more relevant than statist theory in explaining policy outcomes.

1

Industrial Structure, Internationalism, and the Collapse of the Cold War Consensus: Business, the Media, and Vietnam

Erik A. Devereux

Since the mid-1960s, the Vietnam War has emerged as one of the most important foci in the growing debate over the origins of U.S. foreign policy. Anyone interested in U.S. actions in Southeast Asia from 1945 to 1975 now confronts a voluminous literature that spans military, diplomatic and social history, international relations, U.S. politics, media studies, and public opinion research. Foreign policy scholars ranging in theoretical traditions from behavioral neo-realism to structural Marxism have offered their own explanations for the war. Yet with so many thousands of pages already published on the subject, the debate over why the United States fought in Vietnam roars on without any termination point in sight.

This chapter asserts that the lack of closure in the debate over Vietnam is the result of a critical weakness in the existing literature. Simply stated, the scholarship on the war fails to understand the domestic origins of the Vietnam policy. Specifically, the literature lacks an accurate assessment of the role of the U.S. business community—including the U.S. news media—in the evolution of the Vietnam War. This deficiency particularly has injured previous attempts to explain the actions of the Johnson administration during the momentous period between 1965 and 1968, when the United States sharply escalated its military intervention in Vietnam and then made the decision to end the war.

I argue that a correct understanding of the domestic influences on the Johnson administration is necessary for answering two vital questions regarding the formation of policy toward Vietnam: (1) Why did there appear to be such a strong domestic consensus in favor of the 1965 escalation of the Vietnam War?; and (2) How and why did that consensus decline dramatically after the first year of the escalation? These two questions pertain directly to the domestic political context within which the escalation decision was made and eventually reversed. A correct understanding of the domestic aspects of Vietnam also sheds considerable light on a third, more consequential, question: (3) Why did the collapse of the Vietnam consensus have a profound impact on the future conduct of U.S. foreign policy? Vietnam looms large in the debate over U.S. foreign policy because the war forever undermined the domestic, bipartisan foreign policy consensus forged in the decade following World War II. Before Vietnam, Republican and Democrat presidents successfully linked regional foreign policy crises in Greece, Egypt, Korea, Iran, Guatemala, Lebanon, and Laos to the overarching goal of containing communism. By the time Lyndon Johnson announced his decision to not seek re-election, the linkages between Vietnam and the cold war were irreparably broken. And, as a very frustrated Ronald Reagan learned some thirteen years later, in the aftermath of Vietnam it was difficult to link situations in Nicaragua, El Salvador, and elsewhere to the Soviet threat. Moreover, U.S. foreign policy emerged from Vietnam as a major focus of party competition, where it remains today a source of considerable dispute between the Democrat and Republican parties.

Reconsidering the Domestic Influences on Vietnam

The body of scholarship on Vietnam certainly acknowledges that there was an important domestic component to the war. In fact, the existing discussions recognize three potential domestic influences: public opinion, the news media, and the business community. But the treatment of these three influences in the literature tends to be both overly dogmatic and remarkably inaccurate.

Public Opinion and the Vietnam Syndrome

The prevalent view is that negative public opinion emerged as an unexpected domestic constraint on the foreign policy process to complicate, and eventually short-circuit, U.S. intervention in Southeast Asia. This view has given rise to the widespread belief in a "Vietnam syndrome," the supposedly novel phenomenon of the U.S. public categorically opposing all future use of military force in the aftermath of Vietnam. Subsequent foreign policy decisions, such as the Carter administration's attempt to rescue the hostages in Iran, the Reagan administration's covert Iran-Contra program, the Bush administration's overt military response to the Kuwait crisis of 1990, and the Clinton administration's actions in the former Yugoslavia, all have been seen as shaped considerably by the lasting legacy of Vietnam.

But with the benefit of two decades of hindsight, it is now known that there was nothing unusual about the trends in public support for the Vietnam intervention: Throughout the twentieth century, Americans have been skeptical about military intervention when their sons and daughters are dying in foreign lands for no clear purpose; public opposition increases in direct proportion to the total number of U.S. combat fatalities. There is no evidence that this feature of public attitude has changed significantly from the time prior to World War I, to that after the Vietnam War[1] This pattern suggests that the Vietnam syndrome itself is a myth, especially when it comes to the claim that Vietnam produced a sea change in public attitudes toward war.

For those who seek to explain the rise and decline of the Vietnam consensus and the long-term implications for U.S. foreign policy, public opinion thus offers little assistance. Across the course of the war, public support gradually declined as the casualties mounted. There was no turning point, or other dramatic pattern in the polls, that might explain the remarkable change of Vietnam policy in 1968. And following the conclusion of the U.S intervention, no evidence surfaced public opinion that could explain the long-lasting influences of Vietnam on foreign policymaking.

The Media Debate

In the case of the media, two opposed views dominate the literature. One perspective claims that the media, operating in the absence of formal military censorship, systematically encouraged domestic opposition to the war by subjecting the U.S. public to a continuous stream of unsettling, violent images while omitting from the news the major military, political, and social accomplishments of U.S. policy in the region.[2] Written several years after he left office, Richard Nixon's statement on the issue vividly evokes this view:

> The Vietnam War was complicated by factors that had never before occurred in America's conduct of a war. ... the American news media had come to dominate domestic opinion about its purpose and conduct ... Whatever the intention behind such relentless and literal reporting of the war, the result was a serious demoralization of the home front, raising the question whether America would ever again be able to fight an enemy abroad with unity and strength and purpose at home.[3]

The second perspective argues that the media generally echoed the "official line" on the war, rarely presented images of violence to the public, and reported favorably only the dissent over the war that developed inside the government while simultaneously downplaying the antiwar movement.[4]

Critics of U.S. foreign policy, such as Noam Chomsky and Edward Herman, evolve this second position one step further and claim that the media were an integral component of the government propaganda effort on behalf of the war:

It would have been impossible to wage a brutal war against South Vietnam and the rest of Indochina ... if the media had not rallied to the cause, portraying murderous aggression as a defense of freedom and only opening the doors to political disagreement when the costs to the interests they represent became too high.[5]

Although they differ completely on the substantive impact of the media, the two perspectives draw on an identical conception of how the media behaved politically with regard to Vietnam: According to both sides of the debate, the U.S. press was monolithic in its treatment of the intervention in Southeast Asia. Notably absent from the debate is a recognition or comprehension of considerable *diversity* in the media's response to Vietnam.

Returning to the fundamental issue of this study, the debate over the media also fails to yield insight into the rise and decline of the consensus on Vietnam. *This is because all participants in the debate define the influence of the media entirely in terms of the effects of Vietnam news on public opinion.* But, as I pointed out previously, the evidence regarding public opinion provides few insights into the course of Vietnam policy. So, regardless of whether the media tended to support or oppose the government position on the war, the entire focus of the media debate is completely misplaced.

Business Interests and Vietnam

Lastly, prior examinations of the role of the business community in Vietnam also offer two opposed and equally dogmatic arguments about how business interests shaped the war effort. Much of the criticism of the war launched by liberal commentators holds that Vietnam was the ultimate example of U.S. imperialism: a war operated for the express purpose of guaranteeing that U.S. businesses would control economic resources in the developing world. This interpretation disallows the possibility that there was systematic opposition to the war in some segments of the business community—even though such dissent existed.

Yet some influential academic quarters espouse the view that Vietnam demonstrates the *autonomy* of U.S. foreign policymaking from the interests of the business community. There are two key premises of this view: (1) U.S. business actually had little direct economic interest in Southeast Asia; (2) the largely negative impact of the war on the U.S. economy certainly was not preferred by the business community. Stephen Krasner made these points rather bluntly in his *Defending the National Interest* when he responded to the imperialism argument:

Vietnam cannot be understood in relation to direct economic interests; there were none. It is hard to make a case for indirect interests. Chomsky has argued that the war was important because it benefitted certain sectors of the American economy. However, these same sectors could have been supported in other ways. Rationalizing high levels of military expenditure would have been easier for the U.S. government to accomplish by picturing the Soviet Union and China as implacable enemies than by engaging in a land war in Southeast Asia. Superpower conflict provides the opportunity for virtually limitless expenditures, with no clear way of measuring what is really needed ... the financial benefits can be channelled more precisely, and the adverse consequences, such as inflation, can be better controlled.[6]

But this view does not recognize that many sectors of the U.S. economy actually did benefit considerably from Vietnam, or that many of these benefits would not have accrued without the war.[7] Furthermore, there is little acknowledgment in the autonomy argument that broader macroeconomic and domestic political considerations favored Vietnam over other alternatives when the decision to escalate was made in 1965.

Moving beyond the particular defects in these arguments, the more pressing problem is that any such monolithic conception of the business community and the war sheds little insight on the course of the U.S. intervention, or on the profound shift in U.S. foreign policy produced by Vietnam, or on the emergence of foreign policy issues after 1968 as a focus of partisan debates. If there was a general business interest in Vietnam, then that interest appeared to have declined markedly in just three years—a pattern not replicated in the cases of many other U.S. interventions documented elsewhere in this volume. And if the business community had little to do with Vietnam, then we are hard pressed to understand why there exists evidence that the war had such a profound impact on business attitudes toward U.S. foreign policy.[8]

Prospectus

The premise of this chapter is that there was a significant domestic component to U.S. policy in Vietnam, yet the standard treatments of public opinion, the media, and the business community leave us with little explanation of that component. In the remainder of the chapter, I present evidence that the crucial factor in understanding Vietnam, especially during the 1965–1968 period, was political competition and conflict within the U.S. business community. Organized primarily along issues of internationalism and macroeconomic policy, business conflict was expressed directly in the party politics of the period and in the behavior of the U.S. media. Furthermore, the media not only reflected business conflict over Vietnam, but it was also a crucial force in the evolution of business consensus behind the escalation in 1965 and in the decline of that consensus after 1965.

The next section considers the domestic economic and political considerations that encouraged the 1965 escalation and presents an account of the way in which a consensus was forged in the business and media communities to support the escalation. Then I present an analysis of how the economic impact of the war destroyed the pro-Vietnam consensus. Finally, the chapter concludes by relating the Vietnam case to the evolution of U.S. foreign policy since the New Deal and then offering a further theoretical analysis of the media and foreign policy making in the United States. This analysis provides insight into contemporary foreign policy problems and international politics in the aftermath of Vietnam.

Business, the Media, and the Decision to Escalate

Setting the Stage: The Triumph of Internationalism in 1964

With the Republican Party captured by its most conservative and nationalist elements under Arizona Senator Barry Goldwater, the logic of postwar U.S. elections was forced to its extreme limit in the 1964 presidential contest. Lyndon Johnson, a liberal-internationalist Democrat from Texas and a former protégé of Franklin Roosevelt, portrayed himself as the voice of mainstream America while successfully vilifying the Republican candidate as a radical and dangerous departure from the status quo whose policies would lead the country into ruin. Goldwater, in turn, directly challenged the framework of postwar U.S. foreign policy, including free trade and the network of security commitments so painstakingly constructed since 1945. In fact, the 1964 GOP (Grand Old Party) platform explicitly contained a commitment to import restrictions.

Given this stark contrast, huge segments of the multinational business community overwhelmingly and noisily flocked to Johnson. The broad coalition of multinational businesses that supported Lyndon Johnson in 1964 was assembled through a fascinating sequence of actions by political and business figures particularly close to the White House. Although the history of that process bears examination in detail, for the present purpose I restrict attention to the outcome: With explicit guidance from the administration, leading internationalist Republicans established the National Independent Committee for Johnson and Humphrey to coordinate the efforts of the multinational business community to turn back Goldwater.[9]

With much of his own party firmly entrenched in the enemy camp, Goldwater and his supporters fashioned an electoral strategy that further heightened the political differences in the election. The basic elements of their strategy included an emphasis on nationalism as a major theme in the campaign and a plan to generate an international financial crisis that might undermine both the Johnson campaign and the foundations of postwar economic policy.[10] When these plans were combined with Goldwater's statements favoring the use of nuclear weapons and opposing the network of global alliances built during the postwar period, the net result was an even

greater sense of urgency in much of the multinational business community—
and much of the media—that Goldwater should be destroyed politically.
With the lines over foreign policy so clearly drawn in the general election,
Lyndon Johnson was the perfect vehicle for preserving the principles of postwar U.S. internationalism in the face of this challenge.

In terms of 1964 newspaper coverage, Table 1.1 presents a breakdown of
newspaper endorsements in the general election. As indicated, Johnson benefited from the support of two different newspaper blocs in the 1964 election: A bloc of pro-Johnson, pro-Democrat newspapers and a much larger
bloc of anti-Goldwater newspapers. With several notable exceptions, the
most interesting cases of media behavior in the campaign occurred in the
middle bloc of anti-Goldwater voices in the press. As I have argued in detail
elsewhere, Goldwater's nationalism was a primary reason that these newspapers defected to the side of the Democrats.[11]

Table 1.1 Newspapers and the 1964 Presidential Election

Pro-Johnson[a]	Anti-Goldwater[b]	Pro-Goldwater[c]
Atlanta Constitution	*Albuquerque Journal*	*Arizona Republic*
Boston Globe	*Baltimore Sun*	*Birmingham News*
Denver Post	*Chicago Sun-Times*	*Charleston News and*
Fort Worth Star-Telegram	*Cleveland Plain Dealer*	*Courier*
Louisville Courier-Journal	*Dallas Morning News*	*Chicago Tribune*
Milwaukee Journal	*Fargo Forum*	*Idaho Daily Statesman*
Minneapolis Tribune	*Hartford Courant*	*Los Angeles Times*
New Orleans Times-	*Houston Post*	*Manchester Union Leader*
Picayune	*Indianapolis Star*	*San Diego Union*
New York Times	*Kansas City Star*	
St. Louis Post-Dispatch	*Memphis Commercial*	
Washington Post	*Appeal*	
	Miami Herald	
	New York Daily News	
	Omaha World Herald	
	Philadelphia Inquirer	
	Providence Journal	
	Richmond Times-	
	Dispatch	
	St. Louis Globe-Democrat	
	San Francisco Chronicle	
	Seattle Post-Intelligencer	
	Seattle Times	

Notes: a. Endorsed the Democrat for president, including Johnson, 1964–
1968. b. Endorsed Nixon in 1960 and 1968, but not Goldwater in 1964.
c. Endorsed the Republican for president, including Goldwater, 1960–1968.

Vietnam, the Fiscal War

The outcome of the 1964 campaign conclusively resolved the very sharp differences between Johnson and Goldwater, but the political situation in the United States remained extremely saturated. In putting together a coalition of interests and voters more than capable of burying Goldwater, the Johnson campaign made diverse policy commitments to multinational business, to labor, to the civil rights movement, and to other segments of the U.S. political arena. These commitments would be difficult to honor with a single, coherent policy agenda.

In fact, no single domestic policy program could hope to keep Johnson's 1964 coalition together; any attempt to formulate such a package could only return the administration to the intense political infighting experienced under Kennedy. *What was required to lend political viability to the Johnson administration was prosperity.* A high rate of economic growth would make possible substantial increases in domestic spending to satisfy a variety of demands on the administration, while reducing the friction likely to result from the aggressive foreign policies of a strongly internationalist regime at a time of growing unrest in the less-developed world. The question confronting the Johnson administration through 1964 and early 1965 was how to get the economy into a high-growth mode that would satisfy its diverse constituencies.

The search for an answer to this conundrum was made all the more difficult by three constraints. First, recent history included several major tax cuts that resulted from organized pressures from the multinational financial community.[12] Additional tax cuts would be difficult to implement on the heels of the 1963 and 1964 measures. Second, by mid-1964 there was growing evidence that the tax cuts and the free trade measures implemented by Kennedy and Johnson would not keep the economy on an high-growth trajectory. Many economists were predicting a sluggish performance for the U.S. economy for the first quarter of 1965. The issue of growth thus was an immediate threat to the political health of the administration. Third, Republicans and conservative Democrats in the Congress were demonstrably opposed to the Johnson administration on many basic issues of economic and social policy. A return to the acrimonius relations with Congress that marred the Kennedy years would be fatal.

Looking at this picture from inside the White House, evidence abounds that the reasoning behind the 1965 escalation of the Vietnam War had as much to do with the economic objectives of the Johnson administration as it did with geopolitical security concerns.[13] Bluntly put, the Vietnam War initially appeared to be a vital component of a plan to immediately stimulate high growth in the economy without resort to tax cuts. As such, the war also uniquely satisfied many of the demands the administration faced following the election.

Vietnam, in particular, was good to multinational business because the huge defense procurements translated directly into entries in the profit column for many firms, while the buildup in *conventional forces* offered guarantees of protection for their foreign operations elsewhere than Vietnam.[14] Vietnam also represented a huge subsidy to many of the older manufacturing interests that traditionally supported the Republican Party. With a military presence of millions of personnel extended across the United States through the Pacific to Vietnam—all requiring vehicles, weaponry, and clothing—the automobile, aerospace, steel, metal mining, textile, rubber, and shoe industries initially found themselves to be the considerable beneficiaries of the major foreign policy of a Democratic administration.[15]

Domestic construction interests, particularly those with close ties to Johnson, benefited spectacularly from the huge construction projects required by the military in Vietnam.[16] As captured in a September 1965 memorandum from then-Under Secretary of Defense Cyrus Vance to the president, Johnson himself intervened in the military planning process to increase the role in Vietnam of construction firms such as Houston-based Brown and Root.[17] On the labor side, the economic stimulus from defense spending would ease the downward pressure on wages, keeping labor unions quiescent while encouraging heavy consumer demand. In fact, many labor unions recognized their stake in the policy and went out of their way to support Johnson on the war.

And if the economy could be kept in a high-growth mode through a combination of defense spending, tax measures, and lower interest rates (this last another feature of the Kennedy-Johnson economic policies), then aggressive domestic programs such as the Great Society could be implemented without too much strain on the federal budget. Besides strengthening the loyalty of minority voters to the Democrats, the poverty programs also held a wide variety of benefits for Johnson's political investors, including the complex of finance, real estate, and construction interests involved in urban economic renewal. Although the willingness of the Johnson administration to combine a progressive domestic program with the Vietnam War often was seen as an appalling contradiction, the two sides of the Democrats' agenda in the latter half of the 1960s in fact went hand in hand.

In this way, Vietnam seemed to span the breadth of the business coalition that rallied behind Johnson in 1964 and, in the case of nationalistic Republican industries such as steel and textiles, held out the prospect of broadening that coalition in preparation for 1968. Vietnam also offered another political benefit: A strong commitment to fighting communism would ease the way in Congress for the passage of controversial domestic legislation. During the first few years of the escalation, powerful conservatives in Congress did restrain their criticisms of the administration's domestic policies because of their support for Vietnam.

If the administration had any doubts about the fiscal logic of Vietnam, those doubts were erased in 1964 and 1965. Throughout these years, as the 1964 tax cut, the Gulf of Tonkin Resolution, and the first supplemental appropriation of $700 million for Vietnam were passed, good economic news kept arriving at the White House that showed substantial growth projections for 1965 and beyond.[18] By the middle of 1965, with the escalation well under way and the economy beginning to adjust to the large defense budgets, the administration was ready to confirm officially the full economic implications of the Vietnam War. The task of performing the evaluation fell to the new chairman of the Council of Economic Advisors, Gardner Ackley. In a lengthy memorandum sent to Johnson on 30 July 1965, Ackley analyzed the crucial problem: "There is still a *$15–$20 billion margin of idle industrial capacity and excessive unemployment,*" and "our *productive capacity is growing by $25–$30 billion a year* apart from any price increase, making room for both more butter and, if needed, more guns"; but "apart from the defense effort, *market demand would not be likely to grow as fast as productive capacity* during the course of FY [fiscal year] 1966, and unemployment would probably be creeping up."

Thus, without a direct stimulus to demand, the administration foresaw a sagging economy with a tremendous excess of production. After assuring the president that the financial and commodity markets could be kept calm in the midst of the escalation, Ackley recognized the fiscal value of impending war: "We are certainly not saying that the Vietnam crisis is just what the doctor ordered for the American economy in the next twelve months. But, on a coldly objective analysis, *the overall effects are most likely to be favorable to our prosperity.*" Finally, Ackley concluded with a caveat to his analysis: Vietnam spending could lead to both inflation and budget difficulties by 1968, threatening the financial outlook for domestic spending programs.[19]

All this evidence suggests the degree to which the Johnson administration viewed the war as a vital component of its fiscal strategy for stimulating growth. Furthermore, the war seemingly offered Johnson the ability to solidify his existing business support while broadening the coalition even further. In the immediate aftermath of the 1964 election, many Democrats pondered the possibility of establishing total political dominance over the Republican Party.[20] In 1965, Vietnam appeared to be the ultimate weapon for achieving that objective.

Building the Pro-Vietnam Coalition

A Strategy for Consensus.   Despite the potential benefits from Vietnam, considerable doubts about the wisdom of escalating the war prevailed in the business community and the media in 1965. As word leaked out of the White House early in that year about plans to pour hundreds of thousands of U.S. troops and billions of dollars into South Vietnam, the Johnson administration found itself facing a groundswell of criticism. Believing that much of the opposition stemmed from a lack of understanding about the broader importance of the Vietnam policy, the White House responded with a multipronged public relations program to solidify support for the escalation.

First, Johnson noisily embarked on a failed attempt to negotiate with North Vietnam (the "peace offensive of 1965"), a move that provided the administration with a public rationale for the subsequent escalation. As documented extensively in the *Pentagon Papers,* the administration intentionally designed the entire framework of the 1965 negotiation to be unacceptable to the North Vietnamese. In opening the negotiations, the administration also intentionally ignored the revolutionary movement in South Vietnam, the National Liberation Front, thus omitting perhaps the most crucial actor from the diplomatic process.[21]

Second, the administration staged a series of luncheons at the White House for important journalists and editors devoted specifically to Vietnam.[22] Proposed by Johnson himself, the idea for these luncheons was seconded by White House aide Jack Valenti in April 1965:

> During the past few days, my talks with editors convince me that your idea to lunch with White House correspondents and their chief editors has much merit. ... During the next few weeks the Viet Nam embroilment will come under heavy attack. Some editors are getting a little edgy. They are not against you— but they are queasy about where it is all leading us. ... I truly believe luncheons—with you—and the chief editors of newspapers would bear fruit.[23]

The White House also targeted an extensive list of newspaper columnists and news reporters to increase media support for the administration. The heart of the project was an organized program of informal contacts between White House aides and journalists.[24] Combined with the "peace offensive," the increased communication between the administration and journalists helped to quiet the discomfort with Vietnam in the media.

Third, the administration staged a variety of public relations activities to further overcome doubts in the business community and the media about the necessity of the war. Among these subsequent activities was a sequence of White House dinners for key business, labor, academic, and media leaders held on 17 August, 16 September, 30 September, and 5 October, 1965. Devoted to both Vietnam and the economy, these dinners featured brief speeches on Vietnam policy by the president, Secretary of State Rusk, Secretary of Defense McNamara, and, in the case of the 17 August affair, General Maxwell Taylor. During these dinners, the participants were asked to provide their comments on the administration's plans for Vietnam. Many subsequently wrote to the White House, and their views reveal the effectiveness of the program in solidifying support among business and media executives.[25]

Another major activity within the White House information strategy occurred in the immediate aftermath of the 17 August dinner. Taking advantage of General Taylor's presence in the United States, the administration sent him around the country in late August and early September of 1965 to speak to gatherings of business and media leaders in five key cities: Los Angeles, where Otis Chandler of the *Los Angeles Times* hosted a breakfast meeting between the California media and Taylor; Denver, where strong Johnson supporter Palmer Hoyt, editor and publisher of the *Denver Post,* was the host of a dinner for Taylor; Chicago, where *Chicago Sun-Times* editor Emmett Dedmon put together a lunch for Taylor that featured a veritable who's who of the Midwestern media; Houston, where *Houston Post* editor Bill Hobby provided Taylor with a dinner attended by a large share of the leading media and business figures in Texas; and New York, where Frank Conniff, the editor of the now-defunct, Hearst-owned *Journal-American,* hosted a similar lunch for Taylor's benefit. In each case, Taylor carried the administration's case for Vietnam to those who could then actively propagate the message.[26] This activity thus drew upon some of Johnson's strongest media supporters to help solidify the Vietnam consensus in 1965.

Finally, the White House also encouraged the formation of an elite committee, the Committee for an Effective and Durable Peace in Asia, to carry on the public relations offensive from outside the White House. Headed by New York lawyer Arthur Dean, whose law firm of Sullivan & Cromwell was particularly well connected to the major money center banks in New York, the committee included leaders from the foreign policy "establishment" (including Dean Acheson), the media (representatives from the Annenberg, Cowles, and Hobby media interests, along with Ralph McGill and Eugene Patterson, the publisher and the editor, respectively, of the *Atlanta Constitution*), industry (Southern California Edison, Detroit Edison, Hewlett-Packard, El Paso Natural Gas, Crown Zellerbach, Campbell Soup), finance (David Rockefeller and John J. McCloy of Chase Manhattan, Andre Meyer of Lazard Freres, and the chief executive officers (CEOs) of Philadelphia National Bank and First National of New York), as well as the presidents of several major colleges and universities. Boosted by President Johnson's public recognition of the organization and its members, in early September 1965, the committee was placing full-page ads in key newspapers across the United States that featured a call for a strong response to "aggression in South Vietnam."[27]

Early Cracks in the Facade. After months of labor, the efforts by the Johnson administration seemed to weld together broad segments of the business community and the media into a consensus in support of the war. At the end of 1965, the vast majority of editorial opinion solidly agreed with the escalation. Public opinion polls conducted as the summer came to a close indicated broad and deep approval for the war, as noted for the president in a White House memo:

Lou Harris called with the results of a recent poll he completed which shows strong support for your Viet Nam policies. ... This poll will not be published until after Labor Day, and Harris asked that it not be released in advance. ... Harris said the summary of the poll is: (a) American public is ready for a long war in Southeast Asia; (b) the people are ready to face up to the loss of American lives there; (c) the people are strongly committed to a "no yield" stand there; and (d) the public is solid behind the President.[28]

The administration's information strategy had transformed most of the earlier doubts, uncertainty, and dissent in the business community and the media into either all-out vocal support for war or, in some cases, silence.

But it is important to note that even as the administration worked to quell dissent, significant fault lines already could be discerned in its pro-Vietnam coalition. First and foremost, the financial community indicated from the start that it had grave doubts about the long-run fiscal viability of Vietnam. As best represented by a letter to Johnson from New York investment banker John L. Loeb (himself a key Johnson supporter in 1964), some leading financiers expressed concern that Vietnam would not be a *sufficient* fiscal stimulus to keep the economy on a high growth path:

Regarding the economy, whatever incremental defense spending will become necessary will undoubtedly, by adding to the volume of final demand, help to maintain a strong forward momentum at a time when the beneficial effects of the 1964 cut in corporate and personal income taxes will have largely spent their strength. However, the impact of defense spending is more selective and less widely diffused than that of a tax cut ... I note that *Fortune* magazine, as well as a number of business economists who had predicted a recessionary 1966, are now raising their sights for next year because of the prospect of additional defense spending. Should a favorable turn of events in Vietnam make our operations there less costly than now anticipated, new doubts about the economy might arise, unless it is made clear that in such a case appropriate tax relief would be forthcoming.[29]

Particularly prophetic were Loeb's comments about the selective impact of defense spending. Between the lines, he was signaling to Johnson that if the war began to hurt the financial sector, then pressure would mount on the administration to remedy the situation. Several other bankers, including Harold Helm of Chemical Bank, George Moore of Citibank, and former Federal Reserve Chairman Marriner Eccles, spelled out similar concerns for Johnson in writing while also warning the administration about the likely prospects for Vietnam-driven inflation.[30]

Second, Johnson failed to grasp the significance of the strong support for Vietnam emanating from the Republican business community and its allies in the more conservative Republican media. On the surface, events in 1965 seemed to anticipate long-run harmony between internationalist Republicans and the administration. For example, in March, April, and May at the invitation of the president of Pepsi-Cola, and on his own initiative, Richard Nixon gave a series of private speeches to Republican business figures and major newspaper publishers in New York, urging them to back Johnson wholeheartedly on the war.[31] Word of these events spread throughout the Republican business community in New York and other parts of the country.[32] And other Republican business figures also took it upon themselves to defend the Vietnam escalation to their peers.[33] When the Republicans realized that Johnson was going to "draw the line" in South Vietnam, almost all of the conservative Republican press swung behind the president. Editorials in the *San Diego Union, Chicago Tribune, Oakland Tribune, St. Louis Globe-Democrat,* and other newspapers in this group praised the president for his policy.[34]

Furthermore, it was evident by the middle of 1965 that many internationalist Republican newspapers and news organizations would be the closest to the administration on Vietnam—if not quite as ardent in their position as the conservative bloc. Here, in particular, the Hearst newspaper chain, the *Kansas City Star,* the *Cleveland Plain Dealer,* and the Scripps-Howard chain proved to be more than willing to support the president on Vietnam.[35] With the exception of the *Denver Post* and the *Atlanta Constitution,* two strongly pro-Johnson and pro-Vietnam newspapers, the ultimate significance of these media behaviors was that the greatest support for the escalation of the war in 1965 was coming from influential media voices that traditionally were tied to the Republican Party.

The White House interpreted all of these actions as a sign of broad support for Johnson and the administration's policies. But the more accurate interpretation is that the expression of pro-Vietnam sentiment by Republicans in the business community mostly was a sign of support for the war, not for the Democrats or their current administration. If Johnson wavered on Vietnam—perhaps if squeezed by the demands on his domestic agenda—then the administration could not count on maintaining such widespread business support. Republican business support also could dry up if the war went poorly, leaving an opening for the Republicans to attack the entire policy as a failure.

This pattern of behavior in the media also reflected the evidence that Johnson shifted considerably to the right on Vietnam during the 1964 campaign, capitalizing on the political opportunity provided by Goldwater's extreme-right ideological positioning. As Goldwater vacated the center-right position traditionally held by the Republican Party, Johnson was able to move right and take away even more business and media support from Goldwater. Combined with the strong fiscal imperatives for the war, this electoral strategy left Johnson with a foreign policy that was destined to appeal more to the

Republican business and media community than to the more progressive elements in the Democratic Party and in the media. The Vietnam consensus of 1965 thus had a very weak foundation: Johnson's own party was less engaged than was the opposition.

The third sign of potentially fatal cracks in the Vietnam consensus brings this last point home. Despite the efforts of the administration to achieve unanimous media support for the war, several important media organizations never agreed with the policy. In particular, the *New York Times* was opposed from the start to the administration's specific designs for Vietnam. As I discuss later, the *Times* clearly was sensitive to the early doubts in the financial community about the war and about the place of Vietnam in the global scope of U.S. foreign policy. As a result, the administration engaged in a constant battle with the preeminent newspaper over its coverage of the war.

By the middle of 1965, the administration was so vexed with the Vietnam news and editorials in the *Times* that W. Averell Harriman felt compelled to confront the newspaper's editorial board. In a memorandum instructing Johnson on what to say in a meeting with retired publisher Arthur Hays Sulzberger, Harriman explained how he had charged the *Times* with aiding the communist cause:

> I was very blunt with the *Times* board. I said that the more people oppose the President's policies, the longer it would be before North Viet-Nam would come to the conference table. I referred to what Russ Wiggins [editor of the *Washington Post*] had told me, that he had met the young man representing the Viet Cong in Moscow. He had a full file of Walter Lippmann and the *Times* critical articles, plus accounts of demonstrations, etc., which had convinced him the American people would compel the United States to withdraw from Viet-Nam.[36]

The *Times* certainly did not go all the way in attacking the war, nor did it ever question the logic or the morality of the United States in seeking to shape the destiny of Southeast Asia; rather, it pursued a cautious but continuous path of investigating and questioning the specific policy and its effectiveness. But the impact was profound: Much of the Vietnam public relations efforts in the White House over the next three years would be devoted to combating the considerable difficulties caused by the *Times*.

Additionally, influential publisher John S. Knight and his newspapers in Michigan, Ohio, and Florida came out against the escalation of the war in 1965, reflecting, among other things, Knight's more cautious brand of U.S. internationalism As the Knight-owned *Detroit Free Press* succinctly put it in July 1965, "South Vietnam is hardly a democracy. It is run by a military dictatorship, sponsored and supported by an outside nation," and "we cannot be the world's policeman and we have no business trying."[37] After years of publishing his own columns against the U.S. involvement in Southeast Asia, Knight would win the 1967 Pulitzer Prize for his editorial writing on Vietnam.

Decline of the Vietnam Consensus

No Way Out:
Economic Predicament Without Political Solution

Once deeply involved in the war, the administration gradually recognized that it had created a terrible economic and political paradox for itself. Vietnam did generate higher growth and drove unemployment to record low levels;[38] but the additional aggregate demand and the tight labor market introduced structural inflation into the economy. By early 1966—only one year into the escalation—the Office of Emergency Planning (OEP) already had diagnosed the proportions of the economic problems created by Vietnam. In a memorandum sent to the president on 21 January, 1966, the OEP analysis systematically surveyed the damage:

> The continued high level of economic activity, increased further by demands for military goods, constitutes the principal basis underlying expectations of further inflationary pressure in 1966. The Vietnam expansion reinforces the supply and demand pressures in many economic sectors, particularly those of skilled manpower, textiles, metals, machinery, transportation equipment, petroleum products, construction materials, and aerospace equipment.[39]

The increased demand for skilled labor not only drove up wages, but also created the climate for increased labor militancy—precisely the opposite outcome desired by the administration. Indeed, already in the latter half of 1965, the White House struggled to end a protracted steel strike that had impacted the entire economy. Johnson's clear commitment to solidifying business support for the Democrats was undermined by a labor climate conducive to high-wage demands and more strikes.

At the same time that they acknowledged these economic difficulties, government analysts predicted that economic disaster would result from a rapid disengagement from Vietnam. The basic issue was the path of business investment induced by the increased defense spending, as explained in a May 1966 memo to Johnson from Walter Heller, the former head of the Council of Economic Advisors:

> Apart from inflation as such, I'm worried about the *investment boom—it's distorting what has been a beautifully balanced expansion.* All that new plant and equipment is great stuff for a Vietnam economy, but it *will soon build up excess capacity and invite [a] post-Vietnam investment slump.*[40]

With the level of investment running ahead of any "natural rate" in the "Vietnam economy," the business community understandably was nervous about a short-term end to the war.

A month later, Heller wrote again to recommend that the administration begin preparing aggressively for the post-Vietnam economy. Noting that *"to keep the economy moving up when Vietnam ends is going to take skill, speed and preparation"* and that "even if there's a truce and a gradual petering out of Vietnam's impact, we'll need *skillful moves to keep economic spirits and demands up,"* Heller laid the basic issue on the line: "If there's a quick end and troop withdrawals, it will be a real *economic jolt."* What was needed, according to Heller, was a very visible effort by the administration to plan for the future: "It would *reassure both business and consumers* that they won't have to head for the economic storm cellars after Vietnam, that *an alert Democratic Administration will be ready with measures to keep sales, jobs, and incomes high."*[41]

Heller's warning about fears in the business community were well founded. One month after Heller wrote to Johnson, Special Assistant to the president (and former President of NBC) Robert Kintner filed the following report on that issue:

> When I was in New York, Andre Meyer [senior partner at Lazard Freres] had gone to Europe on one of his periodic trips, but I had a chance to talk to him before he left on the telephone. His reaction on the economy and his appraisal of the thinking of business leaders was one of uncertainty, and concern on what will happen in the future. His viewpoints are somewhat pessimistic. ... There is a business uncertainty about what will happen to the economy if the Vietnamese operation would end very quickly and concern over whether or not economic plans had been made in the event of this eventuality.[42]

By 1968, the postwar planning being conducted in the Johnson administration emphasized the formidable problem of guaranteeing prosperity without Vietnam. In July 1968, economist Arthur Okun of the Council of Economic Advisors made his concerns clear: "If ... we suffer a postwar recession, no amount of structural effort will solve the transition problems."[43] Thus, the administration confronted severe economic policy difficulties both because of the war and because of fears of a future without it.

Further heightening the problem was the decaying balance-of-payments position of the United States, which threatened to undermine (as it eventually did under President Nixon) the international monetary order established at the end of World War II. Although the Johnson administration did not recognize this as a paramount concern, many multinational business figures were more worried about the downward slide of the dollar than they were about inflation. And here again Vietnam created a real dilemma for the administration.

The deficits and inflation associated with the war clearly increased the already considerable pressure on the dollar. Overseas military costs directly added to the balance-of-payments burden, while the distortions created by the huge defense budgets added indirectly to the problem. As an excellent study of the monetary problems of the period notes, "the inflationary pressure had the effect of worsening the trade balance by pushing up demand for imports and slowing export growth," yet the administration was willing to adopt stopgap measures only to ease some of the pressure.[44] Moreover, as long as the United States planned to retain a basic commitment to East Asia, even the end of the war was unlikely to decrease significantly the drain on the dollar.[45]

By the middle of 1966, it was clear that Vietnam was not the solution to the political problems that the administration faced in the aftermath of the 1964 presidential election. Furthermore, not only did each of the negative economic consequences of the war alienate different segments of the administration's support in the business community, but the alternative solutions were equally repellant to various blocs of Johnson's political investors. The result was a policy deadlock with even more drastic consequences for the administration's political fortunes.

Most commonly debated as a solution to the inflationary and monetary problems created by the war was a temporary income tax surcharge. Walter Heller (among many others) urged the president to propose such a measure in mid-1966, noting substantial support for it in the multinational business community.[46] But Johnson opposed this measure then, primarily because it would be viewed as an admission that the U.S. military effort in Vietnam was in crisis, and because an increase in taxes during an election year would help solidify political opposition to the war and contribute to the revival of the national Republican Party.

Another alternative would be a substantial cut in the domestic budget, a move that was guaranteed to be opposed by many pro-Democrat sectors of the business community and by much of the Democratic electorate. Any reduction in the budgetary commitment to Vietnam was likely to draw fire from Johnson's constituents in the multinational business community that supported the war, as well as the bloc of more conservative Republican manufacturers. As I noted previously, the administration also opposed all but the most ad hoc efforts to stabilize the dollar, refusing to admit that a crisis was pending in the international monetary system.

In the end, despite a heated internal discussion, the administration did little to ameliorate the economic problems caused by the war. Only near the end of his term did Johnson approve a tax surcharge. Vietnam did lead to a gradual de-emphasis of the Great Society as the federal government deficit ballooned after 1965. The administration thus condoned by inaction a shift in budgetary priorities as a response to the economic difficulties created by the war, but this shift occurred very incrementally. Nevertheless, the failure to fund its domestic agenda adequately did incur political costs for Johnson and for the Democratic Party.

One other measure adopted by the administration to deal with inflation had negative political consequences for the Democrats: The administration pursued a variety of agricultural policies to keep food prices low. As a result, support for Johnson in the Midwestern farm belt declined after 1965, especially following some direct confrontations between the administration and the dairy industry. [47] The effect of these policies was to open the door for the Republican Party to regain its hold on the generally conservative farm belt in preparation for the 1968 election.

Business and Media Divergence on Vietnam: A Three-Bloc Analysis

In the face of the economic consequences of the war, the Vietnam consensus forged in 1965 proved in short order to be extremely brittle. By the middle of 1966, the Johnson administration was confronting serious domestic political challenges on Vietnam. The early spring of 1966 had featured the televised Fulbright hearings, which raised many doubts about the wisdom of the conflict and the legitimacy of the process that had led to the 1965 escalation. With the summer of 1966 came disunity over the distorting effects of the war on the U.S. economy.

As correctly predicted by John L. Loeb in his prescient remark that the war would have selective, rather than general, benefits for the economy, the prolongation of the war sent shock waves across portions of the U.S. industrial structure. [48] The result was the emergence of at least three blocs of opinion in the business community about what do to with Vietnam as the war extended through 1966 and 1967. And orbiting each of the these blocs, and representing their views in public and private debates over the war, were three blocs of newspapers. Thus, the underlying influence of the U.S. industrial structure became expressed through the press.

The basic pattern of media divergence over Vietnam was identified in a variety of news analyses conducted after 1965. In the case of the three major television networks, critical reporting on CBS and NBC eventually motivated the White House to ask an outside observer to monitor CBS and NBC for antiadministration bias in their Vietnam news. But the White House indicated at the same time that ABC was much more supportive of the war effort. [49] Several other studies have observed that ABC was much more conservative on Vietnam reporting than were NBC and CBS. [50] Some factors that may explain ABC's relative conservatism during the 1960s include its weak international sales during the period and its tenuous relationship with local affiliates. The first factor gave ABC less of a stake in internationalist policies, and the second put the network more at the mercy of traditionally conservative local stations.

In the case of newspapers, a State Department analysis of newspaper opinion on the 1968 bombing pause divided newspapers into three groups: the nationalist press, the internationalist press, and a unique group of generally pro-Democrat newspapers that consistently opposed all bombing of North Vietnam. Similar groupings emerged from media studies conducted by the Department of Defense, by the White House staff, and in a special investigative report in the *Boston Globe* published in 1968. When the information from these various sources is cross-referenced, what emerges is the portrait of media attitudes on Vietnam depicted in Table 1.2. The table divides newspapers according to their preferences for the overall direction of U.S. intervention in Southeast Asia, as indicated by their editorial treatment of various developments in the war.

In the left column of Table 1.2 are the newspapers and newspaper chains that generally advocated measures to end the war. These newspapers themselves spanned a range from those desiring an exit from Vietnam without

Table 1.2   Media Attitudes Toward the Vietnam War by 1968

Favored Negotiations and De-escalation of the War	Favored Johnson Administration's Approach to Vietnam	Favored "Total" Escalation of the War
Cowles newspapers	Hearst newspapers	*Chicago Tribune*
Field newspapers	Newhouse newspapers	*Cincinnati Inquirer*
Knight newspapers	Pulliam newspapers	*Dallas Morning News*
Arkansas Gazette	Scripps-Howard newspapers	*New York Daily News*
Baltimore Sun	*Atlanta Constitution*	*Oakland Tribune*
Boston Globe	*Denver Post*	*Omaha World Herald*
Cleveland Plain Dealer	*Detroit News*	*St. Louis Globe-Democrat*
Louisville Courier-Journal	*Hartford Courant*	*San Diego Union*
Milwaukee Journal	*Kansas City Star*	
New York Post	*Los Angleles Times*	
The New York Times	*Philadelphia Inquirer*	
Richmond Times-Dispatch	*Providence Journal*	
St. Louis Post-Dispatch	*Salt Lake City Tribune*	
San Francisco Chronicle	*Washington Post*	
Toledo Blade		
Wheeling Intelligencer		

Sources: Memo, R. C. Bowman to Colonel Ginsburgh, 10/17/67, "Vietnam 7D(1) 7/67–11/67 News Media Coverage of Vietnam," NSF, Vietnam Country File, LBJ Library; news analysis, Min S. Yee, "The U.S. Press and Its Agony of Appraisal," *Boston Globe,* 18 February 1968; "Recent Discussion of Viet-Nam (to Jan. 24 1968)," *American Opinion Summary* (Department of State, Bureau of Public Affairs, Ex PR 16, Box 350, WHCF, LBJ Library).

conditions to those that believed sincere negotiations would produce a more "honorable" settlement to the conflict. In the middle column are those newspapers and newspaper chains that retained their support for the actions of the administration in Vietnam. This generally implied an endorsement of both diplomatic and military initiatives, but with a limit on the further escalation of the U.S. military commitment. Lastly, the right column lists those newspapers that were committed to a definitive U.S. victory in Vietnam, without any limits on further escalation.

Newspapers in the left column also were those that tended to endorse Democrats for the presidency across the 1960s, while the newspapers listed in the right column were those most likely to endorse Goldwater in 1964. Newspapers listed in the middle column generally were more internationalist than those in the right column, but most of the newspapers in the middle column also tended to endorse Republicans for the presidency in 1960, 1968, and thereafter. As the war progressed, the Johnson administration increasingly found media support for the intervention coming entirely from the Republican press, while its greatest opposition was centered in those newspapers most likely to favor the Democrats electorally.

The Conservative Republicans.   As I discuss earlier in this chapter, the bloc of basic manufacturing industries, such as steel, rubber, and textiles, favored the large defense budgets associated with Vietnam and the continuation of the war. At the same time, these sectors were troubled by the tight markets for skilled labor that resulted from the high level of aggregate demand in the economy, as well as by the rising inflation rate, which impacted their cost structures and pricing systems.

According to business opinion surveys circulated to the president by Gardner Ackley, for this bloc, "The *most favored remedy,* proposed by a majority and opposed by a few, was *a cut in nondefense Federal expenditures.*"[51] In other words, this bloc was willing to continue the war but sought a sharp downturn in domestic spending. Vietnam could stay, but the Great Society and other aspects of the Democrats' poverty program were expendable in the face of an overheated economy. This stance emerged as the official position of the National Association of Manufacturers (NAM) by early 1967, following a fact-finding visit to Vietnam by NAM chairman Guy S. Peppiatt.[52]

The basic manufacturing bloc, long tied to the conservative and nationalist voices in the Republican Party and in the press, found newspapers such as the *Chicago Tribune* ready and willing in 1966, 1967, and 1968 to combine a call for further escalation in Vietnam with continuous attacks on the domestic programs of the Johnson administration.[53] By constructing a trade-off between Vietnam and the Great Society, the *Tribune* and other newspapers in its bloc helped set the stage for the Republican Party to take the war issue away from the Democrats while abandoning much of Johnson's domestic programs. Gone from the discussion by 1968 were the implicit linkages between the war and the Great Society that were so evident in 1965.

Newspapers in the conservative Republican bloc also were ready and willing to attack the Johnson administration whenever the president seemed poised to consider a softer line on the war. In St. Louis, for example, the *Globe-Democrat* kept up constant pressure on the White House to escalate the war even further, to do whatever was necessary to win.[52] The same editorial line was adopted at the *San Diego Union* and the *Manchester Union Leader.*

The Liberal Democrats.   For the business bloc centered in the multinational financial community, including commercial and investment banking and the satellite sectors such as real estate and home construction, spiraling inflation and the deepening balance-of-payments deficits were of grave concern. As mentioned before, leading investment bankers also were worried about the distortions in capital spending induced by Vietnam—and the likely problems that would follow once the war was concluded.

The major commercial banks, and some of their close allies in the multinational business community, had another issue on their agenda as well: Beginning in 1966, these interests with extensive investments in Latin America became convinced that the deepening commitment to Vietnam was crowding out U.S. attention to other important and turbulent areas of the Third World. This concern emerged clearly in the 1966 meeting between Vice President Humphrey and the David Rockefeller-chaired Business Council for Latin America:

> Mr. Rockefeller indicated that one question on the minds of some of the members of the Council as they met with officials of the U.S. Government at this time was whether our involvement in Southeast Asia would lead to a neglect of our relations with Latin America. He expressed the hope that the Vice President would comment on the subject. He added that it was the feeling of many that although we would necessarily focus a great deal of attention on Asia in the foreseeable future, it would be highly desirable if one high-ranking official in the U.S. Government paid special attention to Latin American affairs.[55]

To remedy the economic problems created by Vietnam, the finance bloc favored a sharp increase in taxes to put a damper on the economy, combined with some measures to reduce federal spending across the board. Those with interests in Latin America and elsewhere outside East Asia also pushed for a redirection of government attention to foreign policy objectives broader than containing *"indigenous"* communism in Southeast Asia.

Like the nationalist manufacturing bloc, the finance bloc also could count on significant media support, including that of the *New York Times*. Besides questioning the role of Vietnam in U.S. foreign policy, the *Times* strongly pushed the problems of Latin America and the negative impact of Vietnam on U.S. efforts there. The Latin America concerns at the *Times* emerged during two meetings between the publishers and editors of the newspaper and the U.S. Ambassador to the Organization of American States (and the major shareholder in Xerox), Sol M. Linowitz. The first of these meetings occurred in September of 1967 and focused primarily on the newspaper's reporting on Latin America and Vietnam.[56] When Linowitz met with the *Times'* editorial board again in September of 1968, they stated their concerns more openly:

> The discussion moved to Viet-Nam, and I was asked whether the countries of Latin America did not resent our involvement there. I pointed out that virtually everywhere I went, the Latin American people with whom I met recognized that we had undertaken a commitment which we must honor; and that so long as we had the commitment, very major portions of our resources would necessarily have to be devoted to Viet-Nam—and they understood this.[57]

Thus, the reaction in the financial community to the Vietnam War found a parallel expression in the *New York Times* and other newspapers sensitive to its views. The *Times* also was sensitive to the impact that Vietnam had on the ability of the United States to control events in the Middle East, a situation brought dramatically into focus by the Six-Day War in 1967.

By 1967, additional liberal, pro-Democrat newspapers, such as the *Louisville Courier-Journal,* the *Milwaukee Journal,* the *Minneapolis Tribune,* the *Des Moines Register,* the *St. Louis Post-Dispatch,* and the *Boston Globe,* had broken strongly with the administration over Vietnam.[58] These newspapers all advocated a redefinition of the U.S. role in world affairs and a solution to the economic problems created by the war, a stance that strongly reinforced the preferences of the financial community.

A similar drift occurred at the *Denver Post,* although that newspaper retained much stronger support for the war. Editor and publisher Palmer Hoyt's dedication to the Vietnam policy was being tested as he learned that the high price of Vietnam would take away federal budget dollars from urban renewal and economic development programs in Denver and Colorado.[59] Apart from his newspaper's general ties to the Denver-area economy, members of Hoyt's family were personally invested in Denver real estate and were suffering through a deepening housing recession.[60] But the administration was not prepared to take steps to limit the impact of Vietnam on the economy; consequently, through 1966 and 1967 the close relationship between Hoyt and Johnson deteriorated.[61]

Besides breaking with Johnson over Vietnam in print, high-ranking managers at the *Louisville Courier-Journal* joined in the most systematic expression by the business community of its unhappiness with the war. Under the name "Business Executives Move for Vietnam Peace," some 500 executives actively began lobbying the White House to end the war in early 1967. Organized by Henry E. Niles, chairman of the Baltimore Life Insurance Company, and dominated by business persons from insurance, banking, and small-to midsized manufacturing, the effort prominently included Lisle Baker Jr., the executive vice president of the *Louisville Courier-Journal.*

The executives' antiwar movement created great difficulties for the administration. On 8 February 1967, the organization published a full-page advertisement in the *Washington Post* calling on Johnson to stop the war on both practical and moral grounds. On 28 May, a similar advertisement appeared in the *New York Times.* Niles used his personal contacts with Maryland Senator Joseph Tydings to get the message into Congress. After a series of contentious interactions with the White House, including a meeting with National Security Advisor Walt Rostow, Niles staged a conference in Washington, D.C., in late September 1967 that featured speeches by Marriner Eccles and other business figures opposed to the war. Business Executives Move for Vietnam Peace also began contacting members of the "President's Club" of large campaign contributors, urging them to lobby against the war.[62] By early 1968, the organization had joined forces with other antiwar groups seeking to transform the New Hampshire primary into a referendum on Vietnam.

The Internationalist Republicans. The third bloc of opinion on Vietnam within the business community consisted of nonfinance multinational firms. As I noted in the second section of this chapter, many multinationals benefited from Vietnam both from their defense-related production and from the increased military presence of the United States around the world. But as the economic distortions created by the war induced inflation and increased the balance-of-payments deficit, the consensus on Vietnam within the multinational business community began to fragment. To state the case concisely, this bloc found itself in between the bloc of basic manufactures that advocated a further escalation and the bloc of financial interests that pushed for a de-escalation.

Pulled from both sides, many multinational firms supported the Johnson administration's path of implementing a moderate tax increase and maintaining the same level of commitment in Vietnam. Newspapers that carried forth the position of the multinational bloc included the few southern ones in the pro-Democrat group (the *Atlanta Constitution,* and *New Orleans Times-Picayune*—the publishers of both notably close to Johnson) and many in the internationalist Republican group. Some multinationals, particularly those with most of their operations centered outside Southeast Asia, found themselves in the same position as the finance bloc and benefited from the same set of media voices. Furthermore, by 1968 newspapers such as the *Cleveland Plain Dealer* and the *Richmond Times-Dispatch* had backed away from their early commitment to the war.

Conversely, those multinationals with heavy investments in Southeast Asia found themselves in the same position as the bloc of basic manufacturers and advocated a stronger commitment to Vietnam. These interests benefited from both nationalist and internationalist newspapers that maintained editorial support for the war, including the Hearst chain, the Newhouse chain, the Scripps-Howard chain, the *Kansas City Star,* and most of the newspapers listed in the middle column of Table 1.2.[63]

But the fragmentation of opinion in the multinational business community was evident in many internationalist newspapers, including the *Baltimore Sun* and the *Washington Post*. As the war dragged on, the *Post* in particular developed a split personality on Vietnam. On the one hand, various media analyses conducted by the administration concluded that the *Post* generally was pro-administration in news and editorials. Yet specific incidents after 1965 suggested a rising level of tension between the White House and the newspaper. Additionally, the administration encountered serious difficulties with *Newsweek* magazine, owned by the Washington Post Company and controlled by Katherine Graham.[64] Graham attempted to reassure the president of her support late in 1967, when she wrote to Johnson, "I want you to know I am among the many people in this country who believe in you and are behind you with trust and devotion."[65] But her newspaper clearly was worried about the economic impact of Vietnam on the U.S. economy.[66] In the end, the *Post* gradually drifted from its strong support for Vietnam and the Johnson administration to occupy a much more agnostic position.

The Administration Response

The Johnson administration had demonstrated in 1965 the capacity to mobilize a consensus and suppress dissent over the Vietnam War. As that consensus began to decline as broad divisions in the business community and the media emerged, the White House gradually formulated a strategy for shoring up support for its foreign policy. But unlike the situation in 1965, Johnson found himself in a position in 1966, 1967, and 1968 that proved increasingly indefensible. Ultimately, the administration was unable to contain the mounting disagreement with Vietnam.

The first element of the administration's post-1965 strategy was a constant program of off-the-record meetings and briefings with journalists, editors, and news executives.[67] These contacts often involved rather blunt attempts by the White House to limit anti-Vietnam statements in the press. By 1967, the White House formally established a Vietnam "Information Group," which included National Security Advisor Walt Rostow to coordinate interactions with the media.

As part of its information efforts, the White House group sought to counteract the slow but continuous decline of support for the war in public opinion polls by locating and promoting polls that portrayed the contrary trend. Such polls were inserted into the *Congressional Record,* sent out to journalists, and used in private meetings with media personnel to convince them that the war was not becoming more unpopular.[68] The administration also considered means for reducing the media's attention to Vietnam: Driving the war off of the front page was a key goal, especially at times when the image of a stalemate in Vietnam seemed verified by the military developments.[69]

Second, the administration attempted to constrain the inflationary effects of Vietnam, often by cajoling the business community to voluntarily curb prices and limit capital spending. Accordingly, the White House hosted a dinner for key business figures on 30 March 1966, devoted to discussions of the war and the inflation problem.[70] These efforts proved particularly futile; the White House lost a series of battles with the automobile and steel industries over price increases in those key sectors of the economy. And the financial sector (with some exceptions) was not interested in joining such an anti-inflation effort. Rather, financial interests wanted policy changes that would slow down the economy, limit the cost of Vietnam, and address the balance-of-payments problem.

Third, the administration implemented the program for establishing formally democratic political institutions in South Vietnam. The sequence of South Vietnamese national elections in 1966 and 1967 was aimed directly at domestic critics of the war.[71] To help maximize the impact of the 1967 election on U.S. opinion, the White House selected a team of observers from business, academia, politics, and the media to travel to South Vietnam in late August. Among those included were Eugene Patterson, the editor of the *Atlanta Constitution,* and John S. Knight, the publisher whose newspaper chain continued to criticize the war. The Vietnam elections did help the administration to defend its actions in Vietnam—at least through the second half of 1967.

Finally, the White House planned and implemented another elite private committee to counter criticism of the war from outside the government.[72] The bipartisan "Committee for Peace with Freedom in Vietnam" was headed by former Senator Paul Douglas and included former presidents Truman and Eisenhower along with many of the strongest supporters of the war in business, the media, and academia.[71] Like its predecessor, the Committee for an Effective and Durable Peace in Southeast Asia, this new committee in 1967 began an aggressive lobbying effort aimed at the press, all the while attempting to disguise its close connections to the Johnson administration.[72]

The Douglas committee portrayed itself as the representative of the "silent center"—the majority of U.S. citizens who supported a "middle path" in Vietnam, one lying between all-out war and surrender. The committee also portrayed domestic dissent against the Vietnam intervention as raising the dangerous specter of U.S. isolationism—a particularly effective strategy for countering the criticism of the war in the multinational financial community. And much of the American press proved receptive to the committee,

giving it excellent editorial play when the committee released its initial statements in October 1967.

But the Douglas committee found itself unable to draw on the backing of
the most important names in the foreign policy establishment. In particular,
the organization found itself rebuffed by John J. McCloy. Reminding Henry
Cabot Lodge in a letter that he had already agreed in 1965 to participate in
the Committee for an Effective and Durable Peace in Southeast Asia, McCloy
subtly revealed his state of thinking on Vietnam: "I do want to add that I
would always be ready to do whatever is necessary to help the President and
the country bring this Vietnam affair to a constructive conclusion."[75]

The Committee for Peace with Freedom in Vietnam also discovered through
its reception in the media that it would not be able to overcome totally the
major political divisions on the war. In particular, newspapers including the
New York Times, New York Post, and the *Des Moines Register* were hostile
to the effort, calling it misguided and out of touch with the true feelings of
the U.S. public. Moreover, the committee soon found its own membership
unwilling to adhere completely to the administration's line on Vietnam, especially with regard to the bombing of the North.

All four components of the Johnson administration's strategy for address-
ing the domestic political problems caused by Vietnam culminated in a burst
of pro-war publicity in the fall of 1967. Coinciding with the period immediately preceding the 1968 presidential primaries, the effort did appear to have
rebuilt some of the elite consensus on the war and to have silenced some of
the dissent. This accomplishment was recognized in mid-December 1967 by
a Defense Department memorandum on recent press coverage of Vietnam.
Referring to an article in the *New York Daily News* of 9 December ("Reporter on the Scene Finds We Are Winning the War"), the memo observed,
"There is a definite trend by the U.S. press in reporting the war more favorably. Attached is a current example; a report such as this was unheard of
several months ago."[76]

A month and a half later in January 1968, the Tet Offensive revealed the
newly solidified consensus to be paper-thin. As infighting within the Democratic Party over Vietnam came to the forefront in the early primaries, the
so-called Wise Men group of elite foreign policy advisers—many of them
strongly tied to the multinational finance bloc—delivered their judgment that
the United States must de-escalate the war. Several days later, Johnson announced his decision not to seek re-election.[77] Hubert Humphrey, respond-
ing to business discontent with Vietnam and its impact on domestic programs, took up the call for a rapid negotiated end to the war. But with the
backing of much of the multinational business community and the nationalist bloc of basic industries, Richard Nixon and a revitalized Republican Party
ended the Democrats' post-1964 quest for political hegemony.[78] And, consistent with the preferences of his business supporters, Nixon maintained the

U.S. involvement in Southeast Asia for six more years despite the domestic opposition to the war.

Conclusion

Explaining the Rise and Fall of the Vietnam Consensus

At the beginning of this chapter, I posed two questions about the origins and decline of the Vietnam consensus during the period 1965–1968. My historical examination of those questions yields concrete answers. These answers reinforce the importance of considering *accurately* the domestic influences on the U.S. intervention in Southeast Asia.

Why did there appear to be such a strong domestic consensus in favor of the 1965 escalation of the Vietnam War? Coalescing in the immediate aftermath of the 1964 election, that consensus occurred because the Vietnam policy appeared to be the optimum one to the Johnson administration for sustaining high growth in the economy while supplying direct and indirect economic benefits to its political constituencies in the business community. Procedurally, the Johnson administration successfully forged consensus among business, labor, and media leaders based on the macroeconomic importance of Vietnam. Proponents of the view that Vietnam decisionmaking was autonomous from business interests have failed to recognize the critical importance of the political and macroeconomic components of the war, just as other commentators have over-emphasized the economic benefits of Vietnam for specific sectors.

How and why did that consensus decline dramatically after the first year of the escalation? The negative economic impacts of the war divided the business community and the media into three durable blocs of opinion: the bloc of conservative nationalist manufacturers and related media that favored Vietnam and opposed the Great Society; the bloc of multinational financial interests and related media that favored de-escalation and a general reduction of fiscal pressure on the economy and the dollar; and the bloc of multinational manufacturers and related media that varied in preferences about Vietnam depending on the strength of connections to Asia. With the Johnson administration increasingly frozen by this dissensus, the war yielded an economic policy stalemate that paralleled the military stalemate in Indochina until the crucial developments in early 1968 forced the Democrats to choose de-escalation.

Business Internationalism in the Aftermath of Vietnam

At the beginning of this chapter, I also posed a third question regarding the long-term impact of Vietnam. The evidence presented here provides the answer to that third question, but first it is necessary to examine the broader relationship between the business community and U.S. foreign policy since the time of the New Deal. Vietnam represents an important turning point in that relationship because it accelerated the emergence of new conflicts within the business community over the scope and definition of U.S. internationalism.

In a seminal article, Thomas Ferguson argued that political competition within the business community during the New Deal was organized in terms of two variables: the labor sensitivity of industries and the international orientation of firms. The era of Republican political dominance prior to the New Deal was driven by a coherent bloc of labor-intensive nationalist industries led by steel, textiles, and rubber. This bloc achieved very high levels of tariff protection and opposed U.S. involvement in such internationalist ventures as the League of Nations. But the high-growth sectors in the 1920s were capital-intensive, multinational firms including petroleum, banking, and electronics interests. The Depression provided a perfect opportunity for the emerging bloc of multinational business investors to mobilize within the Democratic Party to overturn the protectionist and isolationist policies of the previous thirty years.[79] World War II and the cold war then facilitated the installation of a fully internationalist U.S. foreign policy.

The continued transformation of the economy after World War II further increased the relative influence of the bloc that invested to bring about the New Deal. As trade barriers continued to fall, the older industries of the core Republican bloc found themselves facing stronger foreign competition. Meanwhile, the multinational interests increasingly were able to press their agenda within the GOP and the Democratic Party. Placed on the political and economic defensive, nationalist manufacturers invested heavily in the 1964 presidential campaign of Barry Goldwater. This challenge united all sectors of multinational business behind Lyndon Johnson and facilitated the 1965 decision to escalate in Vietnam.

Why did the collapse of the Vietnam consensus have a profound impact on the future conduct of U.S. foreign policy? What developed in the latter half of the Johnson administration was a deep fracture in the foundations of the cold war framework of U.S. foreign policy. As it became increasingly evident that the aggressive counterinsurgency policies developed under Kennedy and Johnson would incur fantastic costs to the United States, leading figures in multinational business and its subsidiary foreign policy establishment began to question the viability of that more aggressive style of containment.

This criticism eventually led to wider concerns about the limits of U.S. power in world affairs and to partisan debates over military spending in the 1970s and 1980s. Fueling the broader decline of the cold war consensus after Vietnam, therefore, was the increasing importance of political conflict within multinational business. This conflict, organized along issues of global financial policy and the distribution of U.S. attention to various regions of the world in an era of binding limits on foreign policy resources, remains today an essential feature of post-Vietnam U.S. politics. The aftermath of Vietnam thus goes well beyond public opinion effects or the actual costs of the war to involve a much more permanent transformation in U.S. foreign policy. Vietnam was not the cause of this transformation; but it did serve as an effective catalyst in the ongoing evolution of the U.S. political economy.

The Media and Foreign Policy

Before closing this chapter with a further consideration of how my arguments pertain to contemporary problems in international politics, it is necessary to analyze the view of media behavior expressed in the previous discussion of Vietnam. Essentially, I have presented a picture of the media as being strongly influenced on foreign policy issues by blocs of opinion in the business community. Diversity of opinion in business thus translates into diversity of opinion in the media.[80] More precisely, I have found that news corporations are vital components of the larger coalitions of economic interests that determine the course of party politics and policy debates in the United States.

This process involves an interaction between other sectors of the economy and the natural economic interests of media corporations. Internationalism in broadcasting corporations and news magazines may be understood straightforwardly from their status as large multinational corporations with global sales. In the case of broadcasting, at least two of the major networks—NBC and CBS—traditionally have been associated with the liberal internationalist bloc in U.S. politics.[81] So it is not very surprising that in recent years CBS and other networks have given unfavorable treatment to presidential candidates who attempt to place protectionism back on the public agenda.[82] Nor was it surprising that NBC and CBS broke with the Johnson administration on Vietnam at the same time as did multinational financial interests. Similarly, the major news magazines have been major internationalist voices in the universe of U.S. journalism.

The issue of newspapers and internationalism, however, is more complicated. For most urban daily newspapers, lack of national and international sales and distribution has made local concerns the driving force behind their editorial positions. Turning this statement around, without a direct stake in foreign policy many newspapers often have to look to influential business voices in their regions when setting editorial policy on internationalism. In the postwar period, when their local economic base was somewhat insensitive to trade liberalization, many newspapers embraced internationalist policies—and the candidates who advocated them—at a much slower rate than did the broadcasting networks. Moreover, the foreign policy coverage in many newspapers—especially in the Midwest—lagged far behind the efforts of the networks for years.

For a few newspapers, such as the *New York Times,* the *Washington Post,* and other members of the "prestige" press, local influences are linked more to international and national interests. For example, the *New York Times* has widely recognized ties to the New York financial community, important multinational firms such as Ford Motors and IBM, and to the State Department (and the internationalist interest groups associated with it).[83] In fact, the preeminence of the *Times* in U.S. journalism derives less from it being an exhaustive "paper of record" than from the meteoric rise in importance after World War I of New York financiers and the State Department.[84] Many elites look to the *New York Times* for news and analysis because the *Times* is understood to speak for other interests of great importance in international and domestic affairs.

Returning once again to the issues with which this chapter began, the rise and fall of the media consensus on Vietnam indicates the value of looking at the industrial structure of the U.S. economy to understand the media's treatment of U.S. foreign policy. As the major divisions within the business community became organized sharply along the internationalism dimension, three blocs within the press emerged to reflect those differences. The behavior of the nationalist Republican bloc clearly resulted from a natural synergy between the industrial structure of the newspaper industry and the policy positions of basic manufacturing sectors. The actions of the other two blocs of newspapers suggest the degree to which their participation in broader political investment coalitions influenced their treatment of the Vietnam War.

This analysis demonstrates the precise outlines of how the cold war consensus on Vietnam shattered. Contrary to many prior views, the media was not uniform in its treatment of the war. Nor were the differences that emerged the result of any impenetrable "elite influences" in the press. Instead, the major divisions over Vietnam can be explained in terms of very clear-cut differences over how to address the economic impact of the war in the United States. And the range of policy alternatives presented in the media was highly constrained by the political investment of the business community.

Implications for the Present and the Future

As we reflect on the Vietnam War and the end of the cold war, it is possible to discern the outlines of what may lie ahead. Already the Gulf War of 1990 has brought forth major splits within the media over the role of the United States in the New World Order. Clearly the nationalist/protectionist agenda—despite the strenuous efforts of Pat Buchanan—rapidly is fading as a force in U.S. foreign policy. What continues to emerge is a debate over which portions of the globe are the most important for the United States.

But this debate is much different than that conducted in the shadow of superpower conflict. As the *New York Times* recently wrote in a very succinct editorial headline, bold claims about collective security in the post–cold war world now must be contrasted with venal questions such as, "What If Bosnia Had Oil?" In fact, comparisons between the dramatic U.S. military response to the Kuwait crisis of 1990 and the cautious U.S. policy in the ex-Yugoslavia crisis highlight the importance of discernible economic benefits from intervention. In such an environment, the importance of the business community in the formulation of U.S. foreign policy is likely to be *magnified*, making it all the more important for students of that policy to understand the sources of conflict and agreement within business on international issues.

Consequently, careful analysis of the media and foreign policy today is likely to reveal that as the U.S. business community develops positions on new foreign crises, so will the press. Given the decline of the nationalist sector, we can expect to see further decline in support for nationalism in the media—something to which H. Ross Perot and his potential imitators might wish to give heed. Most important, we can move beyond the fixation on the media as an influence on public opinion to utilize the news as an indicator of business conflict over foreign policy. Assessed as such, the press becomes one of our better allies in diagnosing the future directions of the role of the United States in the world.

2

The Military-Industrial Complex, Sectoral Conflict, and the Study of U.S. Foreign Policy
ે

David N. Gibbs

Bureaus have an inherent tendency to expand, regardless of whether or not there is any genuine need for more of their services. In fact, all organizations have inherent tendencies to expand.

—Anthony Downs, *Inside Bureaucracy*

The defense establishment now devotes a large share of its efforts to self perpetuation. ... War justifies the existence of the establishment. ... Standing closely behind these [military] leaders, encouraging and prompting them, are the rich and powerful defense industries. Standing in front, adorned with service caps, ribbons, and lapel emblems, is a nation of veterans—patriotic, belligerent, romantic, and well intentioned, finding a certain sublimation and excitement in their country's latest military venture.

—General David M. Shoup, Former commandant, United States Marine Corps, "The New American Militarism"

The military-industrial complex is a very healthy thing.

—Elbridge Durbrow, Vice Chairman, American Security Council

The question of the military-industrial complex provides an interesting case in the sociology of knowledge. During the 1960s and 1970s, scholars directed considerable attention toward the phenomenon of military-industrial linkages, and numerous titles contained the phrase "military-industrial complex." The attention to this approach was, at least to some extent, correlated with a loss of prestige by the military and, indeed, the entire executive branch of government, due to the Vietnam War, the Watergate scandal, the Church Committee hearings on the CIA (Central Intelligence Agency), and other memorable events of that period. Much of the writing on the military-industrial complex was polemical and journalistic, but there were also serious empirical studies, which tested the approach under controlled conditions. Some well-known and respected political scientists and economists, including Murray Weidenbaum, Samuel Huntington, Robert Art, Bruce Russett, and James Kurth, published research on the subject.[1] In 1973, Steven Rosen concluded that, despite some contrary findings, "it is remarkable how well it [the military-industrial complex approach] has withstood critical evaluation, some of it from an obviously skeptical perspective. ... We conclude that the theory of the military-industrial complex is a most useful analytical construct for both research and policy evaluation purposes."[2]

The phrase "military-industrial complex" (MIC) was first used, of course, in Eisenhower's 1961 Farewell Address, but its basic formulation is usually attributed to C. Wright Mills's *The Power Elite,* which examines the social and political significance of military institutions and weapons procurement companies and treats these groups, collectively, as a vested interest.[3] The concept of the military-industrial complex has been applied to a wide range of empirical questions. Most research on the MIC emphasizes U.S. policy during the cold war era, although some studies analyze the MIC during earlier periods of U.S. history.[4] In addition, the approach has been applied, with some modifications, to military policy in the (former) USSR.[5]

However, research on the military-industrial complex has fallen out of fashion in recent years. Since 1980, there has been almost no scholarly attention to military-industrial linkages, their implications for the functioning of the military, or their overall significance for foreign policy.[6] Instead, the mainstream of the international relations literature has focused overwhelmingly on realist approaches, which emphasize international factors over domestic politics as the driving force behind war. Government officials in the military and throughout the foreign policy apparatus are seen as "autonomous" from interest group pressures, according to the realist approach; foreign policy decisions are made to suit the "national interest," not the interests of the military-industrial complex or of any other pressure group.[7] It is ironic that studies of the military-industrial complex disappeared precisely at the time of one of the largest military buildups in U.S. history, when the military reached exceptional levels of influence and prestige during Reagan's presidency. Despite its fall from fashion, the MIC approach retains considerable value. The approach has been endorsed by several high-ranking officials, and some of these, such as Dwight D. Eisenhower, were certainly well placed to evaluate its validity.

This chapter reevaluates the military-industrial complex perspective. Specifically, it is argued that the military and its associated private sector contractors constitute a political lobby, one that favors international tension and, in some cases, war. I argue also, contrary to realist approaches, that considerations of military-industrial interests significantly influence the substance of policy, with regard to "low politics" issue areas, such as defense procurement, as well as to "high politics" areas, such as the initiation and conduct of military action. I test these propositions in a case study of U.S. responses to the Soviet invasion of Afghanistan during the late 1970s. In my view, the military-industrial complex remains a useful analytical tool.

Toward a Military-Industrial Complex Approach

To develop a detailed military-industrial complex model of U.S. foreign policy, we must first look at the "military" side of the construct. The MIC approach essentially views the military as an interest group (or a cluster of interest groups). Accordingly, conflicts of interest will inevitably emerge between the military's commitment to furthering national security, on the one hand, and its interest in advancing the concerns of itself and its individual members, on the other hand. The MIC approach focuses primarily on the uniformed military, but it also takes into account the interests of civilian employees in the Department of Defense, who have an interest in augmented military expenditures, as well as officers from the CIA, who hold similar interests. In addition, civilians working for research institutes with military connections, such as the Rand Corporation, can be considered a part of the military-industrial complex. In short, a wide range of personnel comprise the military-industrial complex, and this complex, because of its sheer size, constitutes a potent pressure group.

Officers view the world through the lens of their own services, and their views will not always correspond to what an objective observer might conclude. The literature on bureaucracy has firmly established that all institutions are motivated, to some extent, by considerations of self interest, and the older notion of a self-sacrificing bureaucrat has long since been modified, if not outright discarded. Anthony Downs, for example, wrote that "bureaucratic officials, like all other agents in society, are significantly—though not solely—motivated by their own self interests."[8] One of the most important interests, common to nearly all bureaucrats, is the desire to expand their agencies or, at least, to preserve them from contraction. The military will surely seek to increase military expenditures and to protect itself against potential budget cuts. Military officers lobby for augmented budget allocations, for ever-greater amounts of federal land devoted to military exercises, and for continually more up-to-date weapons systems. Most variants of the MIC model emphasize these expansionist tendencies.[9] And, in general, it is emphasized that the military will seek such expansion even when it contributes little or nothing to national security in any objective sense; bureaucratic expansion has its own logic. Some approaches, such as that of Alan Wolfe, also emphasize the importance of rivalries among the four services in the military and how these rivalries will intensify the demands for increased military expenditures.[10]

Despite all of these considerations, it would be mistaken to assume that military personnel always act in a consciously cynical way. It has been generally accepted among sociologists, ever since the publication of Karl Mannheim's pioneering work on ideology, that individuals and groups tend to see their own interests as universal interests. Vernon Aspaturian analyzes the matter this way: "Perception itself is frequently a reflection of self interest rather than objective reality," and there inevitably is some "unconscious distortion of the objective situation through the prism of individual or group self interest."[11] Or as a U.S. admiral once put it, very subtly: "Any step that is not good for the Navy, is not good for the nation."[12] Thus military officers (reinforced, in many cases, by retired officers and veterans' organizations) will constitute a powerful lobby in favor of a promilitary policy. This power will be bolstered by lobbying from the weapons industry.

The "industrial" side of the military-industrial complex has accounted for a substantial proportion of the U.S. economy, between 5 and 10 percent for most of the post–World War II period, and, in 1977, it accounted for almost half of gross fixed capital investment.[13] It occupies a particularly important niche among science-based and advanced technology industries such as microelectronics. In 1982, some 30 percent of U.S. scientists and engineers worked for the federal government, and the government funded about half of all research and development in the United States; according to one study, "the overwhelming bulk of this [federal research] effort is related to defense."[14] It is also worth noting that the military industries tend to be concentrated in specific states, and some of these states—such as California—are of special political importance.[15] In addition, the military procurement corporations, or the "defense" industry as it is usually termed, comprise some of the largest companies in the United States, including such giants as Boeing, Lockheed, McDonnell-Douglas, General Dynamics, and United Technologies.

The economic importance of the military-industrial complex has been widely debated. Paul Baran and Paul Sweezy argue that defense spending constitutes a kind of "military keynesianism," and that these expenditures stimulate the whole macroeconomy.[16] Other analysts, such as Seymour Melman, suggest that military expenditures are really a drag on the economy, which reduce living standards for large parts of the population. Finally, Betty Hanson and Bruce Russett argue that major segments of the business community clearly do not benefit from excessively high military expenditures.[17] Conversely, Ann Markuson et al. present evidence that the defense budget does contribute to the prosperity of at least some regions of the United States (despite deleterious effects on other regions).[18]

The relationship between military spending and the macroeconomy is clearly a complex one, and it would go beyond the limits of this chapter to explore these effects in detail. For purposes of this discussion, I will eschew macroeconomic analysis and, instead, focus on how the MIC affects individual companies. It will be argued that, whatever its effects on the economy overall, *specific companies* clearly do benefit from high military expenditures. Certainly, contractors that obtain a major share of profits from defense procurements have a vested interest in military expenditures. Also, manufacturers of basic weaponry components, especially electronics, will have similar interests. Mining companies, too, will benefit at least indirectly, since defense spending usually augments demand for basic metals.[19] In addition, certain types of foreign investors, particularly those with large capital investments in unstable regions (oil companies in the Persian Gulf, for example) may also favor increased military expenditures.[20] These companies, collectively, will constitute a pro-military bloc within the business community. We would expect such companies to mobilize in support of the uniformed services, all in favor of augmented military spending.

Thus the military-industrial complex represents those segments of the government and the private sector that have vested interests in increasing military expenditures. Both elements—the military and industrial components—can coordinate their activities to some extent, due to the career patterns of military personnel. In the well-known revolving-door pattern, officers often retire and then work as executives for the weapons procurement companies. The practice is widespread and well established. A 1969 congressional study found that some 2,000 former officers, many of flag rank, were employed with the largest defense contractors.[21] The interlinking of powerful bureaucratic and private interests may be viewed as a device to overcome or reduce collective action problems in the MIC. Revolving-door practices, in addition to social connections among former officers built up over years of academy training and career advancement, promote collective self-identification among disparate elements of the MIC and, accordingly, a capacity for collective action.[22] This capacity greatly increases the MIC's political efficacy.

Despite these resources, the military-industrial complex is far from omnipotent. Other elements of the bureaucracy, such as the agriculture or labor departments, compete for funds, and these agencies, too, are linked to powerful constituent groups. It is also important to emphasize that the business community is not monolithic and that some businesses clearly do *not* have interests in military spending. Defense policy will also be influenced by conflicts within the business community. Companies that depend on government contracts in nonmilitary sectors—construction companies that specialize in urban infrastructure, for example—may oppose "excessive" military allocations, since this would reduce spending in other areas. Moreover, commercial banks sometimes oppose military spending on the grounds that such spending can be inflationary, and inflation undermines the international strength of the dollar.[23] In addition, some elements of U.S. society—members of peace groups, for example—remain hostile toward the military on ideological grounds. Some of these various "antimilitary" elements can work together to oppose increased military expenditures.

Defense spending will thus provoke conflicts between promilitary and antimilitary business factions.[24] Overall, we would expect the MIC to have distinct advantages over opponents, at least in the early stages of a controversy. Defense contractors have a direct interest in supporting high levels of defense spending, while antimilitary business interests have essentially indirect interests in opposing such spending. We would expect antimilitary interests to mobilize only in reaction to excessive, potentially inflationary military budgets, and the reactive nature of the antimilitary interests reduces their political effectiveness. Peace groups face other constraints: They must rely on very large memberships for their strength, and such mass movements face serious collective action problems. The core elements in the military-industrial complex—top officers and major executives in defense industries—are a smaller, more cohesive group, and, as Mancur Olson has demonstrated, small groups have systematic advantages in overcoming collective action problems.[25]

Inevitably, the existence of the MIC creates a bureaucratic pressure for conflict and even war. It is well known that an officer must gain combat experience in order to achieve promotion, especially to the higher ranks.[26] The pressures for "action" also exist for employees of the CIA, officers of which must organize covert operations in order to advance their careers.[27] Warfare serves yet another function: It justifies the continued existence of the military, and, if the war is relatively easy and painless, it increases the prestige of the services.

Obviously such uses of force carry risks, and generals will avoid reckless operations; such caution has undoubtedly increased since the debacle of Vietnam. Thus, military commanders are unlikely to favor operations that entail high risk of casualties or ones that lack clearly defined objectives (proposed U.S. intervention in ex-Yugoslavia would fall into this category). Rational self-interest would surely militate against rash adventurism by the military. Nevertheless, the MIC remains enthusiastic over operations that have well-defined objectives and low risks (such as the invasions of Grenada and Panama). General David Shoup, former commandant of the Marine Corps, notes that "civilians can scarcely understand or even believe that many ambitious military professionals truly yearn for wars as opportunities for glory and distinction that are afforded only in combat."[28] The military services, like all bureaucratic entities, seek to demonstrate their capabilities from time to time and to favor policies that enable them to do so.

It is worth mentioning that various "radical" interpretations of U.S. foreign policy emphasize that wars, especially Third World interventions, serve to protect or spread U.S. investments.[29] There is some validity to this view, and, as we have seen, the MIC approach acknowledges that foreign investors can be expected to support a strong military. Nevertheless, the MIC approach eschews the role of foreign investors in influencing policy and considers them to be of secondary importance. In essence, the military-industrial complex approach sees wars as ends in themselves, in the sense that wars advance the political objectives of the MIC and help justify its existence. A war may or may not help U.S. foreign investors, but it augments the fortunes and budget allocations of the military and its associated industries. These objectives will sometimes constitute important factors in motivating war. Concomitantly, members of the MIC will have a vested interest in seeing international events as "crises" and as potential "threats to national security"; such perceptions flow directly from the interests of the MIC. The military, after all, is able to attract greater resources when the public perceives a threat to national security. The military-industrial complex is, then, a permanent bureaucratic pressure in favor of at least some degree of international tension.

The MIC approach to U.S. foreign policy differs markedly from realist approaches. Hans Morgenthau nicely sums up the realist view: "Men do not fight because they have arms ... they have arms because they deem it necessary to fight."[30] The MIC approach would argue, in contrast to Morgenthau, that the existence of a large military will constitute an independent factor, one that will influence decisionmaking processes—including processes leading to warfare.

In the real world, of course, many factors influence defense policy, in addition to pressures from the MIC, and these factors include genuine security interests and assorted ideological objectives. For now, however, I will put aside these other considerations and continue to work with the ideal type of military-industrial complex.[31] Seen as an ideal type, the approach emphasizes the internal determinants of foreign policy. If this approach is correct, then U.S. foreign and military policy is significantly influenced by military-industrial lobbying, and the resulting actions often have little to do with the national interest.

Application

The Soviet invasion of Afghanistan is an excellent case study in the context of this discussion for the simple reason that it was a decisively important event in the history of the cold war. It is generally agreed that it was Afghanistan, more than any other single factor, that ended the policies of détente between the United States and the USSR.[32] Both the Republican and Democrat Parties adopted strongly promilitary positions during the 1980 campaign, and a large-scale military expansion commenced during the decade that followed that election. In short, Afghanistan was the major factor that terminated détente and triggered policies of increased confrontation. Few would quibble with the following commentary by Raymond Garthoff: "The Soviet military intervention in Afghanistan ... and the American reaction to it marked a watershed in American-Soviet relations."[33]

The questions raised are basic: Why did the United States respond so strongly to the Soviet invasion? And why was it considered such a dire threat to Western security? In what follows, I illustrate the use of the MIC approach, and, in accord with the methodology of ideal types, the discussion will be deliberately one-sided. Basically, the military-industrial complex approach argues that the dramatic U.S. response to the invasion resulted, not from security considerations, but from military lobbying. Specifically, I show that elements of the military-industrial complex had been pressuring the public and the Carter administration for higher levels of defense spending and for more aggressive foreign policies to support this spending; the Soviet invasion of Afghanistan presented an ideal opportunity to generate public support for these policies.

First, let us explore some of the background to the case. By the 1970s, the military had lost considerable prestige, and its influence was at a historic low. This loss of prestige was indicated by the antiwar movement, by antimilitary films such as *Catch-22* and *MASH,* and by the relatively pacific détente policies of the Nixon, Ford, and Carter administrations. The military's decline was also marked by the number of academic studies with "military-industrial complex" in the title. More important, the military was gradually losing its share of the budget, and the prodigious growth that the military had enjoyed during the early years of the cold war had, for the most part, ended. Measured in real terms, U.S. military expenditures declined absolutely during the period 1971–1977, and it stagnated until the end of the decade.[34] As a percentage of GNP (gross national product), the decline is even more apparent: Military spending constituted 8.2 percent of GNP in 1964, rising to 9.3 percent during the height of the Vietnam War in 1968. Thereafter, the proportion began to slide, falling to 4.9 percent of GNP in 1980.[35]

The military-industrial complex was also losing ground in the competition for overseas arms sales. During the 1960s and 1970s, the U.S. government was reluctant to support large-scale militarization in Third World countries, and, as a result, U.S. arms exporters lost markets to aggressive European competitors. France became a major weapons producer during this period, and French equipment, especially the Mirage series of fighter planes, offered stiff competition. Latin American countries began to turn to Europe (particularly to France) for advanced weapons, and, by 1973, the United States accounted for only 20 percent of Latin American arms sales.[36]

U.S. arms exporters became increasingly anxious about this new competition. Various other segments of the business community were coming under increased pressure at this time, as well. Specifically, multinational corporations faced ever-increasing economic nationalism in the Third World, with demands for profit sharing, purchases of domestically-produced inputs, and diffusion of technology. Many Third World countries nationalized foreign holdings or circumscribed their autonomy.[37] Finally, political instability threatened foreign investments in many Third World countries, including Iran, Nigeria, South Africa, and even South Korea. Many multinational corporations hired political advisers to help them manage these developments, and the new field of "political risk analysis" became a staple of the business press.[38] However, political consultants were often of questionable value and, in any case, they were inadequate substitutes for the (now diminished) threat of U.S. military intervention. By the end of the 1970s, many multinationals became concerned that the U.S. government was not doing enough to protect their investments.[39] In 1979, *Business Week* ran a special issue that lamented "the decline of U.S. power."[40] Multinational investors thus became one more element in a broad coalition that had a vested interest in augmented military expenditures and an aggressive foreign policy.[41]

The military-industrial complex model would expect these various, dissatisfied interests to mobilize in order to recover their previous level of influence. We would expect that the MIC would argue for increased military expenditures, and that, in order to justify such actions, they would cite alleged national security threats. Finally, we would expect certain foreign investors, especially those operating in unstable areas of the Third World, to align themselves politically with the MIC and to join in the pressure for a stronger military.

This is in fact what happened during the late 1970s. The military-industrial complex did indeed mobilize during this period. Promilitary lobbies included the American Security Council (ASC) and the National Strategy Information Center (NSIC). During the 1970s, these two groups considerably strengthened their financial support. The ASC increased its contributions from $910,000 in 1972 to $1,700,000 in 1977; the NSIC increased its contributions from $620,000 in 1971 to $1,100,000 in 1976.[42] Even accounting for inflation, the increased level of financial contributions was impressive. These contributions may be viewed as an index of the discontent felt by the military and its supporters. In 1976, a wholly new organization was formed, the Committee on the Present Danger, which worked closely with the previously mentioned groups to change the course of foreign policy.[43] By the end of the 1970s, a formidable military lobby was in place. This process of mobilization undoubtedly reflected many factors, in addition to self-interest on the part of the military and its affiliated industries. The political mobilization also reflected the neoconservative movement among intellectuals; increasing anti-Sovietism among U.S. Jews; the rise of Protestant fundamentalism (which had strong conservative and anticommunist overtones); and the traditional cold war views of U.S. labor organizations.[44]

However, there is no doubt that the military-industrial complex was also an important factor. According to one account, the Committee on the Present Danger was launched "by a broad cross section of leading businessmen and onetime military figures and received a substantial start-up grant from David Packard, board chairman of Hewlett Packard."[45] One of the most prominent members of the Committee was Paul Nitze, who as author of the famous "National Security Council Memorandum No. 68," was a major architect of the cold war. With regard to the ASC, for example, Jerry Sanders noted that its backers included some of the country's largest defense contractors, including:

> Honeywell Corporation, General Electric, Lockheed, and McDonnell-Douglas, as well as firms like Motorola. ... In addition, the leadership and policy committees of the Committee include many retired military men of high rank, among them Daniel Graham, and CPD [Committee on the Present Danger] members Lyman Lemnitzer, Andrew J. Goodpaster, and Maxwell Taylor, as well as several congressmen with a stake in military spending. In an interview for this book, Elbridge Durbrow, vice chairman of the American Security Council was asked if the military-industrial characterization bothered him. His reply was emphatic: "Hell no—if our military and industry can't get together how are we going to defend our country?"[46]

Further, an analysis of military publications from this period shows that the military was indeed prepared to lobby for increased military expenditures and major changes in foreign policy.[47] Overall, the promilitary groups spent considerable sums during the late 1970s, sponsoring various symposia, television shows, and other assorted publicity events. The various groups also lobbied against the revised Panama Canal treaty in 1978 and against the SALT II agreement with the USSR in 1979. The lobbying effort reached a particularly high level during the SALT II debate. The opponents of SALT (Strategic Arms Limitation Talks) included military-industrial groups as well as more ideologically oriented conservative organizations. Together, these groups collaborated to lobby the public and the Congress against the treaty. According to Jerry Sanders, "The American Security Council targeted 10 million persons for its direct mail operation," while other anti-SALT pressure groups launched separate mailing drives. A petition against the treaty was organized in all fifty states, and a speakers' bureau with 150 potential speakers was organized. The Committee on the Present Danger effectively used its prestigious membership as expert witnesses against the treaty during congressional hearings; this testimony gained wide publicity. Finally, lobby groups produced anti-SALT films, and these were aired by several hundred local television stations throughout the country.[48]

Examining the lobbying efforts of the period, one is struck by the considerable asymmetry of resources between the promilitary and antimilitary groups. In the case of SALT II, the promilitary groups outspent groups supporting the treaty by a considerable margin. In March 1979, the *Christian Science Monitor* estimated that promilitary groups outspent their opponents by fifteen to one.[49] There was some business support for the SALT treaty, especially among large financial institutions and companies that traded with the USSR, but it played a relatively passive role. (Such interests did, however, become mobilized several years later, in response to the Reagan-era arms buildup.[50]) The peace groups, too, were not very active during the period of study here, while the Carter administration was notably inept in mobilizing support for its foreign policy objectives.[51] Overwhelmingly, it was the military-industrial complex that dominated lobbying efforts. Under the weight of this pressure, the U.S. public was gradually moved to accept highly critical views of the USSR, while the Carter administration, for its part, succumbed and adopted increasingly promilitary policies.[52]

After the Soviet invasion of Afghanistan in 1979, the administration abandoned its relatively mild policies altogether and moved into a position of conflict. The most immediate change in policy was an open material support for the *mujahidin* guerrillas who were fighting the Soviets. And, more important, the invasion was used to justify a generalized shift in policy. The Carter Doctrine was declared, threatening the Soviets with war should they attack the Persian Gulf. The SALT treaty was largely abandoned, while virtually all commercial, scientific, or cultural contacts between the superpowers were curtailed or discarded completely. Carter promised an arms buildup with a particular emphasis on augmented "capability to deploy U.S. military forces rapidly to distant areas."[53]

The incoming Reagan administration expanded these promilitary policies further, and the Soviet occupation of Afghanistan was the administration's main justification. During the period 1980–1985, military spending (adjusted for inflation) increased by 39 percent, and, during the same period, defense spending substantially increased its share of the federal budget, accounting for 27 percent of the total by 1985.[54] There was also an increased willingness to use force, with direct military actions in Grenada, Libya, and Lebanon, as well as "covert" paramilitary operations throughout the world. U.S. arms exports were again encouraged.

There can be no doubt that the military-industrial complex benefited considerably from these new policies. In short, the MIC approach would interpret these events as follows: The U.S. government reacted so strongly to the invasion because of the climate of tension that was created by the lobbying effort. The Soviet invasion of Afghanistan was largely a propaganda issue, which the military lobby used to "sell" its cold war policies to the public and to the government.

Afghanistan: A Second Consideration

There is an obvious counter-explanation to the invasion of Afghanistan, that of the realists. According to the realist view, the invasion was interpreted as a major security threat because it really *was* such a threat. This approach emphasizes that Afghanistan is close to the Persian Gulf, which is where the NATO (North Atlantic Treaty Organization) countries and Japan obtain most of their vital petroleum supplies. Some analysts also note that the Soviets had long sought a warm water port, with direct access to the Indian Ocean. The occupation of Afghanistan positioned the USSR much closer to its historic objectives, bringing the Soviets within several hundred miles of the Persian Gulf and the Indian Ocean.

Virtually all analysts at the time agreed with Jimmy Carter's conclusion that the invasion was "the greatest threat to peace since the Second World War."[55] The "strategic importance of Afghanistan" was immediately and almost universally accepted. Only rarely was it challenged, and even recent analyses still assume that Afghanistan was indeed a strategic prize.[56] Upon close scrutiny, this explanation seems dubious. Afghanistan is not, in fact, very close to the Persian Gulf; Afghanistan and the Soviet Union were actually equidistant from the Gulf. Moreover, Afghanistan's extremely rugged terrain, lack of infrastructure, and general economic backwardness greatly limited its value. Declassified U.S. government documents underscore Afghanistan's lack of strategic importance. During the late 1940s and early 1950s, for example, the United States refused to provide Afghanistan with military equipment and contributed only very limited economic aid.[57] A 1949 report by the U.S. Joint Chiefs of Staff succinctly noted: "Afghanistan is of little or no strategic importance to the United States."[58]

Soviet involvement in Afghanistan was viewed in lackadaisical terms. In 1950, the Soviet role was seen as very minor, and the U.S. National Intelligence Estimate noted that the "Soviet Union has shown no considerable interest in Afghanistan."[59] Soviet influence did increase considerably beginning in 1954–1955, however, when the USSR began establishing a series of commercial and military links with Afghanistan. Thereafter, the USSR became the country's main trading partner, as well as its largest source of economic aid and military training. During the next twenty-five years, Afghanistan became economically and militarily dependent upon the USSR, but U.S. officials were not particularly alarmed by this development. Overwhelmingly, these officials believed that the Soviet involvement in Afghanistan was a direct response to increased U.S. involvement in the region, especially the U.S. decision, in early 1954, to arm Pakistan. A 1954 National Intelligence

Estimate regarded the upsurge in Soviet interest this way: "Increased Soviet attention to Afghanistan is part of a general effort to *counter* recent Western (particularly U.S.) gains in the Middle East- South Asia area."[60] U.S. officials compared Soviet influence in Afghanistan with U.S. influence in Latin America. In 1954, CIA director Allen Dulles commented that "the Soviets were inclined to look on Afghanistan much as the United States did on Guatemala."[61] In 1956, the National Security Council (NSC) explicitly decided not to match Soviet aid activities in Afghanistan, presumably because the country was not considered sufficiently important.[62]

It is tempting, in retrospect, to view such analyses as naive; it may be argued that subsequent events—the fact that the Soviets did eventually invade the country—attest to the fact that U.S. government officials were simply mistaken and were too inclined to trust Soviet intentions in Afghanistan. This interpretation is incorrect. U.S. analysts realized that the country had some geostrategic significance since it bordered the USSR; it was recognized that the Soviets were concerned about developments in border regions.[63] However, U.S. officials generally believed that the Soviets gained little *offensive* strategic value from their relations with Afghanistan.

U.S. officials also recognized that an eventual Soviet invasion of Afghanistan was possible (although it was considered unlikely) and were not very troubled by this prospect. The 1954 National Intelligence Estimate for Afghanistan noted that "physical occupation of the country would offer few if any strategic advantages to the USSR."[64] Elsewhere, the report qualified this conclusion somewhat, noting that the country might be of some importance, because of its location as a buffer between the USSR and the Indian subcontinent, but the report also noted: "Afghanistan's primitive economy, undeveloped resources, negligible military capabilities, and lack of useful strategic facilities severely restrict its positive value to either side in the East-West power struggle."[65]

Despite all of these considerations, a 1954 NSC briefing paper considered the hypothetical possibility of a Soviet invasion of Afghanistan and suggested the following U.S. responses to such an invasion: First, the United States should use "diplomatic measures" to encourage Soviet withdrawal. Second, if such diplomatic efforts were unsuccessful, the United States should "decide in light of the circumstances existing at the time what further action to take through the UN [United Nations] or otherwise."[66] The wording in this memorandum is vague, but it is interesting to note that only diplomatic or UN pressure is discussed; military responses or even economic sanctions are not mentioned at all.

The range of documents, unfortunately, becomes quite scarce for most of the period after the 1950s, but all available evidence suggests that U.S. officials never really changed their view that Afghanistan was a very low priority. The United States continued to provide only limited aid to Afghanistan

and never attempted to match the Soviet aid program. The general lack of
U.S. interest in Afghanistan persisted through the mid-1970s, through both
Democratic and Republican administrations. In general, observers stressed
Afghanistan's lack of strategic importance, and dissenters were very infre-
quent. Analysts who emphasized Afghanistan's "strategic" significance were
often dismissed in government circles.[67] A 1973 *Wall Street Journal* article
ridiculed the idea that Afghanistan was valuable and offered this caustic
assessment:

> Petro-pundits tend somehow to equate Soviet influence in land-locked Afghani-
> stan with Soviet control of the Persian Gulf. ... But from up close, Afghanistan
> tends to look less like a fulcrum or a domino or a stepping stone than like a
> vast expanse of desert waste. ... A visitor perhaps may be excused for wonder-
> ing why the Russians, or anyone else for that matter, would particularly want
> Afghanistan.[68]

The article was entitled "Do the Russians Covet Afghanistan? If So, It's Hard
to Figure Why" and referred to Afghanistan as "a vast wasteland" and a
"nation probably no one wants."

In April 1978, the People's Democratic Party of Afghanistan—the Afghan
communist party—seized power, and the country quite suddenly came into
the center of world attention.[69] Soviet conduct over the next ten years did
not give strong evidence that Afghanistan was strategically important for the
West. The Soviets took no action that suggested that they would use Afghanistan for further aggression in the region.[70] The Soviets did not mass
their troops on the border with Pakistan or Iran.[71] They did not bring in
strategic equipment, such as long- or medium-range bombers, which could
have been used for expansion beyond Afghanistan; nor is there any evidence
that they brought in antiship missiles, which would have been effective for
interdicting Western oil shipments in the Persian Gulf. Most important, U.S.
intelligence repeatedly indicated that the Soviets failed even to lengthen the
runways of their Afghan airfields or to make the improvements in these airfields that would have been necessary to accommodate long-range jets.[72] The
Soviets' postinvasion military buildup provided no evidence that they sought
to use Afghanistan as a staging area for additional aggression.

It is very interesting to note that when the Soviets finally withdrew from
Afghanistan, U.S. officials publicly acknowledged, once again, that the country
was *not* of major strategic significance. Shortly before the last Soviet troops
withdrew in 1989, a *New York Times* correspondent wrote the following:

> [American officials] say Afghanistan has little intrinsic strategic significance.
> "There's no compelling political interest there," a senior administration offi-
> cial said. ... [According to a former State Department official], "Afghanistan

could turn into one of those chronic third world conflicts ... and our tendency would be to close the book." ... "The bottom line is that Afghanistan is not Iran," said an administration official. "It has no oil reserves and isn't located on the Persian Gulf. It's not a particular strategic prize. We have to be realistic about that."[73]

U.S. views of Afghanistan have thus come full circle: U.S. officials now acknowledge that Afghanistan is not very important.

In short, the realist explanation for the U.S. response is quite weak. The Carter administration interpreted Afghanistan to be strategic, due to intense and continuous pressures from the military-industrial complex, specifically, the various promilitary lobby groups discussed earlier. There is no reason to doubt that representatives of the MIC sincerely believed that the Soviet invasion of Afghanistan was strategically important—such an interpretation was consistent with their group interests. But their perceptions were heavily colored by these interests. Overall, it seems much more plausible to view the invasion as a *pretext* to justify implementation of a promilitary policy that the MIC favored. And the invasion of Afghanistan was clearly a major asset for the military-industrial complex, as an *Air Force Magazine* editorial candidly noted in early 1980. The editorial perfunctorily regretted the invasion, but pointed out that, nevertheless, it would help reverse U.S. policy and would "provide a catalyst for putting U.S. foreign and defense policy on the road to renewed credibility." The invasion could "be turned into opportunity and opportunity into advantage."[74]

Conclusion

This chapter is intended to be only suggestive; a full analysis of the Afghan crisis would go beyond the scope here and would require access to classified materials that are not yet available. A full account of the crisis would surely be more complex than the sketch presented here. U.S. actions were undoubtedly motivated by a range of different factors, of which the military-industrial complex was only one. Yet it is interesting to note that the MIC model seems more consistent with the facts of the case than is the generally accepted realist explanation. Overall, the military-industrial complex approach is a model that is well worth reconsidering, and it deserves far more attention from political scientists.

The model may be especially appropriate at the present time. The U.S. military is, to a significant extent, a product of the cold war. It was largely created and sustained over four decades mainly for one (purported) objective: to deter and/or roll back the Soviet Union. Now that the main enemy has literally ceased to exist, we can expect a new era of military-industrial lobbying and the creation of new foreign "threats" and national security "crises." It is worth mentioning that the 1989 invasion of Panama makes little sense in a realist framework. At the time of the invasion, the *Economist* noted, "The security of the [Panama] canal, which matters rather less than it did 80 years ago, was not at stake; and U.S. interests are unlikely to benefit much from the removal of General Manuel Noriega, who, though corrupt and brutish, posed no threat to regional stability, still less to the United States itself."[75] The military-industrial complex may have a lot to tell us about U.S. motivations in that invasion, as well as U.S. participation in the 1991 Persian Gulf War.

Anthony Downs presciently notes that "a bureau threatened by abolition because of a decline in the social significance of its functions must either find new functions or reinstate the importance of its present ones." And inevitably, there will be the "hunt for new business."[76] We should now expect a hunt for new business by the military-industrial complex.

3

Business Mobilization and the New Right: Currents in U.S. Foreign Policy

❧

Amy Ansell

This chapter examines the material basis for the New Right's symbolic construction of the Soviet threat in the late 1970s and early 1980s—what will be labeled here as "the second cold war." Rather than view the emergence of the second cold war as a rational response by governing elites to increased Soviet aggression, or as an ideological reaction fueled by democratic ideals, intraelite bickering, or the paranoid delusions of "cold warriors," this chapter pursues a basically business-centered analysis. Without discounting the relevance of these other variables, the aim of this study is to examine divisions within the international business community and to explore how such divisions contributed to the "right turn" in foreign policy debate. In so doing, I hope to contribute to scholarly debates on the meaning of the end of the cold war, as well as on the dynamics of foreign policy formation more generally.

The business conflict approach to the emergence of the second cold war is offered here as a challenge to the conventional view that increased anti-Soviet rhetoric and policy during the Carter and Reagan eras was solely a response to an objective problem or threat (i.e., increased Soviet aggression).[1] The approach argues that such a geostrategic view, although valid and in many respects revealing, cannot by itself explain the emergence of the second cold war. It asserts that East-West tensions during this period derived, at least in part, from societal disputes among different business actors and the way in which those disputes manifested themselves politically. Such a business-centered analysis cannot on its own explain the right turn in foreign policy formation, but it can help illuminate the more hidden and often neglected material dimensions of power and conflict that operate in the field of international relations.

This chapter attempts to examine the generalized move to the right among influential business groups in the late 1970s and early 1980s and to explore the extent to which this shift contributed to the right turn in foreign and military policy during the Carter and Reagan administrations. Declining economic confidence in the 1970s as a result of the relative deterioration in the U.S. share of world exports, in production of industrial goods, and in the share of overseas investments, as well as the relative increase in the cost of energy and burgeoning revolutionary movements in the less-developed world, all contributed to a marked rightward shift in the policy preferences of significant sectors of the business community. Broad-based support for a more conservative domestic policy and a more assertive foreign and military policy emerged within the business community, cutting across its conventional divisions. Liberal commitments shared by a majority of business groups throughout the early postwar era came increasingly under challenge. The economic and political conditions that had previously supported these commitments changed, with the effect that conservative and nationalist sentiment within the business community began to soar.[2]

As this case study will reveal, business groups were more likely to move to the right if: (1) they had labor-intensive foreign investments; (2) they faced threats to their investments (whether labor- or capital-intensive) from insurgent movements in the less developed world; (3) they were tied to the military-industrial complex; or (4) they were ideologically oriented to the far right, regardless of explicit material interests. Of key import here is the argument that at the root of the right turn in foreign and military policy was not a shift in electoral sentiment, to which much of mainstream political science points but, rather, the transformation of elite industrial coalitions.[3]

My argument, in summary, is as follows: Developments in the less-developed world (including the Iranian and Nicaraguan revolutions, as well as the Soviet invasion of Afghanistan), together with the right turn of significant sectors of the business community in response to declining rates of profit at home and weakening political influence internationally with the fall of key U.S. allies, provided a set of circumstances that intensified the split within the governing core industrial coalition and helped allow for the rise of other groups associated with the military-industrial complex and the New Right. Thus, although the emergence of the second cold war must be understood as developing within a determinate set of circumstances that realists discuss, such an analysis is incomplete without consideration of business conflict over the direction of U.S. foreign policy.

Case Study

The "second cold war" is a period commonly associated with the election of Ronald Reagan to office. Reagan came to power promising to combat what he described as persistent Soviet expansionism. The 1980 Republican Party Manifesto committed itself to restoring U.S. military superiority. Military expenditures grew by 32 percent between 1981 and 1985 in real terms, or from $199 billion to $264 billion in constant 1986 U.S. dollars, thus making the Reagan-initiated peacetime military buildup the largest in the nation's history.[4] Arms control negotiations such as SALT II were abandoned, and the Carter administration's human rights policies were denounced as "unilateral moralism." A more interventionist strategy toward Soviet allies in the Third World was adopted, as evidenced by U.S. support for the Contras in Nicaragua, the mujahideen in Afghanistan, and the National Union for the Total Independence of Angola (UNITA) rebels in Angola. Such cold war policies were justified with fierce anti-Soviet rhetoric, the most notorious of which was Reagan's speech in which he denounced the Soviet Union as an "Evil Empire."

While the foreign policy and rhetoric of the Reagan administration certainly heightened the intensity of second cold war, it is important to note that the turning point from liberal internationalism to containment militarism actually occurred during the Carter administration. By the middle of his term, Carter took a number of measures that departed from his early "Trilateralist" approach to foreign and military affairs, an approach that emphasized global cooperation and economic, as opposed to military, options.[5] Carter took definitive measures toward a more hard-line policy as early as 1978: increasing overall military expenditure, deploying U.S. military forces to the Caribbean, creating a Rapid Deployment Force, and granting covert aid to the Afghan guerillas. The articulation of the Carter Doctrine in a 23 January 1980 State of the Union Address marked the demise of the Trilateralist approach: "Any attempt by any outside force to gain control of the Persian Gulf region will be regarded as an assault on the vital interests of the United States of America, and such an assault will be repelled by any means necessary, including military force."[6]

The Reagan Doctrine merely took the Carter Doctrine to its logical conclusion. Armed with the belief that the decline in U.S. relative power on the global scene had all to do with the misguided policies of previous administrations (i.e., détente) and little to do with long-term cycles of hegemonic decline, the Reagan administration set out to reverse almost every policy element of the détente era. Reagan's election signaled the political triumph of the view that a preoccupation with the Soviet threat should be placed at the center of U.S. foreign and military policy.

This shift was not simply ideological, but was the result of a coalition of business and political elites who had something to gain from exaggerating the Soviet threat. This coalition was constituted by: (1) conservative business internationalists (i.e., those with labor-intensive investments); (2) right-wing business groups that faced threats to their investments (whether labor-

or capital-intensive) from insurgent movements in the less developed world; (3) business groups tied to the military-industrial complex; and (4) policymakers and intellectuals of the New Right driven by anticommunist ideology. Such a "hegemonic coalition" came into conflict during the period under study with those liberal internationalists who favored free trade and economic, as opposed to military, solutions.[7]

Business Realignment and Mobilization

Significantly, this coalition emerged precisely at the time that the New Deal coalition began to disintegrate. Originally constituted as an elite coalition of capital-intensive industries, investment banks, and internationally oriented commercial banks, the New Deal coalition began to break apart in the 1970s as a result of a combination of factors described later. The New Deal system, associated as it was with global U.S. military superiority and an international monetary system that revolved around the dollar, at one time worked to the benefit of the majority of the U.S. corporate community. In the words of the president of Business International: "This was one of the periods of freedom: freedom to invest, freedom to trade, freedom to have economic intercourse, stability and freedom."[8] Changed circumstances altered this equation so that new divisions were created between those sectors of capital that continued to benefit from the system of liberal internationalism and those that either no longer did or never had.

Although there are many political factors relevant to the story of the breakup of the New Deal system, the effect of economic factors on the political constitution of core industrial sectors was perhaps the most crucial. The appearance in 1971 of the first absolute trade deficit in recent U.S. history, the abandonment of the Bretton Woods monetary system that same year, the 1973 OPEC (Organization of Petroleum Exporting Countries) price hikes, and the 1973–1975 "Great Recession" all contributed to growing anti-New Deal sentiment within relevant sectors of the business community, including its multinational wing.[9]

Illustrative of this shift in business sentiment is the Trilateral Commission's report *The Crisis of Democracy*. The report's basic argument was that democracy had overextended itself and was threatening the very health of capitalism. Samuel Huntington, the report's main author, wrote:

> Some of the problems of governance in the U.S. today stem from an excess of democracy. ... Democracy is more of a threat to itself in the U.S. than it is in either Europe or Japan where there still exist residual inheritances of traditional and aristocratic values ... In the United States, the strength of democracy poses a problem for the governability of democracy in a way which is not the case elsewhere.[10]

Such antidemocratic sentiment was all the more significant coming from the Trilateral Commission—a backbone institution of the New Deal coalition itself—and is thus suggestive of how the policy preferences of elites adapt and correspond to basic changes in the structure of the economy and U.S. industry's strategic position within it.

Broad-based support for a more assertive foreign and military policy emerged within the business community, cutting across its conventional divisions. For several years, debate had raged within respectable business journals over what were essentially two foreign policy positions: the one favoring trade and diplomatic maneuvering (i.e., liberal internationalism); the other advocating increased military involvement in the Third World (i.e., containment militarism). By 1980, the latter position had clearly won the day. In a speech in April, for example, David Rockefeller criticized a foreign policy based on "fuzzily defined moral issues—such as human rights," and the Trilateral Commission ceased publication of its human rights report.[11] Although rising hard-line sentiments were of course informed by political factors, such as the wave of fourteen Third World revolutions in a period of six years, newly informed economic considerations also played an important role in détente's demise.

Military force and preparedness increasingly were understood by certain sectors of the U.S. business community as being necessary to protect U.S. economic power against the challenges posed by the growing internationalization of the economy, the OPEC price hikes, the wave of Third World revolutions, and the declining competitiveness of U.S. firms vis-à-vis the economies of West Germany and Japan. Thus, changes in the basic structure of the economy crucially affected the policy preferences of relevant business groups that, in turn, influenced the logic of U.S. foreign policy formation.

This logic, it must be emphasized, did not apply to the whole of the U.S. business community, but only to certain sectors of it. To argue otherwise would be to accept the instrumentalist idea of a single, unified business interest. The business conflict model, by contrast, assumes that disputes will arise among business actors depending on the firms' position in both the domestic and the global economy.

With concern to this case study, disputes emerged inside the multinational business community leading to a split between conservative and liberal internationalists.[12] Conservative internationalists with labor-intensive investments and thus sensitive to wage constraints (mining, lumber, agribusiness, chemical production, etc.),[13] as well as those multinational corporations (both capital- and labor-intensive) that perceived that insurgent movements in the less developed world were a threat to their investments,[14] broke away from those liberal internationalists with capital-intensive investments (commercial banks, petroleum firms, telecommunications, aerospace, computers etc.) who continued to benefit from the free market in trade.[15] This breakaway wing of conservative internationalists joined, in turn, with domestic-oriented business groups already gaining in power (shoes, steel, tobacco, independent oil, textiles, parts of the chemical industry, most small enterprises, etc.).[16] Such an emerging coalition of conservative internationalist and right-wing business groups was born of a shared concern to insulate themselves from growing international competitiveness and revolutionary insurgencies via more assertive foreign economic and military policies.[17]

In the one- or two-year period building up to the 1980 presidential election, then, new lines of political conflict and convergence within the business community were appearing as a result of broad changes in the structure of the economy and the U.S. position within it. The commitment to liberal internationalism shared by a majority of business groups throughout the New Deal era was coming increasingly under challenge. The economic and political conditions that had previously supported this commitment had changed, with the effect that conservative, hard-line sentiment within certain sectors of the business community began to soar. Thus, while the system of multinational liberalism met with fierce opposition from its very inception, it was not until the mid-1970s that such opposition gained a real political voice.[18]

This opposition was not merely defensive, but also formative. Relevant business groups submerged many of their specific concerns in the late 1970s and mobilized in an unprecedented manner for their collective interests. As Thomas Edsall comments, "During the 1970s business refined its ability to act as a class, submerging competitive instincts in favour of a joint, cooperative action."[19]

Old pro-business organizations, such as NAM, the National Federation of Independent Business, and the U.S. Chamber of Commerce, were revitalized.[20] The transformation of the U.S. Chamber of Commerce, for example, into an organization actively involved in politics illustrates the new mood of corporate America. With board members including August Busch III, Joseph Coors, and William May of American Can, the Chamber accrued lobbying resources that surpassed the combined budgets of the Republican and Democratic National Committees.[21] The Chamber's national budget for research, communications, and political activities increased threefold between the years 1974 and 1983, from roughly $20 million to $65 million.[22]

In addition to the revitalization of long-standing business organizations, new ones were formed in response to the changed economic and political climate. By far, the most important of these was the Business Roundtable. Composed of nearly 200 CEOs of major corporations, such as General Motors, General Electric, DuPont, IBM, and AT&T, and born of a sort of siege mentality in the post–Watergate era, the Business Roundtable became a symbol of a new breed of militant direct-lobbying business organization. By the end of 1976, *Business Week* described the Roundtable as "the most powerful voice of business."[23]

Corporate political action committees, known as PACs, also mushroomed during this period. According to the Federal Election Commission, the number of corporate PACs grew from 89 in 1974, to 433 by the end of 1976, to 784 in 1978, to an incredible 1,512 by 1983.[24] Examples of corporate PACs include those of Dart Industries, General Electric, and the Business/Industry Political Action Committee. The explosive growth of political action committees has allowed business leaders to influence the evolving political debate without, significantly, getting involved directly in specific political battles.

By late 1980, significant sectors of the business community were moving to the right and lending their support to the Reagan candidacy.[25] As a result, the range of foreign policy preferences shifted considerably to the right during the Reagan era as compared with the 1970s détente era. This transformation demonstrates the ability of capital to reorganize itself in the political arena in response to changes in the basic structure of the economy, with telling effects on foreign policy formation.

The Military-Industrial Complex

Associated with the rightward shift of the U.S. business community was the growth in power of the military-industrial complex. The military-industrial lobby was particularly involved in pressuring Congress to support the turn to a more hard-line foreign and military policy. Military production had become a major industry in many states, especially in the so-called Sun Belt states where the New Right was, and continues to be, most strong. As Jerry Sanders documents in *Peddlers of Crisis,* political organizations representing the military-industrial complex "linked the architects of Containment Militarism abroad to the recipients of Keynesian Militarism at home."[26]

Perhaps the most important of all the hard-line anti-Soviet organizations connected with the MIC was the Committee on the Present Danger (CPD). The CPD was founded by a large number of prominent business and former military figures in the immediate aftermath of Carter's electoral victory in November 1976, with a large start-up grant from Hewlett-Packard's David Packard and considerable support from Richard Mellon Scaife. CPD members included: Eugene Rostow, Professor of Law, Yale University; James Schlesinger, former Secretary of Energy and campaign adviser to Reagan, former head of the CIA and Secretary of Defense under Nixon; Paul Nitze, one of the writers of NSC paper no. 68 and a key foreign policy and defense adviser in every administration from Truman's to Nixon's; and Frank Barnett, president of NSIC.[27] The CPD was founded as a forum for the defense industry and its infrastructure of supply firms, as well as for cold warriors motivated by anticommunist ideology, to work together to discredit the assumptions and policies associated with the détente era.

In a speech before NAM, CPD member Frank Barnett argued that "the Soviet Union today, in a period of so-called détente, is really a far more deadly challenge than it was under Stalin when everybody knew that the cold war was for real."[28] Barnett concluded with a plea for the mobilization of the U.S. military-industrial complex as "the last and the only shield between the free world and heirs of Lenin and Genghis Khan."

The CPD repeatedly warned of persistent Soviet expansionism. The committee's military inferiority complex is illustrated in its founding statement:

> The principal threat to our nation, to world peace, and to the cause of human freedom is the Soviet drive for dominance based upon an unparalleled military buildup. ... For more than a decade, the Soviet Union has been enlarging and improving both its strategic and its conventional military forces far more rapidly than the United States and its allies. Soviet military power and its rate of growth cannot be explained or justified by considerations of self-defense."[29]

Armed with such a vision of relentless Soviet global expansion, the CPD was instrumental in advocating huge increases in defense spending and mobilizing the political opposition to the ratification of the SALT II treaties. The views of the CPD were well represented within the Reagan administration, with as many as thirty-three committee members (including Reagan's secretary of state, George Schultz) serving in the White House, the State Department and the CIA.

Another important political vehicle for the MIC was the Coalition for Peace Through Strength. Formed in 1978 under the auspices of the ASC, the coalition served as an ad hoc lobby aiming to rally the "silent majority" in Congress in opposition to Carter's defense policy and in favor of military superiority over the Soviet Union. The coalition brought together Southern Rim congressmen with a stake in defense spending and their business constituents, neoconservative and New Right organizations concerned about the Soviet threat, and hawks from the national security establishment under one national defense umbrella.

The New Right

It is in this context of shifting business interests and the emerging coalition with groups representing the military-industrial complex that the New Right materialized as a key player in U.S. politics. Those business groups that were ideologically oriented to the far right, regardless of explicit material interests, represent the fourth and final part of the coalition of business groups that moved to the right during the period under study to help bring the conservative Reagan administration to office.

The New Right appeared in the mid-1970s as the section of the right wing that is distinct from both traditional conservatism and more extreme, far-right groupings. The emergence of the New Right was to some extent consciously encouraged (not to mention actively funded) by conservative business leaders, and to some extent it was an independent development that nevertheless complemented the aims of the newly-emerging elite industrial coalition.

The New Right is important to study when analyzing the emergence of the second cold war since it, more than any other section of the right wing, served as a catalyst in connecting right-wing business interests and hard-line anticommunist sentiments with the electoral strategies and policy goals of the Republican Party. The New Right (in its secular-political, religious, and intellectual manifestations) was a central political actor in justifying the revival of military intervention as a legitimate instrument of government policy.

While much has been written on the New Right's domestic agenda, there has been a relative paucity of attention to its active engagement in the evolving political debate around foreign and military issues. For example, Paul Weyrich's Committee for the Survival of a Free Congress (now known as the Free Congress Foundation) organized regular luncheon meetings on foreign policy issues with congressmen and their aides to brief them on defense and foreign policy topics. In 1982, the Free Congress and Education Foundation created a committee to support the Contras.

The Heritage Foundation, a New Right think tank with offices on Capitol Hill, presented Reagan with a blueprint program for "raising defense spending by 35 billion dollars, unleashing the CIA, using food as a foreign policy weapon, and restoring Congressional internal security committees."[30] New Right leaders were also instrumental in forming the Madison Group, a group of conservative Congressmen concerned with foreign policy and security issues, which met regularly to coordinate lobbying strategies. Other key New Right groups more peripherally involved in foreign policy issues include the National Conservative Political Action Committee (NCPAC) directed by Terry Dolan (now deceased) and the Conservative Caucus directed by Howard Phillips.

A group of conservative intellectuals commonly referred to as "neoconservatives" was also instrumental in facilitating the right turn in foreign policy consensus. Although different in many important respects from the New Right groups mentioned above, especially with concern to the question of political style, this group of mainly New York, Jewish intellectuals shared the obsession with the specter of ceaseless Soviet global expansion and concern with reviving military intervention as a legitimate instrument of government policy.[31] Besides organizing the Committee for a Free World and the National Endowment for Democracy, neoconservative intellectuals such as Norman Podhoretz, Jeanne Kirkpatrick, and Walter Laquer wrote articles for the neoconservative journal *Commentary* (and elsewhere) with titles such as "The Present Danger," "Why the Soviet Union Thinks It Could Fight and Win a Nuclear War," and "Soviet Global Strategy."

In addition to the secular-political Right and the intellectual Right, the religious Right was also involved in forcing a concern with Soviet behavior to the forefront of national politics. New Christian Right organizations such as Religious Roundtable, the Moral Majority (now the Liberty Federation), and Christian Voice were instrumental in discrediting Carter's foreign policy record and legitimating what came to be known as "low intensity conflict" as a form of humanitarian project.[32] Christian Voice, for example, an organization born of the budding relationship between conservative secular-political and religious leaders in the late 1970s, frequently included foreign policy issues on its report cards instructing good Christians on which electoral candidates were deserving of a moral vote.

Ed McAteer, the president of Religious Roundtable and a Tennessee millionaire, sent a letter in which he denounced the passage of the Nuclear Freeze Resolution in Congress, warning that it would lock the United States in a position of military inferiority. McAteer added, "Besides which, the godless Russians have violated treaty after treaty. The one goal and purpose of the Russian War Machine is total world domination." Even today, in the wake of the collapse of the Soviet Union, New Christian Right organizations such as Pat Robertson's Christian Coalition continue to oppose disarmament efforts. In a 1991 special report to Christian Coalition members, Robertson stated, "History clearly records that unilateral disarmament by the leading peaceful powers invariably invites aggression."[33]

Other conservative organizations concerned with foreign and military policy, but not formally within the New Right orbit, include: think tanks such as the Hoover Institution at Stanford University, the Ethics and Public Policy Center in Washington D.C., and the Center for Strategic and International Studies at Georgetown University; foreign policy pressure groups such as the Coalition for Peace Through Strength and the New York–based NSIC; Democratic organizations advocating hard-line foreign policy initiatives such as the Coalition for a Democratic Majority (CDM); and lobbying groups on Latin America such as the Committee of Santa Fe and the Council for Inter-American Security. Together, these institutes, despite their often small size and organizational differences, crucially influenced the rightward shift of the Carter administration and the election of the hard-line Reagan administration to office.

Many of these groups were formed with enormous financial support from relevant sectors of the business community. New Right organizations received millions of dollars from both right-wing oriented businesses (for example, independent oil companies, protectionist textile producers represented by Jesse Helms, weapons manufacturers, and Western mining interests) and from rightward-moving multinationals. Key corporate donors promoting hard-line national security studies included: John M. Olin Foundation (agricultural chemicals, sporting weapons), Fred C. Koch Foundation (energy, real estate); Bechtel Foundation (construction); Adolph Coors Foundation (brewing); Smith Richardson Foundation (Vicks Vaporub, national defense policy think tanks); Sarah Mellon Scaife Foundation (Gulf Oil); Lilly Foundation (pharmaceuticals); J. Howard Pew Freedom Trust (Sun Oil); and Samuel Noble Foundation (oil and drilling). Other corporations instrumental in funding the New Right included: Weyerhaeuser, Ford, Reader's Digest, Potlatch, Mobil, Coca-Cola, Consolidated Foods, Ashland Oil, Tennessee Gas Transmission, Firestone, Pizza Hut, Castle and Cook, Hershey, Exxon, Citibank, General Motors, IBM, and many others.[34]

In sum, the New Right emerged in a historical context characterized by a rightward shift in the policy preferences of a part of the U.S. business community, and the volume of its political voice during the late 1970s and early 1980s was crucially dependent on this shift. Although many commentators describe the New Right as a counterestablishment and many New Right leaders themselves claim to be anti–big business, in reality the New Right served as a spokesperson of sorts for a particular sector of the business community (right-wing nationalists and conservative multinationalists) against another (liberal multinationalists).[35] Once the focus is on conflicts within the business community, it is possible to render consistent the New Right's business mobilization rhetoric and its anti–big business diatribes without writing off either as a smoke screen for "something else." The New Right's ideology of populism is thus arguably as much a legitimating tool of the elite industrial coalition as a genuine expression of popular support or antibusiness sentiment.

Tracing the emergence of the New Right to divisions within the international business community need not, however, obscure the importance of New Right anti-Soviet ideology in justifying the revival of military intervention as a legitimate instrument of government policy. A brief survey follows of the key assumptions—or categories of meaning—that appear in New Right discourse on foreign and military topics.

The most overarching category of meaning is that of the "Soviet threat." For example, the former director of the National Security Task Force of Conservative Caucus, Brigadier General Albion Knight (also a member of Reagan's defense transition team) warned of the "clear and present danger" at a 1982 New Right conference at Harvard University: "The United States is in serious trouble. I have traveled around the country these past eighteen months admonishing that, unless major changes take place in the politics of government and the attitude of our people, we may have fewer than one thousand days left as a free, independent sovereign nation."[36]

Not only is the Soviet threat still a reality, according to national defense conservatives, it is a threat that has grown as a result of the misguided policy of détente. Such a view was vindicated in the eyes of many in the wake of the 1979 Soviet invasion of Afghanistan. For example, in an article for the neoconservative journal *Commentary,* Edward N. Luttwak (author and visiting lecturer at the School of Advanced International Studies of Johns Hopkins University) argued:

> Thus we are now facing a Soviet Union that has changed in a way most ominous. The Soviet Union of ceaseless opportunism that would fill any local vacuum as a sneak thief in a hotel tries every door, but which would not deliberately go to war for fear that its forces would make a mess of things, has now evolved into a different kind of enemy, one that is plainly willing to add direct warfare to its abundant array of expansionist instruments.[37]

Luttwak concluded with a warning: "Afghanistan was merely the weakest and least protected of the countries unfortunate enough to be directly adjacent to the Soviet Union. Now the others wait their turn, facing a Soviet military empire once again on the move."[38]

It is important to note that not only Republicans fill the ranks of national defense conservatives warning of the mounting Soviet threat; Democrats do too. The most notable organization in this respect is the CDM. Begun in 1972 as a forum of opposition to the then reigning soft-line position on foreign policy within the Democratic Party, the CDM mobilized to coordinate dissenting hawkish positions within the party. The Foreign Policy Task Force of the CDM, whose ranks included its chairman, Eugene V. Rostow (Professor of Law at Yale and former undersecretary of state), Norman Podhoretz (editor of *Commentary*), John P. Roche (columnist and former president of Americans for Democratic Action (ADA)), and Albert Shanker (president of the American Federation of Teachers–AFL-CIO), issued a statement in Richard Viguerie's New Right journal, *Conservative Digest:* "The nation is in great danger. Our danger is increasing every day. The Soviet Union continues to pursue a policy of expansion that threatens our vital interests in Europe, the Middle East, and other parts of the world."[39] After admonishing the U.S. defense budget as "an invitation to disaster," the article concludes with a plea to Congress to reaffirm its commitment to maintaining an appropriate balance of world military power: "If we fail to uphold this balance, we Democrats could not escape our share of the responsibility for greatly increasing the prospects of political despotism and eventual war. The United States should be the master, not the victim, of its fate."[40]

A second key category of meaning found within New Right discourse is the belief that the Soviet Union has never been, and is not now, a status quo power. Since it was just such a belief that justified détente and arms control negotiations, such an argument provided a powerful critique of both. The Soviet Union is conceived by national defense conservatives as inherently expansionist. For example, Norman Podhoretz wrote an article for *Commentary* entitled "The Present Danger" in which he argued that the invasion of Afghanistan was merely the newest stage of Soviet expansionism and, as such, "not easily compatible with the notion that the Soviet Union had become a status quo power."[41] The Soviet Union is an expansionary state bent on the destruction of all non-communist states. Podhoretz continued:

> One would think from most of what has been said in recent months that the Soviet Union is a nation like any other with which we happen to be in competition ... the Soviet Union is not a nation like any other. It is a revolutionary state, exactly as Hitler's Germany was. ... In short, the reason Soviet imperialism is a threat to us is not merely that the Soviet Union is a superpower bent on aggrandizing itself, but that it is a Communist state armed, as Solzhenitsyn says, to the teeth, and dedicated to the destruction of the free institutions which are our heritage and our glory."[42]

Such views directly contradict those of respected foreign policy analysts, such as Stanley Hoffmann or George Kennan, who argued that the Soviet Union should be understood as a status quo power on par with the United States with a shared interest in preserving international stability and peace.

New Right answers for why the USSR was not a status quo power vary. Alternative explanations include: historical factors such as the imperial legacy of the czars or Russia's Stalinist past ("How Conservative Is Reagan's Foreign Policy?" by Burton Yale Pines); the distinctive background and character of the Soviet elite ("Why the Soviet Elite Is Different from U.S.," by Robert Conquest); domestic defects of either a political or an economic nature ("Can the Democracies Survive?" by Jean-Francois Revel); the inevitable outgrowth of communist ideology ("Why the Soviet Union Thinks It Could Fight and Win a Nuclear War," by Richard Pipes); or the ineluctable conflict between civilization and barbarism ("The Future Danger," by Norman Podhoretz). [43]

Another major assumption found within New Right ideology is what could be termed the "delusion of détente." Détente is conceived as being an extremely ambiguous concept; an ambiguity, moreover, which has worked to the Soviet advantage. New Rightists insist that the French word was translated through the lens of the U.S. and Soviet political cultures respectively, only to come out the other end with diametrically opposed meanings. Robert Moffit, the founding director of the Washington-based Council for Inter-American Security, puts it thus:

> Détente withered like a delicate flower in the Russian winter. While Washington policymakers looked hopefully toward a new and lasting era of relaxed

tensions, precedent to even broader international cooperation, the Soviet elite saw détente as a reflection of relative American military weakness vis-à-vis the Soviet Empire and a time to consolidate and expand the international gains made by the "Socialist camp", as well as to assist the ubiquitous, anti-capitalist forces of "national liberation" on a global scale.[44]

Such opposition to détente and its architects derives not merely from the view that it is naive or has failed to work, but also from the New Right equation of détente with appeasement. Analogies with the granting of Western concessions to Hitler in the 1930s are continually drawn within New Right discourse, and calls for "No More Munich's" abound. Détente is understood as a humiliating attempt to buy the Soviets off with the granting of unilateral concessions, having already accepted the fact of Soviet dominance. It is in this vein that the New Right opposed arms control agreements that allegedly worked to the Soviet advantage (such as SALT), the "great grain robberies," and advanced technology trade. What was needed, according to New Right ideologues, was not more concessions but, rather, increased U.S. military power.

Closely related to the above is the fourth key category of meaning: military (im)balance. It is a category closely linked to the New Right's engagement in the debate over the ratification of SALT II. National defense conservatives opposed SALT II on the basis that it would lock the United States into a position of military inferiority. New Rightists insisted that U.S. military power had already been allowed to decline to intolerable levels of risk. In an article entitled "Waging War on SALT," former presidential candidate Patrick J. Buchanan warned: "The United States has surrendered strategic superiority; we are in the process of losing parity; we are entering an era in which the West will be militarily inferior to the East—ripe for Soviet blackmail, Soviet bullying and, conceivably, Soviet attack."[45]

The final key category of meaning found within New Right ideology relates to the theme of the decline of the West. The West, and particularly the United States, is said to be suffering from a loss of will, intellectual confusion, and national humiliation. U.S. loss of will is believed to carry serious consequences for the survival of the free world. Walter Laquer warns, "With the West in retreat, the issue at stake is not the arrogance of power, but the defeatism generated by impotence. ... The survival of free societies, including America, is no longer a sure thing."[46] Elsewhere Laquer analyzes the reasons why the West is in retreat and concludes, "It is the internal American crisis—the loss of self-confidence and the political paralysis entailed by this loss—which has been the most important factor."[47]

Such sentiments were reinforced with an added degree of urgency in the aftermath of the Iranian hostage crisis. The seizure of U.S. hostages in Teheran in 1979 created a wave of nationalist-patriotic feelings in the United

States. The use of the Iranian crisis by national defense conservatives as a sort of vaccine against the so-called Vietnam syndrome was crucial to the garnering of popular support for the New Right project to increase defense spending and employ military force to once again protect U.S. interests abroad.

New Rightists charge that such a renewal of Western resolve has been frustrated by what they term the "new foreign policy establishment" and the associated emergence of neo-isolationism.[48] In the New Right worldview, the West is facing a battle on two fronts: on the one front, the enemies without (i.e., communism); on the other, the Eastern liberal foreign policy elite deemed responsible for the decline of the United States as a global power.[49] Asking himself why there seems to be so much opposition to its rightful role as the world's policeman, Walter Laquer surmises:

> Some have written and talked for so long about America's impotence and inevitable decline that they have acquired almost a vested interest in the realization of their nightmare; some are deeply convinced that the country is so irresponsible in the exercise of its power that it has to be kept in a state of weakness; some think that to go under in style is preferable to an outcome more positive but aesthetically less pleasing.[50]

Together, these five categories of meaning—the Soviet threat, the Soviet Union as a non–status quo power, the delusion of détente, military (im)balance, and the decline of the West—interact to produce what I have referred to throughout as the New Right ideology of containment militarism. It is important to emphasize, however, that the emergence of the second cold war was by no means a mere result of a particular combination of New Right ideas. The significance of studying ideology is precisely to examine the role of ideas in constructing which sociopolitical problems are significant and which insignificant, and accordingly, which political solutions are judged beneficial and which misguided.

The New Right and Reagan

New Rightists have not only engaged in the struggle of ideas, but also contributed to the policy formation process. The New Right proposed a whole range of foreign and military policy initiatives, some of which were instituted during the Carter administration, others during the Reagan administration, and some not at all. Yet, irrespective of the timing or degree of impact, government rhetoric and policy initiatives in the area of foreign policy during the period under study dovetailed in important ways with the key categories of meaning produced and circulated by the New Right. Indeed, from 1978 and throughout most of Reagan's first term, New Right ideology emerged at the very center of national foreign policy debate.

From the very beginning, Ronald Reagan made public his belief that the central issue of our time was the conflict between the United States and the Soviet Union. In now-notorious words, Reagan depicted the issue as a conflict of good versus evil; of the free world versus the "Evil Empire." Reagan portrayed U.S. behavior as purely defensive in nature: "The Soviet Union underlies all the unrest going on. If they weren't engaged in this game of dominoes, there wouldn't be any hot spots in the world."[51] Reagan issued a call to arms for the United States to defend tyranny and freedom against "Godless communism." He referred to the Vietnam War as "a noble cause" and to the Soviet military buildup as the "greatest in the history of mankind."[52] In arguing for a new "grand strategy for the 1980s," aiming at military superiority over the USSR, Reagan remarked, "We're already in an arms race—but only the Soviets are racing."[53]

The necessary first step, according to national defense conservatives within the new administration, was to significantly increase defense expenditures in order to close the purported Soviet "window of opportunity." The 1980 GOP platform committed the party to the goal of military superiority.

The Reagan administration made more or less good on its commitment to increase military spending. Defense spending increased from $199 billion to $264 billion between the years 1981 and 1985, an increase of 32 percent in real terms during Reagan's first term alone.[54] As a share of national GNP, defense spending grew from 5.2 percent in 1980 to 6.6 percent in 1985.[55]

The administration justified the military buildup by issuing warnings of U.S. military weakness and statements about the imperative to reverse military asymmetries, warnings that clearly resonated with New Right discourse on the topic. For example, in 1982 Reagan declared that "in virtually every measure of military power the Soviet Union enjoys a decided advantage."[56] In a similar vein, Caspar Weinberger, Reagan's defense secretary announced: "In the United States' view, it must be the Western purpose to strengthen its defense in the face of Soviet military expansionism. ... The West cannot allow the military balance to swing further in favor of the Soviets."[57] Besides vastly increasing the defense budget, the Reagan administration also revived the B-1 bomber killed by Carter, encouraged the development of a new land-based ICBM (intercontinental ballistic missile), added tactical fighter wings to the Air Force and submarines, expanded U.S. air and sea life capacity, and reformed Carter's largely symbolic Rapid Deployment Force into a genuine military muscle.[58]

The Reagan administration's first term was also characterized by a marked de-emphasis on arms control. In a 1981 speech to West Point, Reagan warned of the dangers of the "Treaty Trap" and promised to increase U.S. military strength: "No nation that placed its faith in parchment or paper while at the same time it gave up its protective hardware ever lasted long enough to write many pages in history."[59] In many instances, the administration took affirmative steps to openly subvert arms control efforts. For example, Reagan stacked the Arms Control and Disarmament Agency (ACDA)—an agency set up by Congress to lobby for arms control efforts within the government— with national defense conservatives who opposed such efforts.[60] With Eugene Rostow as the agency's newly appointed director under Reagan, a man who at the time categorically rejected the strategic assumptions behind arms control, the ACDA worked against what little momentum already existed for arms control and instead attempted to mobilize opposition to the growing peace sentiment.[61] Moreover, such de-emphasis on arms control was matched by growing belligerency in Third World policies.

In summary, a preoccupation with the Soviet threat had emerged at the very center of national political debate by the time Reagan was elected to office. A coalition of labor-intensive foreign investors, business groups threatened by insurgent movements in the less-developed world, and sectors connected to the military-industrial complex succeeded in overcoming their conventional differences and united to back Reagan's candidacy. The rightward shift in the foreign policy preferences of relevant business sectors was justified by a group of New Right ideologues motivated by anticommunist ideology. As demonstrated herein, the first years of the Reagan administration remained largely faithful to its campaign promises vis-à-vis U.S.-Soviet relations.

As early as 1982, however, divisions reemerged and the second cold war coalition began to slowly break apart. In keeping with the assumptions of the business conflict approach defended earlier, an explanation for this must look not to objective changes in Soviet behavior, nor to popular sentiment but, rather, to new divisions within the business community and how those divisions influenced the evolving political debate on foreign and military policy. Tensions manifested themselves almost immediately after Reagan assumed office over the grain embargo put in place by the Carter administration. The Reagan administration vacillated over whether or not to uphold the embargo. During the election campaign, Reagan had promised to end the embargo since it was unfair to U.S. farmers. Yet he backed off from that promise during his first press conference, announcing that no decision had yet been made one way or the other. Two months later, the embargo was lifted, appeasing U.S. farmers but infuriating New Right cold warriors and many in the Pentagon who charged the administration with betraying its principles and providing the capitalist rope with which the USSR would hang the West.

Throughout the next year, the administration's policy preferences were riddled with contradictions, suggesting that tensions between those sectors favoring free trade and those favoring economic sanctions and military force could not be so easily resolved. Having pledged conflicting promises to each during the electoral campaign, Reagan faced difficult decisions once in office. For example, again on the issue of trade policy, a battle developed between two groups: on the one hand, those business groups (led by Texas Instruments) with few ties to Soviet Bloc markets that supported the termination of shipments of new technology, and on the other, those business groups (led by Control Data) with extensive ties to the Soviet Bloc markets that supported free trade policies.[62] The dispute was eventually resolved in favor of the former group, culminating in the launch of "Operation Exodus" (a plan to stop the transfer of U.S. technology to the Soviet Bloc), but much political ground was lost, and tensions heightened within the coalition that had helped bring Reagan to power.[63]

Shortly thereafter, another conflict occurred over the issue of European credits to the Soviets for the building of a natural gas pipeline. Again divisions emerged within the administration between those who opposed the plan (independent oilmen, such as George Bush, and neoconservative intellectuals) and those who supported it (State Department officials, such as Warnke, liberal internationalists, and bankers with a financial stake in Europe). Although many may have overlooked the contradiction between the implementation of Operation Exodus and the beginning of wheat exports, the hypocrisy of the administration's opposition to the pipeline in the context of ongoing grain sales was not missed by many opponents of Reagan's hawkish policies. Under fire from liberal internationalists, the administration finally ceased its opposition to the pipeline project, again leaving the New Right feeling betrayed.

This sense of betrayal was heightened in the wake of yet another dispute involving potential economic sanctions against Poland after the December 1981 imposition of martial law. Under pressure from liberal internationalists, the administration granted certain credit concessions to Poland in 1982. Some sanctions remained, but they were largely symbolic in nature. Thus, once again the conflict between the neoliberal concern for free market relations and the neoconservative concern for military force and anticommunist principle had been resolved in favor of the former. By the midterm elections of 1982, much of the sense of coherence that had characterized Reagan's candidacy and first year in office had been lost.

Conflicts emerged over the direction of foreign policy among principled New Right ideologues who criticized the Reagan administration for betraying campaign promises to take a tougher stand against the Soviets (including those associated with the Heritage Foundation and the Free Congress Foundation), intellectually oriented conservatives who were in many instances the key architects of the Reagan policy (for example, neoconservative members of the administration and writers associated with *Commentary* magazine), and neoliberals who advocated economic over military solutions (including members of the Trilateral Commission and many Republican moderates)—divisions that continue to mark the conservative movement to this day.[64] When pushed, the administration resolved the emerging differences in favor of the neoliberal side of the second cold war coalition, leaving the New

Right increasingly disaffected. As James Kurth notes: "In almost every case of economic sanctions, when the Reagan administration had to choose between the pro-business policies of its conservative members and the anti-communist policies of its neoconservative members, it chose the former."[65]

This lack of coherence and shift to a more moderate tone was reflected at the level of policy formation. Real defense spending was frozen. A bipartisan movement emerged in the direction of fiscal orthodoxy with the realization that the budget deficit created by such high military expenditure was harming the economy. There was also a return to an emphasis, however symbolic, on the need for arms control, as illustrated by the Reagan-initiated Strategic Arms Reduction Talks (START). Although future scandals would reveal that the New Right's agenda had not entirely disappeared but, rather, had gone underground (i.e., Contragate), it is nevertheless true that the public posture of the Reagan administration vis-à-vis U.S.-Soviet relations had clearly changed by the end of its first term in office.

There are several reasons for this change in public posture. The burgeoning peace movement both at home and abroad is a significant factor to consider. Another important reason is the moderating trend in public opinion vis-à-vis defense spending and U.S.-Soviet relations.[66] Perhaps most important, however, is the existence of a seemingly irreconcilable contradiction between the goals of a minimalist foreign economic policy and a strong national security strategy contained within the second cold war coalition that had helped bring Reagan to power.

Reagan proved unable to resolve the tensions that continued to exist between the late-arriving conservative internationalists and the right-wing nationalist business groups that had long been his bastion of support. Tensions mounted within Reagan's team of advisers over a number of issues: trade with the Soviet Union, the proper scope of arms limitations negotiations and pace of new weapons acquisitions, and the percentage of GNP to be devoted to defense. The practical economic effects of Reagan's program of simultaneously lowering taxes and increasing military spending heightened these tensions and ultimately served to alienate conservative business internationalist support for Reagan's cold war policies and rhetoric.[67] With such key business support in jeopardy, the Reagan administration moderated its policy and rhetoric and, in doing so, retained most of its business support in the 1984 election. However, the coalition that had helped bring Reagan to power had by 1984 disintegrated, and the process that had driven the emergence of second cold war began to reverse itself.

Conclusion

The business conflict approach advances our understanding of the emergence and decline of the second cold war, as well as of the dynamics of U.S.

foreign policy formation more generally, in ways other approaches do not. It challenges the realist assumption that the state possesses a realm of autonomous behavior and, by virtue of that, pursues a "national interest" that transcends the particularistic concerns of any societal group. Rather than to view the state as insulated from the pressures of private interest groups, the task of the business conflict approach is to find the connection between patterns of economic conflict and the dynamics of U.S. foreign policy formation (that is, between business influence and national security concerns). Business groups are, of course, not the only influence on policymakers, and so there is no need to prove that business influence is determinate in any or every case. Our task is a more modest one: to locate the developments realists point to within the context of business conflict over the direction of U.S. foreign policy.

By the same token, the business conflict approach challenges society-centered approaches to the end of the cold war, and pluralism in particular, by situating the influence of various societal pressures within a contextual examination of the structural and competitive tensions among U.S. capitalists. In other words, the business conflict approach argues that the ability of societal groups such as the New Right to influence policy was conditioned by splits among the capitalist class. Thus, while an appreciation of the dynamics of interest group competition and ideological struggle is important to any explanation of the emergence of the second cold war, the business conflict approach locates such competition within a broader context of capitalist competition. In doing so, the business conflict approach provides an important corrective to the conventional view that the New Right emerged on the political scene as that societal force best equipped to pressure government to take action to protect democracy against the growing threat of worldwide Soviet expansionism.

Analysis of the hidden dimensions of power and conflict that help shape the foreign policy process indicates that business groups did indeed influence the shift to more hard-line foreign and military policies during the Carter and Reagan administrations. More specifically, labor-intensive multinational business sectors concerned about wage constraints, conservative internationalists threatened by insurgent movements in the less-developed world, the military-industrial complex and its array of cold warriors, and New Right politicians driven by anticommunist ideology united in the late 1970s and early 1980s to pressure government to abandon the policies and assumptions associated with the détente era.

This hegemonic coalition was opposed from the beginning by capital-intensive multinational business sectors that continued to benefit from the liberal free trade regime and that were less sensitive to wage constraints. These business groups emerged as early critics of the Reagan-style military buildup. Thus, this case study provides compelling evidence to suggest that the policy preferences of business elites are informed by their sectoral location in the domestic and international economies and that business actors play an important role in pressuring policymakers to pursue new foreign policy initiatives conducive to their particular economic interests.

4

Business Conflict and U.S. Trade Policy: The Case of the Machine Tool Industry
ۮ
William N. Stant

The Transformation of U.S. Trade Policy

United States international trade policy was transformed between 1960 and 1990. In the early 1960s, the agenda of U.S. trade policy, with a couple of notable sectoral exceptions, turned upon liberal-internationalist principles. Policy focused on lowering tariffs through the multilateral negotiating forum of the General Agreement on Tariffs and Trade (GATT).

By May 1989, however, the focus of U.S. policy had changed substantially, as President Bush invoked the Super 301 provisions of the Omnibus Trade and Competitiveness Act of 1988 for the first time, naming Japan, Brazil, and India as the most unfair competitors of all U.S. trading partners and threatening them with retaliatory sanctions if they failed to lower barriers to U.S. exports within eighteen months. Exceptions to liberal internationalism seemed to become rules in the 1980s, as foundational and strategic industrial sectors received protection under one guise or another. What explains this transformation in U.S. trade policy?[1]

This chapter begins by setting aside the tenuous claims of pluralism, statism, and neorealism. Pluralism treats business interests as if they were not significantly more powerful and influential than other interests. Statism, also known as institutionalism, insists that government institutions and the policy process are autonomous from business interests. Neorealism treats U.S. leadership in the post–World War II international system as a "public good" and assumes that states can be understood as unitary rational actors. In place of these claims, the analysis presented here relies upon a synthesis of the business conflict model of U.S. foreign policy[2] with neo-Gramscian historical materialism[3] and the theory of the product cycle.[4] Simply put, explaining the transformation of U.S. trade policy requires accounting for the policy impact of ideological conflict among various business interests.

Neo-Gramscian Historical Materialism and Business Conflict

Neo-Gramscian historical materialism explains U.S. hegemony in the post–World War II international system by applying two of Antonio Gramsci's contributions to Marxist theory: the concepts of the historic bloc and ideological hegemony. A historic bloc is a particular configuration of power within a state-society complex: a complex of relations between classes, within classes, and between classes and the state.[5] A historic bloc includes an ideological consensus that legitimates the wielding of state power in the interests of the most powerful classes and class fractions. Ideological hegemony is the preponderance of influence derived from the consolidated power of a historic bloc. This influence enables the individual and institutional representatives of dominant classes or class fractions, the "organic intellectuals" of the historic bloc, to capture and control key policymaking and policy-advisory positions in the state. From these positions they define the ideological consensus on matters such as trade policy: They set agendas, set the terms of debate, and draw the boundaries of legitimate state authority.

In the early 1960s, a liberal-internationalist historic bloc reached the peak of its influence in U.S. domestic politics and in the international system. This historic bloc originated in the reshaping of state-society relations during the Great Depression and World War II, a reshaping that required the defeat of isolationist forces.[6] In the 1980s, ideological business conflict destabilized this historic bloc, thus weakening its control over trade policy and allowing a transformation from tolerant multilateralism to aggressive unilateralism.

Trade policy was central to the business solidarity required to hold the historic bloc together. The ideological business conflict that undermined business solidarity was materially rooted in the combined impact of the product cycle and the business cycle. Together, these generate a "trade-political cycle" consisting of periodic intensification of structural conflicts of interest among domestic, trade-dependent, and multinational firms and sectors over the definition of the national interest in trade policy. At sufficient levels of intensity, this conflict breaks out of the business world's preferred custom of private conflict resolution, as trade policy losers seek to alter the balance of power among trade-political interests. International differences over the place of business in the structure of state-society relations (e.g., between the United States and Japan) propels this conflict to the international level.

While Gramsci did not develop the international implications of his concept of hegemony in great detail, he was aware of connections between social structure within nations and power relations among states in the international system:

> Do international relations precede or follow (logically) fundamental social relations? There can be no doubt that they follow. Any organic innovation in the social structure, through its technical-military expressions, modifies organically absolute and relative relations in the international sphere too. ... International relations react both passively and actively on [national] political relations.[7]

Gramsci understood the connections between domestic and international politics to be "organic," meaning structural and long-term. Domestic social structures constituted the foundations of international relations. Thus, the U.S. projection of power onto the international system presupposed conclusive outcomes to struggles among domestic social forces whose interests in relation to international markets were contradictory. According to Robert Cox, "[Gramsci] was saying that basic changes in international power relations or world order, which are observed as changes in the military-strategic and geopolitical balance, can be traced to fundamental changes in social relations."[8]

This chapter's focus on ideological business conflict exposes the material roots of a "crisis of hegemony" in which U.S. international trade policy became entangled in the 1980s:

> One can ... prudently speak of a crisis of hegemony as having opened in some of the leading countries of the capitalist world. Its symptoms are an uncertainty of direction among the dominant groups and a fragmentation and absence of cohesion among subordinate groups. ... The crisis of hegemony is a crisis of representation: one historic bloc is dissolving, another has not taken its place.[9]

The historic bloc that was dissolving in the 1980s depended upon the ideological hegemony of liberal-internationalist ideas. It could lead the international system only so long as its ideas remained minimally legitimate in U.S. domestic politics. Ideological business conflict eroded this legitimacy among key fractions of U.S. manufacturing capital. This conflict was materially rooted in the evolution of trade dependence, import penetration, and multinationality.[10]

It is this type of conflict and its policy ramifications that are explored in the machine tool case study. The next section explains how the product cycle governs the evolution of trade dependence, import penetration, and multinationality.

The Internationalization
of U.S. Manufacturing Interests

According to product-cycle theory, the evolution of trade dependence, import penetration, and multinationality is largely a function of the age of products and the diffusion of knowledge of the processes that produce them.[11]

When a product is the first of its kind, substitutable alternatives are scarce. The achievement of scale economies puts firms producing such products in oligopolistic positions from which exporting to foreign markets is easier and more profitable than foreign production. The environment was hospitable to manufacturing firms in such positions in the United States in the 1950s and 1960s. These firms operated in a relatively high-wage, high-income market. This led them to produce leisure-time and labor-saving products, such as household appliances and high-tech industrial automation. U.S. exports faced undeveloped local competition in European and Japanese markets for these products in the period immediately following World War II. Exporting was thus feasible, in terms of both profitability and meeting foreign demand. Gradual increases in foreign demand required, at this stage, exporting on a larger scale. But exporting on a larger scale eventually required, in turn, some minimum foreign direct investment (FDI) in marketing and distribution, which would, at least initially, spur demand for greater exports.

As products "aged," their technology diffused. Domestic and foreign firms copied new products and the processes that produced them, often in violation of "intellectual property rights." The number of firms producing competing alternative versions of the same product increased. As production technology standardized and competition increased, foreign production became more economical than exporting. Maintenance of foreign market share then required locating assembly and production facilities in overseas markets.

Thus FDI can be fundamental to defending a firm's oligopolistic position, a position originally based on the advantages of technological innovation, but that is defended, after the diffusion and standardization of technology, only through economies of scale on an international level, often achieved with the aid of trade barriers and subsidies. Over time, FDI evolves from being a complement to U.S. exports to being a displacing substitute for them.[12] Profitability at the beginning of the product cycle and at the end leaves little choice of where to set up production.

The transition from exporting to FDI produces protectionist price dynamics. Firms dependent on exports have ample reason to oppose protectionist initiatives aimed at countries to which they export. They could suffer from retaliation. Protection aimed at other countries, or universal protection, could increase competition in third-country markets. Firms with assembly or production facilities overseas may fear strategic retaliation. Firms dependent on imports, whether finished goods or production inputs, have reason to oppose protection. In a variety of ways, the price dynamics of protectionism result, either directly or indirectly, in increased costs for manufacturing firms.[13] Efforts to avoid these costs put different types of manufacturing firms at odds over trade policy.

Not all firms within an industry will become trade dependent. Those that are risk-averse, lacking in the resources required for product innovation, or just plain "set-in-their-ways," will be least likely to pass through the product cycle. They may harbor nationalistic resentments toward those among their competitors who, for competitive reasons, begin outsourcing overseas for parts. They will certainly oppose those who import cheaper finished products with cost advantages against which they cannot compete without major adjustments. In short, the substantive representation of a sector's increasingly conflicted interests in the trade policy process becomes an increasingly contentious issue. The stage is set for intrasectoral trade-political business conflict.

Firms that become trade dependent may not move on to the level of international production if they lack the resources to do so. Those that do move on to international production may gain unbeatable cost advantages in foreign markets against their competitors who do not. This can result in the displacement of one's own exports by one's competitors, who are likely also to be one's fellow members of a trade association in Washington, D.C. In addition, international production can reach a stage at which a firm is multinational but no longer as trade dependent as before. At this stage, the firm may well benefit from protection for its products either in its overseas markets or in its home market.

This conflict easily spills over into the realm of international politics. The United States, for example, traditionally protects less competitive, older industries using higher tariffs and quotas. Europe and Japan, by contrast, tend to protect nascent high-tech industries, using nontariff barriers (NTBs), government procurement, and other industrial policies.[14] Thus in the postwar period, U.S. firms faced foreign trade barriers at the "top" of the product cycle, when their foreign competitors were getting into the market with government assistance to sell newer versions of what were, for U.S. producers, "older" products. This could only reinforce the decision of U.S. firms to leave exporting behind entirely, or, for our purposes, to undergo the transition from trade dependence to multinationality. Setting up production overseas, in addition, provides an opportunity to bring one's technology up-to-date with that of one's foreign competitors.

Foreign firms, on the other hand, face protectionism in the U.S. market toward what is for them the "bottom," that is, the beginning, of the product cycle, as they enter competition with older and less competitive U.S. firms, marketing newer versions of their products on the basis of newer and more efficient technology, giving rise to another cycle of diffusion and standardization.

Although the common wisdom has associated MNCs with support for open markets, this analysis suggests that their support is at best qualified and abstract.[15] There are two kinds of MNCs in U.S. trade politics: MNCs with greater stakes in free trade; and MNCs with lesser stakes in free trade. Conflict between these types weakens support for liberal-internationalist trade policies and opens the door to the subversion of the trade-political consensus.

The transition from more trade-dependent to less trade-dependent multinationality generates additional politically potent conflict: increased unemployment and the export of "U.S. jobs"; a worsened balance of payments; an unfavorable balance of trade; generally worsened national economic conditions; and decline in the competitive position of the United States. These issues were not new to the 1970s and 1980s. They were hotly debated as early as the 1920s and 1930s.[16]

Figure 4.1 offers a statistical picture of trends in the internationalization of the U.S. economy as a whole from 1960 to 1988. It shows that in the 1970s nontrade international involvement of U.S. capital tended to increase along with, though not as rapidly as, exports and imports. In the 1980s, however, nontrade involvement, relative to trade, leveled off and declined. In 1982, at their highest point of the period from 1960 to 1988, the value of U.S. assets abroad was 52 percent of the value of domestic and foreign exports by U.S. firms. This relation dropped to 25.3 percent in 1988.

Figure 4.1 suggests that there was an increase in the number of U.S. firms that "went international" in the 1970s and 1980s, and that a primary means of doing so was exporting. This suggests a potential for trade-political conflict between established MNCs benefiting from trade restrictions at home and in foreign markets, on the one hand, and on the other hand, newcoming U.S. exporters, fearing foreign retaliation against increasing U.S. protectionism, seeking access to foreign markets, and complaining of unfair foreign trade restrictions. The consistently low relative level of new FDI indicated in Figure 4.1 lends support to this suggestion. Imports, however, increased more consistently and ominously than the other four indicators, suggesting that increased exports in the late 1980s were as much imperatives of survival as opportunities for growth.

In sum, the 1980s were rife with potential for trade-political business conflict—conflict that took on increasingly public ideological overtones as it raised issues such as the nature of the "proper" relation between business and the state and the consequences of three decades of policy commitment to liberal-internationalist principles.

(continues)

Figure 4.1 The Internationalization of the U.S. Economy, 1960–1988

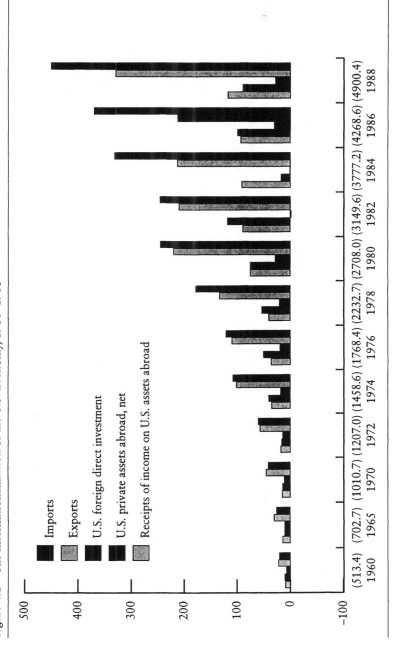

- Imports
- Exports
- U.S. foreign direct investment
- U.S. private assets abroad, net
- Receipts of income on U.S. assets abroad

86

Figure 4.1 (*continued*)

Sources for Figures 4.1–4.6: U.S. Department of Commerce, Bureau of the Census, *U.S. Imports of Merchandise for Consumption: Commodity by Country of Origin,* FT110, calendar years 1960–1963; for 1964 to 1980, *U.S. Imports: Consumption and General,* BIC-Based Products by Areas, FT210, Annual; for 1981 to 1991, Bureau of the Census and Department of Labor, Bureau of Labor Statistics, *Trade and Employment,* Quarterly; for exports 1960 to 1964, *U.S. Exports of Domestic and Foreign Merchandise,* Country of Destination by Subgroup, FT420, Annual; after 1965, *U.S. Exports of Domestic Merchandise,* BIC-Based Products and Area, FT610, Annual, and *Trade and Employment,* Quarterly. Also: U.S. Internal Revenue Service, *Sourcebook: Statistics of Income,* various years; Statistics of Income, 1962, *Supplemental Report: Foreign Income and Taxes Reported on Corporation Income Tax Returns,* July 1961 to June 1962; *Statistics of Income: Compendium of Studies of International Income and Taxes,* Pub. 1267; *Statistics of Income - 1974: International Income and Taxes: Foreign Tax Credit Claimed on Corporation Income Tax Returns;* IRS, Supplemental Statistics of Income, 1966–1972, *International Income and Taxes: Foreign Tax Credit Claimed on Corporation Income Tax Returns,* Pub. 479; Statistics of Income, Supplemental Report, 1976–1979, *International Income and Taxes: Foreign Income and Taxes Reported on U.S. Income Tax Returns.* Also: U.S. Department of Commerce, Bureau of Economic Analysis, *Business Statistics, 1961–1988: A Supplement to the Survey of Current Business,* December 1989; International Trade Administration, *U.S. Industrial Outlook,* various years.

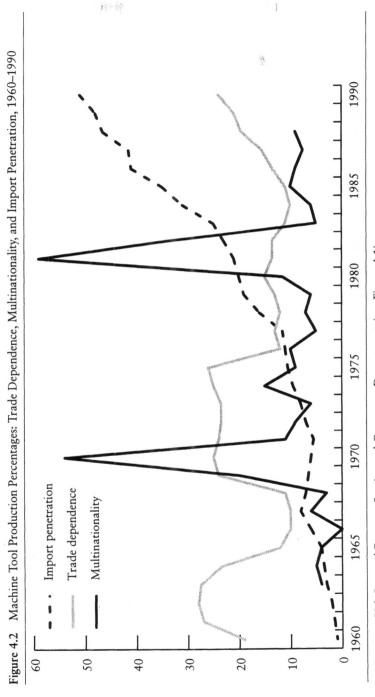

Figure 4.2 Machine Tool Production Percentages: Trade Dependence, Multinationality, and Import Penetration, 1960–1990

Source: U.S. Internal Revenue Service and Commerce Department (see Figure 4.1).

The Case of the Machine Tool Industry

Trade Dependence

Figure 4.2 shows machine tool trade dependence bottoming out in the mid-1960s, improving until the mid-1970s, and leveling off thereafter, with minor fluctuations, until the mid-1980s, after which it began to increase. The export component of trade dependence was particularly strong in the period between 1968 and the mid-1970s, a period marked by the worst machine tool recession since the Great Depression of the 1930s. Export dependence in recessionary conditions stands out in stark relief when export figures are disaggregated by markets (Table 4.1).

Table 4.1   Factor Increases in Exports to Selected Markets

Market	Factor Increase in Exports	Time
West Germany	2.25	1968–1974
Australia	2.44	1969–1975
Mexico	4.0	1968–1974
Venezuela	6.0	1968–1976
Spain	10.0	1969–1975
Brazil	10.0	1969–1976
Soviet Bloc	25.0	1967–1975

Source: Glenn Fong ("Export Dependence Versus the New Protectionism: Constraints on Trade Policy in the Industrial World," Ph.D. diss., Cornell University, 1984, p. 210) derived these estimates from: U.S. Department of Commerce, Bureau of the Census, *U.S. Exports: Schedule B Section by Division by Group by Number by Country of Destination by Customs District of Exportation and Method of Transportation,* EM 522.

Note: Other major export markets during this period included France, Italy, Britain, Canada, and Japan.

The industry began the 1970s increasingly dependent on exports, and this trend continued throughout the decade, though it slowed down somewhat in the late 1970s. The largest firms led the export charge of the 1970s. Exports were publicly recognized by the National Machine Tool Builders Association (NMTBA) in the 1970s as a source of employment and output, and as sources of funds for research and development and capital expansion that were vital to the long-term health of the industry. Such export dependence was not without precedent. Exports were considered to be the difference between bankruptcy and survival in the business downturns of 1921, 1923, 1938, and 1946–1949. Thus exports naturally took on heightened importance in the 1969 to 1971 downturn.[17]

By the early 1970s, a basic shift in the U.S. position in the world machine tool market lent even greater importance to machine tool exports. Between 1966 and 1967, the United States consumed 30 percent of world machine tool production. By 1971, however, the United States consumed only 10 percent of world production. The U.S. market was shrinking relative to a growing world market. The NMTBA conveyed the long-term implications of this shift to Congress in Senate testimony in 1976:

> The world market is the answer to our industry's problems. If the U.S. industry would really market its products on a global scale, it would become almost immune to the vagaries of the domestic business cycle. ... *The health of the American machine tool industry is heavily conditioned upon our industry's ability to expand its global markets.*[18]

Increasing receipts of foreign income in the 1970s (see Figure 4.3) suggest that at least some firms were expanding their foreign presence. Similarly, U.S. machine tool exports improved from 1968 until the mid-1970s, and again after 1977 (see Figure 4.4). Relative to world production and exports, however, the U.S. machine tool industry was in decline.

Between 1945 and 1971, the United States was the world's largest producer of machine tools. It fell to second place behind West Germany after 1971, and to fourth behind Japan, West Germany, and the Soviet Union in 1982. Between 1970 and 1986, world production increased by an average of 7.7 percent per year, from $8.27 billion to $28.5 billion. This improvement reflected, among other factors, globalization of production, as South Korea, Taiwan, India, Brazil, Eastern Europe, and the Soviet Union entered the market as serious producers and exporters. In 1969, world exports accounted for 29 percent of world production. In 1986, they accounted for 47 percent. But the share of world production exported by the United States in 1964 was 6 percent. This dropped to 2 percent in 1986.[19] The U.S. share of world machine tool imports, on the other hand, increased from 7 percent in 1976 to 22 percent in 1985, matching exactly the increase in Japan's share of world exports in the same period. Finally, while labor productivity in the U.S. machine tool industry increased by 1 percent per year between 1959 and 1973, it fell by 0.7 percent per year from 1973 to 1981.[20]

Despite the declining state of the industry in 1973, the NMTBA supported liberal-internationalist trade policies. The NMTBA testified in support of the Trade Act of 1974. It strongly supported renewing presidential authority to negotiate further tariff reductions, in some cases to zero. Philip Geier, president of Cincinnati Milacron, articulated what became the NMTBA's basic trade policy posture for the 1970s:

> While the NMTBA is concerned over the inroads into the U.S. market made by foreign competition, particularly in certain machine tool lines, it believes that

Figure 4.3 Machine Tool Foreign Income, 1964–1989 (in millions, unadjusted)

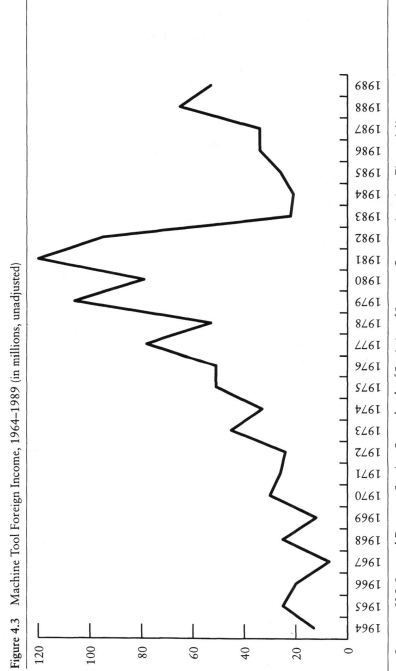

Source: U.S. Internal Revenue Service, *Sourcebook of Statistics of Income, Corporations* (see Figure 4.1).

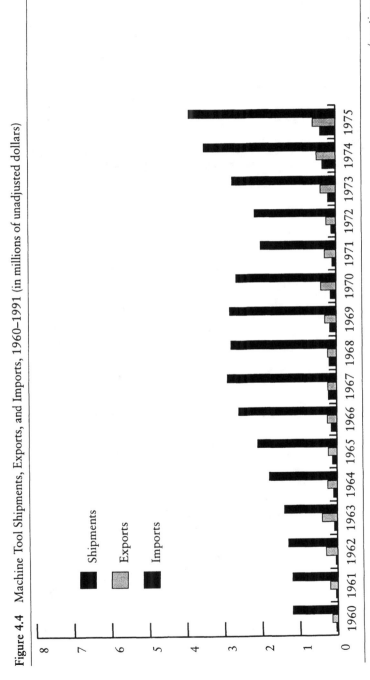

Figure 4.4 Machine Tool Shipments, Exports, and Imports, 1960–1991 (in millions of unadjusted dollars)

(continues)

Figure 4.4 *(continued)*

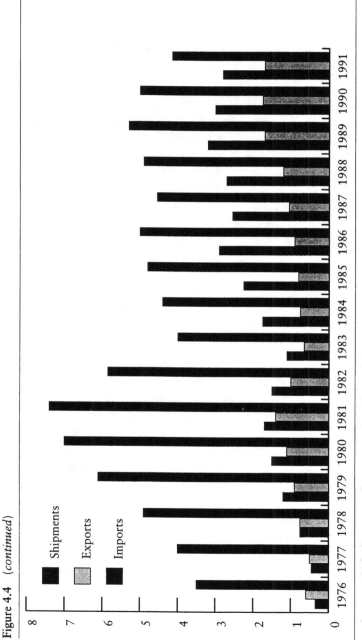

Source: U.S. Commerce Department (see Figure 4.1).

in the long run free trade—assuming reciprocity, fair trading practices on all sides, and adequate governmental authority to deal with emergency situations—is both inevitable and desirable.[21]

Ralph Cross, president of Cross Company, an internationally integrated producer of transfer lines, contradicted his own 1968 testimony: "We do not favor general tariff increases or the widespread imposition of quantitative restrictions on imports."[22] Until the early 1980s, the NMTBA's public statements supported free trade policies. The association supported the Tokyo Round GATT agreement of 1979, including both its tariff reductions and its codes on government procurement and subsidies.[23]

These positions cut against the protectionist tide that was gaining headway among U.S. businesses and in Congress. In fact, at the time the NMTBA took these positions, the machine tool industry had suffered relatively more from import penetration than had some of the industries jumping onto the protectionist bandwagon. Between 1968 and 1974, machine tool imports increased by 80 percent. The foreign share of the U.S. market increased from 12 percent in 1968 to 20 percent in 1974.

The NMTBA had the traditional rationales at its disposal with which to justify demands for protection: increasing import penetration in the context of recession. These are the prime instigators of protectionist demands in U.S. trade politics, particularly when both of them occur simultaneously in a number of industries, as was the case in the early 1970s. The NMTBA's stance in support of the liberal-internationalist trade policies was therefore anomalous. The presence within the U.S. machine tool industry, however, of a small minority of larger, technologically sophisticated, internationally positioned firms with strong traditional ties to the largest U.S. manufacturing MNCs suggests an explanation.

These firms had progressed through product-cycle competition farther than had the great majority of firms in their industry. Their trade-political interests, unlike those of the majority of the firms in their industry, had come into alignment with the underlying material interests expressed in the historic bloc's liberal-internationalist trade-political consensus. It was executives from these firms that were elected to leadership positions in the NMTBA in the 1970s as trade dependence increased. These were the executives who testified before Congress and served in the Private Sector Advisory Committee System established by the Trade Act of 1974. And these were the executives whose liberal-internationalist statements were, until Houdaille Industries somewhat sensationally broke ranks in 1982, frequently and repeatedly quoted in the metalworking and business press. Press attention to the majority of smaller, less internationally integrated firms in the industry, by contrast, was consistently negative, holding these firms up to critical scrutiny for their relative failure to invest in research and development and maintain international competitiveness.

In the early 1980s, the loss of major export markets,[24] increasing competition in the world machine tool market and in the U.S. market in particular, a recession even more severe than those of the 1970s, and the loss of long-established domestic customers with whom relations were steadily deteriorating all combined to send the U.S. machine tool industry into a crisis of unprecedented proportions from which large sections of the industry never recovered.[25] The political upshot of the crisis was an open rift within the industry as the NMTBA, under pressure from the majority of the industry, turned toward overt protectionism. This took the form, first, of the Houdaille petition for protection under Section 103 of the 1971 Revenue Act, and second, of the NMTBA's petition for quotas under Section 232 of the Trade Expansion Act of 1962.

The Houdaille Petition

In May 1982, Houdaille Industries assumed leadership of a growing protectionist movement in the machine tool industry. Houdaille Industries was a privately held conglomerate based in Ft. Lauderdale, Florida, with annual sales of more than $500 million in industrial equipment. The company owned plants in eleven states. Five of its divisions produced machine tools or machine tool accessories, generating 25 percent of total sales.[26] In 1970, Houdaille attempted to sell machining centers in Japan but was allegedly "held up until it agreed to license its technology to Yamazaki."[27] Yamazaki was allowed to sell, under license, Houdaille machines in Asia but not in the United States. Two years after the licensing agreement expired, however, Houdaille discovered that Mazak, Yamazaki's subsidiary in the United States, was selling machines in the United States identical to those previously licensed to Yamazaki. Houdaille's machine tool operations, suffering from the recession of the early 1980s, were running at 40 percent of capacity. These circumstances prompted Houdaille to file a Section 301 unfair trade practice petition. This petition made little progress, allegedly due to Japanese government interference with Houdaille's legal investigation in Japan.[28]

Facing increasing import competition in his other machine tool lines as well, Phillip O'Reilly, president and CEO of Houdaille, acted on a tip from NMTBA public affairs director James Mack and filed a petition under Section 103 of the 1971 Revenue Act on 3 May 1982.[29] Filing under the previously obscure Section 103 could set a precedent in U.S. trade law and politics. Section 103 empowered the president, without congressional hearings or action, to disqualify purchases of imported capital goods from the investment tax credit. This confronted Reagan with "a basic policy decision ... on whether ... to trigger what amounts to a retaliatory strike against Japanese trade,"[30] and whether to provide protectionist forces with a potent new weapon.

The NMTBA endorsed Houdaille's petition. By early 1983, the Houdaille case had generated some international conflict. After the U.S. Senate unanimously endorsed Houdaille's petition in a nonbinding resolution,[31] the Japanese Minister of MITI (Ministry of International Trade and Industry), Sadanori Yamanaka, responded:

> The action sought by Houdaille, if taken, will not only seriously discourage joint efforts of the U.S. and Japanese governments to maintain free trading but also invite various reactions including the rights under GATT. I cannot but fear that it will trigger similar protectionist actions in other industries and other countries.[32]

This thinly veiled threat of retaliation could only have abetted the divisions within the Reagan administration over the Houdaille petition.[33]

Secretary of State George Schultz, a close economic adviser to the president, predictably opposed the petition on the grounds that trade should not be used as a weapon in foreign policy.[34] Other advisers pointed to the lack of protection for the import-challenged auto and steel industries. The cabinet agreed in February that the petition was technically in accordance with the requirements in the law. A favorable decision was legally justified. But cabinet members from the Treasury, Office of Management and Budget, and the Council of Economic Advisors vigorously opposed a favorable decision on ideological grounds. Houdaille supporters in the Office of the United States Trade Representative (USTR), the Commerce and Defense Departments, and the National Security Council had decided to pursue relief under Section 301, the so-called catchall unfair trade provisions. They suspected that several other GATT signatories were waiting for an opportunity to use their own tax laws for trade-protective purposes and thus feared retaliation if the United States used the investment tax credit as a weapon. In addition, Section 301 gave the president a wider variety of remedies from which to choose.

The dispute reached its highest official and political levels when Japanese Prime Minister Nakasone appealed to Reagan for support, claiming that a decision in favor of Houdaille could hurt his prospects in upcoming elections. On 22 April 1983, President Reagan formally rejected Houdaille's petition, acting against the objections of the Secretary of Commerce, the USTR, and other cabinet officials.[35] He announced, however, that the USTR would pursue negotiations to end Japanese "industrial targeting."[36] In response to Reagan's decision, Houdaille closed its 250-employee Di-Acro division plant in Lake City, Minnesota. According to O'Reilly, "I think they're telling American industry that they don't have a trade policy and they're not even prepared to consider one. I think they're telling American industry to go to hell."[37]

Meanwhile, Houdaille's temporary leadership of the swelling protectionist tide stood in sharp contrast to other U.S. machine tool interests. Bendix chairman William Agee, for example, had recently signed a five-year contract to market Japanese Toyoda machining centers in the United States and Canada.[38] According to Frederick Searby, president of Bendix Industrial Group:

> The life cycle of industrial machines is compressing from twenty to three or five years. Some technology you develop yourself. Some you acquire from international partners. ... We're hoping that as we and Toyoda get to know each other, we'll find that we can work together in other areas of the world and in other fields: robotics, material handling, controls, and flexible manufacturing systems, for example ... Toyoda and Bendix presently have no plans to acquire equity in each other. But if Toyoda equity were available, Bendix would consider buying a part of it. I wouldn't rule out a merger.[39]

Toyoda was part of Toyoda Group, which included Toyota Motor Corporation, a partner with GM (General Motors) in developing assembly facilities in California. Bendix, a major auto parts supplier to GM, already had licensees in Japan supplying auto parts to Toyota before signing its contract with Toyoda. According to Agee: "This kind of technical cooperation is the wave of the future. To survive and prosper, you need worldwide cooperation. Toyoda has the technological edge in machining centers worldwide."[40]

The National Machine Tool
Builders Association National Security Petition

With the defeat of the Houdaille petition the NMTBA publicly assumed leadership of the industry's movement for protection. Strategy shifted from the narrow and product-specific demands of Houdaille to a broader, more inclusive demand for protection on national security grounds. By playing the national security card, the NMTBA shifted the nature of the struggle, appealing to values that ostensibly cut across the cleavage that divided nationalists from internationalists and protectionists from free traders. The industry could point out that its efforts in the 1970s to expand exports to the Soviet Bloc, while refraining (at least in public) from protectionism, had been stymied in the name of the same national security values from which it now demanded protection.[41]

NMTBA president Gray justified the demands by claiming that the U.S. machine tool industry was as important to the nations economic strength and military security as either Lockheed or Chrysler.[42] The NMTBA submitted its petition in March 1983 as it was becoming clearer to many observers that President Reagan would not support Houdaille. Under Section 232, the national security clause of the Trade Expansion Act of 1962, the petition required no finding of unfair trade. Rather, it required a finding that machine tool imports represented a genuine threat to national security.[43] In a little-noted but significant exception, two types of tools would *not be covered* by the quotas: station-type transfer machines and metal forming presses, *machines vital to the auto industry.*

The NMTBA's decision to file a petition under Section 232 was not a unanimous one. Neither was the decision greeted with unanimous acclaim in the industry. Several association members had their own active import programs. *American Machinist* reported a divided reaction to the announcement: "A few firms have tended to participate effectively in the Japanese market and tend to be privately derisive of the attitude of those who have not."[44] According to *Business Week:*

> If nothing else, the trade friction underlines a similarity between the machine tool and auto industries. In the past year, some of the best-known U.S. names— including Bendix, Acme-Cleveland, and Danly Machine—have linked up with Japanese partners to market Japanese-made machines in the U.S. or build their own versions. If only because it saves major investments for U.S. companies, that trend seems bound to continue, even while the domestic industry pleads for government help.[45]

Ingersoll Milling Machine Company of Rockford, Illinois, the sixth largest builder in the industry at the time of the petition and a firm with no interest in import-vulnerable market segments, became an outspoken opponent of the Section 232 petition. Edson Gaylord, the company's president, did not mince words:

> Who believes the machine tool industry is going to pull itself up by its boot- straps if it gets five years of grace? There is no historic evidence anywhere … that any industry so protected ever did anything for itself. How can the gov- ernment give aid to the machine tool industry without giving it to steel, diesel engines, ships, foundries … you name it?[46]

Ingersoll later resigned from the NMTBA in protest over the petition. While the majority of the membership supported the NMTBA's petition, "the association no longer relied on any semblance of member unanimity before taking action in the political sphere."[47]

In a 1984 guest editorial for *Industry Week,* Houdaille's O'Reilly argued that machine tool builders were being *forced to abandon what they knew to be in the nation's best interests.* Saying that it was time to take, "whatever steps are necessary to protect our economic well-being," he listed as such steps the shutting down of plants, importation of foreign products, and off- shore production of machine tools. He then pointed to the consequences of such steps:

> I do not want to mince words. These actions are not in the best interests of our nation. They will not protect our industrial base, they will not secure high

paying engineering and manufacturing positions for our citizens, and they will not provide ready access to machine tools for our manufacturers. ... Unfortunately, there is no longer any choice for those companies in the bull's-eye of foreign targeters...This is not an isolated tragedy. It has occurred and is occurring in other industries. It will occur in still others as less-developed nations adopt the Japanese model and learn to use it successfully.[48]

In 1985, Houdaille joined the if-you-can't-beat-them-join-them movement among U.S. capital goods producers, forging links with a Japanese machine tool producer, Okuma, in addition to establishing extensive marketing and licensing agreements with German, French, English, and Italian manufacturers.[49]

The U.S. machine tool industry reported a net loss of $175 million for 1983. In a pattern reminiscent of U.S.-Japan auto competition in the 1970s, U.S. builders retreated further into their niches in the high-tech, low-volume end of the market, increasingly abandoning high-volume standardized segments to the imports.[50] The result was mass layoffs and cutbacks in capacity.[51] Although companies that could do so were implementing international survival strategies, the U.S. industry was sharply contracting. Fully one-fourth of all U.S. machine tool firms went out of business between 1981 and 1983. Industry unemployment reached 39 percent.[52] At this point, the industry began to receive more attention in Congress and the news media. In his home state of Illinois, where the industry lost 5,000 jobs, Senator Percy held hearings of the Foreign Relations Committee on the industry's petition for protection.[53] The CBS news program "60 Minutes" featured a story critical of the government's handling of the machine tool crisis.

A spring 1984 *Industry Week* staff report on the machine tool industry reached what were, for a mainstream business magazine, some rather startling and far-reaching conclusions. The report showed the ideological depth of the machine tool crisis. The staff concluded their report under the heading "Preserving Political Stability":

> The answer seems to be that the U.S. needs toolbuilders of various sizes for various reasons. ... For unless we preserve the U.S. employment base, in machine tools and in the industries that rely on machine tools, the American people may eventually conclude that the private-enterprise system doesn't work anymore. ... In ... Germany after World War I the need to restore economic well-being was among the forces that brought Adolph Hitler to power. And in Communist countries there is no unemployment, which helps them to maintain political stability.[54]

The severity of the U.S. machine tool crisis in early 1983 reached into the policy process in Japan, as MITI moved quietly to raise the prices of Japanese tools in the U.S. market. While the Japanese move was not fully understood, it appeared to be intended to head off the growing protectionist movement in the United States.

The NMTBA initially spent $800,000 on its lobbying campaign in support of the petition. It appointed a public relations expert known to be "close" to President Reagan to head the campaign. Senate Finance Committee Chair Robert Dole endorsed the petition's demand for quotas, as did Commerce Secretary Malcolm Baldridge. In February 1984, Baldridge, supported by a "fairly united" Commerce Department,[55] formally recommended that the president impose quotas. But President Reagan limited himself to ordering the National Security Council to study the industry's problems.[56] After the annual spring meeting in 1984, the NMTBA board allocated another $1 million to the lobbying campaign.[57]

Neither the Big Three auto companies nor aircraft manufacturers actively opposed the NMTBA's petition. These major machine tool users could have opposed protection for machine tools on grounds that it would increase their costs of production. In the case of the auto companies, however, two key types of machines, of which they were major purchasers, were quietly exempted from the NMTBA's petition. In addition, since the Big Three U.S. auto companies had recently obtained protection for themselves, they "did not think it wise to straddle both sides of the trade policy debate."[58]

As major defense contractors, the aircraft companies were able to pass any costs resulting from protection-induced machine tool price increases on to the public via government contracts. In addition, the auto companies saw some validity in at least one of the industry's arguments:

We want to get the best production technology in the world in order to get the lowest possible cost of doing business. But if you buy the best from the Japanese, it has already been in Toyota Motors for two years, and if you buy it from West Germany, it has already been in BMW for a year and a half.[59]

Thus large multinational manufacturing mainstays of the U.S. economy had reason to prefer protection for the U.S. machine tool industry.

The NSC completed its study of emergency machine tool capacity in the summer of 1984 and sent its results to the Commerce Department. Meanwhile, a "fair amount of consensus"[60] had developed in favor of the industry's petition in the Defense Department. Administration officials who remained opposed to machine tool protection added to their ideologically based free trade arguments the more pragmatic warning that accepting the Section 232 petition might encourage other industries to claim similar special national security status. The debate in the administration was becoming "fairly acrimonious," and the investigation was repeatedly "stalled for months at a time."[61] The investigation and debate dragged into 1985 as machine tool import penetration increased.

At this point the NMTBA was, "forced to step up its efforts in Congress."[62] Vocal congressional pressure in turn led Commerce Secretary Baldridge to turn up the heat in his department. After the leaking of an internal Department of Defense memo on the inadequacy of the defense industrial base, House Republicans began to pressure Reagan, asserting that the industry had a compelling case. Finally, in early 1986, the Commerce Department won a chance to present its case in favor of the machine tool industry's need for protection at a meeting of the NSC with President Reagan in attendance. Reagan decided to support the request for protection, but not to honor the Section 232 petition.[63]

On 20 May 1986, one day prior to the beginning of congressional deliberations on new omnibus trade reform legislation, President Reagan announced that he had postponed a decision on the petition until 20 November, pending the USTR's negotiation of voluntary export restraints (VERs) with Japan, West Germany, Taiwan, and Switzerland, who together accounted for 74.3 percent of all machine tool imports. The negotiations were to cover eight of the NMTBA's eighteen specified categories of machine tools.[64]

The VER negotiations dragged all the way to the deadline. On 20 November, the Japanese signed an agreement limiting exports to the United States of six types of tools to 1981 levels. Two weeks later, Taiwan accepted VERs limiting standardized conventional tools to 1981 levels. United States negotiators, applying a lesson learned in the auto VER case, won agreement from the Japanese to freeze their export product mix and not to use the VER as an opportunity to "go upscale."

The Swiss and the West Germans were unwilling to sign VER agreements. But they reportedly communicated privately their willingness to cooperate and refrain from taking advantage of the Asian VERs. Reagan nevertheless threatened, "in a move then designed for public consumption,"[65] to take action against West Germany and Switzerland if the West Germans did not cut certain tool exports back to 1981 levels and others back to 1985 levels, and if the Swiss did not cut exports back to 1985 levels. There was, apparently, no immediate protest from either the Swiss or the West Germans. Meanwhile, the Commerce Department announced that it had warned Britain, Spain, Italy, Sweden, Brazil, South Korea, and Singapore that their exports to the United States would be unilaterally restrained to 1985 levels if they tried to take advantage of the VERs imposed on Japan and Taiwan.[66]

Machine tool protection was a long time coming. Deliberations on the NMTBA's petition dragged on for two years, allowing imports to capture another 10 percent of the U.S. market. According to one Commerce Department official, there was "no excuse" for the delay.[67] Although on one hand, it is an open question whether a larger industry would have received more prompt results, on the other hand, the results of the industry's efforts were surprisingly successful, given the industry's size. The metalworking and business press repeatedly attributed the slowness of the policy process to the relative smallness of the U.S. machine tool industry. But the strategic importance of the industry could not have been overlooked. It was, and is, repeatedly used as a key economic forecasting indicator, was the subject of continual monitoring and encouragement by the Department of Defense, and was widely recognized as vital to the overall ability of U.S. manufacturing to compete internationally.

The size of the U.S. machine tool industry is misleading if it leads one to perceive the 1986 VERs as unexpected or surprising. But the strategic and economic importance of the industry does not offer a full enough explanation of the process by itself. Any number of industries could plausibly claim to be vital as indicators of economic and social health, or as strategically key to national defense. Indeed, as the machine tool VERs were being finalized, a Department of Defense advisory committee issued a report calling for massive government aid to protect the semiconductor industry, on the grounds of its strategic importance to national defense.

Conclusion

The Semiconductor Industry

The semiconductor industry was trade dependent and multinational from its inception in 1959.[68] Predictably, it supported the free trade side of the debate, just as the machine tool industry did, when protectionist pressure heated up in the 1970s. Some of the largest semiconductor firms supported reductions in the U.S. tariff rate into the 1980s, even in the absence of reciprocal reductions in Japan. In the mid-1970s, the U.S. semiconductor industry faced a Japanese challenge from companies producing dynamic random access memories (DRAMS), then the high end of the semiconductor market. A majority of U.S. producers objected to restrictions on access to the Japanese market. They charged Japanese firms with dumping chips in the U.S. market. In addition, they pointed to "unfair practices" in Japanese government-industry relations.

In June 1985, the Semiconductor Industry Association (SIA) filed an unfair trade petition under Section 301 of the Trade Act of 1974 asking for retaliation if more access to the Japanese market was not granted. The petition accused the Japanese of predatory pricing in the U.S. market. Later in 1985, Intel, Advanced Micro Devices (AMD), and National Semiconductor filed charges of dumping, alleging Japanese firms were dumping erasable programmable read-only memories (EPROMS). The SIA and the filers of the EPROM petition aimed to obtain a 20 percent share of the Japanese market by the early 1990s. In July 1986, the United States signed agreements with Japan that were based on the industry's demands. When the Japanese allegedly violated this agreement, the industry demanded retaliation against Japanese electronics that contained semiconductors, rather than the semiconductors themselves. The administration imposed 100 percent tariffs on $300 million worth of such imports. This precipitated a flurry of special-case pleading by firms dependent on imports of the restricted products. "The association made clear that closure of the U.S. market [for semiconductor chips] was not its goal; rather it wanted the government to threaten the use of antidumping and unfair trade sanctions to force the opening of the Japanese market."[69]

The semiconductor industry was, by comparison to the machine tool industry, similarly divided going into the 1980s. International ties were heavily concentrated in the largest ten firms. The largest of these, IBM and Texas Instruments, were the only ones with established facilities in Japan. Neither was party to the Section 301 petition. Other large semiconductor producers had foreign operations but were generally less multinational in the 1970s than IBM and Texas Instruments. All of the top ten semiconductor firms, however, were particularly sensitive to trade restrictions, as they relied on internationally integrated production systems, shipping components to foreign subsidiaries for assembly and processing, and reimporting them for final assembly and sale.[70]

As Japanese imports of semiconductors increased in the 1970s (Figure 4.5), a number of larger semiconductor firms formed the SIA to pursue a trade strategy independent of the Electronics Industry Association (EIA). Intel, Motorola, AMD, Mostek, National Semiconductor, and Fairchild Camera circulated complaints against the Japanese and developed a Section 301 petition in 1978–1979. While they claimed their intention was limited to scaring the Japanese into "fairer" trade practices, they ran into opposition both in the Carter administration and from other U.S. producers.

The USTR was preoccupied with avoiding yet another trade confrontation with Japan. Other semiconductor firms opposed the petition for two reasons: First, corporations with captive semiconductor operations (e.g., IBM and Western Electric) and computer manufacturers (e.g., IBM, DEC, CDC, and Hewlett Packard) purchased substantial amounts of semiconductors from Japan and feared a disruption of supplies; and second, Texas Instruments and IBM were concerned about retaliation against their operations in Japan. The SIA accommodated the opposition by backing down from filing its petition. IBM and the other opponents to the petition then acquiesced in the strategy of using the threat of a petition to win greater market access, and, except for Texas Instruments, joined the SIA and pressured the USTR and the president to open negotiations with the Japanese.[71]

The SIA had been formed in 1976 because the EIA was dominated by multinationals that were not sufficiently concerned about domestic semiconductors production. International Business Machines, Texas Instruments, and

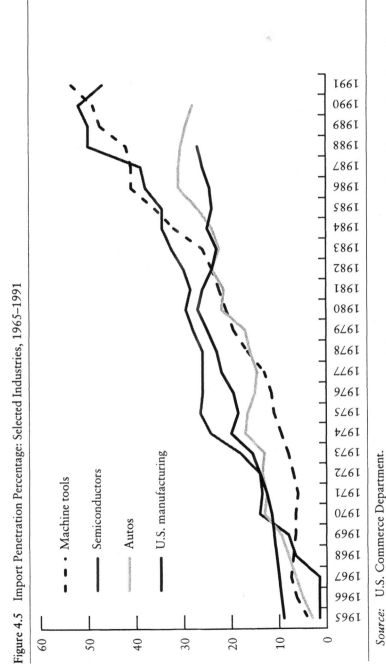

Figure 4.5 Import Penetration Percentage: Selected Industries, 1965–1991

Source: U.S. Commerce Department.

Note: Import penetration = imports as a percentage of shipments + imports − exports. For U.S. manufacturing, shipments = durable + nondurable goods production; and exports and imports = total seasonally adjusted merchandise trade.

major semiconductor users among electronics firms kept SIA at arm's length, disagreeing with the SIA on the need to pursue a political response to Japanese import penetration of the U.S. market. The SIA found that without these key players on board, its trade interests could not be pursued effectively. Thus, in 1979, the SIA pursued a consensus building strategy. Its political focus shifted toward broader issues of industrial policy on which an industry-wide consensus could be built. According to Helen Milner, this change "seems to have increased its political influence, since only after this expansion were its preferences for greater access to the Japanese market acted upon by the U.S. government."[72] By the late 1980s, however, even the "consensus-building" issues of industrial policy had become divisive issues among U.S. semiconductor firms.[73]

Like the machine tool industry, the semiconductor industry was divided internally by varying levels of trade dependence and multinationality among its firms. It was also divided, more specifically, between the few with successful presence in Japan and the rest. The semiconductor industry contained at least one major MNC, IBM, whose international presence and recognized clout was comparable to that of GM, Ford, or General Electric. This at least suggests a reason for its ability to win somewhat quicker response to its demands for aggressive market opening measures against Japan. There was no such firm in the machine tool industry. In addition, the machine tool trade demands were much more clearly protectionist than those of the semiconductor industry. Although I do not agree with the claim that demanding the negotiation of greater openness in foreign markets under threat of retaliation is consistent with a liberal-internationalist position, it is at least more consistent with liberal internationalism than were the quotas and tax credit denials demanded by the NMTBA and Houdaille Industries.

The Trade-Political Cycle

Combined with the preceding theoretical discussion, the cases of machine tools and semiconductors suggest a model of a "trade-political cycle."[74] In this model (Figure 4.6), varying levels of international integration divide U.S. manufacturing firms into four types: The nonrubber footwear industry is typical of industries in which, at least at the beginning of the period from 1960 to 1990, most firms had low trade dependence and low multinationality (Type I). Similarly, the machine tool industry is typical of industries whose leading firms had high trade dependence but, with a few exceptions, relatively low multinationality (Type II); the semiconductor industry is typical of industries that are both highly trade dependent and multinational (Type III); and the auto industry is typical of industries that have high multinationality but low trade dependence (Type IV).

At the heart of any liberal-internationalist historic bloc, with significant components in the manufacturing base of the U.S. economy, we would ex-

Figure 4.6 A Business Conflict Model of the Trade-Political Cycle

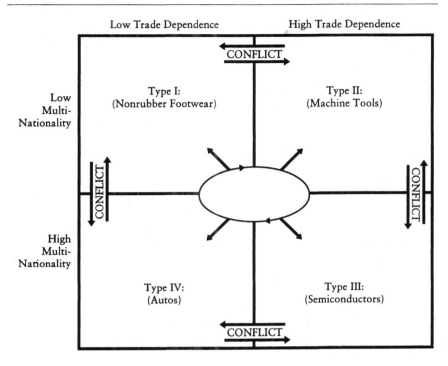

Low Trade Dependence   High Trade Dependence

CONFLICT

Low Multi-Nationality

Type I: (Nonrubber Footwear)

Type II: (Machine Tools)

CONFLICT

CONFLICT

High Multi-Nationality

Type IV: (Autos)

Type III: (Semiconductors)

CONFLICT

pect to find firms whose configuration along the dimensions of trade dependence and multinationality would fit the above descriptions of Types II and III. Historically three of these four industries (excluding semiconductors) started as Type I, producing solely for the national market on the basis of domestic production. Some of them, such as the auto industry, however, evolved from one type to another. And some proceeded further than others in this evolution. Figure 4.5 shows that the three industries chosen to exemplify Type II, III, and IV industries have all sustained increasing levels of import penetration.[75] While the rate of increase of import penetration for autos and U.S. manufacturing as a whole slowed somewhat in the 1980s, machine tools and semiconductors experienced consistently increasing rates of import penetration. All three suffered severe trade deficits in the 1980s. Thus, as illustrated clearly by the machine tool case study and its brief comparison with semiconductors, substantial and increasing trade dependence and import penetration within the same industry will generate objectively contradictory trade-political interests among the industry's firms.

The placement of sectors within each category is determined not by the objective indicators of trade dependence and multinationality but, instead, by the trade-political posture adopted by that sector's political leadership. Thus, for example, in the 1970s, the majority of firms in the machine tool industry were objectively Type I firms. But the industry's political leadership was captured by Type II and III firms that held themselves up as models for the rest of the industry. This leadership crumbled under the impact of precisely those factors discussed in the theoretical sections preceding the case study: Japanese and European product-cycle innovation and industrial policy; increasing levels of import penetration into ever-higher market segments; intensified competition in export markets; and repeated severe recessionary conditions beginning in the 1970s. More specifically, the impact of these factors changed the number of U.S. machine tool firms in each category in the matrix of the trade-political cycle. The change, in terms of the natural progression of the product cycle, was regressive. Firms that had been trade dependent became less so. Firms that had been multinational as well became less so. Only the most competitive and internationally integrated were able to maintain their international positions or progress further toward greater multinationality.

The lines separating the categories of firms and sectors in the matrix in Figure 4.6 should be thought of as lines of trade-political conflict within a sector as much as between sectors. The greater the movement of a sector's firms across the lines of conflict, the more intense the conflict becomes within that sector, and the less certain is the sectoral political leadership, especially in its relations with the heart of the historic bloc.

Alignment with the Historic Bloc: Détente

The model of the trade-political cycle suggests that periods of transition from one type of industry to another will be periods of ideological conflict within and between industrial sectors. Such conflict has not necessarily been restricted to the policy arena of international trade. The machine tool industry's use of national security as a rationale for protection was connected to its earlier support for exports to the Soviet Union and Eastern Europe during détente. Détente, in turn, was an issue of paramount strategic concern to the liberal-internationalist historic bloc..

As the U.S. machine tool industry gradually became more trade dependent in the 1960s, some U.S. tool builders developed an interest in trading with the Soviet Union. As a result, the transition to greater trade dependence among some U.S. machine tool firms was accompanied by ideological conflict over the acceptability of trade with "the communists." In a classic example of liberalism's separation of politics from economics, anticommunism did not stop export-oriented members of what was often described as an ultraconservative industry from demanding greater opportunities to profiteer in the vast and promising "socialist market." Especially in the 1970s, the turn to the East in U.S. machine tool exports stood the industry in good stead with at least three key components of the liberal-internationalist historic bloc: the auto industry, the aerospace industry, and U.S.-based international banking interests.

At the end of the 1960s, the U.S. auto industry had completed a round of investment in southern Europe and Latin America and was looking for other areas in which to invest. At the same time, the aerospace industry had gone into a slump and stood to gain from increased government contracts for the production of strategic missiles. Meanwhile, Chase Manhattan Bank was one of the leading banking interests hoping to make money financing U.S. investments in, and exports to, the USSR and Eastern Europe. And finally, for its part, the U.S. machine tool industry, a key supplier to the auto and aerospace industries, was pursuing an export-led strategy focused on East-West trade in response to challenges from Western Europe and Japan. This constellation of interests, all of which supported free trade in the 1970s, was well positioned to benefit from a policy of détente in East-West relations. According to James Kurth, this constellation of interests and detente did not merely coincide:

> A product cycle theorist would ... have a ready explanation for the U.S. policy of détente with the Soviet Union during the Nixon and Ford Administrations. ... The SALT I (1972) and Vladivostok (1974) arms agreements were skillfully designed so as to create simultaneously an atmosphere for détente (desired by the American automobile industry and by American international banks) and a ratification of increased production of strategic missiles (desired by the American aerospace industry). ... By 1975, the American auto industry had rediscovered that operations in communist countries usually entailed problems which outweighed the profits. And by 1977, American and European international banks had loaned some $50 billion to communist countries, and ... had perceived that this was about the limit of the countries' capacity for orderly repayment. The American industrial and financial interests supporting détente were now much diminished.[76]

Thus the historic bloc components upon which U.S. machine tool builders were most dependent were cutting back their stakes in the Soviet and East European markets, markets that the NMTBA saw as central to establishing and defending an internationally competitive position. Two years later, the U.S. auto industry would complete its turn toward protectionism, joined shortly thereafter by the machine tool industry. The timing and alignment of interests and policy outcomes are suggestive.

They suggest the element of leadership and moral suasion between more powerful (e.g., autos) and less powerful (e.g., machine tools) components of the historic bloc. In historical terms, the NMTBA had only recently joined the auto industry in championing free trade against the swelling tide of protectionism. The auto industry's turn toward protectionism made the NMTBA's liberal-internationalist leadership appear to have joined the free trade cause just in time to see the historic bloc go into crisis. This made it easier to set aside the objections of the erstwhile shining examples of liberal-internationalist cosmopolitanism when the industry turned to protectionism in the early 1980s.

Based on the balance of the evidence presented above, we can conclude that the experiences of the machine tool and semiconductor industries in the trade-political cycle transformed their trade-political postures from liberal internationalism to aggressive unilateralism. Both of these industries occupied strategic positions central to both national security and international competitiveness. This suggests compellingly that the transformation of U.S. international trade policy cannot be adequately explained without accounting for the severe ideological business conflict that precipitated a crisis of hegemony in the 1980s.

5

Explaining Business Support for Regional Trade Agreements
ॠ
Ronald W. Cox

Analysts of the determinants of U.S. trade policy have emphasized ideology, interest group competition, executive-congressional interaction, and cold war rivalry as explanations for U.S. policy. Although each of these approaches offers useful empirical information for scholars of trade policy, they are inadequate for a complete understanding of recent shifts in U.S. policy. This chapter argues for the development of a business conflict model of U.S. trade policy sensitive to the interaction between global macroeconomic conditions and corporate power in establishing the parameters of U.S. trade policy. Specifically, the following is an attempt to lay the foundations for such an approach by linking the macroeconomic trends of industrial restructuring to the development of corporate political coalitions advocating regional trading blocs.

This analysis starts from the proposition that one of the primary roles of the U.S. executive branch in foreign economic policy has been to facilitate the accumulation of capital on a global scale by working to promote the conditions for profitable trade and investment for U.S.-based transnational corporations. In the area of U.S. trade policy, the degree to which the state performs this task is dependent in part on the political mobilization of sectors of business that articulate their demands to influential state actors. In addition, divisions among diverse business sectors often will be reflected in policy debates, with business internationalists joining with the White House, State Department, and Treasury to advocate measures to facilitate increased trade and foreign direct investment and business nationalists and labor groups joining with congressional representatives to promote protectionist measures. Throughout much of the post–World War II period, a dominant liberal-internationalist coalition of business groups, political elites, and intellectuals advocated a U.S. commitment to the policies of multilateralism embodied in the GATT agreements.

Since the mid-1970s, the collapse of the Bretton Woods system has been accompanied by increased divisions among business internationalists previously committed to multilateralism. U.S. foreign direct investors in automobiles and electronics have moved both economically and politically to restructure their operations in order to better compete with Japanese and Western European firms for the triad markets of Japan, Western Europe, and the United States. At one level, firms involved in such restructuring have integrated their North American operations by dividing production of component parts to take advantage of cheap labor and low-cost access to the U.S. market. The project of industrial restructuring represents an ongoing effort by some U.S. transnational corporations to counteract the dual trends of excess capacity and dwindling market share that characterized the late 1970s and early 1980s.[1]

Politically, U.S. foreign direct investors in Mexico, Canada, and the Caribbean Basin have formed coalitions since the mid-1980s to pressure and assist U.S. officials to pursue regional trade agreements that will give them greater protection against foreign competition for the U.S. market. These investors are part of a broad coaliton of business groups that have come together in support of CBI and NAFTA as alternatives to the multilateralism of GATT.

For foreign direct investors facing declining rates of profit and increased foreign competition, regional trade agreements promise numerous advantages. First, they allow U.S.-based multinationals to increase the exploitation of workers by relocating and reorganizing production to low-wage areas. Second, regional operations backed up by regional trade agreements allow U.S. firms proximity to the U.S. market to better compete with foreign rivals.[2] Third, as we will see, regional trade agreements discriminate in several ways against foreign competitors by extending preferential treatment to regionally based firms.

However, it is important to note that not all corporate supporters of CBI and NAFTA view the agreements as a preferable alternative to the multilateralism of GATT. Some firms see these regional agreements as a necessary transition to the renewed promotion of multilateralism on a global scale. For the purposes of brevity and precision, the corporate coalitions behind CBI and NAFTA can be divided into two categories, each of which supports the agreements for different reasons.

The first group can be labeled "multilateralists" or "anti-protectionist" due to their political propensity to support free trade in a variety of different contexts. This group includes retailing, banking and service industries, pharmaceutical companies, and agricultural exporters (especially of grains and oilseeds). Many of the leading Fortune 500 firms in these sectors are heavily dependent on international transactions for their profitability and tend to be highly competitive in global markets. They have been frustrated with the slow progress of GATT and see regional trade agreements as a short-term route to securing important export markets. However, they do not see the regional trade agreements as a substitute for multilateralism. They view the agreements as a first step toward rebuilding the multilateral trading system, and they see CBI and NAFTA as compatible with pursuing free trade agreements through GATT.

The second group can be labeled "regionalists" due to their preference for discriminatory regional trade agreements and their recent opposition to multilateralism. Led by U.S. auto and electronics firms, this group has tended to support nontariff barriers against Japan and Western Europe, while supporting regional trade agreements perceived to give them greater leverage against foreign competition. This group is dominated by foreign direct investors who have struggled to maintain a competitive advantage against European and Japanese companies in the triad markets of Western Europe, Japan, and the United States. These firms see NAFTA as a way to continue the reorganization and rationalization of production necessary to compete with Japanese and European firms who have penetrated the U.S. market.

An example of this regionalist strategy involves U.S. auto firms that successfully won a provision in the U.S.-Canada free trade agreement that has allowed them to continue to bring parts and vehicles into Canada duty-free from any country (including Brazil, Korea, Mexico, Taiwan, and Thailand). Conversely, Japanese firms, including Honda, Hyundai, and Toyota, still have to pay duties on any imports from outside the United States. U.S. auto and electronics firms have insisted on maintaining preferential treatment for North American firms in the trade agreement with Mexico, which places them at a further advantage relative to their Japanese and Western European counterparts.[3] In this sense, these regionalist firms see NAFTA as leverage against foreign competition and advocate restrictive measures that some analysts believe are incompatible with the multilateralism of GATT.

In addition, regionalist firms, especially consumer and industrial electronics, were among the leading advocates of the Caribbean Basin Initiative, which brought together direct foreign investors and export-import interests with a stake in improving the terms of trade with the Caribbean Basin. Like the case of NAFTA, CBI represented a significant departure from GATT in its discriminatory treatment of foreign companies.[4] Regionalists applauded the initiative for giving greater leverage to U.S. firms engaged in global economic competition with their Japanese and European rivals.

The following analysis will focus on regionalist U.S. firms, especially automobiles and electronics, in attempting to explain the appeal of NAFTA. In addition, a focus on regionalist firms will be useful in highlighting the implications of the global restructuring of the world economy for political trade coalitions in the United States. I argue that regionalist firms that supported NAFTA are likely to maintain their opposition to multilateralism, given the current realitites of the world economy.

I will attempt to expand upon these general observations by performing three tasks: (1) locating the process of industrial restructuring within the larger context of global competition for production advantage in the U.S. market; (2) connecting the economic process of industrial restructuring to the development of a U.S.-based political coalition supporting CBI and NAFTA; and (3) drawing lessons from these agreements regarding the future prospects for multilateralism, regionalism, and protectionism on a global scale.

Industrial Restructuring and Regional Trade

The trend of relocating partial production of a product to the less-developed world for reexport to the home market has been occurring to various degrees since the early-to-mid-1960s. This approach was feasible only for companies with access to appropriate capital, marketing, administration, or technology that made relocation less costly than producing the entire product within the domestic market. Multinationals able to take advantage of this approach found partial production abroad to be preferable to other options for maintaining their competitive postition within the domestic market.

Alternative options included automating production in the home market by integrating the latest technological advances into the production process, a method that proved too costly for many firms facing increased foreign competition. Another option was protecting the domestic market against foreign competitors, which was difficult for three reasons: (1) Foreign investors were increasingly circumventing nontariff barriers by investing directly in the U.S. market. (2) Any attempt to increase nontariff barriers was economically risky given the possibility of retaliation by foreign governments and the likelihood of increased costs for imported products. (3) The rise of antiprotectionist groups in the United States posed further political obstacles to protecting the domestic market.

As a result, firms often chose to relocate their labor-intensive operations to low-cost areas abroad as a strategy to maintain their competitive position against foreign firms that had penetrated the U.S. market. As other analysts have noted, this process was facilitated in the case of U.S. firms by tariff codes 806.30 and 807, which permit the "duty-free entry of U.S. components sent abroad for processing or assembly."[5] In addition, U.S. foreign direct investors lobbied heavily for regional trade agreements with Canada, Mexico, and the Caribbean Basin, which allowed them to further integrate their production strategies for the U.S. market. As we will see, the regional agreements also have given (or promise to give) U.S. firms preferential treatment versus their most important international rivals. U.S. foreign direct investors facing declining profitability and increased competition in the U.S. market saw the regional trade agreements as an important political extension of their ongoing efforts to restructure their global operations against increasing foreign competition.

As part of this process, multinational corporations in electronics and automobiles have increasingly viewed Mexico as an ideal location to cut costs and bolster their competitive positions. Since the late 1960s, U.S.-based firms in these industries have used locations in Mexico for production of component parts for export to the U.S. market.

Since the mid-1980s, export production from Mexico has been increasingly important for U.S. firms due to two primary factors. First, U.S.-based firms in electronics and automobiles faced domestic obstacles to lowering the costs of production in the U.S. market. These included relatively high wages and capital costs, which made it difficult to compete with foreign rivals.[6] For electronics industries, the Caribbean Basin and Mexico allowed for the division of production between capital-intensive production in the U.S. and labor-intensive production in cheap labor regions, continuing a trend well established in Asia. For U.S. auto companies, Mexico provided an increasingly important platform for the assembly of component parts and vehicles destined for the U.S. market.

Secondly, these U.S.-based firms faced an internationalization of the U.S. economy that involved increases in foreign direct investment in the U.S. market by Japanese and European competitors. The reaction to such competition was the increased sourcing of component parts to Mexico and (in the case of electronics firms) to the Caribbean Basin, a strategy designed to lower costs of production and maintain profitability in the face of growing competition for the U.S. market. The internationalization of the U.S. market meant that efforts by electronics and automobile firms to limit imports (through voluntary export restraints) had minimal effects on impeding their international rivals, which merely relocated to the U.S. market to avoid voluntary export restraints and other trade barriers. Also, the strategy of reinvesting in new technology and equipment in the U.S. market proved to be too costly in the shortterm.

Thus the preferred option was to locate production of component parts in areas characterized by cheap labor and proximity to the U.S. market. Some electronics firms moved their operations from Asia to Mexico and the Caribbean Basin to lower their transportation costs in exporting to the U.S. market. Auto firms increasingly used Mexico to source component parts for the U.S. market. Furthermore, the beginning of the 1990s have seen auto companies expand their Mexican operations to include production of finished vehicles, including state-of-the-art autos that were previously produced only in the advanced markets of the United States and Europe.[7]

Apparel producers have also used foreign locations for low-cost advantage in producing component parts for the U.S. market. U.S. apparel firms typically subcontract with garment producers in the Caribbean Basin and Mexico for the production of clothing or textiles for export to the U.S. market. As a result, some of the leading U.S. apparel firms have joined other U.S. industries, such as electronics, automobiles, and electrical equipment, to push for CBI and NAFTA. However, as I discuss in detail later, other apparel firms tied to the U.S. market have mounted successful opposition against tariff reductions proposed by their international counterparts in lobbying for CBI.[8]

These foreign direct investors and subcontractors form part of a powerful political coalition lobbying for NAFTA and CBI, often against nationalist firms. The next section of this paper locates the emergence of this coalition in the context of the internationalization of the U.S. market, especially the dramatic increases in foreign direct investment by Japanese companies. In the 1980s, U.S. electronics and auto firms faced with intensified global competition looked to Mexico for increased low-cost access to the U.S. market. Moreover, these firms were facing competitive challenges from Japanese firms toward their East Asian affiliates, prompting them to look toward Mexico as a possible alternative site for long-term foreign direct investment. At the same time, the Mexican debt crisis helped convince Mexican policymakers to loosen the restrictions on foreign capital and to encourage exports to the U.S. market. The result was the formation of a "regionalist" coalition advocating NAFTA as a mutual solution to the problems of industrial restructuring and the debt crisis, respectively.

The Internationalization of the U.S. Market:
The Cases of Automobiles and Consumer Electronics

U.S. auto and electronics firms faced vigorous competition from their Japanese counterparts in the 1980s, which provided the major impetus for industrial restructuring. Prior to 1982, Japanese auto firms did not have a single production plant outside Japan. Instead, Japanese firms, led by Toyota, relied on a "lean production" strategy that emphasized exports to the developed market economies as a method for increasing market share. Innovations in Japanese production provided formidable challenges to U.S. car manufacturers, who had been late in shifting from "mass production" methods to a more flexible production system. As Table 5.1 indicates, Japanese firms were able to increase their penetration of world markets through 1984.

The production strategy employed by Japanese firms involved a number of interrelated changes designed to increase output at considerably lower costs. They included the introduction of sophisticated computer technology to facilitate the designing and engineering phases of production, the relatively low parts inventory achieved by reliance on close functional relation-

Table 5.1   Japanese Car Exports, 1974–1984

Importing Region	1974	1984	Rate of Increase
North America	796	1,990	2.5
European Community	235	790	3.4
Other Europe	109	240	2.2
Asia	177	450	2.5
Oceania	225	230	1.0
Latin America	84	210	2.5
Africa	101	90	0.9
Total	1,700	4,000	2.4

Source: Robert Gwynne, "The Third World Motor Vehicle Industry," in Christopher M. Law, ed., *Restructuring the Global Automobile Industry* (London: Routledge, 1991), p. 69.

ships between customers and suppliers, the multiple tasks performed by Japanese autoworkers to enhance productivity and inhibit the formation of independent unions, and protection from the Japanese government, which limits access to foreign firms and practices discriminatory intervention in favor of domestic producers. Prior to 1982, this productive system was combined with an emphasis on export promotion to successfully penetrate the developed market economies.[9]

Such import penetration posed a considerable challenge to U.S. auto firms, which saw their competitive advantage eroding in the U.S. market. In response, U.S. auto firms most severely affected by Japanese imports joined the United Automobile Workers Union to pressure the government to negotiate voluntary export restraints with Japan. U.S. manufacturers and labor union officials hoped these restraints would help to create a level playing field in the U.S. market by encouraging Japanese companies to reduce exports in favor of foreign direct investment. In this regard, it was hoped that Japanese direct investors would then have to operate under the same conditions as did U.S. companies.

Japanese companies' newfound interest in direct foreign investment went well beyond the expectations of U.S. business and government elites, however. From 1982 to 1989, Japanese auto firms began establishing production plants in the U.S. market that provided further challenges to U.S. companies. Table 5.2 indicates the extent of this investment.

In addition, Japanese firms in consumer electronics were increasing their direct foreign investment in the United States, although this trend began in the 1970s with the television industry (where it had its greatest impact) and continued in the 1980s with the videotape recorder industry. The ability of

Table 5.2   Assembly Plants in the United States Owned or Operated by the Japanese, 1982–1989

	Production Start-up	Production Capacity	Number of Employees
Honda	1982	500,000	4,800
Nissan	1983	220,000	3,200
NUMMI (Toyota and GM)	1984	250,000	2,500
Mazda	1987	240,000	3,500
Toyota	1988	200,000	3,500
Diamond-Star Motors (Mitsubishi and Chrysler joint venture)	1988	240,000	2,900
Subaru/Isuzu	1989	120,000	1,700

Source: R. R. Rehder, "Japanese Transplants: A New Model for Detroit," *Business Horizons* 31, no. 1: 52–61.

Japanese producers to penetrate the consumer electronics market is based on the following five characteristics:

1. Labor costs half or one-third as high as those in Germany and the United Kingdom.
2. Designs requiring up to 30 percent fewer components than Western Europe or U.S. sets because of a greater use of integrated circuits.
3. Automation in the assembly of sets (of 65–80 percent of total components used against 0–15 percent in German and U.K. plants), meaning that a Japanese company could produce a color TV set with an average of 1.9 man-hours against 3.9 in West Germany and 6.1 in Britain.
4. Large scale of plant operations.
5. Superior quality components.[10]

Historically, the Japanese consumer electronics companies, like their automobile counterparts, have relied on these advantages to export to European and U.S. markets. However, the proliferation of voluntary export restraints, coupled with the development of new technology, made it necessary and profitable to engage in direct foreign investments in the United States and Europe. The 1970s saw a wave of Japanese companies invest in television manufacturing plants in the United States, "totally changing the character of the American television industry, as Sony built a plant at San Diego in 1972, Matsushita and Sanyo bought out existing U.S.-owned TV plants by 1976; and Mitsubishi, Toshiba, Sharp and Hitachi ... all launched U.S. factories."[11] Consequently, only Zenith remained as an indigenous U.S. manu-facturer by the end of the 1970s. By the 1980s, Japanese firms were repeat-ing this wave of foreign investment in the area of videotape recorders.

To summarize, the primary factors causing this new trend of Japanese foreign direct investment in automobiles and electronics were threefold. First, Japanese companies relied on direct foreign investment to overcome the ob-stacles to import penetration of the United States. Second, new technologies allowed Japanese firms to tailor vehicles to consumer demand, making it more imperative, and cost-efficient, to locate in foreign markets. Finally, the value of the yen was high against the dollar, allowing for monetary opportu-nity to invest in production plants in the United States.

U.S. firms began to shift production strategies in an effort to withstand the Japanese competitive threat. In order to understand these strategies, one must remember that U.S. firms are fully internationalized themselves, with important stakes in the European and U.S. markets. The broad goals of U.S. firms have included three primary tasks, which are analytically distinct: (1) maintaining a competitive position in the European market; (2) maintaining a competitive postition in the U.S. market; and (3) eventually penetrating the relatively closed Japanese market. In the case of Western Europe, the strate-gies employed by U.S. firms were directed at rationalizing production and supply networks to lower cost and increase efficiency, with the goal being to increase production and sales within Europe itself. In the case of the United States, U.S. producers sought to rely increasingly on supply and production networks in Canada and Mexico in an effort to gain a competitive advan-tage in the U.S. market.

Thus, U.S. auto and electronics firms were solidly behind the free trade agreements with Mexico and Canada, which they saw as essential regional locations for improving their production system in the U.S. market. The re-cent investments by U.S. auto firms in Canada and Mexico represent an effort to integrate production for the U.S. market via the expansion of low-cost supply networks and production facilities. Thus regional trade agree-ments are seen as preferable to GATT in meeting the competitive challenges of global competition. Meanwhile, electronics firms have lobbied heavily for both CBI and NAFTA, reflecting their global production strategies in the face of the internationalization of the U.S. market in the 1980s.

The following sections of this chapter examine the economic and political strategies of U.S.-based auto firms in pursuing regional integration. These firms were part of a political coalition that began lobbying NAFTA in 1986 as part of an effort to increase the regional economic integration already under way. At the same time, electronics firms had pursued both CBI and NAFTA as part of their regional integration strategy. In each case, the strat-egy pursued represented a significant departure from the framework of GATT, as I will explain in the final section of this paper.

Electronics Firms and the Caribbean Basin Initiative

Beginning in 1979, the Caribbean/Central American Action (CCAA) lobby, representing the interests of 90 percent of the Fortune 500 firms with investments in the Caribbean Basin, formed to lobby U.S. governmental officials to ease trade restrictions on products imported from Caribbean Basin countries. The formation of the CCAA anticipated and supported the efforts of the Reagan administration to promote CBI, which lowered tariffs on selected manufactured goods exported from Caribbean Basin countries that qualified. The CCAA took an active role in drafting CBI, with U.S.-based electronics and pharmaceutical firms realizing substantial tariff reduction on products produced and exported by affiliates or subcontractors in the region.[12]

U.S. electronics firms viewed CBI as a means to discriminate against foreign competitors for the U.S. market. The agreement allowed producers of integrated circuits and metal oxide semiconductors to export partially produced products from the region duty-free. These provisions complemented the duty-free provisions already established in Caribbean Basin free trade zones. In addition, CBI implemented a low and flexible local content requirement that gave preferential treatment to U.S. firms. Eligibility for duty-free treatment was contingent on 35 percent of the product being produced in the Caribbean Basin, of which 15 percent could be accounted for by U.S. materials.

U.S.-based electronics firms joined with pharmaceutical firms and producers of baseball gloves, belts, fabricated metals and food processors to lobby for CBI. Electronics firms saw the agreement as a way to regionalize their operations by relying on low-cost, partial production in the Caribbean Basin to compete for the U.S. market. U.S. controlled and/or operated firms accounted for five of the top ten imports from the region eligible for duty-free treatment.[13]

U.S. electronics firms, including Texas Instruments, Dataram, Kay Electronics, Beckman, and AVX Ceramics, were attracted to the Caribbean Basin in the mid-1970s as an export location for low-cost access to the U.S. market. From 1973 to 1978, for example, each of these firms abandoned previous low-wage havens for the more favorable economic conditions offered by Caribbean Basin countries. Dataram moved to El Salvador the year it closed down its Malaysian operation. Texas Instruments began production in El Salvador the same year it closed its Curaçao plant. Finally, both Beckman and AVX corporations moved their plants from Ireland to El Salvador to take advantage of cheap labor, proximity to the North American market, and numerous export incentives.

The move of U.S. multinationals into El Salvador was part of a broader trend of corporations subcontracting part of their operations to the Caribbean Basin for the U.S. market. In Haiti, 150 U.S., and 40 other foreign-owned, firms in electronics, computer parts, and clothing were producing for the U.S. market between 1975 and 1981, when the dollar value of international subcontracting in the Caribbean increased fourfold. In the Dominican Republic during the 1970s, over 50 percent of the products shipped to the United States were assembled by foreign contractors. By the late 1970s, foreign multinationals were increasingly viewing the Caribbean Basin as an important subcontracting area for enhancing international competitiveness and market position.[14]

The Business International Corporation, a consortium of business executives and advisers who offer publications and marketing seminars for corporate executives, has written extensively about the advantages of sourcing in the Caribbean Basin for multinationals competing for access to the U.S. market. In a publication entitled *Improving International Competitiveness Through Sourcing in Latin America,* the authors argued that the Caribbean Basin, by the late 1970s and early 1980s, had become an increasingly important region for U.S.-based multinationals faced with intensified global competition. The following advantages of the region were noted:

1. Proximity to the world's largest and most sophisticated marketplace: North America.
2. Increased use of export processing zones, which offer numerous tax incentives and investment options.
3. Inexpensive, stable, and skilled labor supply relative to other areas such as the Far East. This was especially true during the 1980s, as the Latin American countries realigned their exchange rates and the dollar itself depreciated relative to other hard currencies.[15]

Additionally, U.S. multinationals have turned toward sourcing arrangements in the Caribbean Basin to compensate for increased competition from Japanese firms, in both the United States and the East Asian markets. In the 1950s and 1960s, U.S. direct foreign investment (DFI) dominated the East Asian region. By the early 1970s, Japan acquired what one analyst termed a "hegemonic" position in DFI throughout East Asia.[16] Japanese corporations accounted for the majority of DFI in South Korea, Taiwan, Malaysia, Thailand, and Indonesia, while U.S. DFI continued to lead only in the Philippines, China, and Hong Kong.

Some U.S. multinationals, especially in electronics, have responded by relocating operations closer to the U.S. market. The relocation strategy was especially attractive in the late 1970s and early 1980s. The most substantial benefits accrued to firms engaged in partial production for the U.S. market. As the Business International Corporation noted, by the late 1970s and early 1980s, the Caribbean region offered two distinct advantages for U.S. foreign investors: proximity to the U.S. market and lower wage costs. This was enhanced by the preferential local content requirements of the CBI, which discriminated against non-U.S. firms.

The battle over CBI reflected the diverse business interests involved in trade legislation. First, there were the regionalist firms represented by electronics companies that saw the agreement as leverage against foreign competition for the U.S. market. Spokespersons for AVX, Dataram, and other U.S. electronics firms testified before Congress that CBI would give them a necessary competitive advantage in competing against Japanese and European firms for access to the U.S. market. These firms saw CBI as further institutionalizing an ongoing trend of corporate relocation and restructuring necessary to reverse declining profitability and intensified global competition. As a result, U.S.-based electronics firms lobbied for local content laws that would give preferential treatment to U.S. firms.

The second group of firms in favor of CBI were the multilateralists in pharmaceuticals, services, and banking. These firms were more competitive in global markets and did not seek the restrictive local content laws preferred by electronics firms. Instead, they saw the regional trade agreement as complementary to broader efforts to revitalize the multilateralism of GATT on a global scale. They valued the agreement because it allowed for a further reduction in U.S. tariff barriers, which in turn furthered free trade goals.

Reagan administration officials supported CBI mainly because it complemented broader security goals in the region. The administration insisted that the largest percentage of CBI money should go to El Salvador, where the administration was actively engaged in bolstering the military regime against rebel insurgents. As such, much of the aid attached to CBI reflected the Reagan administration's policy of bolstering a Salvadoran government that was facing an economic and political crisis.

Opponents of the regional trade agreement included domestic firms that stood to lose the most from reducing tariff barriers, especially the domestic textile and clothing industries tied to the national market. An examination of congressional debates over the content of CBI reveals that business nationalists also had some influence on the final legislation. The American Textile Manufacturers Institute and the American Apparel Manufacturers Association joined with the American Clothing and Textile Workers Union and the International Ladies Garment Workers Union to lobby Congress, especially the Subcommittee on Trade of the House Ways and Means Committee, to maintain import restrictions. These business nationalists and their labor counterparts succeeded in excluding all textile and apparel products from the duty-free provisions of CBI.[17]

By the late 1980s and early 1990s, many of the same coalitions that had been active in the battle over CBI would again intervene in the NAFTA debates. An examination of regionalist, multilateral, and nationalist firms active in the NAFTA debate allows us to draw some important lessons about the prospects for multilateralism in the coming decade.

Auto Firms and the
North American Free Trade Agreement

The U.S. automobile industry has developed a corporate production strategy that seeks to combat the effects of increased global competition. An important pillar of the strategy is regionalization of production along continental lines. This regionalization has proceeded along three general dimensions, involving: (1) moving phases of the production process (including the fabrication of engines and transmissions) from the United States to lower-wage sites in Mexico, Brazil, and Argentina, with Mexico becoming a preferred location since the 1980s. (2) developing a North American production scheme characterized by knowledge-based or lean production in order to better compete with Japanese rivals for the U.S. market; and (3) lobbying for a NAFTA agreement that extends preferential treatment to North American producers in Mexico. [18]

The strategies of United States auto firms cannot be separated from the arena of capital-labor relations. U.S. firms facing increased global competition have attempted to reduce labor and supply costs in order to prevent further erosion of market share in the United States. With this in mind, relocation of parts of the production process to cheap labor regions has been viewed as an important strategy in competing with foreign firms for the U.S. market. Through relocation, U.S. firms have been able to take advantage of lower wages in Mexico, Brazil, and Argentina and force numerous concessions from U.S. workers.

From 1970 to 1984, U.S.-based transnationals dramatically increased their investments in plants and equipment in Latin America. According to Robert Ross and Kent Trachte, this trend was related to "a declining rate of profit and to rising price competition from foreign exports."[19] The result is illustrated by data comparing motor vehicle production in the United States to that in Latin America from the early 1970s to 1980. Between 1973 and 1980, the U.S. to Latin American ratio for General Motors declined from 28.8–to–1 to 14–to–1: for Ford from 12.1–to–1 to 4.5–to–1; and for Chrysler, from 14.2–to–1 to 6.4–to–1. Overall, by 1980, "37.2 percent of the total motor vehicle production of the four leading U.S. automobile firms was located abroad."[20]

By the late 1980s, U.S. firms increasingly looked to Mexico as a preferred site for relocation of motor vehicle production for the U.S. market, including the production of auto parts, engines and transmissions, and finished motor vehicles. A number of factors converged to make Mexico especially attractive to U.S. producers. First, the Mexican government implemented a series of trade liberalization measures that facilitated and encouraged U.S. transnationals to export more finished motor vehicles and auto parts. Second, the Mexican state implemented neoliberal reforms that have resulted in a devaluation of the peso and a reduction in wages in the auto industry and elsewhere, making Mexico more attractive to foreign investors. Finally, U.S.-based auto firms have been able to take advantage of Mexico's proximity to the United States, which has given them a cost edge over European and Japanese competitors in the production of parts and finished vehicles for the U.S. market.[21]

This combination of Mexican incentives and corporate interests has already resulted in dramatic increases in U.S. foreign direct investment in auto parts and assembly in Mexico. For example, since the last years of the 1980s, U.S. auto firms have significantly increased their production and export of auto parts from Mexico to the United States. This continued a trend established by the late 1970s and early 1980s. Gary Hufbauer and Jeffrey Schott provided statistics on the overall increase in auto parts trade between the two countries:

> Mexican auto parts trade, almost all of which is with the United States, has grown dramatically. U.S. auto parts imports from Mexico grew from $2.1 billion in 1985 to $3.6 billion in 1989 and now represent 12 percent of total U.S. auto parts imports. U.S. exports of auto parts to Mexico likewise grew by 79 percent, from $1.9 billion to $3.4 billion, over the same period. Most of the recent growth can be attributed to original equipment parts manufactured by the big three and sold in both directions across the border.[22]

In addition to auto parts production, U.S.-based transnationals also have increased dramatically their production of finished vehicles in Mexico. Big Three vehicle production for the first half of 1992 jumped to almost 363,000— 9 percent over the same period in 1991. Ford captured first place, followed closely by Chrysler, with GM third. About half of all production of finished vehicles is for export to the U.S. market, while the other half involves production for the Mexican market.[23]

The production of finished vehicles is increasingly being accomplished with the use of knowledge-based or lean sourcing techniques pioneered by the Japanese. This involves a shift to a workplace organization characterized by flexible work rules and job rotation, broadly defined job classifications, quality circles, work teams and other measures designed to defuse labor-employer tensions and further motivate workers.

At the insitutional level, U.S. auto firms have worked with the Mexican state, especially the Confederation of Mexican Workers, the state's party labor organization, to consolidate the shift to a flexible labor system. This has meant shifting automotive production from Mexico City to northern and central Mexico in order to reduce labor costs and facilitate an export-promotion strategy geared toward low-cost supply for the North American market. As other analysts have noted, U.S. auto companies have attempted to consolidate their control over Mexican labor in order to pursue this flexible production strategy.

At the same time, U.S. firms have asked for dual rules of origin requirements that extend preferential treatment to U.S. firms and discriminate against new entrants into the North American market. In free trade agreements, rules of origin requirements are used to determine what goods were actually produced in the member countries and therefore qualify for preferential treatment. In negotiations over NAFTA, U.S. auto firms have insisted on 50 percent rules of origin agreements, which gives preferential treatment to firms already established in North America.

The discriminatory measures embedded in regional trade agreements contrast with the multilateralism advocated by GATT. Although clearly allowing for regional trade agreements, GATT established criteria "designed to ensure that free trade arrangements lead, on balance, to growth in world trade and can thus be considered building blocks of a more open world trading system."[24] To the extent that NAFTA institutionalizes preferential treatment for U.S. firms and discriminates against foreign competitors, it can hardly be seen as compatible with the broad principles of GATT. As Ernest Preeg has noted,

> The U.S. intent for NAFTA was not directed at ... tariff circumvention, which is likely to be small in any event, but to limit benefits to Japanese and other foreign direct investment in Mexico, in the automotive, computer and other high-technology sectors. A high level of North American value added, as the rule of origin test, and a narrowly drawn definition of value added constitute a form of performance requirements for foreign investment—ironically, just the kind of trade distorting investment measures the United States was trying to eliminate in the Uruguay Round negotiations. [25]

In fact, NAFTA brought together a coalition of corporate supporters advocating both discriminatory treatment against foreign investors and reduced tariff barriers. On the one hand, foreign direct investors in autos and electronics advocated tough rules of origin requirements that privileged existing market players and penalized late entrants, resulting in what Preeg has called a concept of "high-tech regionalism." On the other hand, multilateralists represented by banks, U.S. exporters, and retailers supported NAFTA for its liberalized trade provisions.

These corporate coalitions came together to lobby for NAFTA against import-competing industries who stood to lose market share if trade was liberalized. Opponents of NAFTA included labor-intensive industries producing footwear, glassware, luggage, brooms, and ceramics, and agricultural producers of asparagus, avocados, canned tomatoes, citrus, sugar and sugar beets. Other powerful critics of NAFTA included labor unions, religious organizations, and consumer and environmental interest groups that feared the consequences of liberalized trade and investment for U.S. labor, Mexican workers, and the environment.[26]

The battle over NAFTA suggested that multilateralists faced stiff opposition in securing a regional trade agreement that was compatible with the multilateralism of GATT. This was true for two reasons. First, corporate supporters of NAFTA included an uneasy alliance of foreign direct investors, multinational banks, and exporters, each of which supported the agreement for different reasons. These interests came together to lobby for NAFTA, but they have often been on opposing sides of the free trade debate in other, nonregional contexts. Second, NAFTA became a lightning rod for popular discontent, influenced by the legacy of corporate-labor battles of the 1980s that resulted in considerable union concessions in autos, steel, and textiles. The concessions were often won as a result of corporate flight or threats to close down plants in lieu of reduced wages and/or benefits.

Multilateralism, Regionalism, and Protectionism in the Wake of the North American Free Trade Agreement

There are several noticeable trends that have affected trade politics from the late 1970s to the present. The first has been a defection of some multinational firms from the free trade coalition that previously dominated U.S. trade policy. Firms were more likely to defect if they faced the following conditions: increased import competition leading to loss of market share in the United States and elsewhere, reliance on foreign direct investment geared toward regional markets, and low levels of trade relative to direct foreign investment. U.S.-based firms in electronics and autos have geared production around regional markets via foreign direct investment in North America, the EEC (European Economic Community) and Asia. The international character of these firms has not meant continued support for multilateralism but, instead, has resulted in support for regional trading blocs designed to increase protection against foreign competitors. In addition, electronics and auto firms supported nontariff barriers to trade throughout the late 1970s and 1980s, including voluntary export restraints.

Does this mean an end to the multilateralism of GATT in favor of regional trading blocs? Not necessarily. Another trend in trade politics has been the emergence of antiprotectionist political organizations based among exporters, business and industrial import users, retailers and other trade-related services, and foreign governments of exporting countries. In general, the degree to which firms are dependent on exports as a percentage of overall production is a determining factor in their commitment to antiprotectionsim. One well-documented trend in the late 1970s and 1980s was the fact that the U.S. economy as a whole saw substantial increases in trade dependence as a percentage of GNP. This trend meant that certain U.S. firms in selective industries developed a greater interest in antiprotectionist activity.

Since the mid-1970s, groups with a high export dependence, including the National Association of Wheat Growers and the American Soybean Association, have increased their antiprotectionist lobbying efforts. However, these efforts tend to selectively lobby against trade restrictions involving particular foreign customers and do not usually involve a defense of multilateralism as a general principle. In addition, certain export-dependent groups, such as cotton growers, have joined the American Textile Manufacturers in lobbying for textile protection. Cotton growers identify their interests with domestic textile producers who would be hurt by free trade measures. Other industries that were export dependent, such as aircraft, included firms with an interest in opposing trade restrictions with steel-producing countries, since these countries constituted 21 percent of all aircraft exports and 8 percent of aircraft production. However, aircraft firms had less interest in opposing trade restrictions on countries producing shoes, since only 2 percent of industrial output went to these countries.[27]

The selective nature of antiprotection interests indicates significant limits in the development of an aggressive political coaltion advocating multilateralism. However, other political interests have developed Since the 1990s with a more widespread interest in antiprotectionist legislation. These groups tend to be concentrated in retailing and service firms with a stake in importing automobiles, textiles and footwear, all targets of protectionist efforts in the 1970s and 1980s. In fact, retailers formed several antiprotectionist coalitions in the 1980s designed to lobby against trade restrictions on textiles, automobiles, and footwear. According to I. M. Destler and John S. Odell, retailers were most likely to lobby against trade restrictions under the following conditions:

1. If a particular group of retailers sold primarily to a market niche for which imports were a large share of current supply, and domestic substitutes were only available in lesser quantity and at higher prices.
2. If the price elasticity of demand for a major product class were such that the higher prices caused by import restrictions would reduce sales volume substantially.
3. If import curbs were to be imposed quickly without warning, disrupting the delivery of goods already contracted from overseas sources.[28]

These conditions, again, are fairly narrow and do not imply a generalized coalition prepared to advance multilateralism. Furthermore, many of the antiprotectionist organizations established by retailers are burdened by "a younger and weaker tradition of collective political action on trade, and the uneasy coexistence of such action with the fierce commercial revalries that characterize the retail business."[29] Also, most of the lobbying organizations are established at the local level, "aimed at strengthening community ties (and bringing in customers) while avoiding controversial policy stands that might drive them away."[30]

With these limitations in mind, one has to search elsewhere to find stable political coalitions or interests that advocate a generalized commitment to multilateralism. The leading proponents of multilateralism are difficult to readily identify, since they often eschew overt lobbying efforts used by the previous antiprotection groups. Instead, multilateralists often work with the exective branch in promoting multilateralism in specific institutional contexts, such as the GATT talks, U.S. bilateral negotiations with foreign governments, and multilateral organizations such as the World Bank and the IMF (International Monetary Fund). The most notable multilateralists include banking and service firms that have numerous financial and trade interests connected to open markets.

The top Fortune 500 U.S.-based banks dramatically expanded their overseas lending throughout the 1970s and 1980s to both foreign governments and firms. Bankers have been consistent proponents of multilateralist policies in negotiations with less-developed countries over terms of debt repayment. In addition, bankers have promoted U.S. policies toward Europe designed to maximize trade and foreign investment. Bankers are not as subject to the limitations of sectoral politics as are other firms, since their capital is more fluid and their interests are tied to a wide range of investments in foreign governments and private firms. As a result, bankers have consistently advocated a commitment to multilateralism consistent with their varied interests in collecting government debts and reaping a return on investments in foreign and U.S.-based multinationals.[31]

With those general observations as a starting point, it must be said that not all bankers will be vigorous proponents of multilateralism. Bankers will be more likely to support multilateralism if they exhibit the following characteristics: (1) commercial banks that are thoroughly multinational in character, with loans dispersed around the world to both foreign governments and foreign firms; (2) investment banks linked to multinational firms heavily dependent on foreign trade relative to foreign investment; and (3) bankers ideologically committed to multilateralism as a means to facilitate debt repayment from governments in the less-developed world.

The fact that not all bankers will be committed to multilateralism weakens the potential free trade coalition. In fact, a striking development that may illuminate future trade patterns is the extent to which multilateralists in the banking community have been increasingly isolated from other multinational firms in recent decades, as support for multilateralism has steadily eroded. The only context in which a wide range of multinational firms have been able to coalesce around a trade agreement has been the case of NAFTA, where such diffuse organizations as the Chambers of Commerce, the National Association of Manufacturers, and the Business Advisory Council have taken strong positions in favor of the agreement.

However, as I have argued, the extent of interest group agreement around NAFTA is a product of the regional nature of the agreement, which attracts different multinationals for different reasons. While multilateralists see it as an important step for reinvigorating GATT, regionalists view it as additional leverage against foreign competition. The likelihood of such a powerful free trade coalition emerging in another, nonregional context is minimal at best. What is equally interesting is that, even with such a high degree of unity in the corporate community over NAFTA, the agreement is politically divisive, with nationalists being led by the unlikely bedfellows of organized labor and Ross Perot in opposing the accord. If, in fact, multilateralism is in part the product of interest group pressure, then the future for the global trading regime looks increasingly shaky in the 1990s.

6

The Business of Strategy:
The Political Economy of U.S. Trade
Policy Toward the USSR, 1945–1975

Jerri-Lynn Scofield

Discussions of U.S. trade and investment policies toward the former Soviet Union have been dominated by realist explanations, which linked U.S. policy to national security concerns. These explanations predicted that the United States would pursue competitive economic policies with the Soviet Union during periods of Soviet strength, and cooperative policies during periods of Soviet weakness. In the immediate postwar period, the United States pursued a competitive policy with the Soviet Union and refined this strategy throughout the 1950s. But, paradoxically, as the Soviets expanded their military and their willingness to intervene in foreign states during the 1960s, both the Kennedy and Johnson administrations began to prepare for closer economic cooperation. This cooperative trend culminated in the Nixon administration's policy of détente, a trend not forestalled by continued Soviet aggression in Africa.

This chapter offers an alternative explanation of U.S. trade strategy toward the USSR. Rather than relating U.S. policy fluctuations to national security concerns, I argue that shifting interest group pressures helped shape the transition in U.S. policy from regarding the Soviet Union as a threat to viewing it as an opportunity. These pressures were strongly correlated with two variables. First, the Soviet Union's switch in its commodity pricing policy away from undercutting Western producers resulted in relaxed opposition from influential business interests—primarily oil producers—toward increased U.S.-USSR cooperation. Second, this shift was accompanied by increased pressure from other business interests—agricultural producers, capital equipment manufacturers, automobile producers, and computer manufacturers, to name a few—that had always regarded the Soviet Union as a business opportunity. The interaction between interest groups and political institutions generated the pattern of shifting U.S. policies.

This chapter is drawn principally from archival material from the Kennedy, Johnson, Nixon, and Ford administrations. The trade preferences of U.S. business interests suggest profitable avenues for future explorations of the shifting pattern of competitive and cooperative behavior in the history of U.S.-USSR economic relations.[1]

Background

U.S. trade relations with socialist countries in the postwar period were characterized by different goals and practices than those nominally applied to trade with capitalist states.[2] Whereas the general thrust of postwar trade policy was to liberalize commercial relations, the United States had begun to restrict trade with socialist states in the late 1940s and was initially successful in encouraging other Western countries to follow suit.[3] More than in any other area of trade, Congress was willing to delegate wide authority to the president to set East-West trade policy. Under the authority of the Export Control Act of 1949, the United States controlled exports of strategically sensitive goods and required special licenses for commercial or financial transactions with certain socialist countries. Before this legislation, the president could only restrict exports in narrowly defined cases of war or special emergency; afterward, the president's authority was extended to include restricting peacetime commercial transactions. High tariffs were also imposed on East-bloc imports under the authority of the Smoot-Hawley Tariff Act. Since Section 5 of the 1951 Trade Agreements Extension Act denied most-favored nation (MFN) treatment to most East-bloc countries, goods originating from socialist states received none of the benefits of tariff reduction initiated in the Reciprocal Trade Agreements Act of 1934 and extended through legislation authorizing successive rounds of GATT negotiations. Tariff rates thus remained at the high levels that prevailed in the 1920s and early 1930s.

Some U.S. business sectors and affiliated business organizations developed an interest in liberalizing East-West trade in the late 1950s, as one part of a general search for new markets. But not all business voices called for liberalization. In a revealing letter to National Security Advisor McGeorge Bundy in 1965, former High Commissioner to Germany John J. McCloy asserted, "If this trade with the East is to be something more than a mere subsidization of exports over the long run, there will have to be a continuing basis for it. This means their supplying us with things we need and our supplying them with their needs, and the needs have to be in rough balance if the trade is to prosper."[4] In particular, McCloy recognized that two products would be central to any future East-West commercial relationship:

The Soviet Union and, to a large extent, the satellites have some acute needs for the things we have—modern machinery and plants embodying all the latest technological developments of Western science. Most of the things they can supply us with are, except for some minor products, things of which we have a generous or perhaps an over supply already. The most spectacular of these are oil and timber. I do not see how any objective consideration of the East-West trade issue can fail to take this into account. The real potential the Soviet has in the way of export is oil. They are building an enormous tanker fleet, according to reports. Moreover, oil is one of the great fundamentals of all international trade today and will be for a long time to come. It has great strategic implications both for our own security and that of Europe. Just where this fits into the East-West trade complex will have to be considered. If it is not, the study will not be realistic. ... The Russian oil imports to Europe would also be of strategic as well as economic importance to us. There is much more to it than the hope for a bonanza of consumer goods sales to the Sino-Soviets financed by Soviet gold.[5]

McCloy's later acknowledgment of the importance of oil to East-West commercial exchanges was anticipated by the actions of leading business figures attempting to influence U.S. trade policy. Throughout the 1950s, these oil producers remained strongly opposed to expanding trade with the USSR, motivated by concerns over the competitive threat increased trade would represent. Before the revolution, Russia had been the world's largest oil producer. Production thereafter declined, reaching a low point after World War II. Yet following the war, the Soviet Union began to promote increased production of oil and natural gas, in the first instance for domestic and East-bloc use, and then later for sale to Western European markets. With this latter goal in mind, the Soviet Union began an aggressive price-cutting campaign in 1956.[6] Thus, John K. Evans, who had been chairman of a National Planning Association study group on East-West trade, explained that the group failed to release a report in 1959 "because while the majority of the sub committees involved wanted trade liberalization, the oil sub committee was so afraid of 'Russian Oil' its members were able to stop any Committee report."[7] Yet, Evans continued, "Fortunately, the latter is no longer true [writing in 1967] and now most oil companies know from the experience of the past few years that the West can successfully compete with the Russians."[8]

What brought about this change in attitude? The shift poses a difficult explanatory dilemma for advocates of a realist position, for the shift does not coincide with a clear change in the USSR's strategic policy. Indeed, Soviet strategic policies during the 1960s were as aggressive as its policies in the 1950s. In the 1960s, the Soviet Union had not relaxed its hold on its affiliated socialist states. Moreover, throughout that decade and the next, it pursued aggressive policies in Cuba, Czechoslovakia, and parts of Africa.

Although support for a realist explanation is not strong, the evidence suggesting an economic explanation for changed Western policies is. Significantly, the Soviet Union's revision of its oil-pricing policy provides a convincing rationale for the shift. By the mid-1960s, the USSR had stopped undercutting Western oil prices and had even begun to collude on restricting supplies, so as to maintain higher prices.[9] In addition, socialist countries were actively seeking out commercial opportunities with Western firms and trying to convince capitalist countries to relax their policies prohibiting commercial transactions. Socialist states also amended export policies so as to be less vulnerable to charges of dumping goods and disrupting markets.[10] These changes in pricing, commercial, and export policies convinced some earlier business opponents to moderate their opposition to increased East-West trade and led to a more welcoming U.S. policy toward Soviet goods.[11]

The Johnson Administration's Policy

Shortly after the 1964 election, the Johnson administration began to acknowledge business support for easing U.S. trade restrictions toward socialist states. The administration appointed a full-scale presidential commission to examine East-West trade issues. Appointing such a commission allows an administration to establish consensus for controversial policy changes.[12] Such commissions are nominally independent, thus allowing administrations to distance themselves from any recommendations that are unpopular with important constituencies or inconsistent with administration policy preferences.[13] Yet by appointing the commission's membership, providing its staff assistance, and controlling its access to policymakers, an administration can influence the output of presidential commissions—a fact the Johnson administration well-appreciated.[14]

In March 1965, McGeorge Bundy announced Johnson's appointment of a special committee "to explore all aspects of the question of expanding peaceful trade in support of the President's policy of widening our relations with [Eastern Europe and the Soviet Union]."[15] The membership of the committee—the Miller Committee, named after J. Irwin Miller, the chairman of Cummins Engine Company—included businessmen with a particular interest in East-West commercial issues.[16]

The committee purportedly based its recommendations for greater liberalization of trade with East-bloc states not on commercial opportunities, but on strategic advantages: "The case for expanding peaceful trade comes down to the proposition that we can use trade to influence the internal evolution and external behavior of communist countries" (p. 18), and "the Committee feels that the national interest clearly lies on the side of a more active use of trade as an instrument of foreign policy" (p. 19). But it is hard to see that the committee was called into being to contribute new thoughts to a debate on sound strategic policy; there is no reason to credit the chairman of Cummins Engine or the president of Caterpillar Tractor with any particular insights into such issues. Indeed, the report leaves the grounds for the committee's strategic conclusions quite unspoken.

But this criticism, of course, misjudges the purpose of the Miller Committee. The point of establishing it was not for it to provide an in-depth study of the advantages, commercial or otherwise, of increased trade with the East (the committee's work was completed in just eight weeks). Rather, the committee was intended to provide one more voice supporting the already-established position of the administration. Moreover, the committee's conclusion buttressed the administration's position at its weakest point. The commercial case for expanded trade was widely accepted: Few doubted Kennedy's 1963 claim that "we must not be left behind" as other countries expanded their trade with the East.[17] The focus for opposition to the expansion of trade had to be strategic not commercial, and it was to such objections that the Committee spoke.

It is instructive (and ironic) to consider the report's emphasis on strategic issues in light of Johnson's efforts to convince a representative of organized labor to serve on the committee. AFL-CIO president George Meany initially opposed labor participation in the study. Bundy recommended that Johnson take a strong line in discussions with Meany:

> The point you might wish to make to Meany is that if we follow his current line, *his constituents will be hurt.* (You might wish to leave him with a sense that he should worry more about *his* job to help labor, and let *you* worry about the Berlin Wall, which is your job. Some of his people tell him that we can get political concessions as part of commercial bargains; this is nonsense, in the light of the other markets that are open to Bloc countries—and on the historical record it is not the way the Commies trade, in any case.)[18]

After a direct appeal by Johnson himself, Meany allowed AFL-CIO research director Nathaniel Goldfinger to be appointed to the commission. But Goldfinger's participation failed to produce a shift in either the committee's or the AFL-CIO's positions. Indeed, in a vigorous dissent to the committee's final recommendations, Goldfinger insisted on expounding the very position that Bundy had characterized as nonsense.

In June 1965, Under Secretary of State for Economic Affairs Thomas Mann conveyed the State Department's endorsement of the Miller Committee's approach. Mann recommended that the administration "should sound out the congressional leadership on specific legislative proposals" and "should take advantage of the momentum created by the Miller Report, the CED [Committee for Economic Development] report, the Chamber of Commerce resolution, the favourable reaction in the Business Council, and the Congressional soundings made at the request of the President in connection with the publication of the Miller Report."[19] Following the Miller Committee's suggestions, Mann's memo also proposed legislation giving the president discretion to award or withdraw MFN status to socialist states, so as to increase presidential leverage in political dealings with these countries. The State Department preferred to provide this authority in separate East-West trade legislation, rather than as an amendment to the Trade Expansion Act, to "make clear how MFN could be used as part of bilateral trade agreements with communist countries and how this trade could serve our foreign policy objectives." Among the foreign policy objectives Mann defined were: encouraging movement toward national independence and internal liberalization in Romania; furthering economic decentralization in Czechoslovakia; stimulating pressures for change in Poland, Hungary, and Bulgaria; and using trade negotiations to increase Soviet interest in broader relations with the United States.[20]

But even though the expansion of East-West trade enjoyed some strong business support as well as support from the State Department's foreign policy specialists, the administration proceeded cautiously in preparing its legislative proposals. Indeed, the administration was divided over the political viability of pursuing the conclusions outlined in the Miller report, and even Mann gradually changed his mind as to the most desirable course to pursue. The objections to pursuing the Miller approach arose from growing U.S. participation in Vietnam. Although two State Department officials prepared a memo for Johnson under Secretary of State Rusk's signature strongly recommending that "the President give the proposed East-West Trade Relations Bill a priority position in his legislative program and prominent attention in his State of the Union Address," both Mann and Rusk were more attuned to the domestic political context in which the administration was operating.[21] And after consultation with members of Congress, George Ball, an influential adviser to both Kennedy and Johnson, had decided postponement might be in order as well. In a conversation with the new National Security Advisor Francis Bator:

> George was surprisingly negative. He asserts that [Senators] Mansfield and Fulbright are convinced that it would be very difficult to pass a bill unless there is a breakthrough on Vietnam. (George agrees that, in terms of the President's posture, proposing and getting a bill through *without a bloody fight* would be a plus—but, with Vietnam, he does not think it worth the risk. He did not say so, but I suspect that he is worried about the *foreign policy* consequences of a really nasty fight and *narrow* victory.[22]

In early January, Rusk sent a cautious memo to Johnson, in which he outlined the consequences to U.S international relations of a negative vote on an administration East-West trade proposal:

> My own personal view is that (a) we should continue to be in the posture of favoring an improvement in our relations between ourselves and Eastern Eu-

rope, but (b) we should not press a bill to a vote if there is any chance that it would be defeated. This obviously depends upon a very careful nose count in Committees and in the two Houses before pressing for action.

My own recommendation would be that you continue to support the idea of building bridges with Eastern Europe, including a further development of East-West trade, in your State of the Union message. This would be an important part of a comprehensive attitude toward peace as a major objective. I would recommend, however, that you stop short of throwing your full personal prestige behind the immediate enactment of legislation but rather let the rest of us work with the Committees to see what can be done despite the general impression created by Viet-Nam.

This may appear to be a somewhat cautious approach. My caution, however, is not due to my attitude toward East-West trade but because of the extremely negative effect on our international relations of a vote in the Congress which would reject the kind of East-West trade legislation which we would like to have. If my own political judgement is too timid, I would be prepared to take a bolder line.[23]

The warning that Rusk is giving here is that a conspicuous failure to pass a bill dedicated to more open East-West trade would have an adverse effect on U.S.-Soviet relations at a time when the Johnson administration was looking to the Soviets for help in extricating the United States from Vietnam. But despite this cautious counsel, the Johnson administration adopted the Miller Committee's general policy outline, with Johnson's senior staff willing to defer to this president's superior ability to assess its congressional prospects:

My own prejudice is that the President should be given a free choice. ... He is a far better judge of the Congressional mood than Mansfield and Fulbright— and a better judge of how much of his political capital he is willing to spend to demonstrate his determination to be accommodating where no vital interests are in conflict, even while we have to be tough in Vietnam. (My own guess would be that even if the current peace exercise fails completely, the Congress would find it harder to resist a Commander-in-Chief [illegible] request for discretionary authority than [Mann and Ball] appear to think. On an issue of this sort, the swing group on the Hill does not know what it thinks until it finds out what Lyndon Johnson thinks. To be sure the request would have to be put rather more in cold war terms than it would in an environment of detente.

On the merits, I think the issue is worth serious Presidential consideration, even if Vietnam heats up again. Not that we would make extensive trade deals with the Russians, or even with the East Europeans—we probably would not. The case for moving is essentially the case for a balanced, peace-oriented Presidential posture, even as we escalate in Vietnam.[24]

The case that Bator makes in this memo is the mirror image of Rusk's warning. If the cost of failing to liberalize East-West trade and failing is the loss of any Soviet willingness there might have been to help the United States

get out of Vietnam, then the cost of not pushing the legislation is the continued flight of liberal support from Johnson. Bundy appears to reflect both
points in his memo to the president:

> I think the truth is that everybody believes in the Miller Committee's approach,
> but both Rusk and Mann have doubts about the political course of action on
> the Hill this year. My view is that we can have our cake and eat it on that. The
> bill will not be in hostile hands. Wilbur Mills will have it in the House and Bill
> Fulbright in the Senate, and in their quite different ways I think they would be
> reasonable and helpful.
> Since we can control the legislative course of the bills, I think we can safely
> take the advantage of presenting it. That advantage will be substantial among
> "sophisticated" observers in connection with our desire for peace and our ef-
> fort to show that we know there are different kinds of Communists. It will also
> give substance to our bridge-building policy which is otherwise open to criti-
> cism as more words than action.[25]

Johnson announced the new policy in his 1966 State of the Union Address
and presented the East-West Trade Relations Act of 1966 to Congress shortly
thereafter.

Despite the momentum provided by business pressure and careful administration planning with labor, the media, and Congress, the East-West trade
expansion legislation was unsuccessful. Congressional attitudes to Soviet
support for the North Vietnamese prevented the bill from coming to a vote
in the House or Senate (and, indeed, even the influential chairman of the
Ways and Means Committee, Wilbur Mills, who normally supported administration policies, refused to hold hearings on the legislation). This lack
of success came as no surprise to the administration, which had realized by
mid-March, even before it sent the legislation to Congress, that it would not
pass. But by that point, success or failure was not the object. The administration clearly saw liberalizing East-West trade relations as a long-term project
and came to view this legislation as a first step toward educating Congress
on its new policy proposals. White House aide Joseph Califano's reaction
was that "the bill must be reshaped and efforts made on the Hill to clear the
way for passage."[26]

In 1967, the administration again considered bringing liberalization legislation to Congress and seemed to believe that congressional opposition had
softened, for it even secured a commitment from Mills "that it is entirely
likely that the Committee will get to hold hearings [during the] session."[27]
The administration began by meeting with prominent business executives
who, it was thought, could help convince Congress of the need to extend
East-West commercial relations.[28] Independently, some major business groups
maintained their pressure for liberalization. But at this point, the response of
the Republican Party convinced the administration that the effort would

again be futile. Although some Republican members of Congress favored an outright ban on East-West trade, "the most serious opposition from the Republicans will be based on an effort to delay or otherwise restrict any East-West trade legislation until there are further developments in the Viet-Nam War. We would expect some Democratic support for that position."[29]

The opposition was again successful, this time spurred by Soviet support for the Arab States in the 1967 Middle East war. And in 1968, another version of the legislation failed to receive serious consideration, this time a victim of the Soviet invasion of Czechoslovakia. Thus, despite earnest efforts by the Johnson administration, major reform of commercial policy toward the Soviet Union remained incomplete as the Nixon administration entered office.

Nixon Administration's Policy

Although Nixon had first achieved national prominence for his crusades against communism, throughout the 1968 presidential campaign he remained uncommitted on East-West trade issues; the result was an ambiguous Republican Party platform.[30] Nixon entered office intending to expand East-West trade contacts in exchange for geostrategic concessions by the Soviet Union. Before acting, however, he first requested an NSC study of the issue. Various administration members began to lobby for their policy preferences even before the report was finished. Secretary of Commerce Maurice Stans led the way early in April 1969, arguing strongly for expanding East-West trade:

> I would favor a positive promotional attitude even now, looking toward obtaining authority for extending Eximbank credit guarantees and MFN treatment along with bilateral negotiation of other measures to improve East-West trading relations. ... I am prepared to move ahead on a positive program if you decide that this Administration clearly favors the promotion of such trade and expanded trade relations with Eastern Europe.[31]

Stans's initial memo to the president made a narrow, self-interested case for expanding such trade. This support was motivated by the expected gains that would follow from such opportunities and an awareness of the potential losses of lucrative contracts to foreign competitors unencumbered by U.S export restrictions. Stans did not postulate any broad economic benefits to the U.S. balance of payments from such activity; rather, he thought the opposite was true: The proclivity of "the Communists ... [to] do business on a bilateral, rather than a multilateral basis" limited the positive contribution East-West trade could make to the U.S. balance-of-payments position. Nonetheless, Stans emphasized, "From an economic and commercial viewpoint ... such trade can be quite important to the firms, laborers, and industrial and agricultural communities involved."[32] The emphasis of Stans's memo echoes the advice National Security Advisor Bundy earlier provided to Democratic presidents.

Indeed, Stans eloquently articulated the position of business advocates of East-West trade expansion, an interest that later National Security Advisor Henry Kissinger highlighted in his memoirs:

> The Commerce Department's view was the most interesting because it reflected the surprising attitude of much of the American business community. Business leaders are of course vocally anti-Communist. In the abstract they preach hard bargaining with the Communists and they are quick to blame their government for "giveaways." But when it comes to trade, their attitude changes. During my period in office the most fervent advocates of East-West trade without strings were in the group of capitalists so vilified by Leninist theory. They are dedicated to the free market, at least if it means more business for their companies. They resent as "government interference" the apparatus of regulations and restrictions that is the only way to subordinate economic relations to political goals. If the Soviet Union can enter our market for credit or goods on the basis of purely economic criteria, all political leverage disappears. Perhaps businessmen are in addition especially susceptible to the bonhomie with which Soviet officials flatter those whom they wish to influence—a style of slightly inebriated good fellowship not totally unknown in some of the reunions of capitalist trade associations.[33]

Stans' efforts notwithstanding, the NSC was decisive in defining East-West trade policy during the Nixon administration, including preparing a position paper, collecting comments from affected departments—including State, Commerce, and Treasury—and presenting an overall policy design to the president in May 1969.[34] Lamar Alexander, a White House aide, wrote to one of Nixon's top advisers, Bryce Harlow:

> The issue is essentially political. The Republican Party has traditionally taken the hard stance against expanding trade with the East. Perhaps more important, those who advocate a liberal trade policy are generally those who believe that the Soviet threat is less now than it has been in the past.[35]

While the administration was still trying to formulate its policy (and thus merely requested a four-year extension of existing legislation when it came up for renewal in early 1969), members of Congress had aggressively begun to promote liberalization and, indeed, threatened to seize the initiative. Democrat Senators Edmund Muskie, J. William Fulbright, and Walter Mondale heeded the increased pressure of U.S. business in seeking greater trade opportunities and proposed significant liberalization of export control criteria. Administration inaction thus almost led to wholesale liberalization. This loss of control is significant, for it somewhat contradicts the trade policy predictions of two prominent writers, I. M. Destler and Robert Pastor, who emphasize the importance of institutional constraints and biases in shaping trade policy. In particular, both have highlighted Congress' sympathy for protectionist policies that benefit local constituents, while the president has greater freedom to pursue liberalizing policies. Yet these standard trade policy models fail to account for the legislation at hand: In a climate often described as protectionist, with intense organizing efforts on behalf of various protectionist initiatives, liberalization legislation was almost passed *despite* the administration's intentions.[36]

In part motivating the congressional liberalization proposals was the continued visibility of business:

> There seems to be more acceptance in Congress this year for establishing trade with the East. For example, Sol Mosher reports that all of the business witnesses at the Senate Committee hearings have favored a more liberal trade policy. In the last session of Congress, most businesses were afraid to express such a position.[37]

The administration, however, was unwilling to push for further liberalization at this time. Despite Alexander's expressed fears about the NSC's "liberal" drift, amending the existing Export Control Act was not the vehicle the administration wished to use to effect a serious substantive shift in trade policy with socialist states. Kissinger noted:

> Any acceptance of Committee Amendments would imply a more liberal East-West trade stance by the administration. This would signal a change in policy, which the President does not wish to do at this time. We should therefore respond to any requests for the Administration's views by stating that we are opposed to such amendments. The relevant agencies should be instructed to continue their efforts to defeat them.
>
> The President does not wish the Administration to take an uncompromisingly hard-line on East-West trade. He does not want to deliberalize from where we are now. He simply feels that the present legislation is sufficiently flexible to do whatever liberalizing he might want, short of a dramatic new initiative, and that our relations with the USSR at this time do not warrant support for trade liberalization. Therefore, the White House itself should not take initiatives with the Congress to try to defeat proposed amendments. And we could indicate to sophisticated Congressmen that we have the issue very much under review and will be quite willing to move when the overall political climate changes.[38]

The administration refused to go as far as many liberal Senators would have liked and award conditional MFN status to the USSR, but it did acquiesce in a modest reform of existing legislation, the result of which was the compromise Export Administration Act of 1969. The legislation significantly tightened the criteria for requiring products to be placed on the export control list, while at the same time extending general presidential authority to control exports by alleging national security or foreign policy reasons without having to prove their national security significance. The 1969 legislation also addressed the major complaint that U.S. business had hammered out throughout the Kennedy and Johnson administrations: U.S. suppliers were now able to sell goods to socialist states whenever those products were already freely available from European and Japanese sources. Indeed, the bill now required detailed explanations for restrictions on U.S. exports of non-military goods when such products were readily available from other sources.[39] In contravention of Stans's view, the legislation also asserted that "the unwarranted restrictions of exports from the United States has a serious adverse effect on our balance of payments,"[40] although perhaps this assertion was mere rhetoric.

Designing the Nixon Administration's Policy

Once the new stopgap legislation was passed, the Nixon administration turned to preparing its comprehensive policy for liberalizing East-West commercial relations. As in other trade areas, these preparations occupied the better part of Nixon's first term and were presented to Congress in his second. When the administration later recommended reform of East-West trade proposals, the lesson of the 1969 experience was taken to be that liberalization would not pose the political problem that Alexander (and indeed Nixon, in his cautious approach to the 1968 Republican platform) had earlier assumed. Doctrinaire anticommunism no longer enjoyed its earlier prominence; instead, the emphasis shifted to a combination of Stans's commercial and economic rationale and Kissinger's strategic conception. But further events proved that the administration's 1969 decision not to press for awarding MFN status to the USSR was a serious mistake. When such a proposal was finally made in 1973, Senator Henry Jackson's determination to link granting MFN status to loosening restrictions on emigration of Soviet Jews resulted in the collapse of the East-West trade liberalization movement.

As the Nixon administration prepared its trade policies, it followed the consensus-building procedures that both Kennedy and Johnson had used. Johnson had appointed the Miller Committee to consider East-West trade issues exclusively. Nixon did not appoint a separate commission to study East-West commercial relations but, instead, requested that the Commission on International Trade and Investment Policy (later dubbed the Williams Commission) would consider this as one of many international economic policy topics.[41] Several Williams Commission members were affiliated with companies that had concluded, or were to enter into, significant cooperation agreements with the Soviet Union or other socialist states.[42] Two members of the commission were affiliated with banks heavily involved in East-West transactions: Gaylord Freeman of First National Bank of Chicago and Ernest C. Arbuckle of Wells Fargo Bank.[43] Agricultural producers—who sought access to socialist markets—were represented by Kenneth D. Naden of the National Council of Farmer Cooperatives.

Not altogether surprisingly then, the Williams Commission recommended increasing East-West trade opportunities in its report:

> Within the bounds set by strategic considerations, the United States should attempt to expand its trade with the Communist countries. To this end, we should align our export restrictions and related regulations with those of other Western nations. ...
>
> The President should be given authority to remove the existing tariff discrimination against imports from Communist countries, in return for appropriate benefits from the United States.
>
> We should explore with other Western governments possible multilateral arrangements designed to loosen the existing bilateral constraints on East-West trade.[44]

At the same time as the Williams Commission deliberated, an internal interagency task force also produced a general report analyzing U.S.-Soviet commercial relationships and strongly urging expanded East-West trade.[45]

While the administration designed its East-West trade policy, U.S. business actors separately fostered East-West trade initiatives. In addition to appointing CED president Alfred C. Neal as a Williams Commission member, the CED—which had long advocated increasing East-West commercial contacts—produced a report arguing for expanding such trade. The CED report closely followed the Williams Commission report.[46] In addition, the Atlantic Council produced a study recommending a similar policy. The U.S. Chamber of Commerce sponsored a trade mission to Moscow. The New York Regional Export Expansion Council maintained a permanent committee of members with obvious interests in expanding trade opportunities—including large banks, chemical companies, travel conglomerates, and electronics firms—to promote trade with Eastern Europe. The Emergency Committee on American Trade (ECAT) was active—on both the organizational and the individual level—in sponsoring a conference on East-West trade, while ECAT members David Rockefeller (Chase Manhattan Bank) and Donald Kendall (Pepsico) were instrumental in establishing the U.S.-China Trade Council.[47] But all these efforts were somewhat circumscribed, since one major complaint of U.S. business—that U.S. producers be allowed to sell goods whenever their European or Japanese counterparts could do so—had already been addressed in the 1969 renewal of the Export Control Act.

The Trade Act of 1974
and the Jackson-Vanik Amendment

Early in 1973, the Nixon administration finally presented comprehensive trade proposals, asking Congress to authorize participation in a new round of GATT negotiations, reform U.S. antidumping law, improve the remedies for alleged "unfair trade practices," and increase East-West commercial ties by awarding MFN status to the Soviet Union. All these objectives save the last were achieved when the Ford administration presided over passage of the Trade Agreements Act in December 1974.

Nixon/Kissinger trade policy toward the USSR was derailed by the Jackson-Vanik Amendment, a provision that linked U.S. trade concessions to Soviet concessions on Jewish emigration. When it became clear that the Ford administration could not muster the votes necessary to jettison the amendment, the Soviet Union backed out of the bilateral agreement for mutual granting of MFN status.

Although the Jackson-Vanik Amendment has often been presented as a purely humanitarian gesture, it also had a deeper commercial significance. It was neither proposed nor initially supported by those groups that had long-standing interest in the USSR's Jewish emigration policies. Nonetheless, the amendment quickly became a flashpoint for many groups with strong reasons for opposing increased East-West commercial links or the general trade liberalization promoted throughout the entire postwar period. Indeed, as the legislation was considered, two major opponents of trade liberalization—declining industries and labor unions—developed pressing interest in Soviet emigration issues almost overnight.

The administration well recognized the different uses to which the Jewish immigration issue was being put. So, in October 1973, White House aide Peter Flanigan cautioned Nixon not to threaten to veto any bill containing the amendment lest that very threat provide added encouragement to foes of liberal trade: "I recommend you do *not* dwell on your intention to veto any Bill including Jackson-Vanik, though I agree with that conclusion. This position only inspires Labor and those opposed to any trade bill to work harder in support of the Jackson-Vanik Amendment."[48] Nonetheless, other policymakers did not see Jackson-Vanik as a mere smokescreen for increased East-West trade or, indeed, all trade. These policymakers, instead, believed that the most effective way to stop Jackson-Vanik (and those interests that used the excuse of Jackson-Vanik to promote their own trade agendas) was to convince Jewish leaders to change their views, since "the Jewish leadership is the only group that can move."[49] If Jewish groups were to shift their position, "there will be many people who are standing under the 'emigration' tent for their own personal reasons and interests who will find they are left out in the cold if the Jewish position changes."[50] Indeed, "some Senators who are against the [trade legislation], desire to keep the Jackson-Vanik as is, to stall the [trade legislation]."[51]

The evidence suggests that the Nixon administration misperceived the Jackson-Vanik Amendment as an excuse for pursuing self-interested motivations only, with no independent humanitarian significance. This cynical assessment led the administration to pursue an ineffective strategy for derailing the amendment, since at least initially, the administration instructed its lobbyists to oppose the amendment on straightforward economic grounds. But what was needed was a more sophisticated approach that acknowledged both the commercial and humanitarian significance of the amendment and adjusted lobbying strategies accordingly.[52]

Senator Henry Jackson is credited with the success of the amendment that bears his name.[53] Jackson's success in tying trade concessions to increases in Jewish emigration was largely due to the work of his chief national security aide, Richard Perle, whom Henry Kissinger later credited with scuttling the Nixon administration's U.S.-Soviet trade liberalization proposals.[54] In the leading study of the Jackson-Vanik Amendment, Paula Stern acknowledges that, at minimum, "Jackson's amendment had a dual diplomatic aim: to liberalize Soviet emigration policy and to retard the development of trade and detente between the two superpowers."[55] Bruce Jentleson, however, goes one step farther and suggests that Jackson, a well-known hawk and outspoken critic of détente, "had been searching for a legislative vehicle to block the new economic relationship" between the United States and the USSR.[56] Jackson first sought to scuttle détente by raising the issue of the Soviet Union's continued failure to settle its World War II lend-lease debts. Only after that failed did Jackson turn to the Jewish emigration issue, and this in advance of the established Jewish lobbying groups (many of which had historically supported trade liberalization). Indeed, initial discussions over linking trade and emigration issues were fiercely opposed by representatives of organized Jewish groups, as well as by leading Senate staff members.[57]

Paula Stern suggests that Soviet emigration reveals a reversal of the standard assumptions as to how lobbying relationships work, since Jackson's amendment was an initiative, not a response, and led the way toward linking trade and emigration. Yet perhaps Stern rushes too quickly to a conclusion about the relationship between Jackson and organized lobbies. Stern recognizes that it was neither solely out of concern for Jewish votes nor from a desire to secure Jewish campaign donations that led to the linkage between trade and emigration. Surely it is worth exploring what other constituency pressures could have influenced Jackson's decision. Indeed, as perspicacious an observer of legislative motivation as Wilbur Mills questioned Jackson's underlying motivation for offering the amendment. Rather than exploring any of these issues, Stern notes only that "Jackson was opposed to develop-

ing a trade relationship on the grounds that American national interest was
not being served."[58]

Jackson had ties to both the defense and the timber industries so crucial
to the economy of his home state of Washington. It is of course difficult to
determine whether Jackson's views on proper defense policy had made him a
natural ally of that industry or whether the importance of the industry decisively shaped his views. Yet, by the time of the Jackson-Vanik Amendment,
Jackson had a significant interest in ensuring that East-West relations did
not improve. His general preferences were reinforced in this particular case
by another constituency-imposed pressure: Washington (state) was a significant producer of timber. As McCloy had made clear in his 1965 letter to
National Security Advisor Bundy, the most significant export potential of
Soviet Union was in primary products. One product it could supply more
cheaply than could U.S. suppliers was timber.[59] It should come as no surprise, then, that the major campaign against increased U.S.-Soviet trade was
led by a Senator from a state highly dependent economically on defense production and timber.[60]

The actual result of the Jackson-Vanik Amendment was to shut off the
flow of Jewish emigration entirely; the plight of Soviet Jews further deteriorated once the Soviets withdrew the mutual MFN agreement. Thus, in this
light, it is interesting that the architect of the amendment's "successful" linkage of emigration and trade shortly thereafter exhorted the Ford administration to consider increasing trade with the Soviets, in a letter sent to the chairman of the Council of Economic Advisors, Alan Greenspan, in September
1975:

> As you know, the United States produces far more grain than it needs for inter-
> nal consumption On the other hand, dwindling domestic oil production has
> required us to import substantial quantities of oil from abroad to meet our
> needs.
>
> The Soviet Union is one of the world's largest oil producers. And, because
> of a poor harvest this year, the Soviet Union has purchased substantial amounts
> of grain from us. Administration officials have stated that other major sales to
> the Soviet Union are anticipated this year. Perhaps major grain sales will be
> made in future years.
>
> The obvious question that arises, therefore, is whether we have seriously
> explored the possibility of trading our grain for Soviet oil. Accordingly, I would
> appreciate your comments as to whether such a proposal is feasible. Specifi-
> cally, I would like to receive your opinion as to the lack of statutory authority
> to implement such a program and what legislation would be needed to permit
> such bartering.[61]

The implication of these facts is that Jackson was not overly concerned with
the substantive issue of Jewish emigration; this letter to Greenspan clearly

advocates increasing bilateral trade contacts with the USSR within a year of the Jackson-Vanik Amendment. Such a seeming reversal is more consistent with a vision of Jackson as influenced by certain constituency pressures than it is of him influenced by the substantive merits of competing proposals.

Conclusion

In this chapter, I have tried to develop an alternative explanation of U.S. trade strategy toward the USSR. Rather than relating U.S. policy fluctuations exclusively to national security concerns, I emphasized the importance of shifting interest group pressures on shaping the transition in U.S. policy from viewing the Soviet Union as a threat to viewing it as an opportunity. These pressures were strongly correlated with two variables. First, the Soviet Union's move in its commodity pricing policy away from undercutting Western producers resulted in relaxed opposition by influential business interests—largely oil producers—toward increased U.S.-USSR cooperation. Second, this shift was accompanied by increased pressure from business interests—capital equipment manufacturers, agricultural and construction machinery producers, automobile producers, and computer manufacturers—that had always regarded the Soviet Union as a business opportunity. The interaction between interest groups and political institutions generated the pattern of shifting U.S. policies. Archival evidence presented in the chapter suggests that interest group competition may be a profitable avenue to explore for further insights into the shifting pattern of cooperative and competitive behavior in U.S.-USSR economic relations.

Table 6.1   U.S. Corporations with Long-Term Cooperation Agreements with the
USSR, 1976

Corporation	Sector of Cooperation
American Can	Packaging and containers
Armco Steel	Metallurgical and chemical equipment
Bendix	Electronic and scientific instruments
Boeing	Civil aviation
Brown & Root	Gas and oil transport engineering
Burroughs	Computer technology and applications
Coca-Cola	Food processing, water purification
Control Data	Computer plants and networks
Dresser Industries	Oil and gas extraction
Food Machinery Corporation	Food processing and packaging machinery
General Dynamics	Aircraft, shipbuilding, communications
General Electric	Electrical and electronic engineering
Hewlett-Packard	Electronics, measure instruments
Industrial Nucleonics	Automatic production control
International Paper	Timber exploitation
ITT	Telecommunications, electronics
Joy Manufacturing	Heavy machinery
Kaiser Industries	Aluminum, iron and steel, cement
Monsanto	Rubber, new chemicals and processes
Phillip Morris	Tobacco, packaging, chemicals
Rank Xerox	Copying, duplicating machines
Reichhold Chemicals	Chemical products and processes
Singer	Textile machinery, measurement equipment
Sperry-Rand	Computers, measurement and control systems
Universal Oil Products	Petrochemicals, plastics

Source: This table is a condensed version of a table entitled "Long-Term Cooperation Agreements Concluded by Selected Multinational Corporations with the
State Committee for Science and Technology of the USSR," in J. Wilczynski, *The
Multinationals and East-West Relations* (London: Macmillan, 1976), pp. 26–27.
Wilczynski's original table includes non-U.S. corporations; only U.S. corporations
are listed here. Wilczynski's table is based on "daily and periodical literature published in the USSR and Western countries" (pp. 38–39).

Table 6.2 U.S. Multinationals with Significant Commercial Dealings with
Socialist Countries, 1973

Corporation	Product	Socialist Partners
American Can	Engineering, containers	Bu, Ch, Ro, USSR
Allis Chalmers	Engineering	USSR
Armco Steel	Metallurgy	USSR, Yu
Boeing	Aircraft and equipment	Ch, Ro, USSR, Yu
Borg-Warner	Engineering	Ch, Po, USSR
Burroughs	Office machines, computers	USSR
Caterpillar Tractor	Construction machinery	Ch, Po, USSR, Yu
Clark Equipment	Construction equipment	Hu, Po, USSR
Coca-Cola	Beverages, foods	Bu, Cz, Hu, Po, USSR, Yu
Combustion Engineering	Industrial equipment	USSR, Yu
Continental Can	Packaging, containers	Ch, Po, USSR
Control Data	Computers	Bu, Ch, Cz, GDR, Po, Ro, USSR, Yu
Corning Glass Works	Glassware, ceramics	Hu, Yu
Dow Chemical	Chemicals	GDR, Hu, Ro, Yu
Dresser Industries	Petrochemicals	Hu, USSR
Dupont	Chemicals	GDR, Hu, Ro, Yu
Exxon	Petrochemicals	Bu
FMC	Machinery, chemicals	Po, USSR
Ford Motor	Means of transport	Cu, Ch, Cz, Hu, Yu
General Dynamics	Engineering, chemicals	USSR
General Electric	Electrical engineering	Cz, Hu, Ro, USSR, Yu
General Motors	Means of transport	Ch, Hu, USSR, Yu
General Tire & Rubber	Rubber products, equipment	Ro, USSR
Gillette	Steel, engineering	Cz, Yu
Gulf Oil	Petrochemicals	Ro, USSR
Hewlett-Packard	Electronic measuring instruments	Cz, USSR
Honeywell	Electronics, computers	Ch, GDR, Hu, Po, USSR, Yu
Illinois Central Industries	Transport equipment	USSR
Ingersoll-Rand	Engineering	Ro, USSR, Yu
IBM	Computers, office equipment	Bu, Ch, Cz, GDR, Hu, Po, Ro, USSR, Yu
International Harvester	Agricultural and construction machinery	Hu, Po, Ro, USSR
ITT	Telecommunications equipment	Bu, Ch, Cz, Hu, Po, Ro, Ussr, Yu
Kaiser Industries	Metallurgy, engineering	Bu, USSR

(continues)

Table 6.2 *(continued)*

Corporation	Product	Socialist Partners
Lockheed Aircraft	Aircraft	USSR, Yu
Minnesota Mining and Manufacturing	Metallurgy, engineering	Hu, USSR
Mobil Oil	Petrochemicals	Ch, Hu, Po, Ro, USSR
Monsanto	Chemicals	Ch, GDR, Po, USSR
NCR	Office equipment, computers	Bu, Cz, USSR
Occidental Petroleum	Petrochemicals	Bu, Po, Ro, USSR
Pepsi-Co	Beverages	Cz, GDR, Hu, Po, Ro, USSR, Yu
PPG Industries	Chemicals, engineering	Po, USSR
Pullman	Industrial equipment	Bu, Ch, Po, USSR
RCA	Telecommunications equipment	Ch, USSR, Yu
Rockwell International	Engineering, apparatus	Ch, Po, USSR
Singer	Sewing machines, apparatus	Hu, Po, Ro, USSR, Yu
Sperry-Rand	Computers, communications equipment	Hu, Po, USSR, Yu
Tenneco	Petrochemicals, gas	USSR
Textron	Helicopters, apparatus	Po, USSR, Yu
Union Carbide	Mining, chemicals	Cz, Po, USSR
United States Steel	Metals, mining	Ch, USSR, Yu
Universal Oil Products	Petrochemicals, plastics	GDR, Po, Ro, USSR, Yu
Westinghouse Electric	Electronics, engineering	Ch, Hu, Po, Yu
Xerox	Office equipment	USSR

Source: This table combines data from Table 2, "The Largest Industrial Multinational Corporations Significantly Involved in Commercial Dealing with Socialist Countries," and Table 3, "Medium Industrial Multinational Corporations Significantly Involved in Commercial Dealings with Socialist Countries," in Wilczynski, *Multinationals,* pp. 36–39 and pp. 42–45, respectively. Wilczynski's original tables include non-U.S. corporations; only U.S. corporations are included here. Wilczynski's tables are based on published Soviet and Western Sources.

Note: Bu = Bulgaria; Ch = China; Ro = Romania; Yu = Yugoslavia; Po = Poland; Hu = Hungary; Cz = Czechoslyvakia; GDR = German Democratic Republic; Cu = Cuba.

Business Conflict and the Shadow State: The Case of West Africa

William Reno

In this chapter, I challenge the reasoning behind standard theorizing about political and economic crises in Africa that assume that states will evolve into more capable unitary actors as a basis of political order and the focus of international relations. Contrary to this reasoning, novel forms of "deviant" behavior among rulers are giving rise to political practices and relationships that are not centered on territorially defined or institutionally autonomous entities. My focus here is this new political cooperation among rulers of some disintegrating African states and foreign firms. These arrangements are replacing territorially and institutionally distinct states as the dominant authority in these political communities.

Sierra Leone's President Momoh admitted foreign firms under IMF pressure. Ironically, they became partners in his essentially private use of state power to reward loyal clients with personal privilege. Charles Taylor's "Greater Liberia" does not receive international recognition as a state at all, even though it has at times occupied 95 percent of Liberia and portions of three neighboring states. Yet foreign firms constitute a major component in Taylor's strategy of building political authority independent of state institutions or the normal requirements or privileges of internationally recognized state sovereignty. Both rulers manipulate foreign firm interests and their home government backers to support a new kind of politics in Africa based upon elite coalition capacities to exploit competition among international economic interests.

Increasing numbers of African rulers behave in this manner that seems irrational to those who assume that rulers perpetually seek to maximize their power though strengthening states. Rulers' political strategies in Sierra Leone and "Greater Liberia," as well as in Somalia, Zaire, Angola, and Sudan, are increasingly based upon essentially private arrangements between rulers and foreign firms. Is this interaction between rulers and foreign firms bringing African politics beyond rules and norms of a state system? Are the "discontinuities" of ruler-foreign firm collaboration outside state institutional and territorial borders becoming more prominent than the "continuities" that state-centric analyses posit as proper and inevitable? If so, then a reconceptualization of African political communities outside the conceptual prison of "the state" is ever more warranted.

The Shadow State

Most scholars of Africa's economic crisis focus on the dynamics of the state's institutional reconstruction, as opposed to exploring the possibility of fundamental discontinuities in the system of African states.[1] Yet, with few exceptions, Africa's economic decline and official corruption continue unabated through the early 1990s. Why are states disintegrating in Africa? The state itself is one of the most privatized sectors of society. This abdication of autonomous state interest is most often expressed in the massive channeling of state resources into private hands. Richard Joseph calls this use of state office for the personal benefit of the officeholder "prebendal politics."[2] Where reforms are designed to limit private benefits of office, difficulties of convincing officials to get reforms under way remain great. "The boundary between the state and civil society seemed to have dissolved," said Joseph of the consequence of liberal reforms in Nigeria in the early 1980s. "Public institutions had become as much a party to the struggle for gaining particular advantage as were the registered party organizations themselves."[3] In this manner, states are yielding to new forms of political communities.

Most important is the unwillingness of rulers to end systems of privilege and prerogatives that are the foundation of what Jean-François Bayart calls a "hegemonic alliance."[4] The hegemonic alliance is not institutionally or territorially fixed, but it is the primary feature that determines the organization of politics in the disintegrating African state. This intraelite accommodation takes place outside of, and marks a rupture with, politics defined as pursuit of a national interest. The private diversion of state resources is the glue that holds these intraelite accommodations together. The ruler may view disruption of these networks as the primary threat to his survival. Especially where rulers view prospects for widespread legitimacy to be slim, impersonal state institutions may pose threats to rulers to the extent that they can become avenues of opposition by strongmen or be taken over by enterprising elements of the hegemonic alliance itself. The ruler's solution to his security dilemma is thus not to pursue greater state autonomy but, rather, to develop new forms of societal control.[5]

Some rulers find that foreign firms can provide them with resources and services independent of inherited state institutions. Firms bring a ruler a host of business and foreign state rivalries that can be manipulated to play firms off one another or to exploit foreign governments' anxieties over the activities of rival states' firms. The ruler finds that encouraging these various external actors to align themselves with his political network's private interests maximizes the resources available to clients, reinforces his personal capacity to control resource distribution, and hence increases the political authority at his command.

This "shadow state" model of politics in Africa should be distinguished from dependency theory. Where dependency approaches hold that international relations center on a global class conflict between core and periphery, this study emphasizes divisions within and among core interests. Dependency theory focuses largely on the effects of the core on the periphery. The shadow state model centers, instead, on the capacity of actors on the periphery of the global economy to manipulate linkages to the center. Shadow state elites prove remarkably adept at altering relations with external actors and manipulating diverging interests among these actors to counter both internal and external threats without committing themselves to building strong state institutions. Rulers add accommodations with some foreign firms to their hegemonic alliance. Rulers often desperately need the resources foreign firms have to offer. But this desperation does not necessarily imply a relationship of extreme inequality. The ruler of the privatized shadow state can offer foreign investors preferential access to prerogatives of sovereign state power. This offer to use political power for private profit attracts foreign businesses and political organizations that seek these rewards.

This development poses the possibility that the state-centric system in Africa that reformers seek to reinforce is increasingly bounded within a more encompassing foreign firm-elite relationship. This represents a structural change beyond the "grafting" of nonstate actors onto a state-dominated system that some neorealists use to explain conditions in which new international actors and processes become significant.[6] This development also belies instrumental Marxist analyses of economic reform in Africa that stress the subordination of African elite interests to the coercive nature of reform-oriented toward core state interests.[7] But it still recognizes the high level of African rulers' dependence on foreign investment. Rulers play one firm off another, as well as firms off of creditors and foreign governments.

Under such conditions, rulers' relations to foreign firms and creditors closely approximate elements of the business conflict model.[8] The conceptualization of "business conflict" here applied to the shadow state stresses the escape from presumptions that a state interest ultimately bounds a ruler's pursuit of authority. Rulers recognize and exploit diverse interests among competing foreign investors. Creditor policies that demand greater reliance on foreign investment enhance the shadow state ruler's incentives to incorporate foreign firms into the intraelite accommodation. And as certain kinds of investors find that they can profit from lax enforcement of regulation and private uses of state power, conflict develops among other external economic and political interests concerned with making money or promoting reform in Africa. This conflict provides greater political space for the ruler of the shadow state to rationally advance his own private interests and continue to manage the allocation of resources that hold the intra-elite accommodation together.

As Robert Jackson quips, "They [rulers] have the right to say no. Multinationals realize this. The relationship is therefore less like rape or even seduction and more like legalized prostitution: the partners may be unequal, but any business they transact must involve the consent of both."[9] And from this, both profit. Foreign firms in the shadow state gain from the privileged access resources and political protection that their participation in the hegemonic alliance offers. In return, rulers subcontract the tasks of accumulation and control over networks of exchange to foreign firms that would otherwise be assigned to state institutions. The shadow state ruler's resources and political authority derive from his control over subjects, but also from his control over a hegemonic alliance's extension outside the boundaries of the juridically recognized state and into overseas business networks.

This focus on foreign firm-elite coalition relations does not negate still-significant influences of state power in some parts of Africa. But nor does a business conflict perspective on shadow states ignore the wide range of issues and processes that underpin local political authority but that take place outside the formal authority of states. But our tracing of shadow states' exploitation of business conflict does defy conventional notions of systemic levels of political action centered on state structures. In this way, the notion of "shadow state" better captures the merging of increasingly diverse and competitive global business networks and African elite networks. Hence it better explains why, despite years of predicted demise, rulers such as Mobutu of Zaire survive the nearly total disintegration of the states in which they built their rule. It is difficult to put into state compartments these elite networks that rule less with reference to boundaries or internal legitimacy and more to economic practices and capabilities. The structural basis of the shadow state rests upon this process—that is, rulers' ingenuity and experience in playing business interests off one another, introducing new economic practices, utilizing their capacity to exploit local people and resources, and attracting new partners in a highly competitive global economy.

Fallacies of State-Centric
Analyses of African State Decay

State-centric analyses of politics recognize the existence of nonstate actors. But in local and global settings, the state remains the independent variable, the focus of study, and the explanation of politics. At the level of the state, this capacity to shape the formation of groups and their political capabilities signifies "state autonomy."[10] Theda Skocpol argued in her study of state policies during the Great Depression that the strength of nonstate actors is caused by previous declines in state autonomy to make and enforce rules of politics.[11] Nonstate actors' strengths are seen as a function of policy failure. The "solution," either implicit or explicit in state-centric studies of strong societal actors, is of course to make the state stronger. The goal—strong, effective states—defines systemic views of politics and relegates counterevidence to the status of dysfunction or deviation.

The "realist" school of international politics also view states as the primary structure shaping political action. Realists explain the rise of nonstate actors by insisting that these deviations are meaningful only in a context defined by states. "When the crunch comes," says Kenneth Waltz, "states make the rules by which other actors operate."[12] The prevailing orientation is that global politics will, according to Robert Gilpin, "remain intact even as change swirls through its component parts."[13] Questions remain, however, concerning the increasingly apparent role of nonstate actors in global politics. On the same page as the preceding quote, Gilpin avers that "this argument does not presume that states need always be the principal actors, nor does it presume that the network of states need always be the same."[14] Like Skocpol's state under internal pressure, this teleological analysis predicts that states will change rules that no longer suit them, forming instead new "international regimes."

Where decentralization of state authority does occur, it is explained as a by-product of hegemonic (state) decline, rather than as a consequence of nonstate actors' rise. Some call this synthesis of nonstate actors into a state-centric focus "neorealism."[15] Even those who conclude that nonstate actors do cause declining state capacity and are not simply a by-product of its result retain a state-centric teleological focus. As Susan Strange and John Stopford claim in their study of transnational capital and national policy, "The strong state is less effective in international competition." But then they posit a need for a "shrewd state" very much like the strong, autonomous state that state autonomy and realist scholars seek, since "it is good judgement and a clear vision of priorities that counts."[16]

That there are rulers who appear to abjure a state interest is widely recognized among observers of Africa. But the ways in which hegemonic alliances are separate from the institutional state and sustain or alter the system of states in Africa have not been central to investigation. Instead, we are told that African states are "weak," "soft," "lame Leviathans," or "swollen."[17] Defining these challenges to state power as consequences of state decline, many scholars define African political communities in state-centric terms of what they *should* be. For example, Richard Sandbrook views efforts to create a single, coherent definition of a state interest as essential for economic development: "States must facilitate capitalist accumulation. The phenomenon is universal. ... Who finances industrialization, if not the state?"[18] Africa's creditors concur with this prescriptive focus on state institutions. A recent World Bank report lauds Japan's Meiji Restoration as a model for a top-down "societal consensus" to be emulated.[19] Creditors prescribe reform "where the state assumes a leading role in building human resources, while the goods-producing and non-infrastructure service sectors are left to the flexibility and incentives of private enterprise and market discipline."[20]

In this regard, much of the so-called governance literature that takes up the cause of democratic reform in Africa traces the state's problems there to "a failure of the exercise of power to manage a nation's affairs."[21] It is more accurate, however, to view state decline in Africa as a consequence, rather than a cause, of nonstate actors' rise. In many instances, shadow state-firm alliances are difficult for even so-called strong states to disrupt. The governments of the United States, France, and Belgium oppose Zaire President Mobutu's continuation in power. Yet Mobutu survives and even extends his direct control across international borders through his trade in diamonds with the help of DeBeers, Lebanese syndicates, and Antwerp buyers.[22] Meanwhile, state-centric literature dismisses this behavior as a "pathology of state decay,"[23] cataloging it as merely another effect of state disintegration, not its cause. This focus on states alone reifies conceptions of state and market. In assuming that both function in predetermined ways, such views relegate power relations—the struggles of hegemonic alliances to dominate through control of markets—as a function of incomplete state autonomy or a result of peripheral status in world markets.

Some students of Third World states do accept that limited capacities may cause rulers to behave in rational ways that do not result in their pursuit of power through the maximization of state autonomy. Mohammed Ayoob observes that rulers of weak states attend to personal security concerns to the detriment of long-term development of state institutions.[24] The central problematic facing the African ruler is his lack of legitimacy and the existence of competing foci of power, often exercised by descendants of rivals cultivated by colonial powers. But Ayoob does not question the overall structure of politics. He considers nonstate actors to be elements of processes that do not determine structures. Ayoob is thus concerned that "the sequential phases of the historical process of nation-state-building have been telescoped into one and dramatically shortened in terms of the time required to complete them successfully."[25] Charles Tilly, like Ayoob, concludes that Third World leaders pursue state power through a distinct path of militarization of institutions. But in this process, he also sees a struggle to replicate European state forms, not their replacement.[26]

There is a tendency to thus explain "dysfunctions" of Third World states—including the decay that shadow states replace—in terms of what they are not. And since so much of the focus of studies of state disintegration *is* on states, they ignore or minimize the actions of individuals and foreign firms that may be a source of at least regional systemic transformation. Skocpol argues that states condition such expression of class interests;[27] failure to consider the reverse precludes examining the exploitation and struggle for domination that characterizes shadow state politics.

It should be emphasized, however, that the corrective to these shortcomings demands more than crude explanations of how hegemonic alliances "made" shadow states. Instead, as in the following case study, the focus should be on how these societal forces—themselves constantly redefined by links to foreign capital, local production, and what remains of the old institutional state—combine control of market relations with the project of political domination.

Sierra Leone: From State to Shadow State

Sierra Leone's president faced strong IMF pressure to service loans, particularly after arrears began accumulating in 1980. By the mid 1980s, IMF field negotiators privately complained to Washington that massive official corruption weakened the government's resolve to carry out meaningful reforms.[28] Ninety percent of Sierra Leone's diamond production, the country's main export, was smuggled out of the country.[29] Field negotiators saw this development as especially troubling, since most of the larger diamond smuggling operations were organized and operated on behalf of senior politicians.[30] But although the small and extremely poor country of Sierra Leone appeared to be at the mercy of creditor demands for reform, high-level IMF and World Bank officials worried about threats to their own organizational goals if official corruption continued to sabotage their programs in Sierra Leone.

Brigadier General Joseph Momoh, president since 1985, was also deeply implicated in informal market activity. Creditors despaired that reform would be slow where top political leaders were themselves becoming rich at the expense of state revenues.[31] But Momoh and creditors found unexpected common ground, though for drastically different reasons. In particular, Momoh shared local agents' views that some state officials and their associates were becoming too independent of State House control in their informal market businesses. But his concern was not backed by an interest in imposing a stronger state control over renegade elites to enforce a national interest. Instead, the president discerned that his personal control over an intraelite accommodation that he had inherited in 1985 was collapsing as state officials found that they could profit from their offices without the president's direct approval. This political challenge gained public visibility when the gunmen of a state official heavily involved in illicit diamond mining attacked the home of a high-ranking official critic.[32] This attack exposed the president's inability to even offer physical protection to high-ranking political allies.

On the surface, Momoh appeared to face two mutually exclusive choices: He could either accept creditor advice to marginalize errant elites and defend the formal economy with strengthened state institutions, or he could alienate creditors and discipline elites by regaining personal control over the distribution of state resources. Despite creditor protestations to the contrary, the first option was not viable. Most state resources were already in private hands. Even if these resources were reclaimed to finance stronger state institutions, the president would have to call upon the strongmen identified as the obstacles of reform to implement policies and carry out the enforcement and policing operations designed to undermine their own interests. The president rationally concluded that the latter option, regaining personal control over resources in the informal economy, was the most viable means of disciplining strongmen. This option also offered him the greatest chance to ensure his own political (and physical) survival.

Ironically, the anxieties among creditor officials to produce some results from "reforms" gave President Momoh the means to pursue this second strategy. The IMF did not directly offer the president new resources. But officials from Washington did make clear to Momoh in 1986 that if State House gave greater priority to attracting foreign investors to generate revenue for arrears payments, the IMF could clear the way for bilateral concessional aid, renegotiation of multilateral debt servicing terms, and, eventually, significant loans within the framework of a final agreement with the IMF.[33] IMF negotiators in Sierra Leone also indicated that they trusted foreign firms to pay local taxes through transparent channels that would check the private ambitions of corrupt officials. But foreign firms for Momoh were just what he needed to attack the independent economic power of strongmen. In the meantime, foreign firms would also service arrears and keep creditor demands from impinging upon his domestic political strategy.

The president's strategy of balancing creditor interests with his own political agenda received its first test with the appearance in 1986 of LIAT Finance and Trust Company and Shaptai Kalmanowitch, an Israeli businessman. Kalmanowitch promised the president that if he were given preferential rights to market the country's diamonds, he would drive illicit mining operations out of business and use his profits to directly service some of the country's arrears to the IMF and World Bank.[34] Remaining royalty payments and the rice that Kalmanowitch promised to import on State House's behalf offered the president new resources to service his political network. Kalmanowitch also offered to privately finance vital oil imports, a task that Momoh previously ceded to renegade politicians and their associates in return for speculative rights.

LIAT appeared to deliver on Kalmanowitch's promises to subcontract state "capacity building" tasks. Official diamond exports rose 280 percent in the 1986–1987 mining season.[35] LIAT's payment of official arrears reversed the rapid increase of 120 percent of the year before and actually reduced total arrears by over $1 million to about $13 million.[36] In return, Kalmanowitch found that the president's exercise of state sovereignty for private gain offered him a hospitable environment from which to trade with South Africa in violation of existing sanctions.[37] After selling South African diamonds in Europe via Sierra Leone, LIAT imported technical equipment and military supplies to Sierra Leone. These items were then shipped to a LIAT subsidiary in the South African "homeland" of Bophuthatswana.[38] The president used prerogatives of sovereignty to provide Kalmanowitch, a man constitutionally ineligible for Sierra Leone citizenship, with a diplomatic passport. Kalmanowitch was made a "cultural attaché" and was thus exempted from customs formalities in Sierra Leone and abroad.

Kalmanowitch's willingness to direct at least some revenues through formal channels enabled President Momoh to promote "correct" policies to attract creditor support. In late 1986, Momoh decreed "Public Economic Emergency Regulations" (PEER) that appeared to commit State House to supporting legal market activity to boost official revenue collection. Although creditors reported concerns over PEER's emphasis on draconian enforcement, one field negotiator indicated satisfaction that PEER enforcement included paramilitary attacks against renegade politicians' mining sites.[39] Some local IMF officials believed that LIAT's performance allowed the president to distance himself from corrupt officials and attend to an independent state interest.[40] But Momoh treated LIAT as a tool in his quest to control the shadow state—the elite accommodation held together with the private distribution of state resources.

LIAT failed both Momoh and creditors, however. Renegade politicians used private armies to retaliate against paramilitary attacks. Some politicians had developed financial links with various Middle Eastern political organizations via their diamond trade, and they now used those contacts to bring in armed men from Lebanon.[41] Some of these ties ran deep. For instance, Nabih Beri, head of the Lebanese Amal militia, was born and raised in the Sierra Leonean town of Port Loko, as was a prominent financier of politician mining syndicates. This partnership culminated in a March 1987 coup attempt. Some in Freetown speculated that the financial links of Middle East political organizations to Sierra Leone prompted the Israeli government to arm and advise Momoh—and to provide some initial support for LIAT as a local counterbalancing force. Momoh thus gained additional benefits from these competitive interventions.[42] The Israeli Foreign Ministry cultivated influence with Momoh after Momoh's predecessor allowed an Iranian-backed Palestinian group to establish an embassy in Freetown in exchange for private access to oil imported from Iran on easy credit terms.[43] Kalmanowitch's May 1987 arrest in North Carolina on fraud charges and the Israelis' discovery that Kalmanowitch was selling sensitive information to other governments limited Momoh's options with this organization, however.[44]

LIAT served creditor interests well for a brief time, but President Momoh's main troubles lay in LIAT's inability to displace renegade politicians in the diamond fields. Since most of LIAT's diamonds were not Sierra Leonean, illicit mining continued unabated through 1986–1987 despite LIAT's presence. Indeed, by early 1989, after LIAT's departure, official diamond exports fell to .0003 percent of levels of the mid 1970s.[45] Arrears payments ceased. The World Bank placed Sierra Leone on nonaccrual status in late 1987. As they departed, IMF agents in Sierra Leone "reiterated deep regret over Sierra Leone's continued failure to fulfill its financial obligations to the Fund."[46]

Salvation for President Momoh and his creditors appeared in March 1989 in the form of SCIPA, another Israeli mining firm. SCIPA's head, Nir "The Skipper" Guaz, set out to gain Momoh's favor. Like Kalmanowitch, Guaz offered to privately provide "capacity building" services. Guaz allegedly paid overdue civil servants' salaries and made financial contributions to civic groups supporting the president.[47] Through royalty payments on diamond exports, Guaz rendered assistance with arrears payments in the amount of $5.5 million against obligations of SDR (Special Drawing Rights) $86 million, which caused IMF field negotiators to report that "this demonstrates actively their intention to cooperate with the Fund ... by making regular and substantial payments."[48]

But Guaz also realized that he could advance his interests through agreements with the president's political enemies. SCIPA's diamond buyers made marketing arrangements with local operators that provided an unusually high return to miners. SCIPA then exported the Sierra Leone diamonds purchased with cash brought from abroad.[49] Guaz's efforts to run this alleged money laundering operation through collaborations with Momoh's enemies now directly threatened the president. SCIPA's presence also undermined ongoing negotiations with a Dallas firm, Sunshine Broulle, for more extensive investments in kimberlite mining.

Sunshine Broulle's offer to invest $70 million was very attractive to creditors, since the firm promised a substantial increase in official revenues. Especially attractive to the president was Sunshine Broulle's offer to provide a security detachment to police the mining lease site.[50] Momoh now saw a way to subcontract military attacks on his opponents, and creditors in Washington appreciated the firm's offer to voluntarily collect the bulk of Sierra Leone's official revenues. Negotiations advanced further with the arrest of Guaz in Freetown in late 1989 on charges of "economic sabotage" and with the April 1990 launch of a paramilitary "Operation Clean Slate" to expel illicit miners from the diamond fields.[51] But Sunshine Broulle abandoned the project in 1991, after a U.S. partner withdrew financial support.[52]

Momoh and creditors scrambled to attract foreign firms to other sectors of the economy. IMF negotiators suggested that foreign firms could collect fishing royalties on behalf of the government. West African Fisheries (WAF) bid for a contract. "Realizing the position of the Sierra Leone Government in terms of foreign exchange," wrote WAF agents, "West African Fisheries is prepared to loan Government U.S. $10 million to meet international obligations."[53] But talks with this firm stalled when IMF officials discovered that this British-registered firm included presidential associates among its partners. A firm with creditor blessings, a joint venture with Britain's McAllisten Elliott Fisheries called Maritime Protection Services of Sierra Leone (MPSSL), took on the privatized capacity building function of collecting fishing royalties—$10 million in 1991.[54] MPSSL paid arrears, which released the president from having to undertake any capacity building measures with respect to policing fisheries or gathering royalties.

With creditors at bay, the president enlisted foreign firms to help him with other domestic political battles. Pioneer Resources NL of Australia received exclusive rights to mine sixty square kilometers of prime diamond land. Again, the promise of displacing renegade miners through the intrusion of a large foreign firm appealed to the president. Agreements with Nigerian investors to take over five rubber estates presented the opportunity to displace various politicians who had taken over these operations during a World Bank-sponsored "privatization" exercise in the early 1980s. This "reprivatization" again attracted World Bank support, now in the form of credits.[55]

World Bank and IMF officials also pressed Momoh to subcontract customs collections to the German firm Specialist Services International (SSI) in 1990. This company estimated that the Sierra Leone treasury lost $62.5 million annually through underinvoicing.[56] Far from offering capacity building assistance, the arrival of SSI signaled that both Momoh and creditors had given up on collecting taxes through state institutions. Evidence suggests that SSI did provide some favors to Momoh's shadow state, however, such as payments of at least $100,000 annually to one of the president's political allies.[57]

Logging firms directed more aid to Momoh's shadow state outside disintegrating institutional channels and managed its relations with creditors in return for monopoly rights. Suakoko Wood Corporation bid for twenty-year exclusive rights over 136,016 hectacres, a two-year rent moratorium, an indefinite tax holiday, and 100 percent earnings retention in the first five years. In return, investors offered $1.8 million to help State House clear debts that blocked access to loans from the International Fund for Agricultural Development. Evergreen, the successful bidder, offered a $900,000 interest-free "loan" and $520,000 for "social development" in return for a three-year tax holiday.[58]

More cynical observers saw Momoh's 1991 decision to send a Sierra Leone army contingent to the Persian Gulf as another step in the privatization of the country's sovereignty in the service of his need to provide resources to his political network. After Kuwait's liberation, Sierra Leone received compensation for expenses from the United States and a $10 million development grant from Kuwait. The evacuation of eighty U.S. military personnel from the country after the May 1992 coup also suggests that Momoh's cooperation on Persian Gulf issues won him additional U.S. help with security threats at home.[59]

Momoh's efforts to strengthen his shadow state through balancing various creditor and foreign firm interests failed, however. This failure suggests that Momoh's nascent shadow state was not merely a grafting of nonstate actors onto a state-centric structure. Momoh and his foreign firm partners did find some advantage from prerogatives that accompanied his hold of the residual sovereignty of Sierra Leone. But Momoh also suffered from the obligations of the sovereign state as enforced by creditors. Unable to find enough resources or exercise enough control over his associates' greed, Momoh left army troops unpaid while they fought a "Greater Liberia"-backed rebel force in the country's eastern region. A twenty-seven-year-old noncommissioned officer, Valentine Strasser, and his twenty-four-year-old associate, Solomon Musa, now run Sierra Leone.

Momoh's political network proved incapable or unwilling to defend its head as long as creditors' demands siphoned off resources from his personal control or even the creditor-supported task of strengthening state institutions. Despite Momoh's strenuous efforts to manipulate foreign investment for his own political benefit, arrears payments absorbed 45 percent of formal foreign exchange earnings in 1990–1991.[60] As the president's authority weakened, renegade politicians also diverted a larger share. This left the president with little to distribute to those allies whose support was crucial to his own political survival, much less pay the army or build strong institutions that creditor rhetoric supported. No doubt the president's own greed undercut his political position. Yet maybe the president would have managed internal threats more efficiently were it not for creditor interference in the distribution of revenue from foreign firms.

Momoh's troubles lay in the tendency for IMF and World Bank conditions to leave him a largely negative capability to use firms to deprive rivals of access to economic opportunity. Most of the revenues that would have financed a positive effort to refashion a private elite accommodation were lost to creditors. Where firms such as MPSSL and SSI took over state functions in order to generate arrears payments, they removed the president from political control over the benefits of exchange and diminished his authority. And since most of this money went to pay arrears, the president found no opportunity to actually build state institutions, much less pay soldiers protecting his regime. With "capacity building" rendered so unattractive, the president struggled to use foreign firms' resources to confront internal challenges while keeping creditors at bay.

These "reform" policies fail creditors since the new government of Sierra Leone now has even less of an institutional base to contemplate capacity building measures and faces even larger international obligations. Additionally, the new regime is threatened with a rebel invasion. Would not an external threat prompt Sierra Leone's young leaders to mobilize resources and seek domestic support through institutional channels? Instead, the country's new leaders choose to manipulate foreign investment for direct gain. Their overwhelming need to obtain guns to reconquer the country's diamond-producing areas overrides creditor demands. Their primary political task is to strengthen intraelite accommodations to do battle with invaders and ensure their own survival. Ironically, it is creditors' own policies that make this nearly total privatization of state sovereignty to attract and manipulate foreign investment for private ends more likely, which reduces creditors' capacity to influence internal policy.

The End of States and the
Rise of Shadow States in Africa

The implications for African international relations of closer business-shadow state ties are significant. Rulers presiding over already weak state institutions will find that closer ties with foreign firms may represent the most viable response to challenges from neighboring shadow state networks. With foreign firm support, rulers turn away from the struggle to build institutions in their states to tax and conscript or seek legitimacy and support from populations. Instead, interstate competition follows contours that increasingly parallel commercial networks. Where this is so, as in Sierra Leone and "Greater Liberia" (another case that I have explored elsewhere), rulers may perceive that abandoning respect for colonial borders and suspending recognition of neighbors' unconditional sovereignty is less costly than remaining committed to the project of building state institutions. We should expect, then, to see greater willingness among shadow state rulers to make transnational alliances with state and nonstate actors to gain comparative advantages against competitors.

This African world containing both states and shadow states is structurally different from one containing only states with institutions capable of mobilizing resources and regulating their distribution. Can state structural theories of state autonomy that inform reformers' policies make sense of the practices and nature of shadow state politics? Or are amendments to them, or possibly new theories, called for?

Approaches that rely upon assumptions of state autonomy and definition of a national interest fail to explain how some African rulers manage internal and external challenges and the conditions that they face. Case studies reveal that a primary shortcoming of these approaches lies in a tendency to define by negation. That is to say, many reformers enunciate clearly what Africa is not (i.e., not fully capitalist). This inclination to view African states in terms of what they are not is a common tendency of developmentalist theories. Many creditor analyses also offer little indication of what African states are and how they function within their internal context. Thus the workings of the shadow state are obscured in the rush to explain what is missing.

This is not simply a matter of avoiding Western concepts. Instead, it signals a more serious reification of state and markets seen to function in separate and ideal ways. Such assumptions ignore the extent to which markets in Africa are arenas of political struggle. Exploitation of markets provides local rulers with political resources in place of state institutions. Market control becomes a means to control subjects and accumulate resources. Markets are also the glue that binds the foreign firm to the ruler's project of control. It is certainly possible to analyze rational resource allocation within this context.[61] But a comprehensive analysis will include consideration of political life and the effect of a political environment marked by interelite accommodations outside an institutional framework.

Herein lies the difficulty of employing state-centered analyses in Africa and the need to adopt a shadow state alternative. State-centric scholarly analyses of weak states propose that leaders divorce themselves from other elite allies. Assumptions that there are no alternatives to states as the basis of political community shifts attention away from strongmen and firms that are in fact integral to internal power relations centered on control of markets, and hence, that should be of major concern to political scientists. Thus intraelite accommodations and struggles—the most prominent features of postcolonial African politics—fade into relative insignificance in state-centered analyses.

Likewise, more radical approaches to studying Africa's economic and institutional disintegration, such as dependency theory, assume that markets are functionally determined by economic interests of dominant classes. This interpretation precludes careful attention to the struggle in internal political realms that the battle to control resources indicates. Nor would assumptions of class interest account for the appearance of "buccaneer capitalists" such as LIAT, SCIPA, or rogue logging firms as components of Sierra Leone's externally supported reform policies. We also see diverging interests among foreign governments and firms in "Greater Liberia." It is these conflicts among external agents that gives shadow state leaders the leeway to manipulate foreign interests to advance their own causes in domestic struggles to control resources.

Ultimately, studies of market efficiency and state autonomy in the African context too often avoid or simplify power relations that define and constrain individual and group strategies. Political conflict often centers on trade and commerce—a struggle that creditors' local agents recognize. This struggle is what reformers hope to redirect into institutional channels. But the struggle is over more than just resources. It is over productive processes: the control of workers and the fruits of their labors. This is why markets often parallel splits in intraelite accommodations. Renegades organize and exploit those from whom they profit and use those profits to extend their political control and legitimate their regional domination via patronage links.

This confrontation is not the state power versus societal power confrontation depicted in state-centric analyses and prescriptions. Shadow state analysis goes beyond considerations of how to build states where they are disintegrating. I find in my case studies that Momoh and Taylor seek to enlist external partners to split external and internal alignments that threaten their control over local society and economic exploitation—the glue that holds this elite accommodation together. And where rivals derive *their* capacity to challenge through exploitation of circuits of exchange, reform from a leader's perspective is not simply a matter of reintegrating "illicit" behavior into institutional channels; instead it is a struggle over political authority. Power in the shadow state is something gained through the direct control and exploitation of circuits of exchange, not their regulation through state institutions. In this regard, the emergence of shadow states in Africa is not indicative of Africa's marginalization in global markets. Rather, it is concomitant with the process of its reintegration into the global economy, but on terms very much determined by nonstate actors.

This study differs from state-centered approaches in its use of the shadow state to refocus analyses of failures of reform on intragroup conflicts, as well as on external (structural) pressures. It examines political networks rather than the state itself. This focus better accounts for interactions among internal and external variables in shadow state politics. "Stateness" is not an irrelevant variable, however. No doubt the talisman of sovereignty aids Valentine Strasser's pursuit of security and effort to dominate circuits of exchange. But Taylor's "Greater Liberia" is not a state in any internationally recognized sense. Yet Taylor's control of territory and alliances with internal and external actors suggests that, rather than focusing on "states without citizens," "states without societies," "overdeveloped states," and "underdeveloped states,"[62] it is better to examine the increasingly transnational private networks that dominate exchange and exercise social control in place of the institutions that we commonly associate with an autonomous state interest.

8

Winners and Losers in the Latin American Debt Crisis: The Political Implications
ze

Jeffry A. Frieden

Latin American debt has been politicized since the financial crisis began in 1982. It is easy to understand why international debt has become an international political issue, for the renegotiation of cross-border loans inevitably involves governments. Continued bargaining over the terms of debt service among debtor states, creditors, and creditor states confirms expectations that this international political interaction will reflect the wide variety of material interests and institutional forces at play.

Foreign debt has also become an extremely important political issue *within* Latin American countries. It has been central to Latin American domestic politics since 1982, affecting such significant processes as democratization, oppositional protests, and repression in a variety of countries. Indeed, domestic political strife over the external debt has often spilled over into the international bargaining process, as countries have found their international negotiating stance constrained by domestic pressures.[1]

Recent experience demonstrates the weakness of existing approaches to Latin American political economy. The modernization tradition, which argued for a positive relationship between economic development and political democracy, was largely discredited by the wave of authoritarian coups that swept Latin America in the late 1960s and early 1970s. The most common alternative, the "bureaucratic authoritarian" approach that suggested a causal link between economic crises and political authoritarianism in countries at middle levels of economic development, had been undermined by the wave of democratization that, in the midst of serious economic distress, swept the region in the early 1980s.[2]

This essay suggests an alternative based on the broader political economy literature. The approach explores how socioeconomic actors, in pursuit of their material interests, interact with existing institutions. The result is not a constant assertion that economic growth leads toward or away from democracy but, rather, a mode of analysis that allows us to understand the relationships among economic interests, political behavior, and social outcomes.

The essay summarizes the domestic political impact of the debt crisis in the five largest Latin American debtor nations: Argentina, Brazil, Chile, Mexico, and Venezuela. It emphasizes how the domestic distributional effects of the financial crisis have been reflected in the domestic political arenas of the major Latin American debtors. A simple analytical framework focusing on the impact of the crisis on different social groups, the distinction between liquid and fixed asset-holders, and the availability of a sympathetic government or attractive oppositional coalition partners is used to explain the responses of different economic agents to financial distress. The evidence mustered is not exhaustive or systematic, but meant to illustrate the analytical points being made. First is a general survey of the distributional effects of international financial relations. The next two sections of the essay discuss these distributional effects during the borrowing process and the financial crisis, respectively. The final section explores the political implications of these distributional effects during the debt crisis.

International Finance and Domestic Interests

Foreign debt is often a source of domestic political conflict, for it can raise important distributional issues. An inflow of capital as debts are contracted, or an outflow of capital as debts are repaid, affects different economic agents variably. Some do especially well during an expansion in borrowing, while others do especially poorly during a contraction in new borrowing or reversal of financial flows. The possibility of an unequal distribution of gains and losses in borrowing booms and financial crises makes foreign debt potentially controversial within borrowing countries.

Beyond market forces, government policy can also affect who wins and who loses in borrowing and financial crises. During financial expansions, the government may channel foreign loans to favored firms; during times of crisis, it may use taxpayers' money to bail out the indebted enterprises. External finance may be used to allow industrialists to purchase cheap capital goods from abroad, while a financial cutoff may be dealt with by repressing industrial wages to increased exports. In such instances, the relative distribution of costs and benefits in both book and bust is amenable to government policy and is thus the focus of political conflict. To clarify the issues involved, I first consider the economic impact of a capital inflow (or outflow) in the absence of government policy, and then I consider how government policy can affect this economic impact.

This analysis begins at the point where financial resources start to flow into the country, which affects three important economic variables: the availability of capital, foreign currency, and government finance. This is, of course, only part of the story—the pattern of borrowing presumably responds to the prior structure of domestic socioeconomic and political interests—but it is ambitious enough for my purposes here.[3] I take as given the structure of economic interests, political institutions, and government policy when borrowing begins.

Inasmuch as foreign finance increases the supply of capital available for domestic investment, it lowers domestic interest rates. A capital inflow thus makes borrowing cheaper and saving less attractive. When the capital inflow is channeled through domestic financial intermediaries, as occurs frequently, it benefits the national financial sector as well. Of course, here, as elsewhere, the capital inflow has a number of crosscutting effects. Borrowers eventually have to service their debts, and savers who are also consumers may benefit in the long run if the capital inflow leads to higher levels of productivity and thus lower prices. Nonetheless, the principal short-term result is straightforward: Borrowers benefit from the increased supply and lowered price of capital.

As external borrowing increases the domestic supply of foreign currency, it cheapens foreign exchange relative to the domestic currency. Without getting into thorny analytical debates about currency "overvaluation," it can safely be said that in most instances the borrowing country's currency is stronger than it would otherwise be; domestic prices rise relative to world prices.[4] This benefits those who purchase imports and harms exporters, although the ultimate result depends on the structure of protection. In the usual Latin American context, in which there are many barriers to the import of finished goods, cheap foreign exchange generally helps protected domestic producers who use imported capital goods or inputs.

When foreign capital is used to cover the public-sector deficit, it has distributional effects analogous to those of more general government spending. Some benefit by the public programs made possible by external public borrowing; others benefit by the short-term reduction in taxation that public borrowing allows. When, as is common, public borrowing is done by parastatal firms, the position of three groups is improved: employees of the firms whose debt allows increased wages or payrolls, suppliers of the firms that use debt to increase orders, and customers of the firms' products.

Of course, the differentiated effects of a capital inflow are reversed in the case of a capital outflow or a cessation of new lending. When a country with previous access to foreign capital is cut off, the supply of capital is reduced and domestic interest rates rise. Foreign exchange dries up and the currency depreciates, while the public spending-revenue gap must be closed without recourse to foreign funds. The society also has to mobilize domestic resources and foreign exchange to maintain service payments on the external debt. National savings, exports, and government revenue have to increase, or investment, imports, and government spending must decrease, or some combination of these. As foreign finance disappears and domestic interest rates rise, borrowers lose and savers gain. As foreign exchange becomes scarce and the currency depreciates, consumers of imported goods suffer and exporters benefit. As it becomes harder to finance the public deficit, spending is cut and employees, suppliers, and consumers of the public sector suffer the consequences.

Government policy can affect the distribution of foreign finance and thus the costs and benefits of a country's international financial position. When loans flow in, the government can channel capital and foreign exchange to favored sectors of the economy, thus concentrating the availability of cheaper capital or imports on a few government-backed borrowers. It is precisely this ability of government policy to affect the impact of international financial flows on different groups in society that makes these flows politically controversial. On the basis of these general observations, we can move on to discuss the Latin American experience, both while finance was readily available and once the financial crisis hit.

The economic effects of Latin American borrowing were the result of both market factors and government policies; therefore, they varied from country to country. Nonetheless, general patterns can be identified among the economic actors who were especially assisted by foreign borrowing; that is, those on whom the positive effects of the capital inflow were concentrated. It should be kept in mind that this analysis uses the borrowing period as a somewhat artificial starting point, especially since many of the effects discussed here were the result of government policies already in place when borrowing began.

In virtually all borrowing countries, the financial and commercial sectors grew very rapidly. The banking system was a major conduit for funds in all countries, and its role as intermediary between foreign lenders and domestic borrowers was extremely lucrative. By the same token, the greater availability of foreign exchange increased foreign trade, which in turn helped the commercial sector.[5]

Other consequences of external borrowing depended on the specifics of national government policy. In Brazil, Mexico, and Venezuela, the significant portions of foreign borrowing that went to finance parastatal investment improved the position of the parastatals themselves, as well as that of the suppliers and customers of the parastatals. This included construction firms and capital goods producers, which received lucrative orders to supply the huge parastatal petrochemical, hydroelectric, mining, and steel projects.

It also included the consumers of industrial inputs produced and sold at subsidized prices by these new parastatal investment projects. At the same time, domestic industry was accorded significant protection from foreign competition, even as it was generally able to purchase relatively inexpensive foreign capital goods. In all three countries, therefore, the public industrial corporations and the private firms tied to them grew very substantially.

In the Southern Cone, neoliberal policies meant that external finance went largely to the financial and commercial sectors. Despite the general availability of cheap imported capital equipment and inputs, trade liberalization made the countries' mostly uncompetitive industrial firms particularly unattractive to external lenders. Meanwhile, concurrent booms in consumer goods, financial, and real estate markets made firms in these sectors especially attractive. Chile is the most striking case: The public sector did almost no borrowing, and most of the country's external debt was accumulated by diversified conglomerates based in financial, commercial, and real estate activities. In Argentina, the pattern was similar, although some military-controlled public corporations were major borrowers there.

Foreign borrowing led to little domestic political conflict in Latin America before the financial crisis. This is easy to understand, since an inflow of foreign resources has far more visibly positive effects than negative ones.[6] Whatever unfavorable impact a capital inflow may have had on savers and exporters was generally overshadowed by the general prosperity it brought. The borrowing phase of recent Latin American financial experience was in fact one of relative well-being, as debt went to finance an expansion of consumption or investment or both.

Although debt-financed consumption or investment booms were generally uncontroversial, two criticisms of Latin American borrowing were voiced in some quarters even before 1982. One explicitly political objection came from opponents of the many authoritarian regimes then in power, who viewed foreign borrowing as a contribution to strengthening the status quo. The most obvious examples of this first criticism were in the Southern Cone, where policies of financial liberalization and resultant borrowing sprees were closely tied to the antilabor bent of the military dictatorships and their supporters. The Left and much of the labor movement in Chile and Argentina were just as hostile to foreign borrowing as they were to the regimes' neoliberal policies.

The second pre-1982 criticism of external debt was explicitly economic, focusing on the role of foreign borrowing in validating or reinforcing undesirable domestic resource transfers. The most egregious target of such critics was the linked financial and currency speculation that went on in most countries, especially after 1979. As international interest rates rose in 1981 and 1982 and domestic interest rates followed suit, financial investors reaped very large profits. At the same time, as currencies became increasingly overvalued, the availability of a "one-way bet" against the national currency led financial investors in many countries to buy dollars and transfer their portfolios to Miami, London, or New York. Moreover, the major currency overvaluation of the early 1980s was generally possible because national monetary authorities could borrow heavily abroad and resell borrowed dollars at home at bargain-basement prices.

Despite some complaints about the distributional effects of foreign borrowing—especially in the Southern Cone—the prevailing affluence among the upper and middle classes, and among parts of the working classes, muted most of the discontent that existed. The external debt did not become a major domestic political issue until the financial crisis began in 1982.

Distributional Effects of the Debt Crisis

The sudden disappearance of external sources of finance in 1982, exacerbated by the need to make service payments on large accumulations of external debt, had important macroeconomic consequences for countries that relied on foreign loans to finance investment and/or to cover their trade and budget deficits. Access to foreign capital dried up, which drove interest rates substantially higher everywhere. The reduced supply of foreign exchange led to rapid currency depreciation and major compression of imports. The public sector's inability to finance its deficit abroad forced it to borrow more at home, driving interest rates up still further. It also forced the public sector to reduce its expenditures (other than debt service) and increase its revenues.

The debt crisis was disastrous for virtually everyone in Latin America. In one sense, of course, the crisis hit the poor hardest, since they had the least reserves to cushion the impact of the worst depression in modern Latin American history. Although this is an important fact to keep in mind, it is far too undifferentiated to be of much explanatory power in understanding the politcal fallout of the crisis. Poverty is endemic in Latin America, the poor are always in conditions of relative deprivation, and most of the region's political systems have long succeeded in systematically excluding the poor from effective political activity.

Leaving aside the undifferentiated mass of the impoverished, the effects of the debt crisis fell unevenly on other economic agents. Those who bore the exchange risk for major foreign debts were probably the hardest hit. In some countries, this was the domestic financial system itself, but in most cases local banks had passed the exchange risk on to local borrowers, and the massive crisis-driven devaluations bankrupted virtually all such ultimate borrowers. In one fell swoop, many of Latin America's leading private firms were made insolvent, with dollar liabilities often many times larger than their assets.

The identity of those hit hardest by crisis-induced devaluations depended on the major borrowers in the financial expansion. In Brazil, where the devaluation was only moderate and most of the borrowing had been done by the public sector, the impact on the private sector was less severe than in Chile, where the devaluation was massive and the vast majority of the borrowing had been done by private firms. Mexico and Venezuela both had important privatesector borrowers that were bankrupted by the crisis, but the public sector still accounted for most external debt. In Argentina, the mix was about half and half. In these last three countries, the devaluations were substantial, and the impact was felt throughout both the private and public sectors.

Another important group of economic actors who shared the brunt of the crisis in many countries was the network of firms tied to the public sector. The crisis forced a major curtailment of public investments expanded by borrowing, which hit hard at the parastatals' former suppliers. This was very much the case in Brazil, Mexico, and Venezuela. By the same token, where debt-financed parastatals had offered subsidized inputs to private industry, the crisis forced them to raise prices to maintain debt service. The resultant increase in utility rates, energy prices, transportation costs, and the cost of basic industrial inputs again hurt important industrial sectors in Brazil, Mexico, and Venezuela. Both of these outcomes—reduced parastatal orders and reduced public-sector subsidies to industry—were far less significant in Argentina and unimportant in Chile, which had fewer orders and subsidies to begin with.

Other beneficiaries of government spending were also affected by the crisis in public finance brought on by external debt difficulties. This was especially important in Mexico and Venezuela, both of which had relatively well-developed social programs for politically important popular-sector groups. The urban working class in both nations was an important source of political support for the ruling parties—Partido Revolucionario Institucional (PRI) in Mexico, and Accíon Democratica in Venezuela between 1974 and 1979—and had received some social programs during the financial expansion. These programs were drastically curtailed during the crisis. And, of course, public employees were major victims of the government budget cutting that inevitably followed the crisis.

Besides the ever-present and disenfranchised poor, then, the crisis was also disastrous for certain economically and politically influential sectors and groups. At the risk of oversimplifying, the modern industrial sector was hit hardest in Brazil, Mexico, and Venezuela. This included especially the capital goods and basic industries that relied heavily on government orders and subsidies; it, of course, included both owners and workers. In Argentina and Chile, the financial sectors were hit very hard. The end of the debt-financed consumption book pulled the rug out from under the middle classes that had experienced unprecedented prosperity in the late 1970s. The economic catastrophe that began in 1982 drove economic actors into the political arena to fight for protection or support. The result was a bewildering array of domestic political battles over economic policy in all Latin American nations.

Latin American Politics in the Debt Crisis

To explain the structure of domestic political activity in the debt crisis, I begin with an analysis of the different effects on various economic sectors. I then take into account the implications that different underlying economic positions, and the availability of viable political coalition partners and institutional settings, have for political activity. The goal of the exercise is to combine our rudimentary map of the economic effects of the crisis with a simple analytical framework that helps explain the patterns of political behavior observed in Latin America since 1982. The focus is on political behavior in the relatively short run—the immediate aftermath of the crisis. Political trends over the long term may differ from the initial response to the crisis.

I use the familiar notions of "exit" and "voice" introduced into the political economy literature by Albert Hirschman.[7] This allows for a distinction between those actors who respond to adversity by leaving their surroundings for greener pastures (exit) and those who respond by attempting to improve the pasture they are in (voice). For our purposes, the analysis is dichotomous and can be regarded as a series of decisions. First, actors decide whether to respond to the crisis by taking their assets elsewhere (exit) or by struggling for economic assistance in the political arena (voice). Second, those who opt for political activity decide whether to exert pressure as loyal supporters of the government (voice) or as defectors to the opposition (exit).

The first step is to examine how the position of various economic actors gave them different incentives to divert resources from economic endeavors to political activity. Throughout Latin America, investors whose assets were very mobile could easily exit from the local economy and thus had less incentive to exert political pressure on the government. Other groups whose assets were relatively immobile had no choice but to engage in political activity to protect their interests.

There is a continuum in the political behavior of economic actors from complete reliance on the market to total dependence on government favors. The end points are unrealistic—few firms devote none or all of their resources to political pressure—but there is substantial variation. Whether social actors exit the system or give voice to their demands is a function of the economic position of the actors themselves (i.e., the economic feasibility of each option) and of the domestic political environment (i.e., the expected results of protest). Leaving aside for now the likelihood of the success of political pressure, there are clear reasons why different sorts of investors with different kinds of assets will respond differently to identical economic events.[8]

Some economic actors can easily move their assets among sectors and jurisdictions, and thus they respond rapidly to changes in economic conditions without loss of revenue. For example, those whose savings are in very liquid domestic financial instruments can easily respond to national economic difficulties and uncertainty by shifting their savings to Miami, where both the currency and the underlying economic and political environment are presumably more stable. Financial institutions can similarly shift their short-term assets from Mexico City to London. Investors with easily marketable assets, such as gold, can readily liquidate their holdings as well.

Other investors, however, have assets tied to activities that cannot easily be liquidated without a significant capital loss. Capitalists may have production facilities with which they are very familiar, informal contracts from which they alone can benefit, expertise that can only be used in certain lines of production, or other sector- or site-specific assets that bind them to the local economy. Managers or employees may have skill, language, or personal ties that make it very difficult to move. Investors with assets that cannot easily be sold at the price they are worth to the investors, and who would have to take a major loss to liquidate their holdings, are relatively immobile economically.

The former investors, whom I shall call "liquid asset-holders," are far more likely to take their investments elsewhere in times of crisis than the latter investors, whom I shall call "fixed asset-holders." In response to serious domestic economic difficulties, which lower local rates of return or introduce unacceptable risk into local economic activities, liquid asset-holders will tend to change their portfolios or even to flee the jurisdiction, while fixed asset-holders will tend to stand and fight to protect the value of their assets.

In all of Latin America, important economic groups with liquid assets responded to the debt crisis with a combination of hedging and capital flight. Some got into extremely short-term deposits (often overnight accounts) indexed to the inflation rate or the dollar or otherwise relatively protected against domestic instability. Others bought consumer durables, dollars, or gold, which could easily be sold at predictable prices in case of further trouble. Still others took their assets elsewhere, to establish dollar accounts or buy condominiums in Miami, San Diego, New York, London, or Geneva.

The precise mix of such asset movements was largely a response to national economic conditions as well as to geographical and historical factors. Table 8.1 presents estimates of capital flight in the five major Latin American borrowers. In Brazil, there was only a moderate currency overvaluation, a long tradition of capital controls, and general confidence in the country's long-term prospects. Liquid asset-holders there generally got into real estate, index-linked Treasury securities, or physical dollars they kept inside the country. In Chile, the principal economic actors had substantial liquid assets and reshuffled them in response to the crisis. Few engaged in capital flight, despite the massive peso overvaluation. The reasons for this are not entirely clear. Investors may simply have believed the dictatorship's continual insistence that there would be no devaluation, or astronomical domestic interest rates may have offset devaluation expectations.

Table 8.1   Estimates of Latin American Capital Flight and Total Debt, 1976–1984

Country	Capital Flight (CF) 1976–1984 (in billions)	Gross External Debt (GED) End of 1984 (in billions)	Capital Flight as Percentage of Gross External Debt
Argentina	$16	$46	$35
Brazil	9	104	9
Chile	–2[a]	20	0
Mexico	27	97	28
Venezuela	30	34	88

Source: Donald R. Lessard and John Willimson, eds., *Capital Flight and Third World Debt* (Washington, DC: Institute for International Economics, 1987), pp. 88, 155, 206.

Notes: Estimates for capital flight vary widely; figures presented here should be regarded only as indicative.   *a.* Indicates unregistered capital inflows.

Recourse to capital flight was most common in Mexico, Venezuela, and Argentina. In Mexico and Venezuela, with long traditions of easy movement to and from the United States and few or no capital controls, many investors already had U.S. bank accounts. The principal response of liquid asset-holders in these countries was to buy dollars and take them overseas. To some extent, relatively inexperienced or trusting Mexican middle-class savers established legal dollar accounts inside Mexico; they were rewarded for their inexperience and faith by having their accounts frozen and converted to pesos at an artificially low rate once the crisis struck. Argentina's chronic economic and political instability since World War II has made many investors wary of fixed assets, so flight into overseas dollar accounts was widespread in Argentina.

While liquid asset-holders responded primarily by protecting their assets—shifting their investments into new instruments or taking them abroad or both—they also engaged in some political action. Their primary concern was to ensure the continued liquidity, availability, and profitability of their assets. Thus they lobbied against exchange controls, for freer financial markets, and for government support for failing financial institutions. Although such demands for economic liberalization were limited in the initial phases of the crisis, since investors with such interest were relatively protected against the worst effects of the financial turmoil, pressures from market-oriented liquid asset-holders mounted over time.

In all countries, liquid asset-holders, many of whom now hold internationally diversified portfolios, have come to support more orthodox macroeconomic measures, financial and commercial liberalization, and a more cooperative stance toward international financial institutions. The most visible such movement has been the increased support for the right-wing Partido Accion Nacional (PAN) by a portion of the Mexican business community, especially those in the north and/or those tied to trade and finance. Whether through Mexico's PAN, Venezuela's Grupo Roraima, or through other means, liquid asset-holders have exerted some political pressure on the government. Nevertheless, because they concentrated most of their resources on economic diversification rather than on political activity during the first stages of the crisis, their initial political successes were quite limited.

All of this explains why the foremost political pressures on Latin American governments in the aftermath of the financial crisis came from sectors that could not easily shift their economic activities and so were forced to fight for state support. The most prominent such group was made up of industrial capital and labor. Everywhere in Latin America, the industrial sector was the strongest opponent of debt crisis-induced domestic austerity measures.

My first step was to explain why some social groups engaged in intense political activity as the financial crisis hit. My second step is to explain why this activity took different forms. Within the political arena, I am primarily interested in explaining a group's choice between exerting political pressure on the government and engaging in oppositional activity. The sort of political activity a group chooses depends on the likelihood that such activity will be effective, which is largely a function of the institutional and political environment faced by social actors. Firms, sectors, and groups are most likely to make demands on governments perceived to be responsive. By the same token, they are most likely to support an opposition that has both the willingness to endorse their demands and some prospect to taking power.

The sort of political action engaged in by a social group thus depends on its assessment of the likelihood of success of the various options. This, in turn, is a function of the strength of the group, its ability to ally with other groups, its existing ties to the government, and the strength and availability of an oppositional alternative. This process can be highlighted by focusing on how and why industrial capitalists, the most important group of fixed asset-holders in industrializing societies, choose to exert pressure on the government or defect to the opposition.

The ability of industrialists in Latin America to obtain the policies they sought without defection from the government was largely due to the economic importance of domestic industry, the degree to which industrial labor and management were able to unite in support of common demands, and the existence of close ties between industrialists and the government. A turn toward oppositional activity depended both on an inability to meet these conditions and on the availability of an acceptable opposition partner with reasonable chances of eventual success.

The general openness of the government to various social demands and the availability of an attractive opposition were indeed important factors in the political behavior of the Latin American private sector after 1982. In Chile, ties between domestic industrialists and the military regime were weak. Leaders of industry had little say in, or sympathy for, the government's neoliberal economic policies after 1973. Indeed, industry had been substantially weakened by neoliberal policies, as manufacturing value added dropped from 25 percent of gross domestic product (GDP) in 1970 to 19 percent in 1982.[9] In addition, labor-management relations were extremely hostile, so industrial capital and labor could not unite to pressure the government. Industrial pressure on the Chilean government was weak, and the industrial sector had almost no success in obtaining government support. The government was willing to assume some responsibility for the financial catastrophe, but mostly in support of the heavily indebted conglomerates whose position affected the country's overall international credit worthiness. After some initial vacillation, however, the dictatorship was generally indifferent to the pleas of the domestic industrial sector.

Despite their inability to influence government policy, Chilean industrialists engaged in little political protest. This was primarily because the existing opposition to the military did not enjoy the confidence of the private sector. The Left, of course, was a traditional enemy, but even the Christian Democrats and the Right were discredited in the eyes of the business community by their pre-1970 behavior. The moderate Chilean opposition complained bitterly that the private sector was cowardly and, at the same time, attempted to tie itself to business discontent by assuring investors that the opposition would respect property rights and otherwise encourage private enterprise. Few businessmen were convinced. Another factor was the apparent willingness of the regime to use brute force to repress most opposition; there seemed little likelihood of anyone dislodging Pinochet. The opposition's ambiguous economic preferences and poor prospect of taking power meant that the business sector, discontented as it might be, remained politically passive. The exception that proved the rule, of course, was the brief participation of business groups in the opposition demonstrations in 1983–1984. The government's success in co-opting business was a key factor in the failure of the protest movement.

In Argentina, industrialists had more options. Although Argentine deindustrialization was almost as significant as in Chile—manufacturing value added went from 17 to 23 percent of GDP between 1970 and 1982—the sector maintained ties with some military factions. At the same time, Argentine labor-capital relations, although not fully cooperative, were better than in Chile, and most of the opposition was less suspect. The industrial sector thus used a combination of pressure on dictatorship and defection to the opposition. The 1981 Viola presidency reversed the anti-industrial course of previous economic policy and bailed out many private firms, raising the hopes of the industrialists. When Viola was eased out by hard-line officers, however, industrialists lost faith in the military. After the Falklands/Malvinas disaster discredited the hard-liners still further, it seemed a safer bet to dissent from the military, and much of the industrial sector openly opposed the country's military-run neoliberal policies. The industrial sector in fact received support during both the 1981 Viola presidency and after Raul Alfonsin's accession to power.

In Brazil, Mexico, and Venezuela, industrial production led the pre-1982 economic expansion, and the industrial sector was both economically and politically influential. The three countries differed primarily in government responsiveness to industrial demands.

In Mexico and Venezuela, the industrialists were economically crucial, and labor-management relations were such that unified sectoral demands could be made. In both countries, the industrial sector worked through the existing political structures of the ruling party, and it received substantial support. Government assistance given in response to industrial pressure ranged from subsidized loans to trade protection. Perhaps the most important aid to industry took the form of schemes allowing industrial firms with overseas liabilities to service their foreign debts at the preferential exchange rate rather than at the vastly more expensive market rate, thus effectively transferring most of private industry's debt burden to the government. After the initial shock of the crisis, Mexican policy did gradually move toward liberalization, but by then much of the industrial sector had been cushioned against some of the most severe effects of the financial distress, whether by access to loans at subsidized interest rates or to artificially inexpensive foreign currency for debt service payments.

In Brazil, there was both a history of government sympathy for the industrial sector and a vibrant opposition. Brazilian industry had grown extremely rapidly during the borrowing period, and both labor and management in modern industry were well organized. Brazilian industrialists thus reacted to the crisis in two ways. First, they protested vehemently to the military government about the policies being undertaken. When their protests went more or less unheeded, the industrialists defected to the opposition, either leaving the official party for the new Liberal Front or joining the leading opposition party, the Partido Movimento Democratico Brasileiro (PMDB). Eventually, the military and its civilian supporters were replaced by a broad antiausterity PMDB-Liberal Front movement of the modern industrial sector, the urban middle class, and parts of the working class.[10]

All of these cases are far more complex than this rudimentary summary allows. The structure of labor-management relations, private-sector ties with the military, the traditional party system, and a host of other considerations need to be integrated in much more detail and factored into an accurate account of the crisis. My purpose has been to only sketch the implications and demonstrate the potential usefulness of an approach that directs attention to the economic position of social actors and, given this economic position, to the choices they made within their economic and political environment.

Conclusion

This chapter has presented a framework for analyzing the political effects of the Latin American debt crisis. International financial relations have differential effects. These distributional effects are filtered through two prisms. The first is economic and determines the probable response of economic agents to economic difficulty, especially the likelihood that they will have recourse to the political arena. The second is political and determines the form of the political response, especially the likelihood that a group's political activities will occur within the existing government's support apparatus, rather than taking the form of oppositional protest.

The first step in understanding the politics of the debt crisis, then, is to characterize accurately the economic interests of the various social forces at work. I have argued that there is a crucial difference between liquid and fixed asset-holders, since the former can easily leave the domestic economic environment, while the latter are tied to it and thus driven to the political arena in times of distress. As the debt crisis hit, the response of the two broad groupings of investors was substantially different: One engaged primarily in asset diversification (such as real estate speculation or capital flight), while the other moved primarily into political action.

The second step is to specify the political environment faced by various social forces. I have explored the circumstances in which a group's political activity takes the form of "loyal" pressure on the government and those in which the group resorts to political opposition. This set of choices is determined by the group's economic importance, its ability to unite with other forces, its ties to the government, and the availability of an opposition attractive to the group in question.

The discussion in this chapter is preliminary and suggestive, rather than detailed and definitive. It does, however, indicate the possibility of going beyond ad hoc description and abstract theorizing to analyze the sources of domestic political conflict in Latin America. The essay demonstrates the utility of the approach put forward and holds out the prospect that further investigation and analysis will help us explain Latin American political behavior, both in the debt crisis and more generally.[11]

International Relations Theories: Approaches to Business and the State
?&

Gregory P. Nowell

How do various international relations theories cope with the relationship between business and the state? The field of international political economy is far from a place of consensus. Some international relations theories downplay or even deny the importance of business. Others aggregate business groups into categories that are familiar by now, such as national and international capital. Still others examine the relationship at the level of the firm. This chapter examines a number of approaches: realism, regime theory, cartel theory, world-system theory, factor endowment theory, institutionalist theory, neopluralist theory,[1] and transnational structuring. This brief survey illustrates each theory's agenda, which means some of the core principles of its description of the international system, and also the kind of business research program that it expressly or implicitly prescribes.

Realism

The realist paradigm sees states competing for power in the same way that economic theory sees individual agents competing for profits. Power considerations overwhelmingly determine the relationships among states; economic relationships are second order, largely internal considerations. The competition among states is "anarchic" because there is no central authority to provide a common set of rules and enforce them. The work of Kenneth Waltz is archetypal to this perspective.[2] The economy, when considered at all, is seen as the financial and technical underpinning of the state's military power. In times of crisis, corporations are, like individual citizens, subject to conscription to serve the needs of the state. Where there are no direct power implications, pure realist theory has nothing to say about how goods are produced and traded, and therefore has no theory of business-state relationships. This omission is an analytic weakness if one thinks that business groups play a determining role in how modern capitalist states compete for power. But it is an analytic strength if it can explain successfully the dynamics of power competition among capitalist and noncapitalist states, and even systems of noncapitalist states. Such noncapitalist states might include the centrally planned economies of the twentieth-century communist interregnum or the precapitalist state systems of antiquity.[3]

In realist theory, states enter into alliances and also break them when convenient. The realist theorist has nothing to say about the state's role in governing the economy unless a strategic military technology (e.g., timber masts in the eighteenth century, coal in the nineteenth, oil in the twentieth) is involved. The thrust of the theory is clear: Power considerations come foremost, and business' second-order importance, not to say irrelevance, comes from the fact that in an anarchic state system war-making capability is the primary concern. The governing principle of states is "self-help" or self-reliance, no matter what kind of economy they have or what business groups are harbored within their borders. The relationship of the state to its firms is of more interest to the study of economics than to that of international relations.

Simple as this formulation may seem, it leaves realist theory with a profound ambivalence regarding state behavior and strategic commodities in the capitalist era. The reason for this ambivalence is that the theory has no a priori determination of what economic policy maximizes power. Just as a profit-maximizing investor may hesitate between the multiple considerations (e.g., risk, relative yields, desired liquidity) that go into the decision between investing in stocks and bonds, the power-maximizing state may not have a clear preference between such common economic policies as protectionism and free trade. Theoretically, a state is better off providing for its own needs, but if it gains self-sufficiency in one commodity at such high expense that military equipment acquisition must be forfeited or delayed, there is no way to ascertain the "best" alternative.[4] Hence it seems that realist theory willfully ignores the potential of business groups to take advantage of the state's ambivalence among possible policies.

Another way of thinking about this theoretical ambivalence is to consider that in capitalist states the primary control of technological development, a crucial resource of war and power, lies in the hands of nonstatal actors called firms. This by itself must mean that as firms pursue profit-related goals, they influence, as a secondary effect, the state's ability to pursue power. This must be so even if we do not get into the complexities of real-life relationships between business and the state. The bottom line is that if one is interested in learning the effects of business groups on states and the consequences for the international system, realism is a poor analytical choice and has no practical research agenda to offer to students of business-state relationships.

Regime Theory

Regime theory emerged in parallel with the "interdependence" theory of Joseph Nye and Robert Keohane. Interdependence theory argues that Waltz-style realism is one "pole" of international relations, while interdependence is another. Power in one domain does not translate into power in another: Military supremacy does not mean an ability to dictate oil prices on the world market, at least not all the time. States have reciprocal and interlocking needs on a broad spectrum of issues. There are different kinds of power, and the competitive arena of nation states is multidimensional. In wartime, states may pursue a "pure realist" mode, and during these times the economic emphasis will be on self-reliance. However, in peacetime, states' needs for cooperation are as real as is their competition on some power axis.[5]

Regimes are formal and informal relationships designed to deal with issue areas: "a set of mutual expectations, rules, regulations, plans, organizational energies and financial commitments, which have been accepted by a group of states."[6] Regime theory is a logical outgrowth of "complex interdependence." At any given time, there are many issues on which states would benefit from established, cooperative modes of behavior. But regimes can break down if the world slips into a phase of "anarchic competition," just as warfare can break the web of complex interdependence. Regime theory is state-centric in that state actors are usually seen as organizing the development of rules that govern the behavior of both firms and states. A firm or group of firms may lobby the state to adopt a particular stance in relation to establishing, maintaining, or breaking a regime; but the expression of their interests occurs through the state.

Regime theory most convincingly describes liberalized trade relationships and cooperative monetary agreements among countries. Establishing or maintaining a regime lowers the cost of trade relationships and establishes conflict resolution practices or expectations that reduce the saliency of disagreements on a given issue. Regime theorists see regimes as normatively desirable: The benefits of cooperation are positive attributes created against the current of selfish action or "anarchy." Charles Kindleberger's description of the decline of international monetary and trade agreements in the 1930s has been influential on this school.[7] Thus Keohane, working with the combined assumptions of realism (one pole of the international system) and complex interdependence (the other pole), acknowledges that it is easier for a victorious power to establish worldwide rules for trade and other concerns.[8] However, he nonetheless labors hard to show that regimes have a value to states by providing collective goods.[9] In his book *After Hegemony,* he assumes that the United States, the post–World War II hegemon, is in a period of relative decline. Trouble surely lies ahead for the world system if the maintenance of world cooperation depends on the efforts of a hegemon that is losing its power to enforce the rules. However, if the tenets of regime theory are true, there are reasons to believe that enlightened self-interest could steer states away from anarchic-catastrophic competitive policies. Even without a hegemon, therefore, there are grounds for hoping that states will maintain the cooperative regimes that are already in place and seek ways to establish new ones.

Because of its realist component, there is an underlying tendency for regime theory to focus on the rationality of the state actors and their reasons for maintaining cooperation. Nonetheless, there is a certain analytic ambivalence to business lobbies and their influence on the state. Both Keohane and Krasner, for example, give considerable attention to business interests in conflicts over U.S. foreign policy. Krasner finds that even the "weak" U.S. government resisted business influences that might impede the national interest. Keohane finds some impacts of business influence undesirable, such as the decision to protect the U.S. oil market from imports, which drained U.S. domestic oil reserves and undermined energy self-sufficiency.[10] Considering these examples along with Kindleberger's study of the Great Depression, a major threat to regimes is that selfish business interests may tempt or force the leaders of states to favor short-term interests over long-term interests. The liberal, cooperative, free trade world economy is threatened by selfish interests that, if they succeed in capturing or influencing state policy, may turn the whole world system into a competitive vicious cycle in which every nation-state player ultimately loses more than it gains.

To approach international relations from the point of view of regime theory, a regime that is either in place, being built, or falling apart is needed. If there are no such regimes, then, as with complex interdependence, the other pole of the international system is operating, and the regime approach would move back toward realist analysis. Regime theorists study domestic business interests in individual states to see how these influence a state's attitude toward cooperation (regime) or noncooperation. It is also possible, however, that state actors, recognizing the constraints of the international system, may rebuff the demands of business groups.

The demands of business groups (at the firm or the sectoral level) on the state are not excluded from regime theory, but they are of secondary importance. The primary concern is the structure of relationships among states. "Irrational" or nonoptimizing behavior may, within that general structure, be attributed to the interference of selfish groups on the state's articulation of its own goals. Moreover, state rationality, when dealing with the many objectives inherent in complex interdependence, is not reduced to power maximization pure and simple. A state may therefore have good reason to assent to a regime or to multiple regimes that do not enhance its power, but that may provide other benefits. The interest groups within the state may therefore have to accommodate themselves as best they can to the imperatives designed by their leaders: This could include, for example, the conse-

quence of adhering to free trade pacts, even if such adherence inflicts disproportionate costs on some members of society. The research agenda of regime
theory targets business groups insofar as these groups influence regime formation, maintenance, or disintegration. Business is also relevant to the extent that its activities contribute to the creation of complex interdependence,
which is one of two major poles of the continuum that constitutes international politics.

Cartel Theory

Cartel theory here refers chiefly to turn-of-the-century works that focused
on the role of cartelized business sectors and their influence on the state. The
major theorists of this approach include J. A. Hobson, Rudolf Hilferding, V.
I. Lenin, Nicolay Bukharin, Karl Kautsky, and Max Weber.[11]

In the more developed capitalist economies, the tendency toward industrial concentration has important consequences in economic and political
development. Cartelized industrial sectors generate surplus profits that are
not reinvested in the domestic economy, in part because the noncartelized
sectors of that economy find both the demand for their products and their
profitability diminished. The flow of surplus revenue to the cartelized sector
depresses the purchasing power of all consumers and hence pushes sales down
in the noncartelized sector. The cartel itself, by definition, restricts output,
and the amount of investment that will occur in its own members' facilities
will be controlled by mutual agreements. The need for markets and for places
to invest surplus capital leads to the need for overseas investment arenas, or
colonies. The attempt to secure these colonies, or imperialism, is a direct
cause of warfare among advanced capitalist states.

Regarding the relationship of business to the state, Hobson's *Imperialism*
presents what is probably the most articulated model. Hobson describes a
true military-industrial complex that benefits directly from the arms race
that its own aggressive policies initiate and aggravate. He discusses relationships among dominant firms, their banks, their political parties, their newspapers, and the secondary effects of imperialist propaganda on the culture of
the country. The propaganda targets adults and schoolchildren. Through it,
citizenship is militarized and racist theory elevated to national doctrine.

Free trade, antitrust policies, trade unionism, and income redistribution
are antidotes to the deleterious impacts of cartels and imperialism. Hobson
does not say how this agenda can be enacted against the overwhelming political power enjoyed by the imperialists.

In Hilferding's *Finance Capital,* by contrast, there is scarcely any mention
of the state. The main focus is a careful scrutiny of how the competitive
dynamic in capitalism can give way to a "market" that is no longer really a
market as such, but a pure power relationship between producers and con-

sumers. A general cartel regulates production and distribution. The interests of the cartel and state are fused; the fusion is implicit in most of Hilferding's book, except toward the final chapter, where the fusion is stated, but not explained in detail. The fusion is more explicit in the writings of Lenin and Bukharin.

Hilferding, unlike Hobson, argues that the cartelized state is essentially an irreversible development. Over time, production techniques become ever-more capital intensive. Eventually, firms cannot by themselves raise the massive capital required for the "highest phase" of capitalism; banks come to play an important role in industry not only as lenders, but also as stockholders. Hilferding lays cartelization (attributed to industry by Hobson) at the doorstep of the banks that have organized it to protect their many loans and investments.[12] These are the operations of "finance capital." The restoration of liberal capitalism that Hobson recommends is impossible. The historical process of competition inevitably creates the capital-intensive firms that inevitably require the backing of banks, which organize and enforce cartels to guarantee profitability. There can be no reform within the framework of capitalism because it is the laws of capitalism that have transformed competition into total cartelization.

However, the virtual fusion of capital and the state makes it easier to envision the nationalization of capital—socialism—as an alternative. The classic liberal critique of centralized production is no longer operative: A totally cartelized economy no longer allocates goods according to the efficiencies of price and market; rather, it does so according to the logic of the cartel. The decision to produce represents the accommodations between the antagonistic power relations of the cartel and consumers. Socialist revolution does not supersede a competitive market. It supersedes a noncompetitive market and replaces oligarchy with more democratic control of production. [13]

For the cartel theory, historical context determines the meaning of a state policy. In the early period of capitalism, tariffs might be intended to provide protection to infant industries, in the manner described by Friedrich List.[14] In a later stage of capitalism, tariff polices are tools to promote cartelization and aggressive export strategies.

The theorists agree that one result of this cartelization is Hobson-style imperialism. Hilferding, Bukharin, and Lenin, unlike Hobson, emphasize that protection allows firms in mature capitalist countries to use their surplus profits to subsidize exports. The firms gain additional benefits from the larger-scale economies that this strategy, predatory dumping, makes possible.[15] Predatory dumping eventually provokes the country receiving the dumped goods to put up its own tariffs in retaliation. The result, for Hilferding, is that the firms originally engaged in predatory dumping may build new production facilities in the export market. In that new market, their new subsidiaries benefit from the tariffs that were originally designed to keep their products out. This implies a competitive dynamic in international investment that runs counter to Hilferding's hypothesis of a totally cartelized market. If his logic were pursued, it would mean either the internationalization of cartels or eventual downward pressure on cartel prices, despite the influence of finance capital.

Kautsky significantly deviated from the analysis of Hobson, Hilferding, Lenin, and Bukharin. He proposed that the movement toward cartelization in the leading capitalist countries of the world could have a peaceful, rather than a bellicose, outcome. "Ultra-imperialism" could result if the major capitalist powers, after their phase of imperialist expansion and immersion in fratricidal warfare, realized the unprofitability of conflict and formed a common alliance to exploit the peripheral countries. The exterior form of national cartelization would be international cartelization. "Peace" as such would be possible, but this peace would be a nightmare for the subjugated peoples, not the liberal-democratic ideal proposed by Hobson. Kautsky's short article does not specify the relationship between business sectors and the state; but a "fusion" between state interests and cartelized capital is, as with Hilferding, implicit.[16]

Unlike regime and realist theory, and very much like world-system theory, this approach requires a consideration of the interactive relationship between rich and poor countries. Less-developed countries serve as the sites for capitalist investment of surplus funds, sale of export goods, and arenas for the establishment of imperial preference zones; they are also the prizes to be gained in war. Such distinctions are less necessary for the realist and regime theories; in fact, the poorer and weaker nations often disappear altogether from the universe of study. A possible implication is that regime and realist theories may have an "imperialist bias" in their focus on relations among the "great powers" or "developed countries."[17]

To conclude, the cartel theories offer an interesting model of the political economic forces that underlay conflict in the first half of this century. The development of great trading blocs, as discussed by Robert Gilpin and more recently by Lester Thurow,[18] could cause a reprise on a grander scale of the imperial conflicts of yesteryear.[19] The specific relationships between the state and business groups, while more developed than in realism, is not much more specific in these theories than it is in regime theory. In the cartel theory, the broad sweep of industry and finance's relationship to the state lies within the logic of the "development of capitalism." The relationship is therefore treated more as a theoretical aggregate than as a specific focus of analysis.

However, this need not be the case. Historical studies based in the period of "finance capital," such as Jame Herbert Nolt's[20] may be what is needed to take the abstract theory and breathe some life into it on the basis of historical evidence; and T. Ozawa shows that the cartel theory is, at a minimum, a useful reference point for looking at Japan (see note 16 to this chapter). Historical analysis may point to the weakness of the theoretical assumption of "total control" by finance capital. It may also suggest that cartelized economies can become capital exporters without becoming imperialists. The cartel theory could probably benefit more from reevaluation than from continued neglect. Research in the style of the neopluralists, discussed later, may elucidate more about the behavior of the component parts of the models (competitive business, cartelized business, export industry, tariff policies, etc.).

As a final point, the empirical validation of cartel theory in the pre–World War II period need not depend on finding that the profit rate in the countries of foreign investment exceeded the profit rate in the cartelized economy, or even that there was any profit at all. To defend a cartelized market, firms require that potential competitors not gain control of the resources they would need to challenge the leaders of the cartel. It is perfectly possible that a cartel would invest in the control of a resource that it not only did not need, but on which it would lose money, to keep that resource from falling into the hands of a competitor. The cartel theory in its historical form is really an ideal type description of imperialism; it is conceptually useful for understanding pre–World War II politics[21] and could help to organize some serious rethinking about the modern dynamics of international investment and export strategies.

World-System Theory

This approach is the descendant of the cartelist theories of imperialism, but cartelization is not the primary mechanism behind imperialism. Market control and cartelization are important and recurring features of a system that is stable in its instability. Immanuel Wallerstein's oeuvre on this approach is exemplary.[22] The capitalist world developed, right from the beginning, with a core, a semiperiphery, and a periphery. The dominant states have managed to turn resources or other endowments into decisive technological and market advantages. As they compete for power, one state gains hegemony over all the rest. Such hegemony is ephemeral; other states compete against the hegemon, and core-country fighting over control of the periphery and control over the terms of international trade is a characteristic feature. The semiperiphery has some of the characteristics of the core and some of the characteristics of the periphery. The periphery is characterized by extremely low wage rates that reflect the incorporation of noncapitalist zones into the world-economy (which is hyphenated to emphasize that the system emerged and operates as a whole, not as an aggregate of independent units). These below-subsistence wages are possible only because they are subsidized by subsistence farming, which is itself continually being gobbled up by the expansion of export agriculture.

In all states, the capitalist class uses the threat of disinvestment to coerce cooperation from the state and from the workers. Low wage rates in the periphery guarantee that capital in other areas will have a place to flee. Low-wage havens in the periphery influence the bargaining among the state, capital, and labor in the core and the semiperiphery. Because subsistence farming is always being absorbed into capital export farming, the capitalist world, to maintain the wage structure and the balance of class power that guarantee the ability to privatize profits in all nations, must be always expanding and always incorporating new, noncapitalist areas into its operations. Should the periphery "disappear"—or, more to the point, should there be no new zones of incorporation of noncapitalist areas—the capitalist system would enter a crisis. Without the threat of disinvestment, a worldwide shift would occur in the balance of power among capital, state, and labor, a shift that would favor the state and labor. This shift would eventually make capitalist accumulation impossible.

The world-system can never be "stable" because the competitive dynamic of capitalism contains too many antagonisms to permit stability. The business relationship to the state, in the world-economy, is an essential element of system dynamics. Relations vacillate between "free trade" or "protectionist" (mercantilist, cartelist, etc.) arrangements, depending on the period in question. For realists and regime theorists, the rise and decline of the United States, its ability to maintain regimes, and so forth, is important. For Wallerstein, the periodic emergence of new hegemons (Holland, Great Britain, the United States) is part of the great capitalist dynamic. Had there been a different series of hegemons in the capitalist world-economy, world history would be radically different, but the system as a whole would still look very much the same. What realism sees as the principle governing all nations is, for Wallerstein, the principle governing only those core nations strong enough to compete with other core nations for dominance of the world-system as a whole.

This tradition has generated some fine case studies, but these works live in the shadow of Wallerstein's great machine of world capitalism.[23] In the world-system approach, the concerns about business groups that animate the work of the neopluralists, for example, exist in much the same way as does the existence of the solar system in the study of the galaxy: The solar system turns around and fits within the larger structure, but it also virtually disappears in the larger structure. As Anthony Brewer observes, "my main criticism ... is that there is little connection between their grandiose general statements and their (often very illuminating) discussion of particular historical cases."[24] It is hard to disagree: The world-system may be in its essence the product of a "creative act" that employs the materials gathered by researchers in other traditions, such as institutionalists and neopluralists. Thus there may be no business research agenda that is a specific outgrowth of the theory. Rather, this theory's principal agenda is the digestion of the products of other research models.

Factor Endowment Theory

Ronald Rogowski's *Commerce and Coalitions* is a recent contribution to the political economy literature.[25] His book builds on the Heckscher-Olin and Stolper-Samuelson theorems regarding international trade. Under the Heckscher-Olin theorem, factor abundance and factor intensities help to explain the specialization of countries in producing one good versus another. As a country specializes and produces more goods for export, an increase in the demand for the "abundant factor" occurs. The Stolper-Samuelson theorem holds that as the price of the exported good—the output price—rises, the price of the factors used to make it (e.g., labor or raw materials) will change in the same direction, but more than proportionally.[26] One consequence of this is a disproportionate loss inflicted on the sector in which the country no longer enjoys a comparative advantage. It is this disadvantaged sector that must "make a sacrifice" in order for the rest of the country to enjoy the increased wealth that comes with specialization.

Rogowski argues that change in relative factor endowments can occur relatively rapidly as a result of technological development. To argue, for example, that the relative factor endowment of Prussia in "land" changed as a result of U.S. grain exports in the latter half of the nineteenth century (because of railroads, mechanical reapers, improved shipping, etc.) may not make intuitive sense, because the quantity of land in each place remained the same; but under the terms of the two theorems, it does make sense to say that, in effect, the reward for owning land in Prussia has declined. The decline means not only that Prussian landowners will earn less, but also that other "factors" of the economy may stand to gain disproportionately more in response to the shift in relative factor endowments. Rogowski argues that shifts such as these can provoke massive political conflicts as the "disadvantaged" strive to use state power to compensate for the "natural" or "exogenous" shock to the previous state of political and economic equilibrium. Shifts in relative factor endowments can be the exogenous cause of radical reorientations in the struggle for control of state power and in the character of rule in each state.

The reliance on the Heckscher-Olin and Samuelson-Stolper theorems is not problem free. As Paul Krugman points out, these theorems do not always appear to describe reality. Contrary to what one would expect, the developed countries trade mostly similar goods, and mostly with one another.[27] This does not mean that the theorems are wrong; but it may indicate that caution is required in adopting them wholesale into a model of political behavior of nation-states. In addition, there is a peculiar circularity to the argument: Changes in relative factor endowments affect the competition for state power, but state power affects relative factor endowments. When the change is effected by instruments, such as the tariff, its "artificiality" is evident. However, the Heckscher-Olin theorem acknowledges that differences in "taste" for a good between countries may translate into changes in relative factor endowments; that is, the difference in relative demand affects the relative price commanded by a good in two different countries and leads to greater reward for the input factor goods in the country of higher demand. The greater reward leads, ceteris paribus, to a "comparative advantage" for the country with the greater demand.[28] This leaves us with some peculiar problems of potential manipulation. Advertising and demand management devices (such as Japan's de facto requirement that automobiles be retired after six years)[29] can help to establish comparative advantages that eventually become entrenched in the economic landscape. If consumers in Japan were to win the right to own their cars for ten years or longer, it would effectively change the country's relative factor endowment.

Rogowski's approach tells us very little about the actual relationship between business and the state, other than that, in its broad movements, this relationship must reflect changes in factor endowments—which perhaps we might construe as a dressed up version of the old "changes in the forces of production" argument. Conflict, adjustment, political alliances, and antagonisms are specified. But to understand the process of political struggle, we would have to leave Rogowski's level of generalization and refer to his sources, where we would find the usual array of class, interest group, and other kinds of analyses. Rogowski's approach would show how the "deck is stacked" in favor of one group or another. The research agenda would appear to reside either in refining and quantifying the factor endowment losses and gains of respective groups, including business (industrial, agricultural, financial) and labor (all types), or perhaps in a more detailed analysis of how political struggle impacts the formation of, as well as derives from, shifting comparative advantages.

Institutionalist Theory

Institutionalist theory, like neopluralist theory, focuses on domestic struggles for control of policy outcomes. These outcomes may in turn impact the international system of which a state is a part or may be considered from the point of view of their "internal" aspect. Unlike neopluralist theory, however, it stresses particular institutional forms of the state, and the influence that these play on all actors, in constraining outcomes. Thus for Peter Katzenstein, industrial policy in "small states in world markets" reflects institutional adaptations that are partially determined by states' environments.[30] Large states have the luxury of being protectionist in the event of major changes in the terms of international trade. Small states cannot survive on such a strategy. The inability to rely on protectionism forces labor and capital to live together in ways that do not happen in a large country like the United States. Democratic corporatism works to facilitate bargaining among players in the small state's national economy.

If we ask what kinds of demands will workers and capital place upon the state, the answer is that their demands and their willingness to compromise are in part functions of their institutional environments; therefore, the character of political struggle and its outcomes will be different. Paulette Kurzer, rebutting Katzenstein but staying within the institutionalist framework, argues that the degree of central bank independence (an institutional arrangement) plays a role in limiting (or not limiting) the ability of capital to leave the country.[31] This, in turn, has an impact on the ability of labor coalitions to resist attempts to dismantle the welfare state.

Other institutionalists also usually try to determine "how the game is played" within existing institutions, how this affects the goals of actors, and therefore, how this affects outcomes. Even though this work usually rejects a naive view of the "public interest" or "national interest" as the motive for state actions, there is a sense in which constraints upon states and institutions can be seen as systemic, and actors must respond to these systemic constraints. To the extent that the "system" is a system of states competing for power, there is a potential for institutionalism to become the internal, or domestic, aspect of realist or neomercantilist theories that stress the external, foreign policy dimensions of state power. Theda Skocpol's statement that "any state first and fundamentally extracts resources from society and deploys these to create and support coercive and administrative organizations"[32] looks very much like the domestic side of the argument advanced by Kenneth Waltz. The struggle to isolate institutional factors and ideology as determinants of political outcomes is characteristic.

The research agenda of institutionalist theory, like that of neopluralist theory, often requires detailed political analysis of specific outcomes in specific countries. The goals of business "count," but they are significantly determined by the impact institutions have on defining those goals. Where business is taken into consideration, it is usually on a sectoral basis. If societal approaches (such as neopluralism) tend to gloss over institutional differences among nations, statist or institutionalist approaches tend precisely to emphasize these differences as having a determining impact on outcomes. Understanding the international system means understanding the sum of the nation-specific institutions that affect states' behavior toward the international system.

Neopluralist Theory

In the good old days, pluralist studies by such writers as V. O. Key, Ida Tarbell, R. E. Schattschneider, and Charles Beard and G.H.E. Smith did an excellent job of describing the jockeying for state power by business groups.[33] The state was a competitive arena for interest group struggles, which were often chronicled in great detail. The theories had no explicit international relations dimension as such. One can deduce an international political economy component from Schattschneider because the subject matter is tariffs. Beard and Smith chronicle the seesaw battles among nineteenth-century interest groups. The international effects of these political struggles for control were sometimes quite dramatic, as with the case of the Philippines. The pluralist theory extended its reach into international relations without, apparently, self-consciously realizing that it was paving a road to pluralist international relations theory, though Beard and Smith's *Idea of National Interest* is a possible exception.

Today's neopluralists continue to emphasize business interests and have added a great deal of theoretical elegance to the original formulations, but the emphasis on business factionalism, the desire to control the state, and the tendency to relegate class struggle to the background remain characteristic.[34] The emphasis of the neopluralists, as a group, is on specifically situating the relationship of business and the state to international outcomes. Examples in this category include the work of David Gibbs, Ronald Cox, Thomas Ferguson, Joel Rogers, Jeffry Frieden, David Abraham, and James Nolt.[35] The posture of states toward the international arena is explicitly derived from the interplay of domestic and internationalist coalitions.[36] This work, however, has typically focused on internationalist coalitions *within* countries and has not described multiple outcomes across many countries at once, as described in the following section. Ferguson's work has the additional characteristic of seeing public opinion as a dependent variable in the struggle among business groups. Gibbs's focus on a struggle that is by definition "international" further refines his point to distinguish among different "internationalists." The work is recognizably descended from the Beard-Schattschneider tradition—a productive one, regardless of gratuitous putdowns by doctrinaire institutionalists like Skocpol and Margaret Weir.[37]

For better or for worse, it is a feature of U.S. politics that to identify state actions as emanating from the business sector delegitimates the state, whereas to emphasize the state's ability to optimize some kind of public goal legitimates it.[38] Important theoretical consequences follow from these attitudinal differences. Statists and institutionalists, identifying state-centric motivations for certain actions, are wont to accuse neopluralists of either oversimplification or ideological obstinacy in refusing to see that state actors do have their own motivations, apart from the dynamics of politically motivated economic actors in society.

If one twists the arm of a neopluralist, he or she will concede that there is no formal reason to discount the possibility of motivations specific to state actors. But the neopluralist is acutely aware of the obstacles in identifying and understanding the complex maneuvering of major business players in politics. Much of the written record is routinely destroyed or never written down. On the other hand, politicians and regulators trumpet to the press and all who will listen the "public interest" rationale for their actions. There is no shortage of preserved records (in the press, in memoranda, published memoirs, etc.) to shore up statist interpretations. But for the neopluralist this means simply that the preservation of the historical record is biased. Institutionalist interpretations of events are suspect of being sloppy research. It is easy to do a superficial reading of materials, decide that business interests were disorganized or not influential, and then conclude that the major influences were ideological or institutional. Consequently, for the neopluralist, statist interpretations can look tautological. Statists often appear to start from a position of not wishing to find conclusive evidence of business conflicts. When that is the case, research may become superficial, and it is easy to come up with a fancy, but perhaps inaccurate, theoretical explanation. [39]

The institutionalist retort to this would be that neopluralists are trying to find a business conspiracy in every closet. A more serious formulation of their objection would be that the kind of "muckraking" discoveries that often "prove" relationships between business and the state may in fact only prove that business was pressuring the state to do what it would have done anyhow, for other reasons. From any theoretical perspective, the attribution of intent and motivation to state activities remains at once extremely problematic and at the core of many serious academic disagreements.

To some extent, the societal or neopluralist approach must rest on the presumption that the development of worldwide capitalism is tending to make politics in different countries follow the same competitive dynamics. To understand outcomes, one must therefore look at the balance of power among groups—especially, but not solely, business groups. In the statist approach, institutions channel and shape the development of capitalist and other forms of struggle; institutions are the rocks that jut out of the sea. For the neopluralist, these rocks are sinking beneath the waves. All over the world, business groups struggle with one another for power. Institutional arrangements are more the dependent outcomes of this process than the determinants of it. The research agenda therefore places a premium on identifying business groups and how they seek to manipulate state power. Where corporations are large enough to stand on their own as interest groups, the analysis becomes firm-specific.

Transnational Structuring

"Transnational structuring" is a term advanced by Gregory Nowell to describe business interest group politics on a global scale. [40] It is in method and assumptions a direct application of the neopluralist tradition. It may therefore be considered either a subset of that work or a logical extension of it. The chief innovation of this approach is that it assumes that international corporations pursue political objectives simultaneously in many countries. The number of countries might be as little as two (simple transnational structuring) or many states across the globe (complex transnational structuring). The emphasis of the approach is not so much on outcomes—since these are constantly changing—as on the continuous process of international struggle.

In this continuous political struggle, state institutions can be created and dismantled. State power is at once an outcome of the process and a partial determinant of that outcome. The posited goals of corporations vary according to time and circumstances. Cumulatively, the process of transnational structuring can lead to the creation of state institutions in many nations. The world oil cartel of 1928–1942, and its surviving fragments (the Texas Railroad Commission, the Direction des Carburants in France, and entities in the Middle East and elsewhere) are examples. The cartel eventually broke up, but it left the world energy market a different place. Therefore, this approach to some extent addresses statist concerns with institutions, since the persistence of the institutions (even after the sponsoring business groups have been evicted or lost interest in them) indicates a role for state autonomy. The transnational structuring approach also concedes the validity of realism as a separate logic that also determines state behavior, particularly in war. Since realist behavior implies that somewhere in the state there are people making decisions that are based on criteria other than those of societal actors, a space has been left in the theory for institutional influences as local (national) phenomena.

On the other hand, the only existing case study is ruthless in dismissing national institutional differences as having any bearing in understanding the operations of the pre–World War II oil market. Countries as widely different as Great Britain, Iraq, France, Germany, the United States, and so on, were caught up in the same dynamic struggle to rationalize world oil markets. From the institutionalist perspective, we would expect that the very different types of institutions and cultures of these states would lead to highly dissimilar oil policy outcomes. Instead, we find a tightly coordinated system of global market coordination, enacted in spite of the member states' many differences, due to the sustained efforts of a closely knit group of oil companies that worked worldwide in many different political environments. If a corner is reserved for institutionalist approaches in *Mercantile States and the World Oil Cartel*, it is a small corner.[41]

Realists see economic actors as resources to be used by states; in transnational structuring, state power is a resource used by firms. The two arenas of action are not antagonistic but, rather, orthogonal, and it is possible for the "power drive" of the state to be thwarted by economic arrangements put together by international interests, often in coordination with local domestic interests. The only way to distinguish among all these possibilities is through detailed analysis of the specific case; as with the neopluralist approach, the difficulty of finding preserved materials (for history) or getting any materials at all (for current events) biases available evidence against the approach.

Transnational structuring differs from regime theory because it does not see "state objectives" as central to the process. Indeed, the promulgation of official "public interest" justifications of either interventionist or liberal trade policies is a dependent variable. The public interest justifications adopted by state officials are an outcome of the process of struggle for control of international markets. Whereas regime theory is most comfortable describing liberal trade agreements organized by states, transnational structuring describes both liberal and nonliberal outcomes as part of one process.

That is, if a regime theorist saw a world of ten states in which five were highly protectionist and five devotees of free trade, the free traders would be assigned "regime status" and the protectionist states would be seen as "the pole of realist competition," described earlier. But from the perspective of transnational structuring, although the regime interpretation is not necessarily excluded, it is equally possible that the five protectionist countries are all organized into a single cartel; their protectionism results from the use of state power to ration the flow of the world commodity into a major consuming area. The five free trade states might be states in which the cartel had reached reasonably stable agreements among its principals without the need for state power to provide enforcement; or it might describe other outcomes. But in the "strong version" of transnational structuring, the policies of all ten countries would be the outcome of simultaneous lobbying by selected firms. To look for a "regime" is to misunderstand the worldwide political process.

From the viewpoint of transnational structuring, the strategic outcomes of "realist" state competition can have an important impact on the process of world competition among firms. Conversely, the resources wielded by corporations and their international market regulation arrangements can have an impact on the ability of states to compete in the realist sense of the term.

Transnational structuring offers, therefore, an opportunity to extend the neopluralist emphasis on business power to a world scale, looking at the cumulative process of interest group struggle as it affects nations, their institutions, and their economic policies and development. Its focus is on the market-regulating behavior of countries within an international capitalist economy. Since it is rare that the member firms of an entire industrial sector have operations in the same countries, the analysis almost of necessity must be firm-specific.

Concluding Thoughts

The summaries of theories offered here cannot do full justice to the various traditions and do not pretend to offer the full menu of major authors in each. Learning these different approaches and defining one's own stance in relation to them is synonymous with becoming professionally involved in the intersecting fields of international relations, international political economy, and comparative political economy. Were it not a cliché, it would be tempting to say that each tradition brings to the combined field of study some grain of truth worthy of consideration.

I believe the cliché to the extent that many of these studies have made important empirical and theoretical contributions, but I cannot entirely concur with such a Clintonesque exercise in compromise. In my view, some of these traditions, especially realism, seriously distort our understanding of the world system. Regime theory is too state-centric and, ultimately, too strongly linked to realist theory as a background set of assumptions. Cartel theory is fascinating, if dated, reading. Hilferding, in particular, provides important insights into how tariff protection can turn into a competitive advantage. It is worthwhile to consider how the cartel theory does and does not apply to world capitalism today; it may be more in need of adaptation than premature consignment to obsolescence. World-system theory could probably assimilate, in some form, virtually all of the approaches surveyed here. As a consequence, it is difficult to see what kind of business-related research agenda would be of special relevance to it; but perhaps its chief value lies, like a figurehead monarch, not so much in function as in the image of grandeur. Factor endowment theory strikes me as worthy of further consideration, but I think that ultimately once the "endowments" are known, the process of "understanding what happened" metamorphoses into the neopluralist or the institutionalist approach.

I am wary of institutionalism because it is extremely easy to underestimate the power of business and also to underestimate the bias in the preservation of historical materials. Furthermore, I believe that the struggle for market control is a fundamental characteristic of politics in the capitalist world: Regardless of each nation's institutional arrangements, the objectives of the struggle for market control are the same in many different kinds of national environments. And, indeed, so are the outcomes.

I find the neopluralist approach to be useful in that it continually adds to our understanding of the dynamics of political competition to control the market (whether in a "regulated" or "deregulated" condition). Such an exercise is fundamental not only to understanding the politics of market economies in a given era, but also to understanding the transitions from one dominant pattern of technology to the next. My particular emphasis, therefore, has been on the extension of the neopluralist approach to worldwide dimensions, even though the descriptive term I use, "transnational structuring," is a regrettable addition to a discipline already overburdened with jargon.

10

Business Conflict and Theories of the State

🎗

Daniel Skidmore-Hess

At a time when neo-Marxist state theory has become, in the opinion of one of its leading practitioners, "esoteric and often inaccessible and/or irrelevant to those working in other traditions,"[1] the development of the business conflict model suggests otherwise. Rather than add another layer to the already sizable literature concerned with defining the appropriate abstract formulation of the state, the business conflict approach augurs a healthy empirical and historical turn in the study of political institutions. The value of the business conflict model lies in its detailed attention to tensions and contradictions within and among intraclass capitalist interests, as well as in the potential payoffs this approach might provide toward a more concrete understanding of contemporary state institutions. In this chapter, I argue that alternative pluralist and Marxist approaches are less adequate to the understanding of business conflict. However, I also argue that a more sophisticated theoretical understanding of the nature of state institutions, and of the ideological means by which state policies are legitimated, will need to be developed by business conflict theorists in order to make the model more adequate (without losing its distinct virtues as an empirically and historically oriented method).

The dominant positions within Marxist state theory have been instrumentalism and structuralism. As these two broad positions are fairly well known to students of both contemporary political theory and political institutions, I will avoid a detailed discussion of them at this point.[2] Nonetheless, a few brief summary comments are pertinent. The instrumentalist view emphasizes the extent to which the state is a tool or device of the capitalist class.[3] In this view, agency is a matter of social class formations acting to attain what is, or what they perceive to be, their best interests. Politics and state policies are determined by economics.

The structuralist view,[4] in contrast, declares that the state is relatively autonomous of direct control by the capitalist class. However, the state is not fully autonomous in the sense of being an independent social agency that acts in its own best interests, à la the Machiavellian prince. To the contrary, in structuralist Marxism, state autonomy is seen as a means by which the authoritative functioning of the legal and political systems on behalf of capitalism is assured. The argument here is that a structurally autonomous state can act against the shortsighted preferences of some business groups in such a manner as to preserve the capitalist system. The historical development of the welfare state has been cited as a premier example of how the state is structurally and functionally capitalist even when it acts against the express wishes of many capitalists.[5]

The problem with both approaches from the point of view of historical and empirical research is that they operate at such a general level of abstraction as to provide little or no ground-level insight into the particular debates, compromises, and infighting between interest groups and factions in contemporary capitalist democracy. As Joshua Cohen and Joel Rogers argue, "after abstracting from the distinctive features of a particular system, one cannot expect to account for everything about its functioning. Since the basic framework is shared by many states, it cannot for example account for the often quite important differences among capitalist democracies."[6] The broad assumptions of capitalist class coherence made in structuralist and instrumentalist Marxism are particularly questionable. Although in other capitalist democracies, business conflict may be heavily mediated by corporatist structures and traditions, business class conflict in such areas as monetary, trade, and immigration policy has been endemic throughout U.S. history.

To summarize the typical critiques of the two major Marxist approaches without going into great detail: In the instrumentalist approach, the business class is a monolithic actor; the mere implication of business conflict as a central determinant of policy suggests schizophrenia. In this approach, one would have to assume that some sector of capital was suffering from false consciousness and failing to maintain intraclass solidarity within the class struggle. In the structuralist approach, there could be some expression of intraclass tension, but it would have to be considered secondary to the state's function as a kind of supermanager, or board of directors of capitalism in general. However, for a structuralist approach to be valid, two problematic assumptions must be made. First, one must accept that the state always acts in the best interests of capitalism, and second, that there is a singular best interest for all capitalists.

It should be acknowledged that even within a non-Marxist framework, it is very nearly a truism to state that the contemporary state acts to preserve existing socioeconomic relations. At least since Hobbes, the overriding assumption of modern political thought has been that the state works to sustain order and, thereby, preexisting social, legal, and cultural systems. Or, when social and political change occurs, the states channels it into legally controlled processes that constrain change to specific issues or policies while perpetuating such social institutions as markets, property, and the corporation. However, historically exceptional regimes have occurred that violate the generalization that the state functions to conserve the social order.

Stalin's and Mao's revolutions from above could be cited as examples of complete state autonomy when the state acted as agency of transformation rather than reproduction of social relations. However, even in these two cases, subsequent Chinese and Russian history suggests the eventual need for the state, even in a command economy, to recognize and protect particular social interests. In these cases (although to differing degrees), the managerial and technical strata, the foreign investors, and the state capitalists that provided the material bases of state power in the form of economic surplus, foreign exchange, and military and civilian infrastructure were ultimately provided with measures of privilege and assurances against expropriation.

The crucial point to be made about structuralist Marxist approaches to the state is that although the capitalist state does act in the interests of the capitalist system, it does not necessarily follow that the state acts in the interests of capitalists. A further point to be made is that although all business groups do have an obvious and fundamental common interest in the continued existence of free enterprise, one cannot logically conclude that this commonality of interests is sufficient to induce all businesses to function as a coherent class formation.

The business conflict model points out that there are deep cleavages and contradictions within and among different business sectors and that these sectoral differences are crucial to understanding the contemporary state. We can make an analytical distinction that would allow that, at least theoretically, at moments of acute systematic crisis the consciousness of common class interests might come to grip the minds of business people in general (perhaps in Chile in 1973?). Or it might be the case that at crucial historical junctures the semiautonomous state will act to conservatively reform the business system over the objections of many corporate leaders (perhaps in the case of the New Deal?). Yet when the system is not in sharp crisis, I would argue, such fundamental commonalities of interests among economic and state elites are secondary to their differences and disagreements over alternative policy options. Thomas Ferguson makes the point with regards to business conflict in U.S. presidential elections: "The chance of one candidate simultaneously satisfying high- and low-tariff advocates, labor-intensive and high-tech firms, or exporters and importers is zero."[7]

Ferguson also provides the example of the change in U.S. trade policy during the 1930s as a crucial historical shift in which business conflict played a central role. He argues that the economic crisis of the period allowed for a shift in political power from domestic-market-oriented manufacturing and protectionist groups to a "multinational bloc" of internationally oriented investment bankers, exporters, and advanced technology firms. Crucial to this example is that the very policies that were geared to benefit the multinationalists (free trade, foreign aid, and public subsidies for education, research, and development) were opposed by, and perceived as extremely detrimental to, the protectionist groups. Indeed, it can be argued that state policies facilitated the near destruction of some older, low-technology, labor-intensive industries (shoe manufacturing, for example) while promoting the growth of others such as the new "information industries."

The past six decades of internationalist-oriented policies that have been highly beneficial to some business sectors, while detrimental to others, are difficult to explain within a structuralist Marxist perspective. A structuralist perspective would suggest that these policies were adopted in order to ensure the reproduction of capitalist social relations; yet unless one assumes that policymakers have insight into the historical evolution of capitalism, this explanation is difficult to accept. Absent historical determinism, one must turn to historical and empirical studies of which particular coalitions of interests succeeded in gaining the adoption of beneficial policies and which failed, in order to better understand the nature of the state in its relation to the political economy.

It might be suggested at this point that there is a certain degree of convergence with pluralist analysis in that the business conflict model adopts sectoral groups, rather than classes, as its unit of analysis. Furthermore, a third strand of neo-Marxism, which defines the state as an arena of class struggle, also seems to have moved in the direction of the pluralist perspective.[8] In this perspective, classes other than capital can gain influence within the state. In this "class struggle" version of neo-Marxism, however, classes, not interest groups, remain the units of analysis. Thus it could be argued that there are two types of nonpluralist theory that are converging upon the idea that state policy is a product of multifaceted business conflicts.

Bob Jessop's summary of Nicos Poulantzas's later thinking shows the clear similarity of class struggle Marxism with the business conflict model: "Contradictions among the dominant classes and fractions in the power bloc and between the dominant and dominated classes are necessarily reproduced within the economic activities of the state."[9] This kind of neo-Marxist analysis, which emphasizes the central role of class struggle, moves very strongly in the direction of a societal-based mode of analysis, without reducing the state to an epiphenomenon of supposedly monolithic dominant class interests. Essentially, the argument, which Poulantzas made in an abstract manner, is that state policy is contingent upon the relative position of classes and class fractions within the class struggle—what Antonio Gramsci referred to as the "war of position" of modern political life. Ferguson makes a similar point when he argues that in nineteenth-century U.S. politics, "state policy could have promoted organizing and political activity among small farmers and labor" but did not due to the influence of powerful political investors. Not until the New Deal, argues Ferguson, "did any important segment of the mass population acquire much importance as political investors. Before that date, the major investors ... consisted entirely of businessmen."[10] The point for Ferguson, as for Poulantzas, is that the role of the state is relative to the strength of the various societal actors who seek to influence it.

Indeed, theoretical convergence can even be said to be three-sided, since pluralists now tend to admit that business interests have more influence than do other groups (a point that class struggle–oriented neo-Marxists would certainly insist upon). The three broad perspectives that societal-based models of the state adopt can be summarized as follows: (1) state policy as outcome of business conflict; (2) state policy as product of interest group conflict within which business groups are most influential (Dahlian pluralism); and (3) state policy as product of class struggle within which capitalists dominate, but not necessarily always. Clearly, there are distinct differences here with regard to what is the proper unit of analysis (respectively, sectoral business interests, interest groups, classes) and to how much power nonbusiness groups might have (none, some, little). Yet these differences do not seem so great anymore as does the vast gulf between, say, Ralph Miliband's instrumentalism and Robert Dahl's earlier pluralist formulations.

At the present time, the crucial divide in state theory and research may no longer be between pluralists and neo-Marxists so much as between statists and societalists. One the one hand, there is a broad tendency among societalists to recognize the dominance of business interests; on the other hand, there has been a developing literature on the role of state elites as historical subjects with their own specific interests and political projects.[11] Statist approaches suggest that all social groups and classes are relatively powerless when the state acts in accord with the *raison d'état,* or national interest. It could be argued that rarely, if ever, do state interests appear to contradict dominant business interests, given the many ways in which state and dominant groups are mutually dependent for material and ideological resources. Certainly, it is exceedingly difficult, if not impossible, to imagine some critical case that would test the relative power of dominant business groups versus state elites.

I argued earlier that the fully autonomous state was the exception, rather than the rule, at the systematic level of analysis. However, in terms of more mundane explanations of policy and state activity, there is some balance to be struck between state autonomy and societal influences. In theory, there appears to be a fundamental divide between these research programs; their central assumptions about the basis of political power seem to be directly at odds. In terms of carrying out empirical state research, however, I would argue that it is not necessary to commit fully to either side of the state/society divide. Although the business conflict model is strongly imbued with a societal perspective, business conflict researchers may pay attention to the mediating and determining roles played by state institutions without accepting the abstract thesis that "national interest" is the last-instance determinant of state action.

To some extent, the business conflict model tends to operate with a "black box" model of the state, out of which outcomes suited to the most powerful business groups or coalitions inevitably emerge. Cox's work on U.S. foreign economic policy presents a subtle, but crucial, shift in business conflict thinking about the role of state institutions in shaping policy outcomes.[12] He describes state institutions as mediating variables and gives the example of how different business interests interact with the branches of the separated powers of the U.S. national government. Specifically, Cox shows that domestic manufacturing capitalists appear to have greater to access and influence with congressional representatives, while multinationalists have greater access to certain agencies of the executive branch (especially the State, Defense, Treasury, and Commerce Departments). Thus far, Cox has not fully developed an explanation as to why these particular nexuses have developed.

To his credit, Miliband had previously suggested that the state be thought of not so much as a unitary entity, but as a "state system" of interrelating institutions in a manner similar to what Cox seems to be suggesting. For Miliband, the elites within the state system were drawn from social elites, all of whom tended to share a common worldview.[13] While Miliband's elite analysis is salient regarding the ideological facets of policymaking, its does little to explain how the state as institutional framework influences outcomes. Hopefully, future development of the business conflict model will develop a means of integrating state institutions as explanatory variables.

Ultimately, I would argue that a situation of methodological pluralism is the preferred condition for scientific practice and that neither the state-oriented nor the society-oriented paradigms can be ultimately falsified. Furthermore, wise and opportunistic scholars might do well to borrow from both traditions. In what follows, I do not attempt to argue for the ultimate value of the business conflict model over either its statist or its societalist competitors; rather, I discuss where the business conflict model provides promising developments as well as where its limitations lie. I also suggest how the business conflict model might allow for a measure of state autonomy without losing its central focus on the dominance of, and conflicts among, business interests.

The business conflict model has been greatly influenced by the investment theory of politics as developed by Thomas Ferguson and his associates. As such, some readers well familiar with this literature may find it perplexing that I approach the business conflict model from the perspective of state theory. Neither Ferguson's investment model nor the business conflict model are theories of the state in the same sense as is the work of Miliband, Poulantzas, Jessop, Fred Block, Theda Skocpol, or any of the other scholars connected with the recent resurgence of state theory. The next section of this paper will address the strengths and weaknesses of "the state" as a political-theoretic category, with reference to its potential value for the future development of the business conflict model.

The Value and Limits of the State As Category

The value and limitation of the state as an analytic concept has been a notably controversial topic among political scientists. David Easton argued famously that "the word [state] ought to be abandoned entirely."[14] Yet even Easton admitted in the very same work that "no one can deny that political science is indeed interested in the state ... as one type of political institution."[15] Easton's rationale for dropping the usage of the state as a category was based upon his conclusion that previous political science had misconstrued the nature of politics by restricting itself to a narrow institutional arena, rather than studying the full range of political activity. For Easton, "the inadequacy of the state concept as a definition of subject matter stems from the fact that it implies that political science is interested in studying a particular kind of institution."[16] The crucial point in Easton's argument for this essay is that politics is understood as a dimension of human behavior that extends well beyond the public legal framework commonly recognized as "the state."

That nonstate agencies such as the family, religion, voluntary associations, and interest groups are crucial elements of any political system is hard to deny. To a certain extent, the business conflict model, as well as neo-Marxist state theory, finds common cause with Easton in his rejection of institutional formalism. In Eastonian behavioralism, as in the business conflict model, politics is conceptually understood as an activity into which goal-oriented individuals and groups participate. The crucial difference, of course, is that business conflict centers on the economic motivations of action, rather than the psychological approach that Easton favored.

Although Easton may well have been correct to emphasize the extent to which politics is an activity rather than an institution—and the business conflict model may be making a valid move to understand politics in terms of actions intended to benefit certain economic groups—it is still important to explain why the state is the particular institutional site around which this activity centers. The old behavioralist argument that there is no clear definition of the state, and hence the concept lacks rigor, is a weak criticism. Many concepts in political science exhibit a similar instability; indeed, the most contested concept of all might be "politics." The lack of a clear consensus on the definition of the state reflects historical variation in the form and function of states. Yet this does not mean, as Easton himself admitted, that the state in any particular instance is not a vitally important political institution.

Recently, a number of statist theorists have continued and extended a theoretical project, which had already to some extent been set in motion by neo-Marxism: namely, that of bringing the state back in. The work of this group, while it cannot be discussed at any great length here, is relevant to consider in that it does not attempt to resurrect the state from a formalist philosophical perspective. To the contrary, the neostatist literature reintroduces the state as institution, existent in a variety of social systems, that crucially affects social development and dynamics. The difference between Skocpol and Krasner, on the one hand, and Poulantzas and Jessop, on the other, is that the state is the central explanatory variable for the first group. Yet both neostatist and neo-Marxists see the state as a useful category in the study of political development.

For example, Skocpol's comparative study of revolutions emphasizes the state's monopoly on legitimate coercive force.[17] In her analysis, consequently, when the military loses confidence in and loyalty to the old regime, revolutionary groups have the opportunity to come to power. By contrast, any Marxian approach would emphasize that revolution is made by a social class. Yet Skocpol does not deny the importance of class or other societal formations; but as state theorist, she looks to the state apparatuses to understand the dynamics of political development. At a basic level, she is on common ground with neo-Marxism, especially its structuralist variant, when it emphasizes the state's vital strategic role in the process of accumulation.

Unlike Easton, business conflict analysts do not studiously avoid use of the concept "state." Yet business conflict theory has not put forth an explicit and fully developed model of the state and its functions, other than the general view that the state reflects the conflicts among business interests. In a seminal study by David Gibbs, who first termed this approach "the business conflict model," fairly minor attention was given to the role of the state qua institution in mediating business conflict and influence.[18] In a manner very similar to Milibandian instrumentalism, Gibbs emphasized the importance of personal contacts and financial connections between state and business elites, as well as the common social backgrounds of state and corporate personnel. Although these contacts and commonalities are no doubt important, they do not provide a full account of why and how business and state actors adopt the cooperative strategies that they typically exhibit in the area of foreign economic policy. Somewhat lacking in Gibbs's account is a fully detailed theoretical discussion of the importance of Zaire to the U.S. macroeconomy.

Like Easton, Gibbs leaves us without an explanation as to why the state apparatuses are the crucial means of achieving business goals such that foreign economic policy becomes a vital concern to many business investors; in other words, what it is about the *function* of the modern state that causes business not to adopt a laissez-faire attitude vis-à-vis politics. The implicit tendency toward instrumentalism in the business conflict literature leaves unstated why influencing state policy is vital from the standpoint of capitalist accumulation, or what is lost if specific business groups fail to influence policy in the manner they seek.

The value of a more refined concept of the state for the business conflict model would be to clarify the importance of public policy for business interests: what they seek to get out of political intervention or when, if ever, they might "go it alone" in the manner called for by classical free market political economy. Insofar as the business conflict model assumes politics to be contentious, it would not be inconsistent to conceptualize politics as a form of *strategic* activity into which business firms and other interests enter as a part of their overall approach to the pursuit of specific economic and social goals within the context of a market economy. To a great extent, this insight is already implicit in Gibbs's formulation of the business conflict model; the point, in the case of business firms, is to make explicit how politics fits into larger investment strategies (as Ferguson suggests).

As a focus of socially strategic action, the state must be assumed to have some resources to make influence over it, or access to it, worthwhile. I would argue, following two central themes in modern social theory, that the key resources that define the state are legitimacy and coercive force. Once any particular business interest is granted favorable state policies, the state tends to provide that interest with the legitimacy of the national interest. An example of this is the position taken by some elites that the protection of certain "key" industries is vital to national defense, or that new "high-tech" industries should be granted favorable tax incentives in order to keep the United States competitive in the world economy of the future. The pseudodemocratic process of U.S. policymaking will tend to grant legitimacy to those firms and interests that achieve success in gaining the adoption of their favored programs. However, the current intensified fiscal crisis of the state may be lessening the legitimacy so gained. Also, the coercive force of the state is of occasional strategic interest—either domestically, in terms of hindering organized labor, or in terms of foreign intervention. Finally, and most commonly, the state is a source of subsidy of various kinds: worker training, infrastructure, price supports, new product research, and so on.

This formulation of politics and the state as strategic action is similar to Bob Jessop's recent formulation of the capitalist state as an accumulation strategy.[19] However, Jessop's approach tends to be a restatement of structuralist Marxism in that it suggests that the state acts as a macro-, even an epochal, strategist of capitalist accumulation. Another recent work that develops, within a more statist perspective, the idea of the state as strategy of accumulation is Robert Bianchi's work on "unruly corporatism" in Egyptian development.[20] What could be of interest in Bianchi's work to business conflict theorists is that he does not assume that state elites achieve effective functional coordination of the institutions that they establish. An interesting theoretical parallel in a liberal context would be to assess to what extent business elites experience an inability to influence the evolution of new accumulation regimes (e.g., Fordism, the New Deal) once they are institutionalized.

Although it is not clear what the limits of business elites as dominant social agents are, it is clear that the business conflict model allows for contingency in public policy. The business conflict framework does not assume a macrofunctional capitalist state in order to understand state activities as part of a strategic interaction process. The business conflict approach allows one to avoid a grand theory of the state, of the kind Jessop himself disparages, yet still come to an understanding of the whys and wherefores of the form and function of the state as an arena of business conflict. One can have state theory within a broader understanding of the nature of political and social conflict without having a theory of the state.

Conceptualizing the state as an institutionalized setting of strategic action allows for the Eastonian insight that the state is but one of a number of sites of political activity (although, probably the most crucial, I would add). Also, construing the state as a venue of strategic action avoids the problem of failing to account for the larger social role of the state and for the motivations of various interests that attempt to influence state action. The important resources of coercion and legitimacy, in particular, provide incentives for businesses and other interests to seek access to the policymaking process. Understanding the state as a locus of strategic action and valuable political resources dovetails nicely with the business conflict model's intellectual debt to Ferguson's investment theory of politics, which largely focuses on the manner in which business interests invest in parties and candidates in order to attain favorable policy returns. What the business conflict model is accomplishing is the extension of Ferguson's insight that "what properly defines American party systems is not blocs of voters but patterns of interest group alignment and coalitions among major investors"[21] to the policymaking process of the state itself.

Like Ferguson's investment model of politics, the business conflict approach is largely predicated upon rational choice assumptions about social behavior. For Ferguson, parties, interest groups, candidates, and think tanks are foci of investment. In other words, the idea of the state as a resource and political action as a profit-seeking tactic is based on the assumption that, by and large, social and economic agents act in a utility-maximizing manner. This kind of macro-ontological framework does tend, however, to leave open many crucial questions when it comes to explaining the behavior of specific individuals and interests in various historical and cultural circumstances.

A rational choice approach faces some difficulty in explaining why some firms pursue certain public policy options with great enthusiasm, while other similarly interested entities remain relatively aloof. Further, there are cases when firms that appear to have very similar interests adopt opposing, or at least divergent, political tactics. These instances raise questions about the methodological problems of moving from the theoretical identification of objective interests to the subjective decisionmaking processes of individual social agents—questions that are underexamined in many economic approaches to political analysis. This aspect of the business conflict model will be discussed in further detail later; first, it will be useful to summarize the discussion thus far before moving on to a discussion of key methodological aspects of the business conflict model, including the problems of rational action assumptions.

To summarize the argument up to this point: The business conflict model provides the insight that politics in capitalist societies can be largely explained in terms of contradictions among divergent economic sectors and interests. Other than at moments of great systemic crisis, I have argued, the assumption of business conflict, rather than intrabusiness class cooperation, is closer to empirical and historical reality. Instrumentalist Marxism assumes that the capitalist class acts as a singular social actor, while structuralist Marxism sees the state as acting on behalf of the business system as a whole. Neither of the two previously dominant modes of Marxist state theory can, as such, adequately account for business conflict expressed in and among state institutions. Lacking in the business conflict model, however, is a sufficiently developed theory of what the role and purpose of state power is within the capitalist political economy as a whole. It would be consistent with the rational choice methodological assumptions of the business conflict model to view the state as the location of key institutional resources (legitimacy and coercive force, as well as public subsidies and revenues) crucial to the accumulation strategies of various economic groups, but most especially, of business.

What the Business Conflict Model Explains

Theoretically developing the business conflict model to address the problem of the state reveals a need for certain shifts of methodological emphasis. State theory is centrally concerned with interpreting the form and functions of a set of public *institutions,* while the business conflict model has been articulated primarily in the study of *policy.* In structural terms, state theory and the business conflict model are operating at different levels of analysis: state theory at a systemic level, while business conflict studies have been concerned to understand specific, conjunctural policy decisions.

Of course, in the social world, "levels of analysis" do not maintain their discretion—policies are made in, by, and through institutional agencies. The point, as I argued earlier, is not whether the model needs a concept of state, but what kind of state concept the business conflict model needs. If the future research focus is to remain on policy decisions, I would argue that attention needs to be given to form. In other words, attention needs to be given to the ways in which state agencies and business groups interact and the ways in which business interests are translated into policy. How the mediation of business interests by state institutions actually occurs and how the organization of interests and institutions allows for influence to be translated into policy become the crucial state theoretic questions in policy studies. A focus on function, conversely, by which I mean the role the state plays in the social system as a whole (reproduction of the mode of production in the terms of Marxian structuralism), would move analysis away from specific historical and empirical studies of state policy formulation. A functional approach, however, might be very useful for a *longue durée* history of business and state interaction patterns. Whether or not a functional approach to the state can be synthesized with business conflict assumptions is a question outside the scope of this chapter.

Previously, I discussed Cox's example of the different strategies employed by protectionist and multinationalist business groups in their efforts to influence policy. In this example, businesses favoring a protectionist orientation gained greater access to the state within the legislative branch of the U.S. national government, while internationalists had their greatest leverage in certain parts of the executive branch (especially the Departments of State, Treasury, and Commerce). This example points out an important dimension of the contemporary state: As a complex institutional matrix, the state is typified by an intricate division of labor. The political division of labor of the contemporary state apparatuses is apparently conducive to certain modes of interaction between the state and various interest groups. The implication also seems to be that the contemporary state is not a univocal entity, but one capable of interacting with, perhaps even gaining the confidence or acquiescence of, contradictory interests. Also possible, then, is that the state can pursue conflictual policies simultaneously on behalf of divergent interests.

Cox suggests that the state "mediates" business interests. One form this mediation might take is disaggregation; that is, by providing a number of subarenas in which interests can seek points of access and influence, the state mediates via disaggregation. In other words, the very goal of U.S. constitutional design expressed by Madison of separating powers and, thereby preempting the dominance of any faction or interest, may be the means by which business conflict is institutionally managed. This point may be even more relevant to considering how a democratic capitalist state adjusts to pressures from below and maintains its legitimacy to subaltern groups. The historical pattern of proliferating new state agencies and congressional committees, which become the institutional points of access for new social movements (e.g., the Labor Deptartment, Environmental Protection Agency, Department of Housing and Urban Development, etc.), might also be reconsidered in light of Cox's point.

Previous approaches, including pluralism, neo-Marxism, and statism (especially this last, with its assumptions of the state as univocal agency), all tend to ignore the phenomena of state disaggregation. Within the business conflict model, however, there may be means to develop a better understanding of how the complex form of the contemporary state interacts with, and facilitates conflictual economic interests for the ultimate benefit of, certain business interests.

Essentially, the business conflict model explains the strategic bases in economic interests of policy decisions. The crucial theoretical question of the state for future business conflict research is to what extent the form of the state as institutional matrix can be added into the business conflict equation without disturbing the core assumptions of this emergent research program. The business conflict model leads us to predict that business interests will conflict based upon their sectoral economic orientations. Yet, as capitalist society's controllers of economic resources, these interests will dominate policymaking overall. The notion of the disaggregated state should provide some means of understanding how lesser business interests, or even nonbusiness groups, can attain some access, even some limited success, in influencing policy, without the state ceasing to be dominated by business interests. By understanding the state as a complex division of political labor, with subarenas of interest group articulation, we can begin to develop an understanding of the political investment strategies of various interests as well.

The view of the state that I am describing here does, however, leave open the extent to which the state is a specifically capitalist state. A disaggregated state is one in which the ruling class does not rule, as Fred Block argues,[22] but instead reproduces existing social relations accidentally, by systematically preempting the possibilities of political change simply by the force of complexity. Here is a crucial theoretical dialogue into which the business conflict model might enter with class struggle oriented neo-Marxism, as well as with pluralism.

Business Hegemony/Business Conflict

Possibly the most critical theoretical problem that the business conflict model faces is the apparent paradox of simultaneous business conflict and capitalist hegemony—especially if the internal differentiation of the state is considered as opening up the possibility that subaltern social groups can, at points, gain access and influence over some areas of public policy. Ultimately, this is not just a question of state institutions, but also one of social formations; that is, which groups are sufficiently well organized to effect policy decisions. There are grounds for arguing that business groups have superior capacity to overcome what Mancur Olson has termed "collective action" problems and form effective interest groups and organizations.[23] Given smaller numbers, strong economic incentives, and lower costs of access to the means of communication and fund-raising, business interests have many social advantages in developing effective interest representation.

In terms of state theory, however, there is a two-sided question that must be confronted about state and business interest mediation: (1) To what extent do business interests limit the state and its ability to respond to popular demands? (2) To what extent does the state as institution, especially the liberal democratic state, limit the ability of business groups to achieve their preferred policy goals, either because they are checked by other interest groups or because state decisionmakers must proceed within acceptable ideological parameters?

James O'Connor's well-known argument that there is an inherent contradiction between the popular and the capitalist demands placed on the contemporary liberal state is relevant to this discussion.[24] The contemporary liberal state, it is said, attempts to please both popular demands for social welfare and powerful business pressures for preferential tax treatment and/or other forms of public subsidy. The result is a fiscal crisis of the state, as well as a tax squeeze on the middle-income groups, which undermines the legitimacy of the welfare state.

O'Connor's view would seem to be consistent with the notion of a disagreggated state. Indeed, the key insight of the business conflict model would suggest further that the contemporary state may be caught in a contradiction between conflicting business interests, as well as popular demands for increased funding of social programs, and middle-class tax cuts.

The current health crisis seems to be a pertinent example that calls for a detailed business conflict study. The current system of public subsidy for the elderly and poor (Medicare and Medicaid, respectively) has been, historically, of great benefit to the health care industry due to the lack of effective cost controls. Yet spiraling health care costs in the public sector have exacerbated the fiscal crisis of the state. Paralleling the public health funding problems has been a crisis of market failure in the private insurance industry, with close to half of the population unable to afford adequate coverage. The crucial element, however, in recent moves toward reform seems to be the increased costs to business of providing coverage to workers. To some extent, companies can seek to roll back employee benefits; but they might also adopt the less confrontational strategy of seeking governmental subsidy. Some firms, especially those in unionized or export-oriented sectors, are now actively supporting an increased level of state intervention in the health care area.

The value of a business conflict analysis in studying the health care issue is that it would lead us to predict that universal, publicly insured health care would likely remain off the public agenda until such time as there was sufficient business support, or at least acquiescence toward reform. In other words, labor unions and liberal reformers may have been calling for these reforms for decades, but it was only when the cost of health care to business became a source of competitive disadvantage that health care reform became possible.

At the present time, business interests in the health care industry (pharmaceuticals, insurance, and medical professionals) and others opposed to employer-mandated health insurance coverage have succeeded in curbing some of the more progressive reform impulses. Yet the likelihood remains that the fiscal crisis problem will only intensify as health industry profits, in effect, become even more publicly subsidized. Either way, this issue will continue to tell us something about the limits of state autonomy, the ability of the state to act in a coherent manner in response to social crisis, and/or the limits of business interest group power.

Power in the business conflict model is understood in terms of resources, organizational and otherwise. The idea is that a bloc of business interests, sometimes with popular allies, will generally succeed in winning control of the state. This approach is similar to the classical Marxist notion that historical blocs of class fractions are crucial to establishing long-term patterns of capitalist development, as Gramsci argued vis-à-vis Fordism.

Gramsci's notion of hegemony suggests that the capitalist ruling class, or fractions thereof, could attain the consent, even the active support, of subaltern classes such as the peasantry or workers.[25] Essentially, this is what Ferguson seems to be arguing occurred in the United States during the New Deal era: A multinationalist bloc of business investors coalesced within the Democratic Party alongside labor and other popular groups, such as civil rights activists. This historic bloc lasted well into the 1960s as the hegemonic power in U.S. politics. Most analyses of the dissolution of the New Deal have focused on the internal cultural contradictions, between the white and the black working class for example, or between lower-class social welfare recipients and middle-class taxpayers.

However, a business conflict approach would suggest that business interests would be hegemonic within any dominant bloc in a capitalist society. Yet there is the critical question of what is the agency of bloc coalescence: Ferguson's work suggests that it is business interests that quietly succeed in forming these blocs, while a more statist approach would see this formation as the role of the political leadership. In either scenario, however, power is a matter of resources and organization.

Although the business conflict approach to power has many affinities to classical Marxism, its more immediate intellectual debts are to rational choice theory. Rational choice assumptions provide powerful simplifying abstractions that allow for prediction of the self-interested behavior patterns of social agents. However, when it comes to the question of integrating ideological factors into analysis, crucial difficulties arise. Individuals in society do not, of course, make their decisions in the rarified air of formal decision models but, rather, in discourses of common social and political concepts and accepted cultural mores.

Of course, many business and investment decisions are phenomenologically quite similar to rational choice theory. The crucial question here is to what extent business "holds politicians more or less like stocks."[26] Business conflict analysis must come to terms with the issue of whether the ideologies by which business interests seek to attain public legitimacy (free enterprise, property rights, increased productivity, national security, etc.) are to be treated in an instrumental fashion, reducible to a strictly utilitarian calculus. Or can the business conflict model allow that ideology is also an independent determinant of policy? Are the discourses by which interest group politics are pursued simply so much obscuration of the underlying interests, or do they somehow partly create public understandings of which interests are at stake in any political conflict?

Recent developments in analytical Marxism use rational choice theory to suggest that popular consent to capitalist hegemony is not simply a matter of false consciousness. One might argue that information costs are too high for many individuals to effectively understand how their interests are at stake in many political issues, thus preempting effective participation. Or, perhaps, as Adam Przeworski has argued, the costs of systemic transformation are too high for the working class—better to seek improvement of one's position within the existing hegemonic framework.[27]

While I do not wish to question the validity of Przeworski's analysis, it does serve to point out a key difficulty in any rational choice approach: that rational choice theory has a problem of *horizon*. What I mean by this term, borrowed from Gadamer,[28] is that utility-maximizing assumptions do not tell us in what secular frame social actors are making their calculations. This is similar to the problem with structuralist Marxism: We must ask if business interests are pursuing strategic action geared toward fairly immediate payoffs (such as a tax cut would bring) or toward much longer-term rewards—such as a better trained workforce in future years (which public investment in education might bring). The concept of the horizon of action should, I would argue, be added to the business conflict model's attention to economic sectoral influences in interpreting business political strategies. Indeed, it is not a particularly radical departure in that contemporary management theory acknowledges differences in business philosophy between managerial conservatives who seek to minimize short-term costs and others who see management as something more akin to corporatist planning. The crucial point here is that there are ideological differences among capitalists as to the nature of how free enterprise is to be pursued, what the proper role of the state is, and on which horizons profit is to be sought. These differences are interrelated with sectoral interests, but probably irreducible thereto.

Jeffry Frieden, whose work on Latin American debt has greatly influenced the development of the business conflict model, has stated that "all else equal, social actors prefer public policies that maximize their incomes."[29] What is lacking in this statement is any notion of time frame. In the long run, the statement is a truism, certainly so far as business interests are concerned. Yet in the short and medium run, it has serious flaws. If by "incomes" Frieden means maximizing profits in the near term, this might cause the firm to lose long-term profitably if profit-reducing reinvestment is not made. Some management philosophies urge revenue, rather than profit-maximizing strategies (since profit is offset by the depreciation accrued from investments). More conservative managers seek to reduce expenses, while others focus more on market share and see cost control as of lesser importance. My hypothesis is that some schools of management practice would lead business executives to emphasize fiscal conservatism in politics, while others would take a more "liberal" approach, favorable to government intervention of various kinds that created new markets or rationalized competition in existing industries.

Within Frieden's utilitarian framework, there is still much room for many divergent investment strategies. To better understand business tactics in politics, I would urge business conflict theorists to pay some attention to the typical managerial approaches of different firms and industries and to seek connections between these practices and their ideological proclivities. Attention to the ideological horizons of political-economic rationality should not fundamentally alter the business conflict model, but serve only to enrich its understanding of how and why business coalitions and conflicts are formed and pursued.

The ultimate goal of including the ideological dimension in state theory is to bridge the gap from business coalitions, investments, and policy preferences to public opinion and the crucial mediating role that political discourse plays in forming political blocs that can be simultaneously popular and hegemonic. Ideological analysis might also help us understand how business conflict and hegemony can coexist. The common terms within which divergent business interests pursue public debate should help reveal what values and institutions are commonly accepted. Gramsci, it should be noted, defined something as ideologically hegemonic when it had attained the status of "common sense." Aspects of public discourse that social interests commonly accept (the superiority of market economies, for example, or that increased productivity is an appropriate policy goal) are in this sense hegemonic.

U.S. political discourse can be said to have a quasi-democratic character that is open to popular demands for reform. Yet the advocates of progressive reform must speak in the terms of dominant discourses. Political leaders' ability to form political blocs is mediated by these discourses, and they must speak to the rationality horizons of various powerful interests. The current Democratic administration, for example, is attempting to articulate a philosophy of public investment in terms of long-term economic benefits that would accrue to corporate interests, not least of all. It is very much an open question at this time whether or not the long-term horizon of benefit that the Clinton administration advocates will prove to be an acceptable investment risk to a sufficient number of business interests (or members of the voting public for that matter).

Some radical analysts, especially those heavily influenced by the Frankfurt School, have perceived contemporary capitalism as a highly effective system of ideological control. To a certain extent, Ferguson even seems to take a similar view when he asserts that "major investors ... are responsible for sending most of the signals to which the rest of the electorate responds."[30] Yet central to a business conflict/investment approach to the study of ideology would have to be the insight that efforts to influence public opinion are similar to business investments; in other words, they carry risks, and they might not succeed. To a great extent, it is imaginable that efforts on the part of both business and political elites to form political support blocs are based on guesswork, a form of entrepreneurial activity in which would-be leaders hope that their own ideological articulation will comfortably fit the horizon of public opinion, or that opinion can be swayed a bit to achieve political success.

The main point of this section of the chapter has been to suggest ways of refining the business conflict model's understanding of the state as an institution about and through which political discourse attempts to legitimate policies and interests, as well as to exert influence. Eric Devereux's work on how various business sectors influence the content of U.S. journalism should open the ideological domain to future business conflict analysis.[31] However, I would urge that attention be given notto simply the content of journalistic ideology, but to its consumption as well. Attention needs to be given to which social groups are being successfully appealed to, in order to better understand how and why hegemonic "consent" is achieved and cross-class political coalitions are formed. Liberal democratic politics is a conflict business at all levels, economic as well as ideological.

Appendix: A Brief Reply
David N. Gibbs

I commend Daniel Skidmore-Hess for his analysis of the business conflict model, which nicely situates the model in the larger context of theories of the state. His criticisms and suggestions for refining the model are most welcome. He and I are not very far apart in our overall perspectives, but there are some specific criticisms of my 1991 book, *The Political Economy of Third World Intervention*,[1] to which I would like to respond.

First, Skidmore-Hess criticizes the book for neglecting the role of state institutions. In fact, the significance of state institutions, and their interaction with business conflict, forms one of the principal arguments in the theoretical section of my book. The role of institutions reappears throughout the empirical analysis of U.S. intervention in Zaire during the 1960s. Institutional issues occupy about one-fifth of the empirical study.

Skidmore-Hess implies that my study focuses excessively on economic determination and does not consider how ideological and other noneconomic variables can influence state action. This is mistaken. The book repeatedly emphasizes the importance of ideological influences, and the fourth chapter concludes: "Thus both economic pressures and anticommunist ideology were crucial in the Kennedy policy" toward Zaire.[2] It is true that my book does not discuss ideological factors as extensively as do previous studies of U.S. intervention, since such factors already have been discussed ad nauseam and are well known.

Finally, Skidmore-Hess criticizes the book for neglecting the "importance of Zaire to the U.S. macroeconomy." This statement assumes—without evidence—that Zaire really was important for the functioning of the U.S. macroeconomy. In fact, there is considerable evidence that political instability in Zaire posed no threat at all to the U.S. macroeconomy,[3] and Skidmore-Hess seems unfamiliar with this evidence. It has long been fashionable to argue the importance of Third World investments in the macroeconomies of core countries. Both left-wing *dependistas* and right-wing anticommunists (with very different political agendas) assiduously promoted this idea during the 1970s. Yet, very little of this analysis has withstood serious scrutiny.[4] Third World instability may pose threats to specific U.S. companies, but seldom to the economy as a whole.

In making the latter criticism, Skidmore-Hess raises an interesting point. Most contemporary social scientists eschew the significance of private-sector influences and assume that some public-spirited objective—the needs of the macroeconomy, the "national interest," or the "epistemic community"— drives foreign policy. Like Skidmore-Hess, we assume that there *must* be some larger interest motivating state processes; accordingly, it seems untidy to argue that weighty matters of foreign policy could be affected by private interests seeking narrow, financial objectives. Yet, such things have been known to occur in the real world. Specific business interests sometimes do influence policy (whether for better or for worse), and our theories might as well take reality into account.

Notes

Introduction

1. Well-known proponents of the statist approach include Theda Skocpol, "Bringing the State Back In," in Peter Evans, Dietrich Rueschemeyer, and Theda Skocpol, eds., *Bringing the State Back In* (Cambridge: Cambridge University Press, 1985). For a useful overview of theories of the state, see Martin Carnoy, *The State and Political Theory* (Princeton, N.J.: Princeton University Press, 1984).

2. This volume is part of a theoretical tradition in international political economy that focuses on the importance of business sectors and classes in understanding the dynamics of international relations. The tradition includes the following representative works: James Kurth, "The Political Consequences of the Product Cycle: Industrial History and Political Outcomes," *International Organization* 33, no. 1 (winter 1979); Thomas Ferguson, "From Normalcy to New Deal: Industrial Structure, Party Competition, and American Public Policy in the Great Depression," *International Organization* 38, no. 1 (winter 1984); Peter Gourevitch, *Politics in Hard Times* (Ithaca, N.Y.: Cornell University Press, 1987); Bruce Cumings, *Child of Conflict* (Chicago: University of Chicago Press, 1983); David Gibbs, *The Political Economy of Intervention* (Chicago: University of Chicago Press, 1991); Ronald Cox, *Power and Profits: U.S. Policy in Central America* (Lexington: University Press of Kentucky, 1994); Gregory P. Nowell, *Mercantile States and the World Oil Cartel, 1900–1939* (Ithaca, N.Y.: Cornell University Press, 1994); James Herbert Nolt, "Business Conflict and the Origins of the Pacific War, 2 vols., Ph.D. diss., University of Chicago, 1994; and Jeffrey Frieden, *Debt, Development, and Democracy* (Princeton, N.J.: Princeton University Press, 1991).

Chapter 1

* An earlier version of this chapter was delivered at the 1992 annual meeting of the Society for Historians of American Foreign Relations, Vassar College and the Franklin D. Roosevelt Library, 18 June–21 June 1992. The author wishes to acknowledge the comments of Tom Ferguson, Benjamin Page, Burton Kaufman, and Ronald Cox on that previous draft. Substantial portions of this chapter are adapted from the larger manuscript "The Guardians at the Gates: Newspapers, Party Competition, and the Limits of the American Democracy."

1. Political scientist Richard A. Brody and *Washington Post* pollster Richard Morin make this point concisely and clearly in their article "The Iraq Syndrome: No Mandate for the Trigger Happy" (*Washington Post National Weekly Edition,* 1–7 April

1991, p. 37). For evidence of the trends in Vietnam opinion, see W. Lunch and P. Sperlich, "American Public Opinion and the War in Vietnam" (*Western Political Quarterly* 32, no. 1 (1979): 21–44) and J. Mueller, "Trends in Popular Support for the Wars in Korea and Vietnam" (*American Political Science Review* 65, no. 2 (1971): 358–375).

2. P. Braestrup's *Big Story: How the American Press and Television Reported and Interpreted the Crisis of Tet 1968 in Vietnam and Washington* (Boulder, CO: Westview Press, 1977), which severely criticizes the media for the coverage of the 1968 Tet Offensive, is the classic statement of this view. See Edward Herman and Noam Chomsky, *Manufacturing Consent: The Political Economy of the Mass Media* (New York: Pantheon Press, 1988, appendix 3), for a systematic refutation of Braestrup's argument.

3. Richard M. Nixon, *The Memoirs* (New York: Grosset & Dunlap, 1978), p. 350.

4. See D. Hallin, *The "Uncensored War": The Media and Vietnam* (New York: Oxford University Press, 1986) for a seminal study of the coverage of Vietnam in the *New York Times* and on the major television networks in these terms. W. Hammond's *Public Affairs: The Military and the Media, 1962–1968* (Washington, D.C.: GPO, 1989) is the official military study that comes to similar conclusions.

5. Herman and Chomsky, *Manufacturing Consent*, p. xv.

6. Stephen Krasner, *Defending the National Interest: Raw Materials Investments and U.S. Foreign Policy* (Princeton, N.J.: Princeton University Press, 1978), p. 324.

7. The best, and regrettably unpublished, proof of this point is J. Galbraith, "The Ammunition Boom: Procurement for the Vietnam War" (honors thesis, Harvard University, 1974).

8. See O. Holsti and J. Rosenau, *American Leadership in World Affairs: Vietnam and the Breakdown of Consensus* (Boston: Allen & Unwin, 1984) and "Consensus Lost. Consensus Regained? Foreign Policy Beliefs of American Leaders, 1976–1980," *International Studies Quarterly* 30 (1986): 375–409; and the response in Thomas Ferguson, "The Right Consensus? Holsti and Rosenau's New Foreign Policy Belief Surveys," *International Studies Quarterly* 30 (1986): 411–423.

9. For an in-depth look at the history of the these development, see Erik Devereux, "Media Coalitions in the 1964 Election: A Political Investment Analysis" (Working Paper 92–38, Carnegie Mellon University, H. John Heinz III School of Public Policy and Management, 1992).

10. For a complete summary of the Goldwater strategy, see the fascinating letter, Leonard Scruggs to Deputy Under Secretary of the Army Harry C. McPherson, undated, attached to memo, McPherson to Horace Busby, 8/7/64, Ex PL 2, Box 83, WHCF, LBJ Library.

11. See Devereux, "Media Coalitions," esp. pp. 16–17

12. See Thomas Ferguson and Joel Rogers, *Right Turn: The Decline of the Democrats and the Future of American Politics* (New York: Hill & Wang, 1986), pp. 51–52, for more on this point.

13. This point, which once was quite controversial, now appears to be widely accepted. In fact, public discussions of the Persian Gulf War often distinguished Vietnam as a "fiscal war" having broad intended and unintended effects on the U.S. and

world economy. Hobart Rowen, writing in the *Washington Post,* noted that "the traditional fiscal stimulus associated with earlier wars such as World War II or Vietnam is not likely to happen [with the Gulf War] unless the war with Iraq lasts more than six months, resulting in a fuller mobilization of the economy—including a military draft" 13 January 1991, p. H-1).

14. See Ferguson and Rogers, *Right Turn,* p. 56, for more on this point. Their entire discussion of Johnson and Vietnam, (pp. 55ff.) is an excellent overview of how different industrial and financial sectors responded to the war as it progressed.

15. See T. DiBacco, "The Business Press and Vietnam: Ecstasy or Agony" (*Journalism Quarterly* 45, no. 3 [1968]: 426–435), for a review of the commentary in the various industries trade publications regarding the likely economic impact of Vietnam on their profitability. Generally, financial publications were much more cautious about Vietnam than were manufacturing newsletters.

16. For a summary of construction-related activity, see "Vietnam Construction 50 Per Cent Done," *Engineering News-Record,* 9 February 1967, pp. 31–33.

17. Memo, Cyrus Vance for the President, 9/8/65, Ex CO 312, Box 80, WHCF, LBJ Library.

18. See the memo, Walter W. Heller for the President, 2/4/64, Ex PR 16, Box 345, WHCF, LBJ Library; the memo, Walter W. Heller for the President, 4/22/64, Ex PR 16, Box 345, WHCF, LBJ Library; and the letter, Donald C. Cook to Jack Valenti, 2/23/65, Ex PR 16, Box 346, WHCF, LBJ Library. For later evidence of this phenomenon, see "Deflating the Fears of a Recession," *Business Week,* 22 October 1966, pp. 122–124.

19. See the memo, "Economic Aspects of Vietnam," Gardner Ackley for the President, 7/30/65, Ex ND 19/CO 312, Box 216, WHCF, LBJ Library (emphasis in original). As I observe in the text, this memo was written well after the decision to escalate had been made, yet it clearly reflects economic considerations that were incorporated into the decisionmaking process. As I also stated, the economic forecasts coming into the White House in 1964 began to improve markedly as the administration planned for the escalation.

20. See the letter, Mickey Polan to Walter Jenkins, 6/18/64, C.F. PL, Box 119, WHCF, LBJ Library. In this letter, Polan, a business figure with strong ties to the Democrats, envisions sixty to eighty years of unbroken Democratic control of the White House.

21. Late in 1965, the administration would be embarrassed by revelations that the North Vietnamese had made a peace overture to Johnson in 1964, which the administration had suppressed entirely from the public and from Congress. For more on the 1965 negotiations, see Hallin, *The "Uncensored War"*; Herman and Chomsky, *Manufacturing Consent*; and G. Herring, *America's Longest War: The United States and Vietnam, 1950–1975* (New York: Alfred A. Knopf, 1986), chap. 4.

22. These events were held for the Cowles newspapers (*Minneapolis Tribune* and *Des Moines Register*), the Hearst newspapers, and the Scripps-Howard newspapers, among others.

23. Memo, Jack Valenti to the President, 4/19/65, Ex SO 3-1, Box 9, WHCF, LBJ Library.

24. For more on this program, see memo, Horace Busby for Bill Moyers, 4/21/65, Ex PR 18, Box 357, WHCF, LBJ Library.

25. See for examples, letter, Arthur B. Krim to the President, 8/20/65, Ex SO 2/8/17/65, Box 5, WHCF, LBJ Library; letter, Howard H. Helm to the President, 8/19/65, Ex SO 2/8/17/65, Box 5, WHCF, LBJ Library; letter, George S. Moore to the President, 8/25/65, Ex ND 19/CO 312, Box 216, WHCF, LBJ Library; letter, Leonard H. Goldenson to the President, 8/18/65, Ex SO 2/8/17/65, Box 5, WHCF, LBJ Library; and letter, Robert E. Kintner to the President, 8/24/65, Ex SO 2/8/17/65, Box 5, WHCF, LBJ Library. Krim was president of United Artists and a major fundraiser for Johnson in 1964; Helm was chairman of Chemical Bank, and Moore was president of Citibank (then officially the First National City Bank)—both pledged the support of the commercial banking community for Vietnam; Goldenson was president of ABC (American Broadcasting Company), and Kintner was president of NBC (National Broadcasting Company)—both gave their strongest endorsement to Vietnam.

26. See the memo, Jack Valenti for the President, Ex PR 18, Box 357, WHCF, LBJ Library, and the attached memoranda and letters regarding Taylor's U.S. trip.

27. See the letter, McGeorge Bundy to Arthur H. Dean, 8/11/65, Ex ND 19/CO 312, Box 216, WHCF, LBJ Library (and attachments); the letter, Douglass Cater to Arthur H. Dean, 8/28/65, Ex ND 19/CO 312, Box 216, WHCF, LBJ Library; the letter, Douglass Cater to Arthur H. Dean, 9/3/65, Ex ND 19/CO 312, Box 217, WHCF, LBJ Library; and the press release, "Bi-Partisan Committee Formed to Support Administration Policy in Vietnam," Ex ND 19/CO 312, Box 217, WHCF, LBJ Library.

28. Memo, Marvin Watson for the President, 8/28/64, Ex PR 16, Box 346, WHCF, LBJ Library.

29. Letter, John L. Loeb to the President, 8/18/65, Ex SO 2/8/17/65, Box 5, WHCF, LBJ Library.

30. See the memo, Henry Fowler for the President, (n.d., Ex SO 2/8/17/65, Box 5, WHCF, LBJ Library), for the administration's lengthy response to Helm's concerns, spelled out in his letter, Howard H. Helm to the President, (8/19/65, Ex SO 2/8/17/65, Box 5, WHCF, LBJ Library). This memo reveals, among other things, early recognition at the Treasury of the inflation problem. Moore's concerns may be found in letter, George S. Moore to the President (Ex ND 19/CO 312, Box 216, WHCF, LBJ Library). Eccles sent the administration a lengthy criticism of the Vietnam escalation: Marriner S. Eccles, "Statement of U.S. Position in Vietnam" (12/22/65, Ex ND 19/CO 312, Box 218, WHCF, LBJ Library). Among other things, this document decried the policy for its savage disregard for human life. The White House dismissed Eccles's views on Vietnam as "hostile and slightly hysterical," and apparently did not bother to acknowledge to Eccles that his views were known by the president (see the memo, Jack Valenti for the President, 1/7/66, Ex ND 19/CO 312, Box 218, WHCF, LBJ Library).

31. See the letter, Donald M. Kendall to the President, 5/4/65, Ex ND 19/CO 312, Box 215, WHCF, LBJ Library; and the letter, Richard E. Berlin to Jack Valenti, 3/23/65, Ex ND 19/CO 312, Box 214, WHCF, LBJ Library.

32. See, for example, the memo, Joseph Kingsbury-Smith to Richard Berlin, (3/19/65, Ex ND 19/CO 312, Box 214, WHCF, LBJ Library), for a report on a mid-March 1965 Nixon address to business figures. Kingsbury-Smith was the publisher of the *New York Journal-American*, a Hearst newspaper.

33. See, for example, the letter, Paul L. Davies to Henry H. Fowler, 5/28/65, Ex PR 4/ST 5, Box 16, WHCF, LBJ Library. Davies, the chairman of the California-based FMC Corporation, and a lifelong Republican, delivered a stinging defense of Vietnam when accepting the award for California Industrialist of the Year.

34. In the case of the *San Diego Union*, a visit by the vice president unleashed a blizzard of pro-Vietnam, pro-Johnson editorials. See the memo, the Vice President to Jack Valenti, 7/19/65, Ex ND 19/CO 312, Box 216, WHCF, LBJ Library; and the *San Diego Union*, 1, 4, 10, and 25 May 1965, all p. B-2, and 9 June 1965, p. B-2.

35. For evidence regarding the Hearst newspapers, see the letter, Joseph Kingsbury-Smith to the President, 6/10/65, Ex SO 3-1, Box 9, WHCF, LBJ Library; the letter, Charles L. Gould to Richard E. Berlin, 5/19/65, Ex ND 19/CO 312, Box 215, WHCF, LBJ Library; the letter, Frank Conniff to the President, 6/14/65, Ex SO 3-1, Box 9, WHCF, LBJ Library; the letter, Joseph Kingsbury-Smith to the President, 5/20/65, Ex ND 19/CO 312, Box 215, WHCF, LBJ Library; and the letter, Richard E. Berlin to Jack Valenti, 5/21/65, Ex ND 19/CO 312, Box 215, WHCF, LBJ Library. For the case of the *Kansas City Star*, see the letter, Roy A. Roberts to the President, 12/21/64, and the attached memo, from Robert Pearman, 12/16/64, both in Ex CO 312, Box 79, WHCF, LBJ Library. For the case of the *Cleveland Plain Dealer*, see the letter, the President to Thomas V. H. Vail, 12/3/65, Ex ND 19/CO 312, Box 218, WHCF, LBJ Library.

36. Memo, W. Averell Harriman, "Memorandum on Arthur Hays Sulzberger," 8/20/65, Ex PR 18, Box 357, WHCF, LBJ Library.

37. See the editorial "The Stakes Rise Again, and War Comes Closer," *Detroit Free Press*, 29 July 1965, p. 6A.

38. As D. Cameron noted of this effect, "It is not facetious to say that if the United States has a full employment policy, it is war" in "The Politics and Economics of the Business Cycle," in Thomas Ferguson and Joel Rogers, eds., *The Political Economy: Readings in the Politics and Economics of American Public Policy* (Armonk, N.Y.: M. E. Sharp, 1984), p. 240.

39. Memo, Frank B. Dryden for the President, 1/21/66, C.F. ND 19/CO 312, Box 71, WHCF, LBJ Library. Dryden was director of the Office of Emergency Planning. In an explanatory note attached to this memo, Dryden notes for the president that the OEP Economic Surveillance Committee was meeting twice a week to monitor the economic impact of the war.

40. Memo, Walter W. Heller for the President, 5/13/66, C.F. "V" Name File, WHCF, LBJ Library (emphasis in original).

41. Memo, Walter W. Heller for the President, Ex ND 19/CO 312, Box 221, WHCF LBJ Library (emphasis in original).

42. Memo, Robert E. Kintner for the President, 7/23/66, C.F. ND 19/CO 312, Box 72, WHCF, LBJ Library.

43. Memo, Arthur M. Okun for Joseph A. Califano, 7/3/68, Ex FG 654, Box 380, WHCF, LBJ Library. For expressions of the same concern in the media, see "And If Peace Should Come? Effects on the U.S. Economy," *Newsweek*, 18 July 1966, p. 73; and "How War's End Will Jolt the Economy," *Magazine of Wall Street*, 21 January 1967, pp. 451–453.

44. See Fred Block, *The Origins of International Economic Disorder* (Berkeley: University of California Press, 1973), p. 183, for an analysis of the administration's response to the problems with the dollar.

45. See the memo, Henry H. Fowler for the President, 10/12/66, C.F. ND 19/CO 312, Box 72, WHCF, LBJ Library.

46. See the memo, Walter Heller for the President, 6/2/66, C.F. PR 16, Box 81, WHCF, LBJ Library. In this memo, Heller notes that the tax surcharge also could be manipulated to stimulate the economy after the end of the war: "Cancelling the tax increase will be the *quickest shot in the arm we can give the economy when the war ends.*"

47. The Governor of North Dakota outlined the political effect of these policies in a mid-1967 letter to the president: "Very unfortunate quotes and actions in the past two years have led many farmers to believe that the Administration's farm policy is *consumer-oriented* to hold the cost of living down, with the farmer, in his minority position, being forced to be the economic shock absorber for stability in food prices as they affect the cost of living" (Governor William L. Guy to the President, 7/15/67, C.F. PL 2, Box 77, WHCF, LBJ Library). Until 1967, Guy was a strong supporter of Johnson on Vietnam, but he broke with the administration in 1968. This reflected the eventual disillusionment in the farm belt with the Democrats over the direction of the economy after 1965.

48. For an intriguing analysis of the differential impact of the war on the U.S. economy, see R. Jallow, "Divided Impact of Peace on the National Economy," *Commercial and Financial Chronicle*, 21 November 1968, sect. 2, pp. 28–30, 40.

49. See the memo, George Christian for the President, 8/14/67, Ex PR 18, Box 360, WHCF, LBJ Library.

50. Hallin (*"The Uncensored War"*) noted that ABC continued to support administration policies in Vietnam even after the Tet Offensive, while first CBS and then NBC became more negative toward the war even before 1968 (p. 111). ABC also kept using "cold war" rhetoric in its Vietnam War news well after NBC and CBS stopped framing the story in terms of a global communist threat (p. 141). For further differences in the Vietnam coverage of the three networks, see G. Baily, "Television War: Trends in the Network Coverage of Vietnam, 1965–1970," *Journal of Broadcasting* 20, no. 2 (1976): 147–158; and O. Patterson, "An Analysis of Television Coverage of the Vietnam War," *Journal of Broadcasting* 28, no. 4 (1984): 397–404.

51. Memo, Gardner Ackley for the President, 6/15/66, Ex PR 16, Box 347, WHCF, LBJ Library (emphasis added).

52. See Guy S. Peppiatt, "Report on Viet Nam," *NAM Reports*, 17 April 1967; and the letter, Warren P. Gullander to the President, 4/18/67, Ex ND 19/CO 312, Box 225, WHCF, LBJ Library.

53. See, for example, the editorial "The Two Wars" (*Chicago Tribune*, 1 September 1967, p.16), which suggested that, without success in Vietnam, the antipoverty programs of the Johnson administration would be meaningless.

54. See the memo, with attachment, Jack Valenti for Marvin Watson, 12/14/67, Marvin Watson Office Files, "Missouri," Box 10.

55. See the memo, the Vice President to the President, 2/2/66, Ex CO 1-8, Box 10, WHCF, LBJ Library; and the attached document entitled "Memorandum of Meeting of the Vice President with the Council for Latin America." Contrary to the rhetoric that Vietnam would demonstrate U.S. resolve against socialist movements everywhere, the history of unrest in areas outside Southeast Asia shows that the level of insur-

gency climbed dramatically during the period 1965–1972. With the U.S. military tied down in Vietnam, the ability of the United States to express force effectively in other regions was sharply limited. This became painfully evident during the 1967 war in the Middle East, when the White House had few options for enforcing its will on the combatants.

56. See the memo, Sol M. Linowitz for the President, 9/11/67, Ex CO 1-8, Box 10, WHCF, LBJ Library.

57. Memo, Sol M. Linowitz for the President, 9/9/68, Ex PR 18, Box 361, WHCF, LBJ Library. For more evidence of the *Times'* position on Vietnam, as well as the increasing tensions between that newspaper and the administration, see memo, Larry O'Brien for the President, 5/9/66, Ex FG 140, Box 195, WHCF, LBJ Library; letter, A. H. Raskin to Bill Moyers, 7/27/66, Ex ND 19/CO 312, Box 222, WHCF, LBJ Library; letter and attachments, Jack Valenti to the Vice President, 3/25/66, Ex ND 19/CO 312, Box 220, WHCF, LBJ Library; memo, Robert E. Kintner for the President, 1/12/67, Ex PR 18, Box 359, WHCF, LBJ Library; memo with attachment, Walt Rostow for the President, 1/14/67, Ex PR 18, Box 359, WHCF, LBJ Library; memo, Tom Johnson for Jim Jones, 1/14/67, Ex PR 18, Box 359, WHCF, LBJ Library; and letter with attachments, Bill Moyers to Lester Markel, 9/29/66, Ex PR 16, Box 347, WHCF, LBJ Library.

58. By the middle of 1967, the White House was so exasperated with the Vietnam reporting in the *St. Louis Post-Dispatch* that it began excluding the *Post-Dispatch's* top national news reporter, Mark Childs, from background briefings. See the letter, Marquis Childs to George Christian, 8/18/67, Ex PR 18, Box 360, WHCF, LBJ Library. For evidence of the anti-Vietnam position in the Cowles newspapers (*Minneapolis Tribune, Des Moines Register*) see the letter, the President to John Cowles, 6/3/66, H-K Cowles Name File, WHCF, LBJ Library; the letter, Phil G. Goulding to Richard Wilson, 10/19/67, Vietnam Country File, "Vietnam 7D(1) News Media Coverage of Vietnam," NSF, LBJ Library; and the memo, with attachment, Marshall Wright for Walt Rostow, 12/19/67, Vietnam Country File, "Vietnam 7E(3) Public Relations Activities," NSF, LBJ Library.

59. See the letters, Palmer Hoyt to the President, 2/4/66 and 2/5/66, Ex ND 19/CO 312, Box 219, WHCF, LBJ Library.

60. For more on this, see the memo, James Rowe for the President, 5/11/66, James H. Rowe Name File, WHCF, LBJ Library.

61. See the letter with attachments, the President to Palmer Hoyt, 3/6/68, Ex FG 11-2, Box 55, WHCF, LBJ Library; the letter, Palmer Hoyt to the President, 3/8/68, Ex FG 11-2, Box 55, WHCF, LBJ Library; and the memo, Mike Manatos for the President, 3/11/68, Ex PL/ST 6, Box 38, WHCF, LBJ Library.

62. Documentation of these developments is in the letter and attachments, Henry E. Niles to Donald Ropa, 6/1/67, Ex ND 19/CO 312, Box 226, WHCF, LBJ Library; the memo and attachments, John Criswell to James R. Jones, 9/19/67, Ex ND 19/CO 312, Box 228, WHCF, LBJ Library; and the letter, and attachments, Henry E. Niles to the President, 9/21/67, Ex ND 19/CO 312, Box 228, WHCF, LBJ Library.

63. In the case of the *Kansas City Star*, see the letter Walt Rostow to William W. Baker (4/27/67, Ex ND 19/CO 312, Box 226, WHCF, LBJ Library), which pertains to an extensive defense of Vietnam published in the *Star* in mid-April 1967.

64. For evidence of the tensions between the administration and the *Post* and *Newsweek*, see the letter, Katherine Graham to the President, 5/16/64, C.F. PR 18, Box 83, WHCF, LBJ Library; the memo, with attachments, John M.Steadman to Lawrence E. Levinson, 8/4/67, Ex ND 19/CO 312, Box 227, WHCF, LBJ Library; the memo, Fred Panzer for the President, 9/26/67, Ex ND 19/CO 312, Box 228, WHCF, LBJ Library; the memo, with attached report, John P. Walsh for Bromley Smith, 8/6/68, Vietnam Country File, "Vietnam 7D(3) News Media Coverage of Vietnam," Box 99, NSF, LBJ Library; the disposition form, MACJ341, 10/11/67, Vietnam Country File, "Vietnam 7E(1)b Public Relations Activities," Box 99, NSF, LBJ Library; and the letter, with attachments, Walt Rostow to Katherine Graham, 10/27/67, Vietnam Country File, "Vietnam 7D(1) News Media Coverage of Vietnam," Box 98, NSF, LBJ Library.

65. Letter, Katherine Graham to the President, 12/8/67, Ex ND 19/CO 312, Box 230, WHCF, LBJ Library.

66. For further evidence of this, see the memo, Joe Barr for the President, Ex ND 19/CO 312, Box 232, WHCF, LBJ Library.

67. See the memo, with attachments, Robert E. Kintner for Bill Moyers, 6/6/66, C.F. PR 18, Box 83, WHCF, LBJ Library. This memo and those attached to it summarize some of the press contacts.

68. See the memo Robert E. Kintner for the President (6/22/66, C.F. PR 16, Box 81, WHCF, LBJ Library), which records Johnson's "desire to disseminate more affirmative polls" through a variety of channels.

69. For example, see the memo, with attachments, Jack Valenti for the President, 3/21/66, Ex PR 16, Box 347, WHCF, LBJ Library. This memo reports an offer by polster Elmo Roper to help the White House divert public attention from the war.

70. See the memo, Robert E. Kintner for the President, 4/5/66, Ex SO 2, Box 3, WHCF, LBJ Library.

71. See Edward Herman and Frank Brodhead, *Demonstration Elections: U.S.-Staged Elections in the Dominican Republic, Vietnam, and El Salvador* (Boston: South End Press, 1984), for an analysis of the Vietnam elections in these terms.

72. Evidence of the deep involvement of the White House in the planning and operation of the new committee are found in memo, with attachments, Walt Rostow for the President, 3/17/67, Ex ND 19/CO 312, Box 225, WHCF, LBJ Library; memo, John P. Roche for the President, 5/19/67, C.F. ND 19/CO 312, Box 72, WHCF, LBJ Library; memo, John P. Roche for the President, 5/26/67, C.F. ND 19/CO 312, Box 73, WHCF, LBJ Library; memo, James H. Rowe for the President, 5/17/67, C.F. ND 19/CO 312, Box 73, WHCF, LBJ Library; and memo, John P. Roche for the President, 6/15/67, C.F. ND 19/CO 312, Box 73, WHCF, LBJ Library.

73. See the list of founding members published in the *New York Times*, 26 October 1967, p. 10. Members included James H. Rowe, Thomas D. Cabot, Thomas S. Gates (Morgan Guarantee), Ralph McGill (*Atlanta Constitution*), George Meany, John Hay Whitney (publisher of the then-defunct *New York Herald-Tribune*), and Lucius D. Clay (Lehman Brothers).

74. See the memo, with attachment, Walt Rostow for the President, 11/28/67, Vietnam Country File, "Vietnam 7E(2) Public Relations Activities," Box 99, LBJ Library; and memo, with attachment, Marshall Wright for George Christian, 3/12/68, Ex ND 19/CO 312, Box 232, WHCF, LBJ Library. The attachments to these

memos are compilations of editorial reactions to the committee and its policy statements in newspapers from across the United States.

75. Letter, John J. McCloy to Henry Cabot Lodge, 10/16/67, "Vietnam 7E(1)a," Country File Vietnam, NSF, LBJ Library.

76. Memo, OASD(PA) for the Record, 12/11/67, Vietnam Country File, "Vietnam 7E(3) Public Relations Activities," Box 100, NSF, LBJ Library.

77. Herring, *America's Longest War*, p. 206.

78. See Ferguson and Rogers, *Right Turn*, chap. 2, for more discussion of business and Nixon.

79. Thomas Ferguson, "From Normalcy to New Deal: Industrial Structure, Party Competition, and American Public Policy in the Great Depression," *International Organization* 38, no. 1 (winter 1984): 41–91.

80. See R. Entman, *Democracy Without Citizens: Media and the Decay of American Politics* (New York: Oxford University Press, 1989), chap. 3, for a more general analysis of the relationship between the media and elite opinion.

81. At times, the multinational character of the broadcasting industry has achieved a level where the potential for conflicts of interest become unbelievably serious, such as when Robert Kintner noted for President Johnson in mid-1966 that "the President may be interested in the attached *Wall Street Journal* article ... which summarizes the awarding of a contract to NBC to assist the South Vietnamese Government in establishing a four-station television network. RCA will sell the equipment; and NBC will manage the stations and train the South Vietnamese. ... For your information, NBC has similar contracts in Nigeria and Saudi Arabia. NBC will receive $250,000 for its first year of service in South Vietnam. These contracts are very profitable to NBC" (memo, Robert E. Kintner for the President, 7/2/66, Ex CO 312, Box 80, WHCF, LBJ Library). Until early 1966, Kintner was president of NBC, when he then became Special Assistant to the president.

82. Ferguson and Rogers, *Right Turn*, and Thomas Ferguson, "By Invitation Only: Party Competition and Industrial Structure in the 1988 Election," *Socialist Review* 19, no. 4 (1989): 73–103: Both present evidence that the networks "targeted" protectionist Democrats and Republicans in 1984 and 1988.

83. J. Alexander, ("The Mass Media in Systemic, Historical, and Comparative Perspective," in E. Katz and T. Szeskö, eds., *Mass Media and Social Change* [Beverly Hills, Calif.: Sage, 1981], p. 31, notes that when Adolph Ochs purchased the *Times* in 1896, "he tied it publicly to the anti-silver campaign," which was the preeminent cause of the New York banks. B. Cohen (*The Press and Foreign Policy* [Princeton, N.J.: Princeton University Press, 1963] describes in detail the relations between the *Times* and the State Department.

84. Several other newspapers competed strongly with the *Times* to be the paper of record, especially with regard to foreign affairs. For years, the international coverage of the *Chicago Daily News* was considered to be superior, yet that paper never achieved the influence and elite readership of the *Times*.

Chapter 2

* I would like to extend thanks to Peter Schraeder and Timothy McKeowan for their comments on a previous draft of this chapter, which has been prepared especially for inclusion in this volume.

1. See Murray Weidenbaum, "The Military-Industrial Complex: An Economic Analysis," in Omer L. Carey, ed., *The Military-Industrial Complex and United States Foreign Policy* (Pullman: Washington State University Press, 1969); Samuel Huntington, "The Defense Establishment: Vested Interests and the Public Interest," in Carey, ed., *The Military-Industrial Complex;* Robert Art, "Why We Overspend and Underaccomplish: Weapons Procurement and the Military-Industrial Complex," in Steven Rosen, ed., *Testing the Theory of the Military-Industrial Complex* (Lexington, MA: Lexington Books, 1973); Bruce M. Russett, "A Countercombatant Deterrent? Feasibility, Morality, and Arms Control," in Sam Sarkesian, ed., *The Military-Industrial Complex: A Reassessment* (Beverly Hills, CA: Sage, 1972); and James Kurth, "Aerospace Production Lines and the American Defense Spending," in Rosen, ed., *Testing the Theory.*

2. Steven Rosen, "Testing the Theory of the Military-Industrial Complex," in Steven Rosen, ed., *Testing the Theory,* p. 25.

3. C. Wright Mills, *The Power Elite* (New York: Oxford University Press, 1959), esp. chaps. 8 and 9.

4. For studies of the military-industrial complex in early U.S. history, see Benjamin Franklin Cooling, ed., *War, Business, and American Society* (Port Washington, NY: Kennikat Press, 1977); and Paul A. C. Koistinen, *The Military-Industrial Complex: A Historical Perspective* (New York: Praeger Publishers, 1980).

5. Vernon Aspaturian, "The Soviet Military-Industrial Complex: Does It Exist?" in Rosen, ed., *Testing the Theory.*

6. A rare exception is James Kurth, "Military-Industrial Complex," in Joel Krieger, ed., *Oxford Companion to Politics of the World* (New York: Oxford University Press, 1993). As this goes to press, it has come to my attention that there has been some revival of interest in the MIL in sociology. See the excellent study by John L. Boies, *Buying for Armageddon: Business, Society, and Military Spending Since the Cuban Missile Crisis* (New Brunswick: Rutgers University Press, 1994).

7. The influence of "security" explanations is pervasive in the literature. For example, Brian Pollins, in an excellent analysis of political versus economic explanations for U.S. trade policy, seems to assume that all political considerations are synonymous with security ("Does Trade Still Follow the Flag?" *American Political Science Review* 83, no. 2 [1989]). The classic statement on the question of the national interest is Stephen Krasner, *Defending the National Interest: Raw Materials Investments and U.S. Foreign Policy* (Princeton, N.J.: Princeton University Press, 1978). For a critique of this approach, see David N. Gibbs, "Taking the State Back Out: Reflections on a Tautology," *Contention* 3, no. 3 (spring 1994): 115–138. See also replies to Gibbs in the same issue of *Contention* by Stephen Krasner, David Lake, John Ikenberry, and Jeffry Frieden.

8. Anthony Downs, *Inside Bureaucracy* (Boston: Little, Brown & Co., 1967) p. 2.

9. See, for example, Seymour Melman, *Pentagon Capitalism* (New York: McGraw Hill, 1970); Sidney Lens, *The Military-Industrial Complex* (Philadelphia: Pilgrim Press, 1970); and John Kenneth Galbraith, "How to Control the Military," in Carroll W. Pursell Jr., ed., *The Military-Industrial Complex* (New York: Harper & Row, 1972).

10. Alan Wolfe, *The Rise and Fall of the Soviet "Threat"* (Washington, DC: Institute for Policy Studies, 1979), chap. 5.

11. Aspaturian, "The Soviet Military-Industrial Complex" in Rosen, ed., *Testing the Theory,* p. 127.

12. Admiral Louis Denfield, 1949, quoted in Peter Karsten, *The Naval Aristocracy* (New York: Free Press, 1972), p. 395n.

13. See figures in Fred Halliday, *The Making of the Second Cold War* (London: Verso, 1983), p. 129n.

14. Ira Magaziner and Robert Reich, *Minding America's Business* (New York: Harcourt Brace Jovanovich, 1982), pp. 228–229.

15. This geographical component is emphasized in Ann Markuson, Peter Hall, Scott Campbell, and Sabina Deitrick, *The Rise of the Gun Belt* (New York: Oxford University Press, 1991).

16. Paul A. Baran and Paul M. Sweezy, *Monopoly Capital* (New York: Monthly Review Press, 1966), chap. 7. It should be noted, however, that Baran and Sweezy regarded military spending as socially wasteful, despite its stimulative macroeconomic effects.

17. Betty C. Hanson and Bruce M. Russett, "Testing Some Economic Interpretations of American Intervention: Korea, Indochina, and the Stock Market," in Rosen, ed., *Testing the Theory.*

18. Markuson et al., *Rise of the Gun Belt.* See also Peter Trubowitz and Brian E. Roberts, "Regional Interests and the Reagan Military Buildup," *Regional Studies* 26, no. 6 (1992).

19. Alfred Eckes Jr., *The United States and the Global Struggle for Minerals* (Austin: University of Texas Press, 1979).

20. Jeffry Frieden, "The Economics of Intervention: American Overseas Investments and Relations with Underdeveloped Areas, 1890–1950," *Comparative Studies in Society and History* 31, no. 1 (1989).

21. Noted in Colonel James Donovan, *Militarism USA* (New York: Charles Scribner's Sons, 1970), p. 54.

22. The capacity for collective action is of course, a well-recognized asset for an interest group. See Mancur Olson Jr., *The Logic of Collective Action* (Cambridge, MA: Harvard University Press, 1971).

23. See, for example, Terence McCarthy, "American Dollar in Jeopardy: Can Flight to Gold Be Halted?" in Seymour Melman, ed., *The War Economy of the United States* (New York: St. Martin's Press, 1971). See also Louis B. Lundborg, Chairman of the Board, Bank of America, "Statement to the U.S. Senate Committee on Foreign Relations," in Melman, ed., *The War Economy.*

24. I have elsewhere argued that business conflict is an important variable in explaining public policy. See David N. Gibbs, *The Political Economy of Third World Intervention: Mines, Money, and U.S. Policy in the Congo Crisis* (Chicago: University of Chicago Press, 1991), chap. 1.

25. Olson, *Logic.*

26. It may be said that the need for combat is part of the informal "standard operating procedures" that are well-established features of any large organization. See Graham Allison, *Essence of Decision* (Boston: Little, Brown & Co., 1971), chap. 3.

27. John Stockwell, *In Search of Enemies* (New York: W.W. Norton, 1978), p. 251.

28. General David M. Shoup, "The New American Militarism," *The Atlantic,* April 1969, p. 55.

29. See, for example, Harry Magdoff, *The Age of Imperialism* (New York: Monthly Review Press, 1969).

30. Quoted by John Mueller, "Quiet Cataclysm: Some Afterthoughts on World War III," in Michael J. Hogan, ed., *The End of the Cold War: Its Meaning and Implications* (Cambridge: Cambridge University Press, 1992), p. 42.

31. See Max Weber, "'Objectivity' in Social Science and Social Policy," in *The Methodology of the Social Sciences* (New York: Free Press, 1949). It should be noted that the MIC might be expected to pressure the government to intervene even in remote areas, which otherwise carry little economic significance. Most mainstream analyses of war and intervention fail to consider this point, and serious misunderstandings can occur. Thus Jeffry Frieden writes: "Any list of reasons for the American interventions in Grenada and Nicaragua, to take more recent examples, would place economic interests far down." However, Frieden fails to consider the economic interests of the defense procurement companies and their role in promoting interventions during this period. See Frieden, "The Economics of Intervention," p. 77.

Frieden's article actually argues that economic interests *did* influence U.S. interventions during the period 1890–1950. However, the article then accepts the conventional view that economic factors played little or no role in U.S. interventions since World War II. This point seems quite dubious. Even apart from MIC influences, there is considerable evidence that direct investments significantly influenced U.S. interventions during the post–World War II period. See the following sources: Stephen Schlesinger and Stephen Kinzer, *Bitter Fruit: The Untold Story of the American Coup in Guatemala* (Garden City, N.Y.: Anchor Books, 1983); Ronald W. Cox, *Power and Profits: U.S. Economic Policy in Central America* (Lexington: University of Kentucky Press, 1994); David N. Gibbs, *The Political Economy of Third World Intervention.*

32. The best summary of these events can be found in Halliday, *Making of the Second Cold War,* chap. 8.

33. Raymond Garthoff, *Confrontation and Detente* (Washington, DC: Brookings Institute, 1985), p. 887.

34. Stephen Gill, *American Hegemony and the Trilateral Commission* (Cambridge: Cambridge University Press, 1990), p. 80.

35. Elmo Zumwalt Jr., "Heritage of Weakness: An Assessment of the 1970s," in W. Scott Thompson, ed., *National Security in the 1980s: From Weakness to Strength* (San Francisco: Institute for Contemporary Studies, 1980), p. 49.

36. See Stockholm International Peace Research Institute, *SIPRI Yearbook* (Stockholm: Almquist & Wiksell, 1973), pp. 308–309.

37. See, for example, Theodore Moran, *Multinational Corporations and the Politics of Dependence: Copper in Chile* (Princeton, N.J.: Princeton University Press, 1974); and Joseph LaPalombara and Stephen Blank, *Multinational Corporations and Developing Countries* (New York: The Conference Board, 1979).

38. See Stephen Kobrin, "Political Risk: A Review and Reconsideration," *Journal of International Business Studies* 10, no. 1 (sping/summer 1979); and Theodore Moran, ed., *International Political Risk Assessment: The State of the Art* (Washington, D.C.: School of Foreign Service, Georgetown University, 1980).

39. This point is emphasized in Dan Haendel, *Corporate Strategic Planning: The Political Dimension* (Washington, D.C.: Center for Strategic and International Studies, 1981), chap. 1.

40. Jerry Sanders, *Peddlers of Crisis: The Committee on the Present Danger and the Politics of Containment* (Boston: South End Press, 1983), p. 238. See also the study by the Business Week Research Team, *The Decline of U.S. Power and What We Can Do About It* (Boston: Houghton Mifflin, 1980).

41. It should be noted that most multinational investors do not fall within my definition of the military-industrial complex. The point here is that the multinationals had common interests with the MIC.

42. Thomas Ferguson and Joel Rogers, "Introduction," in Thomas Ferguson and Joel Rogers, eds., *The Hidden Election: Politics and Economics in the 1980 Presidential Campaign* (New York: Pantheon Press, 1981), pp. 17, 59n. 24; and Robert Sherrill, "War Mongering Chic: Gene Rostow's Propaganda Club," *The Nation*, 11–18 August 1979.

43. For an extended analysis, see Sanders, *Peddlers of Crisis.*

44. On these trends, see Peter Steinfels, *The Neoconservatives* (New York: Simon & Schuster, 1979); and Halliday, *Making of the Second Cold War*, chap. 5.

45. Thomas Ferguson and Joel Rogers, *Right Turn: The Decline of the Democrats and the Future of American Politics* (New York: Hill & Wang, 1986), p. 99.

46. Sanders, *Peddlers of Crisis*, p. 223.

47. During the 1980 election, for example, *Air Force Magazine* published an article that complained about the "steady, cumulative slide in American military power relative to the Soviet Union" and pointedly urged voters to support candidates who would rectify these problems. See "'Dear Voter': An Open Letter to the American Electorate," *Air Force Magazine*, October 1980, p. 53.

48. Sanders, *Peddlers of Crisis*, p. 265.

49. "Anti-SALT Lobbyists Outspend Pros 15 to 1," *Christian Science Monitor*, 23 March 1979. The article anticipated that the spending would even out in the subsequent months (although it did not say why this trend was anticipated); in any event, the article expected SALT "treaty opponents still spending $7 for event $1 by proponents."

50. Ferguson and Rogers, *Right Turn*, p. 99. Regarding anti-Soviet economic sanctions, proposed in 1982, Kenneth Rodman writes that "firms like Dresser Industries, Caterpillar Tractor, and General Electric ... were heavily dependent upon contacts with the Soviet bloc" and stood to lose from the proposed sanctions. Rodman astutely recognizes the phenomenon of business opposition to certain cold war policies, but he is incorrect in his implication that the U.S. business community *in general* stood to lose from the sanctions. Rodman neglects to consider that the defense sector benefited from the prodefense atmosphere that such sanctions tended to foster. See Rodman, "Sanctions at Bay? Hegemonic Decline, Multinational Corporations, and U.S. Economic Sanctions since the Pipeline Case," *International Organization* 49, no. 1 (1995): 135.

51. Halliday, *Making of the Second Cold War*, pp. 120–122.

52. See the excellent study on this period, Sanders, *Peddlers of Crisis*, chap. 7.

53. Jimmy Carter, quoted in Garthoff, *Confrontation*, p. 954.

54. Ferguson and Rogers, *Right Turn*, p. 124.

55. Carter, quoted in Garthoff, *Confrontation*, p. 957. However, there were some differences of opinion with regard to Soviet motivations. Some analysts believed that

the Soviets had invaded *with the intention* of spreading their influence throughout the region; others believed that the Soviets may have invaded due to local or idiosyncratic considerations but that, nevertheless, the invasion did in fact give the Soviets major strategic advantages, whether or not this was their actual motivation.

56. This is emphasized in Milan Hayner, *The Soviet War in Afghanistan* (Lanham, MD: University Press of America, 1991).

57. See David N. Gibbs, "Does the USSR Have a 'Grand Strategy'? Reinterpreting the Invasion of Afghanistan," *Journal of Peace Research* 24, no. 4 (1987): 367–369.

58. Joint Chiefs of Staff, "Program Assistance for the General Area of China," 16 January 1950, in *Declassified Documents,* microfiche series (1979, no. 33A.

59. National Intelligence Estimate, "Soviet Capabilities and Intentions," 11 November 1950, in *Declassified Documents,* microfiche series (1980, no. 226A), p. 20.

60. National Intelligence Estimate, "Outlook for Afghanistan," 1954, in *Foreign Relations of the United States, 1952–1954,* vol. 11, p. 1491.

61. Dulles, paraphrased in National Security Council, "Memorandum of Discussion at the 228th Meeting of the National Security Council on December 9, 1954," in *Foreign Relations of the United States, 1952– 1954,* vol. 11, p. 1149.

62. National Security Council, "Memorandum of Discussion at the 285th Meeting of the National Security Council, May 17, 1956," in *Foreign Relations of the United States, 1955–1957,* vol. 7, p. 237.

63. See Gibbs, "Does the USSR Have a 'Grand Strategy'?" pp. 368–369.

64. National Intelligence Estimate, "Outlook for Afghanistan," p. 1492.

65. Ibid., pp. 1483, 1484, 1492.

66. National Security Council, "Memorandum by the Executive Secretary (Lay) to the National Security Council," 14 December 1954, in *Foreign Relations of the United States, 1952–1954,* vol. 11, p. 1153.

67. A secret CIA report in 1973 analyzed a coup d'état in Afghanistan in that year. It was noted that 200 Soviet technicians were in the country at the time; but the report concluded that "there is no evidence, however, that the Soviets either instigated or were actively involved in the coup" (Central Intelligence Agency, "Biographic Report: Mohammad Daud," 13 August 1973, reprinted verbatim in *Den of Spies* document collection [Tehran], vol. 29, p. 42).

68. *Wall Street Journal,* 27 December 1973.

69. It should also be noted that the period from April 1978, when the People's Democratic Party seized power, to December 1979, when the USSR invaded the country, provides considerable evidence that the Soviets were not at all eager to increase their commitment to Afghanistan. This is strongly indicated by recently declassified Soviet documents from the period prior to the invasion. See verbatim transcripts of these documents in "From Hesitation to Intervention: Soviet Decisions on Afghanistan, 1979," *Cold War International History Project Bulletin,* no. 4, 1994, pp. 70–76. See also the following analysis of Soviet activities in Afghanistan that analyzes recently available Soviet documents: Odd Arne Westad, "Prelude to Invasion: The Soviet Union and the Afghan Communists, 1978–1979," *International History Review* 16, no. 1 (1994).

It is interesting to note that these recent Soviet releases tend to confirm earlier interpretations of Soviet behavior in Afghanistan, which had argued—without access to then-secret documents—that the Soviets were not enthusiastic about the Afghan communist party. See the following: Garthoff, *Confrontation;* John P. Willerton, "Soviet Perspectives on Afghanistan: The Making of an Ally," *Jerusalem Journal of International Relations* 8, no. 1 (1986); and Gibbs, "Does the USSR Have a 'Grand Strategy'?"

70. It is worth mentioning that a vast quantity of U.S. government documents, pertaining to Afghanistan during 1978–1979, are now available. These documents strongly suggest that the Soviets invaded, at last in part, to subdue recalcitrant elements in the Afghan communist party. For analyses of these document collections, see Gibbs, ibid., and Garthoff, ibid., chap. 26.

71. Major Joseph J. Collins, *The Soviet Invasion of Afghanistan* (Lexington, MA: Lexington Books, 1986), p. 152.

72. See G. Jacobs, "Afghanistan Forces: How Many Soviets Are There?" *Jane's Defence Weekly*, 22 June 1985; and Selig Harrison, "Afghanistan Stalemate: 'Self Determination' and a Soviet Force Withdrawal," *Parameters: Journal of the U.S. Army War College* 14, no. 4 (1984).

73. Elaine Sciolino, "To U.S., Afghanistan Seems to Move Farther Away," *New York Times,* 12 February 1989, "Week in Review."

74. The editorial noted that previous communist actions, such as the invasion of South Korea in 1950 helped to trigger increased expenditures on the military. The editorial concluded that "the Soviets [by invading Afghanistan], once again, may inadvertently save us from ourselves" ("Afghanistan: A Watershed," *Air Force Magazine*, February 1980). For a very interesting comparison between crises in Afghanistan and Korea, see Fred Block, "Economic Instability and Military Strength: The Paradoxes of the 1950 Rearmament Decision," *Politics and Society* 10, no. 1 (1980).

75. Quoted in Bogdan Denitch, *The End of the Cold War* (Minneapolis: University of Minnesota Press, 1991), p. 29n.

76. Downs, *Inside Bureaucracy*, p. 200.

Chapter 3

1. Richard Perle and Richard Pipes are key exponents of the very widespread view that legitimate national security concerns, rather than domestic societal interests, shaped the turn to a more assertive U.S. foreign and military policy under Ronald Reagan. Although certain realists differ with this view by acknowledging that the Soviet threat has often been exaggerated, they still share the common assumption that foreign policymakers are motivated—rationally or not—by national security concerns and anticommunist ideology. For an example of this latter view, see: Stephen Krasner, *Defending the National Interest: Raw Materials Investments and U.S. Foreign Policy* (Princeton, N.J.: Princeton University Press, 1978).

2. For a general discussion of the right turn of U.S. business, see Thomas Ferguson and Joel Rogers, *Right Turn: The Decline of the Democrats and the Future of American Politics* (New York: Hill & Wang, 1986); and Mike Davis, *Prisoners of the American Dream* (New York: Verso, 1986).

3. Thomas Ferguson is perhaps the leading proponent of this approach, one he labels the "investment theory of politics." See Ferguson, "From Normalcy to New

Deal: Industrial Structure, Party Competition, and American Public Policy in the Great Depression," *International Organization* 38, no. 1 (winter 1984): 41–91; "Party Realignment and American Industrial Structure: The Investment Theory of Political Parties in Historical Perspective," *Research in Political Economy* 6 (1983): 1–82; and "The Reagan Victory: Corporate Coalitions in the 1980 Campaign," in Thomas Ferguson and Joel Rogers, eds., *The Hidden Election: Politics and Economics in the 1980 Presidential Campaign* (New York: Pantheon Press, 1981).

4. See p. 75 of Barry Posen and Stephen Van Evera's contribution in Kenneth Oye, Robert Lieber, and Donald Rothchild, eds., *Eagle Resurgent? The Reagan Era in American Foreign Policy* (Boston: Little, Brown & Co., 1983).

5. On ties between the Trilateral Commission and the Carter administration, see Holly Sklar, *Trilateralism: The Trilateral Commission and Elite Planning for World Management* (Boston: South End Press, 1980 and New York: Monthly Review Press, 1981); and Stephen Gill, *American Hegemony and the Trilateral Commission* (Cambridge: Cambridge University Press, 1990).

6. Quoted in Fred Halliday, *Soviet Policy in the Arc of Crisis* (Washington, D.C.: Institute for Policy Studies, 1981), p. 21.

7. The term "hegemonic coalition" is borrowed from James Kurth, "The United States and Central America: Hegemony in Historical and Comparative Perspective," in Richard Feinberg, ed., *Central America: International Dimensions of the Crisis* (New York: Holmes & Meier, 1982), p. 54.

8. Quoted in Holly Sklar, "Reagan, Trilateralism, and the Neoliberals: Containment and Intervention in the 1980s," (Boston: South End Press, pamphlet no. 4, 1986), p. 2.

9. For a good discussion of the dimensions of economic decline, see Ferguson and Rogers, *Right Turn,* pp. 79–83.

10. Samuel Huntington, *The Crisis of Democracy* (New York: Trilateral Commission, 1975), p. 115.

11. Rockefeller's statement is quoted in Bruce Cummings, "Chinatown: Foreign Policy and Elite Realignment," in Ferguson and Rogers, eds., *Hidden Election*, p. 218. For a sophisticated rendition of the human rights debate within the Trilateral Commission, see the special issue on human rights in the commission's journal *Trialogue*, no. 19 (fall 1978).

12. Evidence of this split can be found in the journals of multinationals, such as the Trilateral Commission's *Trialogue* or the Atlantic Council's *Atlantic Community Quarterly*, and in the membership lists of conservative business mobilization organizations, such as the Business Roundtable.

13. Labor-intensive firms tend to favor military over economic intervention since they are faced with tight wage constraints, leading them to support U.S. military assistance to governments faced with leftist insurgencies and/or militant labor movements. Many U.S. multinationals (computers, electronics, and clothing, for example) have established export platforms in less-developed countries as a means of lowering production costs. Such firms have long depended on conservative regimes for economic and military assistance to protect their investments abroad.

14. As more and more large U.S. firms have expanded abroad, and as greater proportions of their profits are derived from overseas operations, the U.S. state has served to facilitate the creation of the conditions for U.S. capital accumulation and

reproduction on a worldwide scale. When these conditions are threatened by insurgent movements in the less developed world, multinational corporations support, even urge, the use of coercive (i.e., military) measures in order to protect their interests in the region. James Petras and Morris Morley developed the concept of the "U.S. imperial state" to signify this process of the extension of the state's jurisdiction far beyond its territorial boundaries so as to create and maintain conditions conducive for capital accumulation. See James Petras and Morris Morley, "The U.S. Imperial State," in James Petras et al., eds., *Class, State, and Power in the Third World* (London: Zed Books, 1981).

15. Liberal internationalists, often firms with capital-intensive investments, more often support the use of economic and diplomatic pressure, as they are less dependent on low labor costs to maintain international competitiveness and are relatively insulated from policy shifts associated with regime changes. Moreover, these firms generally oppose militaristic solutions due to the propensity for such solutions to create political instability, thereby undermining conditions conducive to profitable foreign investment.

16. For an elaborated demonstration of the emergence of such a coalition of conservative internationalist and right-wing domestic business groups, see Thomas Bodenheimer and Robert Gould, *Rollback: Right-Wing Power in U.S. Foreign Policy* (Boston: South End Press, 1989).

17. Rich and detailed empirical support for such an argument, as it relates to the case of Central America, can be found in Ronald W. Cox, *Power and Profits: U.S. Policy in Central America* (Lexington: University Press of Kentucky, 1994).

18. Groups opposed to the system of multinational liberalism from its inception include: the defense industry and a whole array of supply firms and consultants, the Pentagon and its associated academics, and declining industrial sectors seeking protection from the pressures of international trade.

19. Thomas Edsall, *The New Politics of Inequality* (New York: W.W. Norton, 1984), p. 39.

20. For further elaboration of this point, see Thomas Ferguson and Joel Rogers, "The Knights of the Roundtable," *The Nation*, 15 December 1979, pp. 620–625.

21. John Soloma, *Ominous Politics: The New Conservative Labryinth* (New York: Hill & Wang, 1984), p. 79.

22. Ibid., p. 79.

23. Quoted in ibid., p. 66. For further discussion of the history of the Business Roundtable, see Ferguson and Rogers, "Knights of the Roundtable."

24. Soloma, *Ominous Politics*, p. 69. Also see Kim Moody, "Reagan, the Business Agenda, and the Collapse of Labour," in Ralph Miliband, Leo Panitch, and John Saville, eds., *Socialist Register* (London: Merlin Press, 1987), p. 166. Moody documents that the total amount of money spent by corporate PACs also went up accordingly: from $8 million in 1974, to $39 million in 1978, to $85 million in 1982.

25. For a detailed description of the final months of the campaign and the shifting alliances of business groups, see Thomas Ferguson and Joel Rogers, "The Empire Strikes Back," *The Nation*, 1 November 1980.

26. Jerry Sanders, *Peddlers of Crisis: The Committee on the Present Danger and the Politics of Containment* (Boston: South End Press, 1983), p. 223.

27. For more information on the CPD, see Robert Sherrill, "Gene Rostow's Propaganda Club," *The Nation*, 18 August 1979, pp. 106–110; and Jerry Sanders, *Ped-*

dlers of Crisis (for a list of committee members in the Reagan administration, see pp. 287–289).

28. Sherrill, "Propaganda Club," p. 108.

29. Robert Scheer, *With Enough Shovels: Reagan, Bush, and Nuclear War* (New York: Random House, 1982), p. 48.

30. Charles Heatherly, ed., *Mandate for Leadership: Policy Management in a Conservative Administration* (Washington, D.C.: Heritage Foundation, 1981). Founded in 1974 by Paul Weyrich, the Heritage Foundation was given $200,000 in start-up money from Joseph Coors. Trustees of the foundation have included industrialist J. Robert Fluor, the ubiquitous William Simon, Justin Dart of Dart Industries, the Scaife family of Pittsburgh, Dow Chemical, and Bechtel Corporation.

31. For more information on the neoconservatives, see Peter Steinfels, *The Neoconservatives: The Men Who Are Changing America's Politics* (New York: Simon & Schuster, 1979).

32. For more discussion on the New Christian Right and "low intensity conflict," see Sara Diamond, *Spiritual Warfare: The Politics of the Christian Right* (Boston: South End Press, 1989).

33. "Pat Robertson's Perspective: A Special Report to Members of the Christian Coalition," October–November, 1991.

34. "Hearts and Minds: The Conservative Network," *Washington Post,* 4 January 1981, p. A14.

35. For examples of New Right claims of being a counter- establishment and/or anti-business, see Sidney Blumenthal, *The Rise of the Counter Establishment* (New York: Times Books, 1986); and Jerry Falwell, *Listen, America!* (New York: Bantam Books, 1980). In addition, the articles and advertisements in the New Right journal *Conservative Digest* (now defunct) are full of anti–big business rhetoric.

36. Brigadier Genderal Albion Knight, in Howeard Phillips, ed., *The New Right at Harvard* (Conservative Caucus, 1983), pp. 41–78.

37. Edward N. Luttwak, "After Afghanistan, What?" *Commentary* (April 1980): 48.

38. Ibid., p. 49.

39. CDM, "The U.S. Defense Budget: Invitation to Disaster," *Conservative Digest* (August 1975): 16.

40. Ibid., p. 17.

41. Norman Podhoretz, "The Present Danger," *Commentary* (March 1980): 35.

42. Ibid., p. 39.

43. Burton Yale Pines, "How Conservative Is Reagan's Foreign Policy" (speech delivered to the American Political Science Association, Chicago, IL, 1 September 1983); Robert Conquest, "Why the Soviet Elite Is Different from U.S.," *Policy Review* (fall 1977), also reprinted in the *Atlantic Community Quarterly* 16, no. 1 (spring 1978); Jean-François Revel, "Can the Democracies Survive?" *Commentary* (June 1984): 19–27; Richard Pipes, "Why the Soviet Union Thinks It Could Fight and Win a Nuclear War," *Commentary* (July 1977): 25–26; Norman Podhoretz, "The Future Danger," *Commentary* (April 1981): 40.

44. Robert E. Moffit, "Soviet-American Relations in the 1980s," in Robert W. Whitaker, ed., *The New Right Papers* (New York: St. Martin's Press, 1982), p. 212.

45. Patrick Buchanan, "Waging War on SALT," *Conservative Digest* (March 1979): 37. The New Right response to SALT II was varied. Howard Phillips's Conservative Caucus organized a petition drive against the treaty. Countless articles were published with titles such as "SALT Is Dangerous," by Patrick J. Buchanan; "SALT: The Deadly Tranquilizer," by Eugene Rostow; and "SALT II: A Soviet Triumph," by the *Conservative Digest* editorial board. It is interesting to note the degree to which New Rightists such as Buchanan moved beyond mere "anti-ism" to propose that SALT II "should be made a casus belli for civil war within the Democratic Party." In much the same way that race served Kevin Phillips's formulation of the "Southern Strategy" during the Nixon era, New Right ideologues proposed that SALT II could serve to divide the Democratic Party between Carter Democrats, who were pro-SALT, and SALT-free Jacksonian Democrats—thus potentially creating a coalition between the New Right and hard-line national defense conservative Democrats.

46. Walter Laquer, "The West in Retreat," *Commentary* (August 1975): p. 44–52.

47. Walter Laquer, "Confronting the Problems," *Commentary* (March 1977): 37.

48. The Eastern liberal foreign policy elite includes organizations such as the Coalition for a New Foreign and Military Policy, SANE, Americans for Democratic Action, and the Institute for Policy Studies, as well as policymakers such as George Kennan (the principal architect of containment as the author of the famous "Mr. X" article of 1947 in *Foreign Affairs*) and Stanley Hoffman of Harvard.

49. For example, see Robert Schuettinger, "America's New Foreign Policy Elite," *Policy Review* (spring 1979).

50. Walter Laquer, "Containment for the '80s," *Commentary* (November 1980): 42.

51. Ronald Reagan, speech to the Heritage Foundation, 3 October 1983.

52. Cummings, "Chinatown," p. 219.

53. Ibid.

54. Posen and Van Evera, in *Eagle Resurgent?* p. 75.

55. Ibid.

56. "Reagan's Strategic Outlook," *New York Times*, 23 November 1982, p. A12; quoted in Posen and Van Evera, p. 81.

57. Caspar Weinberger, "United States Defense Policy," *Atlantic Community Quarterly* 19, no. 2 (summer 1981): 259–263.

58. For details on these developments, see Pines, "How Conservative Is Reagan's Foreign Policy?"

59. Quoted in Fred Halliday, *The Making of the Second Cold War* (London: Verso, 1983), p. 11.

60. While my focus is upon the ideological affinities between the New Right and the Reagan administration, rather than inter-personal linkages between cold warriors and the administration, it is revealing to note the extent of the latter. Eugene Rostow of the CPD was appointed to head the ACDA. Richard Perle, a military adviser to the Pentagon, was appointed as assistant secretary of defense for international security policy. Richard Pipes, the former Harvard historian notorious for arguing that a nuclear war was winnable, was appointed as the senior Soviet specialist on Reagan's National Security Council staff. Former secretary of the Navy and CPD member Paul Nitze became Reagan's key negotiator on European strategic weapons.

Also among those appointed by Reagan to advise on foreign and military matters were: neoconservatives such as Jeanne Kirkpatrick (U.S. Ambassador to the United Nations), Kenneth Adelman (arms negotiator), and Elliot Abrams (adviser on Latin American policy), as well as Hoover Institution fellows Milton Friedman, Richard Staar, and Peter Duignana. Closely associated with the appointment of so many cold warriors to advise on foreign and military matters is the fact that the majority of Reagan's kitchen cabinet had national, rather than transnational, business interests, suggesting a foreign policy that would sharply increase defense spending, legislate fair trade rather than free trade (so as to favor declining U.S. industries by restricting imports), and implement a more interventionist policy in the Third World. Business nationalists in Reagan's kitchen cabinet included Salvatori, a Los Angeles oilman; Justin Dart of Dart Industries; William Wilson, a land developer; Theodore Cummings, who built the Food Giant chain; Holmes Tuttle, an auto dealer; Jack Wrather, oil and entertainment; Earle Jorgenson of Jorgenson Steel; and Alfred Bloomingdale, former board chairman of Diner's Club. See Cummings, "Chinatown," p. 225.

61. Scheer, *With Enough Shovels,* p. 84.

62. During this time many advertisements were placed in *Conservative Digest,* a key New Right journal of the eighties, criticizing the Control Data group for providing the Soviets with the rope with which they would eventually choke the free world.

63. Despite opposition from both the State and Commerce Departments, the Pentagon succeeded in establishing rules that even prevented a machine called "Belle," a computer chess-playing product, from being sent to the Soviets.

64. In personal interviews conducted in January 1995 with Paul Weyrich (executive director of Free Congress Foundation) and Adam Meyerson (executive vice president for educational affairs at the Heritage Foundation), the significance of the end of the cold war in shaping the contours of today's conservative movement was emphasized. Paul Weyrich explains that before the end of the cold war, establishment and anti-establishment conservatives were united in their stand against the Soviet threat, and that with the end of the cold war, this central division has once again manifested within the conservative movement. Adam Meyerson understands the key fissure within the movement as one of sociocultural conservatives versus economic conservatives and explains the diminished status of many key New Right operatives of the seventies and eighties as having to do with their failure to appreciate Reagan's efforts to end the cold war. Indeed, as late as 1984, New Right ideologues writing in a special edition of the *Policy Review* on the Soviet threat criticized the Reagan administration for betraying anticommunist principles. In hindsight, with many conservatives today lauding the Reagan administration for "winning" the cold war, those conservatives who took a principled stand against Reagan have lost credibility within the movement.

65. James Kurth, "The United States and Western Europe in the Reagan Era," in Morris Morley, ed., *Crisis and Confrontation: Ronald Reagan's Foreign Policy* (New Jersey: Rowman & Littlefield, 1988), p. 67.

66. On trends in public opinion, see Ferguson and Rogers, *Right Turn,* pp. 19–21.

67. These practical effects included huge budget deficits, high interest rates, and an overvalued dollar. Many conservative internationalists moderated their position and advocated slower increases in defense spending to control the budget deficit and inflation, and a de-emphasis on militaristic rhetoric so as to maintain stable political

relations for profitable capital accumulation. This moderation is best illustrated by the Trilateral Commission's return, after 1982, to its former "trader" position. Indeed, by 1986, the commission's founder, David Rockefeller, led a business delegation to the Soviet Union.

Chapter 4

1. *New York Times*, 28 May 1989, p. E3; see also 29 May 1989, p. 32. Japan was accused of unfair practices involving satellites, supercomputers, and forest products. Brazil was cited for unfair import licensing requirements. India was accused of unfair restrictions on foreign direct investment and foreign insurance companies. According to the *New York Times:* "In rallying behind domestic industries much as other countries do, the United States is shifting from tolerant economic internationalism toward a more parochial economic nationalism."

2. See David N. Gibbs, *The Political Economy of Third World Intervention: Mines, Money, and U.S. Policy in the Congo Crisis.* Chicago: University of Chicago Press, 1991.

3. See note 6 for citations of the literature of neo-Gramscian historical materialism.

4. See: Raymond Vernon, "International Investment and International Trade in the Product Cycle," *Quarterly Journal of Economics* (May 1966): 190–207; and Raymond Gruber, Dileep Mehta, and Raymond Vernon, "The R&D Factor in International Trade and International Investment of United States Industries," *Journal of Political Economy* 75 (February 1967): 20–37.

5. Antonio Gramsci was a leading Italian communist and a political theorist whose contributions to Marxism are the subject of ongoing debate. Following publication of *Selections from the Prison Notebooks* (1971), Gramsci's political thought influenced a growing school in international political economy (IPE). His most influential theoretical contribution in this regard was his conception of hegemony. The idea of "state-society complexes" is developed in the work of Robert Cox, "Social Forces, States, and World Orders: Beyond International Relations Theory," *Millenium* 10, no. 2 (summer 1981): 126–155, esp. 141; and *Production, Power, and World Order: Social Forces in the Making of History* (New York: Columbia University Press, 1987), esp. pt. 2, and pt. 3, chap. 8. Also in the neo-Gramscian tradition of IPE are: B. K. Gills, "Historical Materialism and International Relations Theory," *Millenium* 16, no. 2 (summer 1987): 265–272; Stephen Gill and David Law, *The Global Political Economy: Perspectives, Problems, and Policies* (Baltimore: Johns Hopkins University Press, 1988), and "Global Hegemony and the Structural Power of Capital," *International Studies Quarterly* 33 (1989): 475–499; Stephen Gill, "American Hegemony: Its Limits and Prospects in the Reagan Era," *Millenium* 15, no. 3 (fall 1986): 311–336; Robert W. Cox, "Gramsci, Hegemony, and International Relations: An Essay in Method," *Millenium* 12, no. 2 (summer 1983): 162–175; Stephen Gill, ed., *Atlantic Relations: Beyond the Reagan Era* (New York: St. Martin's Press, 1989); David P. Rapkin, ed., *World Leadership and Hegemony* (Boulder, CO: Lynne Rienner Publishers, 1990); and Craig N. Murphy and Roger Tooze, eds., *The New International Political Economy* (Boulder, CO: Lynne Rienner Publishers, 1991).

6. See Jeffry Frieden, "Sectoral Conflict and U.S. Foreign Economic Policy, 1914–1940," *International Organization* 42, no. 1 (winter 1988): esp. 83–88; and Thomas Ferguson, "From Normalcy to New Deal: Industrial Structure, Party Competition, and American Public Policy in the Great Depression," *International Organization* 38, no. 1 (winter 1984): 41–94.

7. Gramsci, *Selections,* p. 176.

8. Cox, "Social Forces," p. 169.

9. Cox, *Production,* p. 285.

10. Trade dependence consists of a manufacturing firm's dependence upon either exports or imports. Multinationality consists of a firm's dependence upon foreign direct investment (FDI), international joint ventures, or international licensing agreements. Import penetration consists of the share of domestic markets for a specific sector's products accounted for competing imports. Trade dependence can be measured at the four-digit SIC sectoral level by computing exports as a percent of shipments plus imports. Multinationality can be measured at this level by computing foreign subsidiary dividends plus foreign tax credits plus constructive taxable income from related foreign corporations as a percent of total annual income. Import penetration is measurable at the same level by computing imports as a percent of shipments plus imports minus exports.

11. See note 4.

12. This assertion has been and still is debated in the literature on trade and multinational corporations.

13. See W. M. Corden, *The Theory of Protection* (London: Oxford University Press, 1974), and "The Costs and Consequences of Protection: A Survey of Empirical Work," in Peter B. Kenen, ed., *International Trade and Finance: Frontiers for Research* (Cambridge: Cambridge University Press, 1975); Harry G. Johnson, *Aspects of the Theory of Tariffs* (Cambridge, Mass.: Harvard University Press, 1971); and Morris E. Morkre and David G. Tarr, *The Effects of Restrictions on United States Imports: Five Case Studies and Theory,* Staff Report of the Bureau of Economics to the Federal Trade Commission (Washington, D.C.: GPO, June 1980).

14. Kiyoshi Kojima, "A Macroeconomic Theory of Foreign Direct Investment," in C. Fred Bergsten, ed., *Toward a New World Trade Policy: The Maidenhead Papers,* pp. 75–100 (Lexington, Mass.: Lexington Books, 1975).

15. This point was made in C. Fred Bergsten, Thomas Horst, and Theodore Moran, *American Multinationals and American Interests* (Washington, D.C.: Brookings Institute, 1978).

16. See, for example, Frank A. Southard Jr., *American Industry in Europe* (Boston: Houghton Mifflin, 1931); and Herbert Marshall, Frank A. Southard Jr., and Kenneth W. Taylor, *Canadian-American Industry: A Study in International Investment* (New Haven, Conn.:Yale University Press, 1936). See also Bell, "Private Capital Movements and the U.S. Balance of Payments Position" (pp. 395–491), in *Factors Affecting the United States Balance of Payments,* compilation of Studies Prepared for the Subcommittee on International Exchanges and Payments of the Joint Economic Committee (Washington, D.C.: GPO, 1962), cited in Bergsten et al., *American Multinationals,* p. 54; Martin F. J. Prachowny and J. David Richardson, "Testing a Life-Cycle Hypothesis of Balance-of-Payments Effects of Multinational Corporations," *Economic Inquiry* 13 (March 1975); and Gary C. Hufbauer and F. M. Adler, "Over-

seas Manufacturing Investment and the Balance of Payments," U.S. Department of Treasury, Tax Policy Research Study No. 1 (Washington, D.C.: GPO, 1968).

17. Glenn Fong, "Export Dependence Versus the New Protectionism: Contraints on Trade Policy in the Industrial World," Ph.D. diss., Cornell University, 1984, p. 212.

18. U.S. Congress, Senate, Committee on Banking, Housing, and Urban Affairs, Subcommittee on International Finance, *Extension of the Export Administration Act,* hearings, 94th Cong., 2nd sess., 2 March 1976, p. 329.

19. William J. Corcoran, "The Machine Tool Industry Under Fire" (p. 235), in Donald L. Losman and Shu-Jan Liang, eds., *The Promise of American Industry: An Alternative Assessment of Problems and Prospects* (New York: Quorum Books, 1990).

20. Ibid.

21. U.S. Congress, House, Committee on Ways and Means, *Trade Reform,* hearings, 93rd Cong. 1st Sess., 14 May 1973, pt. 3, p. 803.

22. U.S. Congress, Senate, Committee on Finance, *The Trade Reform Act of 1973,* hearings 93rd Cong., 2nd sess., 26 March 1974, p. 1506.

23. Fong, "Export Dependence," pp. 168–169.

24. Export markets in the Soviet Union and Eastern Europe were lost when the USSR invaded Afghanistan, and the United States responded by renewing the cold war, including the reimposition of export controls. The Brazilian market was lost due to that country's imposition of increased barriers to machine tool imports.

25. For much of the following description of the machine tool crisis of the 1980s I am indebted to Ronald Gutfleish, "Machine Tools," chap. 7 in "Why Protectionism? U.S. Corporate and State Responses to a Changing World Economy," Ph.D. diss., University of California, Berkeley, 1987. Gutfleish's interviews generated insights not available elsewhere.

26. Thomas M. Rohan, "U.S. May Have Found Potent Import-Fighter," *Industry Week,* 15 November 1982, p. 19.

27. Gutfleish, "Why Protectionism?" p. 299.

28. While the Japanese government held the attorneys temporarily at bay, Yamazaki made minor changes in the design of the machine tools in question. As a result of this alleged obstruction, Houdaille was obliged to start the petition process all over again. U.S. Congress, Senate, Committee on Foreign Relations, "The U.S. Machine Tool Industry: Its Relation to National Security," hearings, 98th Cong., 1st sess., 28 November 1983, pp. 4–7; and Houdaille Industries, *Petition to the President of the United States Through the Office of the United States Trade Representative Responsible for the Exercise of Presidential Discretion Authorized by Section 103 of the Revenue Act of 1971,* 3 May 1982, p. 2.

29. According to *Industry Week,* the NMTBA had been searching for ways of imposing quotas and other restrictions on imports for years, and the search intensified *as early as 1975,* suggesting an element of disingenuity in the NMTBA's pro–free trade posture of the 1970s. The NMTBA discovered the possibility of using Section 103 by happenstance when its tax law group compared notes with its trade law group. See Rohan, "Potent Import Fighter," p. 20.

30. Had Reagan sided with Houdaille, he would have found it difficult to turn down hundreds of other manufacturers that were closely watching the case. See Rohan, "Potent Import Fighter," p. 19.

31. "U.S. Senate Supports Houdaille Petition," *Iron Age*, 12 January 1983, p. 12.
32. Quoted in Gutfleish, "Why Protectionism?" p. 301.
33. Ibid., p. 302.
34. The predictability of Schultz's opposition to the Houdaille petition is due to his "historic bloc pedigree." A product of Princeton and MIT, Schultz had been director and president of Bechtel Corporation, and a director of General Motors, Morgan Guaranty Trust, and Dillon, Reed, and Company.
35. "Toolbuilder angered by Reagan 'No'," *Industry Week*, 19 September 1983, pp. 25, 31.
36. Gutfleish, "Why Protectionism?" p. 303.
37. "Toolbuilder Angered,"*Industry Week*, p. 30.
38. Bendix estimated that it would sell between 3,000 and 3,500 Toyoda machining centers per year at an average price of $150,000.
39. "Bendix to Sell Toyoda Machining Centers," *Iron Age*, 12 January 1983, p. 13. Ironically, this item appeared on the same page as a quote from Houdaille's O'Reilly: "Our quarrel is not with Japanese competition. ... *It is with cartel activities* funded with government subsidies" (Emphasis added).
40. Ibid.
41. In the interim, the Soviet Union had invaded Afghanistan.
42. *Industry Week*, 29 November 1982, p. 21.
43. The petition asked that overall machine tool imports be limited to a maximum 17.5 percent while import shares of eighteen specific market segments be limited to 20 percent of consumption.
44. *American Machinist*, December 1982, p. 5.
45. "Japan Parries a Protectionist Thrust," *Business Week*, 11 April 1983, p. 35.
46. "Machine Tools: Will the Cornerstone Erode?" *Industry Week*, 30 April 1984, p. 78.
47. Gutfleish, "Why Protectionism?" p. 304. Gutfleish cites an NMTBA interview in support of this statement.
48. Phillip A. O'Reilly, "Fight Foreign Government Cartels," *Industry Week*, 25 June 1984, p. 8.
49. On this trend, see "How Imports Are Reshaping the U.S. Economy," *Business Week*, 1 April 1985, p. 31; and *Industry Week*, 13 June 1983, p. 69.
50. *Business Week*, 1 October 1984, p. 77; *Business Marketing*, November 1984, p. 112; *American Machinist*, February 1985, p. 5.
51. "Slow Recovery for a Vulnerable Giant," *Financial World*, 17–30 October 1984, pp. 24, 28.
52. Gutfleish, "Why Protectionism?" p. 305.
53. U.S. Congress, Senate, Committee on Foreign Relations, The U.S. Machine Tool Industry: Its Relation to National Security, hearings, 98th Cong., 1st sess., 28 November 1983, pp. 11–13.
54. "Machine Tools," *Industry Week*, 30 April 1984, p. 64.
55. Gutfleish, "Why Protectionism?" p. 306.
56. *American Machinist*, May 1984, p. 33. For more details, see *Industry Week*, 25 June 1984, p. 8; *American Machinist*, May 1984, p. 23; and Gutfleish, "Why Protectionism," p. 310.
57. *American Machinist*, May 1984, p. 33.

58. Ibid.

59. *American Machinist,* January 1986, p. 45, cited in Gutfleish, "Why Protectionism?" p. 45.

60. This is according to the results of one of Gutfleish's interviews, "Why Protectionism?" p. 312.

61. Ibid.

62. Ibid.

63. Ibid, p. 313.

64. Ibid.

65. Ibid, p. 315.

66. Ibid.

67. From interview notes cited in Gutfleish, "Why Protectionism?" p. 316.

68. This brief section on semiconductors is indebted to David B. Yoffie and Helen V. Milner, "An Alternative to Free Trade or Protection: Why Corporations Seek Strategic Trade Policy," *California Management Review* 31, no. 4 (summer 1989): pp. 111–131, esp. pp. 117–119.

69. Ibid., pp. 118–119.

70. Helen Milner, *Resisting Protectionism: Global Industries and the Politics of International Trade* (Princeton, N.J.: Princeton University Press, 1988), pp. 124–125.

71. Ibid., pp. 127–128.

72. Ibid., p. 132.

73. "The Future of Silicon Valley: Does the U.S. Need a High-Tech Industrial Policy to Battle Japan Inc.?" *Business Week,* 5 February 1990, pp. 54–60.

74. This matrix, and the industries selected in it, are inspired by three theses: Glenn Fong, "Export Dependence"; Helen Milner, "Resisting the Protectionist Temptation: Industry Politics and Trade Policy in France and the United States in the 1920s and 1970s," Ph.D. diss., Harvard University, 1986; and Ronald Gutfleish, "Why Protectionism?"

75. I set aside nonrubber footwear from here on since it has neither undergone international integration nor noticeably participated in the product cycle.

76. James R. Kurth, "Political Consequences of the Product Cycle: Industrial History and Political Outcomes," *International Organization* 33, no. 1 (winter 1979): 1–34.

Chapter 5

1. There are a wealth of scholarly studies on different aspects of the politics of industrial restructuring. One of the best recent accounts is Robert Ross and Kent Trachte, *Global Capitalism: The New Leviathan* (New York: City University of New York Press, 1991). See also Saskia Sassen, *The Global City* (Princeton, N.J.: Princeton University Press, 1991).

2. On the importance of global competition for the triad markets of Western Europe, the United States, and Asia, see Kenichi Ohmae, *Triad Power: The Coming Shape of Global Competition* (New York: Free Press, 1985).

3. John Holmes, "The Globalization of Production and the Future of Canada's Mature Industries: The Case of the Automobile Industry," in D. Drache and M. S.

244   Notes

Gertler, eds., *The New Era of Global Competition: State Policy and Market Power* (Montreal: McGill-Queens Press, 1990).

4. For an analysis of the domestic forces behind the CBI, see Ronald W. Cox, *Power and Profits: U.S. Policy Toward Central America* (Lexington: University Press of Kentucky, 1994).

5. Joseph Grunwald and Kenneth Flamm, *The Global Factory* (Washington, D.C.: Brookings Institute, 1985), p. 12.

6. This category of "electronics" firms is very broad, but the trend of industrial restructuring is most apparent in consumer electronics and is represented by RCA, GTE, Sylvania, and Zenith, all of which built up subsidiary plants in Mexico during the late 1970s and early 1980s. In addition, electronics firms producing for computers and the telecommunications industry have also been relocating in Mexico. For details, see D. Ernst, "U.S.-Japanese Competition and Worldwide Restructuring of the Electronics Industry: A European View," chap. 3 in J. Henderson and M. Castells, eds., *Global Restructuring and Territorial Development* (London: Sage, 1987).

7. The best recent account is Christopher M. Law, ed., *Restructuring the Global Automobile Industry* (London: Routledge, 1991). See also Rhys Jenkins, *Transnational Corporations and the Latin American Automobile Industry* (London: Macmillan, 1987).

8. See W. Raymond Cline, *The Future of World Trade in Textiles and Apparel* (Washington, D.C.: Institute for International Economics, 1987).

9. For an overview of these trends, see James M. Rubenstein, "The Impact of Japanese Investment in the United States," chap. 5 in Law, ed., *Restructuring the Global Automobile Industry.*

10. Peter Dicken, *Global Shift* (New York: Guilford Press, 1992), p. 340.

11. Ibid.

12. Much of the following account is based on information contained in bimonthly newsletters published by the Caribbean/Central American Action organization (now the Caribbean/Latin American Action), in addition to material from my book, *Power and Profits.*

13. See Emilio Pantojas Garcia, "The United States Caribbean Basin Initiative and the Puerto Rican Experience," *Latin American Perspectives* 12 (fall 1985): 105–128.

14. For a summary of this trend, see Business International Corporation (BIC), *Improving International Competitiveness Through Sourcing in Latin America* (New York: BIC, 1989).

15. Ibid., pp. 2–4.

16. See William Nestor, *Japan's Growing Predominance Over the World Economy* (New York: St. Martin's Press, 1990), esp. chap. 4.

17. For an account of these business conflicts, see the CCAA report, "A Briefing on the CBI and Legislative History," 7 August 1989.

18. For a good discussion of these trends, see Lorraine Eden and Maureen Appel Molot, "Continentalizaing the North American Auto Industry," in Ricardo Grinspun and Maxwell Cameron, eds., *The Political Economy of North American Free Trade,* pp. 297–313 (New York: St. Martin's Press, 1993).

19. Ross and Trachte, *Global Capitalism,* p. 124.

20. Ibid.

21. For a detailed exposition of these trends, see *U.S.-Mexican Industrial Integration* in Sidney Weintraub, Luis Rubio, and Alan Jones, eds., (Boulder, Colo.: Westview Press, 1991).

22. Gary Hufbauer and Jeffrey Schott, *The North American Free Trade Agreement* (Washington, D.C.: Institute for International Economics, 1992). p. 213.

23. Betsy Lordan, "Wheels of Fortune," *U.S./Latin Trade* 34, no. 1 (July 1993): 66.

24. Ernest Preeg, "The Compatibility of Regional Economic Blocs and GATT," in Sidney Weintraub, ed., *Free Trade in the Western Hemisphere* (London: Sage Periodicals Press, 1993), p. 165.

25. Ibid., p. 167.

26. For an overview of these divisions, see Margaret Cummins, "Interest Group Competition and NAFTA," unpublished manuscript, University of North Carolina-Chapel Hill, 1992.

27. I. M. Destler and John S. Odell, *Anti-Protection: Changing Forces in United States Trade Politics* (Washington, D.C.: Institute for International Economics, 1987), p. 40.

28. Ibid., pp. 50–51.

29. Ibid., p. 56.

30. Ibid.

31. For a general overview of the multilateralism of segments of the banking establishment, see Jeffry Frieden, *Banking on the World* (New York: Harper & Row, 1987).

Chapter 6

1. I explore the nexus between business interests and U.S. trade policy at greater length in my doctoral dissertation, "Foreign Policy as Domestic Politics: The Political Economy of U.S. Trade Policy, 1960–1975," Oxford University (in progress).

2. Michael Mastanduno provides a fairly comprehensive summary from a realist perspective of the origins of these restrictive policies. See Michael Mastanduno, "Trade as a Strategic Weapon: American and Alliance Export Control Policy in the Early Postwar Period," *International Organization* 42, no. 1 (winter 1988): pp. 121–150.

3. Interestingly, during the war, many, such as Roosevelt adviser Harry Hopkins, regarded the Soviet Union as a potential market—thus an opportunity rather than a threat (see Bruce W. Jentleson, *Pipeline Politics: The Complex Political Economy of East-West Energy Trade* [Ithaca, N.Y.: Cornell University Press, 1986], pp. 51–52). Nonetheless, concern over the possible competitive threat—as opposed to strategic threat—posed by the centralized structure of the Soviet economy dates to an even earlier period. See, for example, H. R. Knickerbocker, *Fighting the Red Trade Menace* (New York: Dodd, Mead, 1931).

4. Letter, McCloy to Bundy, 18 January 1965, filed with letter, Bundy to McCloy, 25 January 1965, Ex FG 761, WHCF, Box 408, LBJ Library, Austin, Texas.

5. Ibid.

6. Jentleson, *Pipeline Politics*, pp. 81–87.

7. Letter, Evans to the President, 16 May 1967, filed with letter, Rostow to Evans, 25 May 1967, Gen TA, WHCF, Box 2, LBJ Library.

8. Ibid.

9. J. Wilczynski, *The Multinationals and East-West Relations: Towards Transideological Collaboration* (London: Macmillan, 1976), p. 19.

10. The shift in the policies of socialist states in response to complaints is beyond question. Nonetheless, these complaints may have been overstated, distorted perhaps by political considerations. In the dumping area, for instance, the Tariff Commission was charged with determining whether dumping had occurred and what remedy was in order. In a 1955 decision, three commissioners indicated that regardless of the facts of the case—that is, whether the definition of dumping in the relevant trade statute applied—"in their judgement ... any sale by a Communist Country was in and of itself injurious." Ironically, a decade later, the Tariff Commission was still injecting extraneous criteria into its decisionmaking process, but to opposite effect, arguing that dumped imports from Comecon countries should not be considered injurious since their poor quality and consumer resistance to their origin greatly circumscribed potential U.S. sales. Richard Dale, *Anti-Dumping Law in a Liberal Trade Order* (London: Macmillan, 1980), pp. 178–179.

11. Note that this explanation accords with Jentleson's discussion of the differences that emerged between the United States and Western European allies on the optimal commercial policy to pursue toward the Soviet Union. While Americans were pushing anticommunism to justify their view that trade should be restricted, many Western Europeans argued that increased commercial linkages would help tame the renegade state. There are several factors that account for these differences: One undoubted influence was that Europe, for both historical and geographical reasons, had been a more significant trader with East-bloc states, and in the aftermath of the war, European producers were more interested in reestablishing basic commercial relations than in furthering a U.S. strategic design. Jentleson further argues that one significant reason for the conflict was the different position of the United States from that of Europe in oil production. The United States, as a significant oil producer, had much to lose from reestablishing the Soviet Union as an oil producer; by contrast, most of Europe was merely an oil consumer and, as such, favored increased trade with the Soviets as a means to diversify its sources of supply, particularly after the Suez Canal crisis. Jentleson, *Pipeline Politics*, chap. 1, esp. pp. 38–40.

12. For a general introduction to the Kennedy and the Johnson economic advisory systems, see E. Ray Canterbery, *Economics on a New Frontier* (Belmont, Calif.: Wadsworth Publishing Co., 1968), chap. 10 and 11, as well as Walter W. Heller, "Economic Policy Advisers," in Thomas E. Cronin and Sanford D. Greenberg, eds., *The Presidential Advisory System* , pp. 29–39 (New York: Harper & Row, 1969).

13. Presidents find it relatively painless to ignore findings of presidential commissions that conflict with their overall goals. Thomas R. Wolanin provides a systematic treatment of the responses to commission recommendations in Appendix 3 of his "Responses to the Recommendations of Commissions," in Thomas R. Wolanin, *Presidential Advisory Commissions: Truman to Nixon*, pp. 216–245 (Madison: University of Wisconsin Press, 1975).

14. For an account of the Johnson administration's control of the output of one such commission, see Daniel Bell, "Government by Commission," in Cronin and Greenberg, eds., *Presidential Advisory*, p. 118.

15. NSAM 324, Bundy to Secretaries of State, Treasury, Defense, Interior, Agriculture, Commerce, and Labor; Director of Central Intelligence; and President, Export-Import Bank, 9 March 1965, National Security Files, LBJ Library.

16. After initially considering David Rockefeller for chairman, Johnson chose Miller. Letter, McCloy to Bundy, 18 January 1965, ibid. Several Miller Committee members worked for corporations that later concluded significant cooperation agreements with the USSR or other socialist countries, including William Blackie (Caterpillar Tractor), George Brown (Brown & Root), Crawford H. Greenewalt (Du Pont), and J. William Miller (Cummins Engine Company). For some details of the agreements these companies concluded with the USSR, see Wilczynski, *Multinationals*, particularly the list and index of multinational corporations and their affiliates (pp. 197–232). Some of Wilczynski's data are summarized in Tables 6.1 and 6.2 in this chapter. In addition, Jentleson discusses some of the later activities of Caterpillar Tractor and Brown & Root; see Jentleson, *Pipeline Politics*, pp. 139–141, 204.

17. Memo, Kennedy to the Export Control Review Board, 19 September 1963, "NSC Meetings, Vol. 1, Tab 58 4/16/64, East-West Trade," National Security Files, Box 1, LBJ Library.

18. Memo, Bundy to the President, 3 March 1965, filed with memo, Bundy to the President, 28 April 1965, Ex FG 761, WHCF, Box 408, LBJ Library (emphasis in original).

19. Memo, Mann to Bundy, 17 June 1965, C.F. LE/TA, WHCF, Box 64, LBJ Library.

20. Ibid., pp. 2–5.

21. The quotation is from memo, Stoessel and Solomon to Rusk, 16 December 1965, filed with memo, Bator for the Record, 27 January 1966, C.F. LE/TA, WHCF, Box 64, LBJ Library. Indeed, Mann suggested: "I am not at all convinced, however, that an East-West trade bill would not meet with very strong opposition in the Congress, especially if no end of the Vietnamese conflict is in sight and our commitments there are increased" (memo, Mann to Rusk, 17 December 1965, attached to memo, Bator for the Record, 27 January 1966, ibid).

22. Memo, Bator to Bundy, 4 January 1966, filed with memo, Bator for the Record, 27 January 1966, ibid. (emphasis in original).

23. Memo, Rusk to the President, 7 January 1966, filed with memo, Bator for the Record, 27 January 1966, ibid.

24. Memo, Bator to Bundy, 4 January 1966, ibid.

25. Memo, Bundy to the President, 8 January 1966, filed with memo, Bator for the Record, 27 January 1966, ibid.

26. Memo, Califano to the President, 21 September 1966, Ex LE/TA, WHCF, Box 155, LBJ Library.

27. Memo, Bator to the President, 24 March 1967, filed with letter, Watson to the President, 7 April 1967, Ex TA, WHCF, Box 1, LBJ Library; see also Item for the President's Evening Reading, no date, filed with memo, Califano to Gaither and Bator, C.F. LE/TA, WHCF, Box 64, LBJ Library.

28. For example, the administration considered seeing members of the Chicago Board of Trade on their Washington visit, because "this group is a natural leader on behalf of the East-West trade bill" (memo, Wilson to the President, 10 February 1967, Ex TA, WHCF, Box 1, LBJ Library).

29. Letter, Trowbridge to the President, 8 May 1967, filed with memo, Kintner to the President, 8 May 1967, C.F. LE/TA, WHCF, Box 64, LBJ Library.

30. "Platform for Today," *The Economist*, 10 August 1968, p. 19. Southern influence accounted for some of this ambiguity: Nixon's soundness on the communist question was an important criterion for Strom Thurmond's support for the 1968 nomination.

31. Memo, Secretary of Commerce to the President, 9 April 1969, filed with memo, Burns to the President, 12 April 1969, Ex TA Trade [1 of 57, December 1968–August 1969], WHCF, Box 1, Richard M. Nixon Project (hereafter, RMNP), College Park, Maryland, pp. 4–5.

32. Ibid., p. 1.

33. Henry A. Kissinger, *The White House Years* (London: Weidenfeld & Nicolson, 1979), p. 153.

34. "Apparently a White House decision will be reached by Monday, May 26, on East-West Trade policy. Next week the Administration witnesses will present this policy to the House and Senate Banking and Currency Committees, which are holding hearings on extension of the Export Control Act, which expires June 30" (memo, Alexander to Harlow, 15 May 1969, Ex TA Trade [1 of 57, December 1968–August 1969], WHCF, Box 1, RMNP).

35. Ibid.

36. These arguments are developed at greater length in I. M. Destler, *American Trade Politics: System Under Stress* (New York: Twentieth Century Fund, Washington, D.C.: Institute for International Economics, 1986); I. M. Destler, "Executive-Congressional Conflict in Foreign Policy: Explaining It, Coping with It," in Lawrence C. Dodd and Bruce I. Oppenheimer, eds., *Congress Reconsidered*, 2nd ed. (Washington, D.C.: Congressional Quarterly Press, 1981); and Robert Pastor, *Congress and the Politics of U.S. Foreign Economic Policy, 1929–1976* (Berkeley: University of California Press, 1980). See also Jerri-Lynn Scofield, "U.S. Trade Policy and the U.S. Trade Deficit," in Godfrey Hodgson, ed., *Handbooks to the Modern World: The United States* (New York: Facts on File, 1992), pp. 1478–1503.

37. Memo, Alexander to Harlow, 15 May 1969, ibid., p. 2.

38. Memo, Kissinger to Harlow, 23 June 1969, Ex TA Trade [1 of 57, December 1968–August 1969], WHCF, Box 1, RMNP.

39. This legislation foreshadowed a more general trend toward relaxing restraints on exports for strategic reasons: in 1972, Congress passed legislation requiring prompt removal of export controls not vital to national security and extended the authority of the Export Administration Act until 30 June 1974 (Congressional Quarterly, Inc., *Trade: U.S. Policy Since 1945* (Washington, D.C.: Congressional Quarterly Press, 1984), p. 108.

40. Ibid.

41. The commission was given the charge "to examine the principal problems in the field of U.S. foreign trade and investment, and to provide recommendations designed to meet the challenges of the changing world economy during the present decade" (U.S. Government, *United States International Economic Policy in an Interdependent World,* report to the President by the Commission on International Trade and Investment Policy [Williams Commission] [Washington, D.C.: U.S. GPO, 1971], p. ix) (hereafter Williams Commission Report).

42. Some of these individuals included James H. Binger (Honeywell), Fred J. Borch (General Electric), Richard C. Gerstenberg (General Motors), Charles H. Sommer (Monsanto), William R. Pearce (Cargill), Leroy D. Stinebower (Standard Oil of New Jersey, which became part of Exxon in November 1972), and Albert L. Williams (International Business Machines). See Tables 6.1 and 6.2 for the data upon which these comparisons are based. Some of the activities of Standard Oil and General Electric are explored further in Jentleson, *Pipeline Politics*, pp. 110–112, 139–141.

43. For more on the connections between the First National Bank of Chicago and socialist states, see Wilczynski, *Multinationals*, p. 21n and pp. 121, 147, 209; for Wells Fargo, see p. 230.

44. Williams Commission Report, pp. 15–16. See also pp. 259–271.

45. Peter G. Peterson, *U.S.-Soviet Commercial Relationships in a New Era* (Washington, D.C.: U.S. GPO, 1972).

46. CED, *A New Trade Policy Toward Communist Countries* (New York: Committee for Economic Development, 1972).

47. The birth and subsequent activities of ECAT are discussed at greater length in Scofield, "Foreign Policy as Domestic Politics."

48. Memo, Flanigan to the President, 24 October 1973, Ex TA Trade [50 of 57, October 1973], Box 7, RMNP (emphasis in original).

49. Memo, Staempfli to Brady, 9 November 1973, Ex TA Trade [51 of 57, November 1973], Box 7, RMNP.

50. Ibid.

51. Memo, Eberle to Kissinger, Schultz [sic], Dent, Flanigan, Timmons, Simon, Casey, Haig, 9 April 1974, Ex TA Trade [55 of 57, April 1974], Box 8, RMNP.

52. So, for example, some Jewish labor leaders who otherwise opposed Nixon's trade expansion plans supported the legislation as a small price to pay to get the Jackson-Vanik Amendment enacted as a statute. See Russell Warren Howe and Sarah Hays Trott, *The Power Peddlers: How Lobbyists Mold America's Foreign Policy* (Garden City, N.Y.: Doubleday & Co., 1977), p. 231.

53. The leading study of the Jackson-Vanik Amendment is Paula Stern, *Water's Edge: Domestic Politics and the Making of American Foreign Policy* (Westport, Conn.: Greenwood Press, 1979).

54. See Strobe Talbot, *Deadly Gambits: The Reagan Administration and the Stalemate in Nuclear Arms Control* (London: Pan Books, 1985), p. 16.

55. Stern, *Water's Edge*, p. 21.

56. Jentleson, *Pipeline Politics*, p. 142.

57. Stern, *Water's Edge*, p. 26.

58. Ibid., p. 21.

59. See the earlier quotation from letter, McCloy to Bundy, 18 January 1965, ibid.

60. This is not to imply an unduly deterministic view of this problem. It is just to suggest that Jackson's constituency pressures allowed him to promote the Jewish emigration issue in a way he might not have been able to do if he had been a senator from some other state.

Precisely why these pressures were so successful, in light of the strong pressure for liberalization from other business sectors, is a topic that must await further exploration.

61. Letter, Jackson to Greenspan, 4 September 1975, folder TA3/CO158, 9/1/75–9/20/75, Box 8, WHCF TA3/CO158, Gerald R. Ford Library, Ann Arbor, Michigan.

One unspoken motivation behind this letter is the effect of OPEC's oil embargo on attitudes toward diversifying sources of petroleum supply. Space considerations prevent me from exploring further the efforts oil producers made to cooperate with the Soviets in oil production efforts. Jentleson addresses some significant issues in Jentleson, *Pipeline Politics*, chap. 5, esp. pp. 138–149.

Chapter 7

1. A recent statement of this state-centric teleological approach is found in Richard Sandbrook, *The Politics of Africa's Economic Recovery* (New York: Cambridge University Press, 1993).

2. Richard Joseph, *Democracy and Prebendal Politics in Nigeria*, (New York: Cambridge University Press, 1990), p. 8.

3. Joseph, *Democracy*, p. 180.

4. Jean François Bayart, *L'État en Afrique* (Paris: Fayard, 1989).

5. An analysis of this intentional deinstitutionalization is developed in Joel Migdal, *Strong Societies and Weak States*, (Princeton: Princeton University, 1988).

6. Stephen Krasner, *International Regimes* (Ithaca, New York: Cornell, 1983) and Robert Keohane, "Realism, Neorealism and the Study of World Politics," in Robert Keohane, ed., *Neorealism and Its Critics* (New York: Columbia University Press, 1986).

7. A. Samatar and A. I. Samatar, "The Material Roots of the Suspended African State: Arguments from Somalia," *Journal of Modern African Studies* 25, no. 4(1987): 669–690.

8. David N. Gibbs, *The Political Economy of Third World Intervention: Mines, Money, and U.S. Policy in the Congo Crisis* (Chicago: University of Chicago, 1991), pp. 32–33.

9. Robert Jackson, *Quasi-states*, (New York: Cambridge University Press, 1990), pp. 178–179.

10. Peter Evans, Dietrich Rueschemeyer, and Theda Skocpol, eds., *Bringing the State Back In* (New York: Cambridge University Press, 1985).

11. Theda Skocpol, "The Limits of the New Deal System and the Roots of Contemporary Welfare Dilemmas," in Margaret Weir, Ann Shola Orloff, and Theda Skocpol, eds., *The Politics of Policy in the United States* pp. 293–311 (Princeton, N.J.: Princeton University Press, 1988).

12. Kenneth Waltz, *Theory of International Politics* (Reading, Mass: Addison-Wesley, 1979), p. 94.

13. Robert Gilpin, *War and Change in World Politics* (New York: Cambridge University Press, 1981), p. 18.

14. Ibid.

15. Keohane, ed., *Neorealism and Its Critics*.

16. Susan Strange and John Stopford, *Rival States, Rival Firms* (New York: Cambridge University Press, 1991), p. 217.

17. Crawford Young and Thomas Turner, *The Rise and Decline of the Zairian State*, (Madison: University of Wisconsin Press, 1985); Richard Sandbrook, "Taming the African Leviathan," *World Policy Journal* 8, no. 3(1990): 673–701; Larry Dia-

mond, "Class Formation in the Swollen African State," *Journal of Modern African Studies* 25, no. 4(1987): 567–596.

18. Richard Sandbrook, *The Politics of Africa's Economic Stagnation* (New York: Cambridge University Press, 1985), p. 33.

19. World Bank, *World Development Report, 1991* (Washington, DC: World Bank, 1991), p. 133.

20. World Bank, *Sub-Saharan Africa: From Crisis to Sustainable Growth* (Washington, DC: World Bank, 1989), pp. 186–187.

21. Ibid., p. 60.

22. "Zaire: Les diamants de Mobutu," *Jeune Afrique*, 22 April 1993, p. 8.

23. Young and Turner, *The Rise and Decline*, p. 399.

24. Mohammed Ayoob, "The Security Predicament of the Third World State: Reflections on State Making in a Comparative Perspective," in Brian Job, ed., *The Insecurity Dilemma* pp. 63–80 (Boulder, Colo.: Lynne Rienner Publishers, 1992).

25. Ibid., p. 69.

26. Charles Tilly, *Coercion, Capital, and European States* (New York: Basil Blackwell, 1990), pp. 192–225.

27. Theda Skocpol, "Bringing the State Back In: Strategies of Analysis in Current Research," in Evans, Rueschmeyer, and Skocpol, eds., *Bringing the State Back In*, pp. 25–26.

28. IMF, "1988 Article XIV Consultations" (Sierra Leone Ministry of Internal Affairs, November 1988).

29. Bank of Sierra Leone, *Economic Trends* (Freetown: Government Printer, 1986–1990).

30. Ministry of Internal Affairs, "Assessment of the Visit of the Minister of State for Finance to Ghana," 6 March 1990.

31. IMF, SM/88/68, "Staff Report," 20 April 1988.

32. "Correspondence from Assistant to the Minister of Interior to His Excellency J. S. Momoh," 16 July 1986.

33. IMF, "1988 Article XIV Consultations."

34. [Ministry of Internal Affairs], "Cabinet Minutes," 2 Feb 1986.

35. Ministry of Mines, "Report of the Inspector of Mines" (Freetown: Government Printer, July 1989); and Bank of Sierra Leone, *Economic Trends*, various issues.

36. Data provided by Sierra Leone authorities and IMF staff estimates [Ministry of Internal Affairs].

37. See *Africa Confidential*, 17 September 1986, 7 January 1987, and 24 June 1987; Stephen Ellis, "Les prolongements du conflit israelo-arabe en Afrique noire," *Politique Africaine* 30 (1988): 69–75; and issues of the Freetown weekly *For Di People*.

38. Information provided by a former high official and associates of a South African diamond-buying operation currently active in Sierra Leone.

39. [Ministry of Internal Affairs], "Cabinet Minutes," 2 February 1987.

40. Ibid., 24 January 1987; IMF, EDB/88, "1987 Article IV Consultation," 20 April 1988.

41. For more on Iranian and Palestinian connections, see "Sierra Leone: Rape," *Africa Confidential* (local press), 28 November 1984.

42. *For Di People*, May 1987 issues.

43. *Africa Confidential*.

44. "A Dose Too Much," *West Africa*, 6 July 1987.

45. Ministry of Mines, "Report to the Inspector of Mines."

46. IMF, EBS/89/233.

47. Interview with a former Ministry of Internal Affairs official, Freetown, 18 April 1990.

48. IMF, EBS/89/233.

49. Officials of some foreign states privately concluded that SCIPA was a money-laundering operation. U.S. concern was serious enough to warrant visits by Drug Enforcement Agency delegations.

50. "Sierra Leone: Of Mines and Men," *Africa Confidential*, 8 March 1991; and National Diamond Mining Corporation, "Kimberlite Project Negotiations with Sunshine Broulle of Texas, USA," notes of 6 February 1990.

51. *We Yone* (Freetown weekly), 20 May 1990; and *New Citizen* (Freetown weekly), 26 May 1990.

52. "Sunshine Mining Co. Told to Pay Damages," *Wall Street Journal*, 23 January 1992.

53. Ministry of Agriculture, Natural Resources and Forestry, correspondence "Proposed Joint Venture Agreement for Management and Control of Fishing Rights in Sierra Leone's Territorial Waters," 3 January 1990.

54. Economist Intelligence Unit, *Ghana, Sierra Leone, Liberia*, second quarter, 1991.

55. PF/NA/507/1, Ministry of Interior, correspondence of 5 July 1989, "Corruption and Indiscipline in Private Sector."

56. "At the Bottom of the Pile," *African Economic Development*, 9 September 1991, p. 18.

57. Economist Intelligence Unit, *Ghana, Sierra Leone, Liberia*, second quarter, 1992, p. 23.

58. Ibid., first quarter, 1991.

59. "President of Sierra Leone Ousted; Troops Rule West African Nation," *New York Times*, 1 May 1992.

60. Calculated from Bank of Sierra Leone, *Economic Trends*, and Economist Intelligence Unit, *Ghana, Sierra Leone, Liberia*.

61. For successful examples, see Robert Bates, *Beyond the Miracle of the Market: The Political Economy of Agrarian Development in Kenya* (Cambridge: Cambridge University Press, 1989); and Jean Copans, "Du vin de palme nouveau dans les vielles calebasses?" *Genéve Afrique* 27, no. 1 (1989): 7–43.

62. For example: Victor Azarya, "Reordering State-Society Relations: Incorporation and Disengagement," in Donald Rothchild and Naomi Chazan, eds., *The Precarious Balance: State and Society in Africa*, pp. 3–21 (Boulder, Colo.: Westview Press, 1988); Goran Hyden, *No Shortcuts to Progress* (Berkeley: University of California Press, 1981); Colin Leys, "The 'Overdeveloped' Post-Colonial State," *Review of African Political Economy* 5 (1976): 39–48; and Claude Ake, *A Political Economy of Africa* (London: Longman, 1981).

Chapter 8

1. For some representative examples of the burgeoning literature on this international bargaining, see Charles Lipson, "Bankers' Dilemmas: Private Cooperation in Rescheduling Sovereign Debts," *World Politics* 38, no. 1 (October 1985); Jeffrey Sachs, "Theoretical Issues in International Borrowing," *Princeton Studies in International Finance*, no. 54 (Princeton, N.J.: International Finance Section, 1984); and Vincent Crawford, "International Lending, Long-Term Credit Relationships, and Dynamic Contract Theory," *Princeton Studies in International Finance*, no. 59 (Princeton, N.J.: International Finance Section, 1987).

2. On the approaches and their deficiencies, see, for example, J. Samuel Valenzuela and Arturo Valenzuela, "Modernization and Dependency: Alternative Paradigms on the Study of Latin American Underdevelopment," *Comparative Politics* 10, no. 4 (July 1978); and David Collier, ed., *The New Authoritarianism in Latin* America (Princeton, N.J.: Princeton University Press, 1979).

3. For a more ambitious attempt to explain both the origins and the effects of national borrowing experiences, see my "Classes, Sectors, and Foreign Debt in Latin America," *Comparative Politics* (forthcoming); more detailed references can be found there. Surveys include Andres Bianchi, et al., *External Debt in Latin America* (Boulder, Colo.: Lynne Rienner Publishers, 1985); Carlos Diaz-Alejandro, "Latin American Debt," *Brookings Papers on Economic Activity* no. 2 (1984); Inter-American Development Bank (IADB), *External Debt and Economic Development in Latin America* (Washington, D.C.: IADB, 1984); Jonathan Hartlyn and Samuel Morely, eds., *Latin American Political Economy: Financial Crisis and Political Change* (Boulder, Colo.: Westview Press, 1986); and Joseph Ramos, *Neoconservative Economics in the Southern Cone of LatinAmerica, 1973–1983* (Baltimore: Johns Hopkins University Press, 1986).

4. In the simplest sense, "overvaluation" results when an inflow of resources leads to an increase in the demand for nontraded goods, the prices of which thus move upward. Inasmuch as traded goods prices are constrained by international competition and the exchange rate is set by the traded goods sector, the exchange raite will tend to drift toward "overvaluation" as it rises more slowly than does domestic inflation. See, for example, Arnold Harberger, "Economic Adjustment and the Real Exchange Rate," in Sebastian Edwards and Liaquat Ahamed, eds., *Economic Adjustment and Exchange Rates in Developing Countries* (Chicago: University of Chicago Press, 1987). The well-known and controversial literature on the "Dutch disease" discusses a special case of this phenomenon.

5. In a more nuanced vein, the benefits accruing to the financial and commercial sectors, and to the nontraded goods sectors more generally, depended on the degree to which financial resources flowed to these sectors or "leaked" into them in large amounts. To the extent that government policy limited borrowing to producers of traded goods and forced borrowers to use borrowed funds directly for imports, there was little overvaluation and thus little switching of domestic expenditures from domestically produced traded goods to foreign and nontraded goods. Where government policy allowed significant amounts of borrowed funds to be used for nontraded goods purchases, the resultant overvaluation exacerbated the first-order effort by cutting into the domestic demand for domestically produced traded goods.

6. This implies, of course, that agents were not accurately forecasting the future costs of current borrowing. Given the catastrophic and relatively sudden nature of the crisis, this is hardly a controversial assertion. For an argument that even "prudent planners" would have been swamped by the events of 1982–1983, see Carlos Diaz-Alejandro, "Some Aspects of the 1982–1983 Brazilian Payments Crisis," *Brookings Papers on Economic Activity*, no. 2 (1983).

7. Albert O. Hirschman, *Exit, Voice, and Loyalty* (Cambridge, Mass.: Harvard University Press, 1970).

8. In what follows I focus almost exclusively on real capital; the argument could easily be extended to include human capital, and thus the specific skills of workers. The political implications of the inclusion of human capital are clear and significant. It should also be noted that the following discussion assumes that investors' portfolios are not completely diversified. This is a reasonable assumption, especially in Latin America, where capital markets are extremely underdeveloped and almost all firms are family owned.

9. Manufacturing value added as a percentage of GDP calculated from IADB, *Economic and Social Progress in Latin America: 1986 Report* (Washington, DC: IADB, 1986).

10. For more details on the Brazilian case, see Jeffry Frieden, "The Brazilian Borrowing Experience," *Latin American Research Review* 22, no. 2 *(1987)*.

11. For further reading, in addition to the sources cited in this chapter's notes, see: Jeffrey D. Sachs, "External Debt and Macroeconomic Performance in Latin America and East Asia," *Brookings Papers on Economic Activity*, no. 2 (1985); and Rosemary Thorp and Lawrence Whitehead, eds., *Latin American Debt and the Adjustment Crisis* (London: Macmillan, 1987).

Chapter 9

* The author wishes to acknowledge the help of Deborah Avant, Ronald Cox, James Nolt, David Gibbs, Timothy Sinclair, and Walter Goldstein in the preparation of this chapter.

1. Neopluralism is also called the "business conflict" or "business investment" model. My reasons for calling it "neopluralism" are established in the section that bears its name.

2. See the following works by Kenneth N. Waltz: *Man, the State, and War: A Theoretical Analysis* (New York: Columbia University Press, 1959); "The Myth of National Independence" in Charles P. Kindleberger, ed., *The International Corporation*, pp. 205–226 (Cambridge, Mass.: MIT Press, 1970); and *Theory of International Politics* (Reading, Mass.: Addison-Wesley, 1979).

3. It should be observed that realists, for all their focus on unitary states and their quest for power, never appear to have considered the possibility that a state might self-destruct into component parts. The disintegration of the Soviet Union and Yugoslavia into bitterly antagonistic fragments is an example of a phenomenon that has had a major impact on the international system and is beyond the purview of realist theory.

4. Stephen Krasner, *Defending the National Interest: Raw Materials Investments and U.S. Foreign Policy* (Princeton, N.J.: Princeton University Press, 1978). Krasner

presents a list of economic-strategic objectives, but it is not very convincing. Kenneth Waltz makes similar recommendations in *Theory of International Politics*. For a critique, see Albert O. Hirschman, *National Power and the Structure of Foreign Trade* (Berkeley: University of California Press, 1980).

5. Robert Keohane and Joseph Nye, *Power and Interdependence: World Politics in Transition* (Boston: Little, Brown & Co., 1977).

6. John G. Ruggie, "International Responses to Technology: Concepts and Trends," *International Organization* 29 (summer 1975): 557–584.

7. Charles Kindleberger, *The World in Depression, 1929–1939* (New York: Penguin, 1987).

8. See Stephen Krasner, "Regimes and the Limits of Realism: Regimes as Autonomous Variables," in Stephen Krasner, ed., *International Regimes* pp. 355–368. (Ithaca, N.Y.: Cornell University Press, 1983). Krasner argues that: "The most common proposition is that hegemonic distributions of power lead to stable, open economic regimes because it is in the interest of a hegemonic state to pursue such a policy and because the hegemon has the resources to provide the collective goods needed to make such a system function effectively" (p. 357).

9. Robert Keohane, *After Hegemony: Cooperation and Discord in the World Political Economy* (Princeton, N.J.: Princeton University Press, 1984).

10. Robert Keohane, "State Power and Industry Influence: American Foreign Oil Policy in the 1940s," *International Organization* 36, no. 1 (1982): 165–183.

11. J. A. Hobson, *Imperialism: A Study* (London: James Nisbet, 1902); Rudolf Hilferding, *Finance Capital: A Study of the Latest Phase of Capitalist Development*, trans. M. Watnick and S. Gordon (London: Routledge & Kegan Paul, 1981); Vladimir I. Lenin, *Imperialism: The Highest Stage of Capitalism* (Moscow: Progress Publishers, 1977); Nicolay Bukharin, *Imperialism and World Economy* (New York: International Publishers, 1929); Karl Kautsky, "Ultra-imperialism," *New Left Review* 50 (January–February 1970): 41–46; and Max Weber, *Economy and Society*, trans. by Guenther Roth and Claus Wittich (Berkeley: University of California Press, 1968). It should be noted that Weber offers a characterization of capitalism that includes both cartelization and instruments of foreign investment policies similar to the "finance capital" model of Hilferding; but he refrains from going so far as tying them together into an underconsumption or cartel-driven theory of imperialist expansion. For a positive critique of Hobson, see John Strachey, *The End of Empire* (New York: Random House, 1959). For a negative critique, see Richard Koebner and Helmut Dan Schmidt, *Imperialism: The Story and Significance of a Political Word, 1840–1960* (Cambridge: Cambridge University Press, 1964). I avoid the label "underconsumption theories" because the notion of underconsumption is not as common to the different theories as is the stipulation of a cartelized national economy.

12. Hilferding's interpretation is at variance with that advanced by Alexander Gerschenkron in *Economic Backwardness in Historical Perspective: A Book of Essays* (Cambridge, Mass.: Harvard University Press, 1962). According to Gerschenkron, "At the turn of the century, if not somewhat earlier, changes became apparent in the relationship between German banks and German industry. As the former industrial infants had grown to strong manhood, the original undisputed ascendancy of the banks over industrial enterprises could no longer be maintained" (p. 21)

13. Pre–World War II Germany offers partial grounds for the thesis of total cartelization. See Philip Newman, *Cartel and Combine: Essays in Monopoly Produc-*

tion (Ridgewood, N.J.: Foreign Studies Institute, 1964); and Franz Neumann, *Behemoth: The Structure and Practice of National Socialism, 1933–1944* (New York: Octagon Books, 1963). The latter study offers some additional reasons why Hilferding's model may have gone awry. Like Gerschenkron, Neumann believes there was some room for industry to win independence from the banks.

14. Frederich List, *The National System of Political Economy* (New York: Augustus M. Kelley, 1966).

15. The use of tariffs as an aggressive export tool receives excellent treatment in Hilferding, but is also found in other economics literature. See Jacob Viner, *Dumping: A Problem in International Trade* (New York: Augustus M. Kelley, 1966); William A. Wares, *The Theory of Dumping and American Commercial Policy* (Lexington, Mass.: Lexington Books, 1977); Joan Robinson, *The Economics of Imperfect Competition* (London: Macmillan, 1965); Paul Krugman, *Rethinking International Trade* (Cambridge, Mass.: MIT Press, 1990), pp. 185–198; W. J. Ethier, "Dumping," *Journal of Political Economy* 90, no. 3 (1982): 487–506; Ludger Schuknect and Joerg Stephan, "EC Trade Protection Law: Produmping or Antidumping?" *Public Choice* 80, nos. 1–2 (1994): 143–156; and T. Ozawa, "Japanese Multinationals and 1992," in B. Burgenmeier and J. L. Mucchielli, eds., *Multinationals and Europe, 1992,* pp. 135–154 (London: Routledge, 1991). Ozawa modifies the Hobson-Hilferding thesis of capital export by large firms, noting that in a cartelized economy it is the small firms that may have to locate production overseas first.

16. Kautsky's theorizing about peaceful coexistence among cartelized imperial powers is not purely theoretical. The division of China by foreign powers toward the end of the nineteenth century and the cartelization of the European oil market and sharing of oil resources in Mesopotamia in 1914 would be examples of Kautsky-style shared imperial domination.

17. In *After Hegemony*, Robert Keohane devotes some descriptive energy to OPEC, a kind of Third World regime, but then concentrates on a rather tepid and unconvincing elevation of the International Energy Agency to regime status. The International Energy Agency is a pathetic contrast to the masssive domination of the world oil trade that characterized the post–World War II market until the time of the nationalizations of 1973.

18. See Robert Gilpin, *The Political Economy of International Relations* (Princeton, N.J.: Princeton University Press, 1987); and Lester Thurow, *Head to Head: The Coming Economic Battle Among Japan, Europe, and America* (New York: Morrow Press, 1992). I should mention in this section lateral pressure theory, which attempts to identify developmental factors such as national population, resources, and technology in an effort to correlate these with bellicose state behavior. There is a kinship with the old cartelist theories in the sense that factors related to economic performance are analyzed in relation to war propensity. But there is not an explicit "test" of the theory in the sense that some of its main variables, such as savings, rate of interest and investment, and degree of economic concentration and cartelization are not tested. See Nazli Choucri and Robert C. North, *Nations in Conflict: National Growth and International Violence* (San Francisco: W. H. Freeman, 1975), and Nazli Choucri, Robert C. North and Susumu Yamakage, *The Challenge of Japan: Before World War II and After* (New York: Routledge, 1992) for a later-day application of the theory to Japan; and Richard K. Ashley, *The Political Economy of War and Peace: The Sino-*

Soviet-American Triangle and the Modern Security Problematique (New York: Nichols Publishing Co., 1980). Ashley, by including two command economies, was trying to go beyond the limits of capitalist-specific theories of imperialism.

19. However, the "rationality" of such a conflict, already limited to particular elements of the capitalist class in Kautsky's time, would be zero if eventual warfare among capitalist states led to nuclear exchanges. See Paul Baran, *The Political Economy of Growth* (New York: Monthly Review Press, 1957), for the following observation: "Such harnessing of atomic energy as took place in August 1945 in Hiroshima and Nagasaki would, if repeated, not merely send the capital assets on the way to the scrap heap but also the would-be investors on the way to the cemetery" (p. 132).

20. See James Herbert Nolt, "Business Conflict and the Origin of the Pacific War," 2 vols., Ph.D. diss., University of Chicago, 1994.

21. Hobson's catalog of imperialism's economic and social costs—cartelized prices, armament programs financed by deficit spending, territorial acquisition and expansion, antagonism of neighboring nations, militarization of society, exaltation of antidemocratic norms—was almost perfectly validated by Nazi Germany.

22. See the following works by Immanuel Wallerstein: *The Modern World System: Capitalist Agriculture and the Origins of the European Economy in the Sixteenth Century* (New York: Academic Press, 1976); *The Modern World System II: Mercantilism and the Consolidation of the European World Economy, 1600–1750* (New York: Academic Press, 1980); and *The Modern World System III: The Second Era of Great Expansion of the Capitalist World Economy, 1730–1840s* (New York: Academic Press, 1989). Other examples include Samir Amin, *Accumulation on a World Scale: A Critique of the Theory of Underdevelopment*, trans. by Brian Pearce (New York: Monthly Review Press, 1974); and Samir Amin, ed., *Dynamics of Global Crisis* (New York: Monthly Review Press, 1982).

23. See Immanuel Wallerstein and Terence K. Hopkins, eds., *World Systems Analysis: Theory and Methodology* (Beverly Hills, Calif.: Sage, 1982); and Joan Smith, Immanuel Wallerstein, and Maria de Carmen Baerga, *Creating and Transforming Households: The Constraints of the World Economy* (Cambridge: Cambridge University Press, 1992).

24. Anthony Brewer, *Marxist Theories of Imperialism: A Critical Survey* (New York: Routledge, 1980). In this passage, Brewer is discussing both Wallerstein and Andre Gunder Frank.

25. Ronald Rogowski, *Commerce and Coalitions: How Trade Affects Domestic Political Alignments* (Princeton, N.J.: Princeton University Press, 1989).

26. Beth V. Yarbrough and Robert M. Yarbrough, *The World Economy: Trade and Finance*, 2nd ed. (Chicago: Dryden Press, 1991), pp. 74–78, 98–106.

27. See Krugman, *Rethinking International Trade*, p. 227.

28. On "taste," see Yarbrough and Yarbrough, *The World Economy*, pp. 77–78.

29. On automobile retirement in Japan, see James P. Womack, Daniel T. Jones, and Daniel Ross, *The Machine That Changed the World* (New York: Macmillan, 1990). And, of course, demand management in the Keynesian sense might have even more colossal impact.

30. Peter Katzenstein, Small States in World Markets (Ithaca, N.Y.: Cornell University Press, 1985).

31. Paulette Kurzer, *Business and Banking: Political Change and Economic Integration in Western Europe* (Ithaca, N.Y.: Cornell University Press, 1993).

32. Theda Skocpol, *States and Social Revolutions: A Comparative Analysis of France, Russia, and China* (Cambridge: Cambridge University Press, 1979).

33. V. O. Key, *Politics, Parties, and Pressure Groups* (New York: Thomas Y. Crowell, 1942); Ida M. Tarbell, *The Nationalizing of Business, 1878–1898* (New York: Macmillan, 1936); R. E. Schattschneider, *Politics, Pressures and the Tariff* (New York: Prentice-Hall, 1935); and Charles Beard, G.H.E. Smith, *The Idea of National Interest* (New York: Macmillan, 1934).

34. "Business conflict model," "business investment theory," and "interest bloc conflict" are self-descriptive terms employed by these neopluralist authors. I contend that the work is properly identified as a continuation of an older tradition in U.S. scholarship. I believe that this disagreement (in the end minor) over labels has two causes. The first is that the pluralist tradition has been identified too closely with the conservative and even propagandistic writings of the late 1950s and early 1960s. There is a legitimate worry about distancing oneself from that. the second is that there is room for disagreement as to when one has modified a theory so much that one deserves a new label. For instance, Marx may properly be called a left-Hegelian, but we do not call Marxist history left-Hegelianism because the rupture was too profound. I do not think that the neopluralists have moved as far from the "left-pluralists" (cited earlier) as they seem to think. This is, I hope, a matter of friendly disagreement.

35. David N. Gibbs, *The Political Economy of Third World Intervention: Mines, Money, and U.S. Policy in the Congo Crisis*
(Chicago: University of Chicago Press, 1991); Ronald W. Cox, *Power and Profits: U.S. Policy in Central America* (Lexington: University Press of Kentucky, 1994); Thomas Ferguson, "Party Realignment and American Industrial Structure: The Investment Theory of Political Parties in Historical Perspective," *Research in Political Economy* 6 (1983): pp. 1–82; Thomas Ferguson, "From Normalcy to New Deal: Industrial Structure, Party Competition, and American Public Policy in the Great Depression," *International Organization* 38, no. 1 (winter 1984): 41–94; Thomas Ferguson, *Golden Rule: The Investment Theory of Party Competition and the Logic of Money-Driven Political Systems* (Chicago: University of Chicago Press, 1995); Thomas Ferguson and Joel Rogers, *Right Turn: The Decline of the Democrats and the Future of American Politics* (New York: Hill & Wang, 1986); Jeffry Frieden, "Sectoral Conflict and U.S. Foreign Economic Policy, 1914–1940," in G. John Ikenberry, David A. Lake, Michael Mastanduno, eds., *The State and American Foreign Economic Policy* (Ithaca, N.Y.: Cornell University Press, 1988); David Abraham, *The Collapse of the Weimar Republic: Political Economy and Crisis*, 2nd. ed. (New York: Holmes & Meier, 1986); and Nolt, "Business Conflict and the Origin of the Pacific War."

36. It would be useful if neopluralists gave some thought to the difference between "internationalists" who support protection to use differential pricing (which often requires a tariff shield) in order to export goods (such as steel and many manufactured goods), "national capitalists" who are protectionist because they are not competitive internationally, and "internationalists" who prefer no tariff barriers (world marketers of raw materials such as oil, banks, etc.). This is a key point raised by Hilferding.

37. Theda Skocpol and Margaret Weir, "State Structures and the Possibilities for 'Keynesian' Responses to the Great Depression in Sweden, Britain, and the United States," in Peter Evans, Dietrich Rueschemeyer, and Theda Skocpol, eds., *Bringing the State Back In*, pp. 107–163 (Cambridge: Cambridge University Press, 1985).

38. The rent-seeking theorists, not discussed in this essay but essentially a formal rational choice outgrowth of the neopluralist approach, share the suspicion of the legitimacy of government intervention in the economy. See Gordon Tullock, *The Economics of Special Privilege and Rent Seeking* (Boston: Klumer Academic Publishers, 1989); and Mancur Olson, *The Rise and Decline of Nations: Economic Growth, Stagflation, and Social Rigidities* (New Haven, Conn.: Yale University Press, 1982). Olson provides a rational choice model of national economic decline that is certainly allied with, though perhaps not identical to, some of the premises of the rent-seeking analysis.

39. See on this score David N. Gibbs, "Taking the State Back Out: Reflections on a Tautology," *Contention* 3, no. 3 (spring 1994): 115–138; and David N. Gibbs, "The Emperor's New Tautology: Reply to Krasner, Lake, Ikenberry and also Skocpol," *Contention* 3, no. 3 (spring 1994): 163–170. This issue of *Contention* is devoted to a debate between Gibbs and the leading statist theorists on the concept of "state autonomy."

40. Gregory P. Nowell, *Mercantile States and the World Oil Cartel, 1900–1939* (Ithaca, N.Y.: Cornell University Press, 1994).

41. The distinction between at least some insitutionalist approaches and transnational structuring diminishes to the extent that the institution, in the institutionalist approach, is seen as derivative of the struggle to control the state. An example is Colleen Dunlavy, *Politics and Industrialization: Early Railroads in the United States and Prussia* (Princeton, N.J.: Princeton University Press, 1994): "Thus, in Prussia, the railroads' unprecedented capital-intensity—in this case, their sheer demand for capital—pushed events to the point of [the 1848] revolution and brought a change in political structure, which in turn altered the policy making process."

Chapter 10

1. Bob Jessop, *The Capitalist State* (New York: New York University Press, 1982), p. 24.

2. For detailed discussions of the concept see, Bob Jessop, *Capitalist State*, as well as his *State Theory* (University Park: Pennsylvania State University Press, 1990); and Martin Carnoy, *The State and Political Theory* (Princeton, NJ: Princeton University Press, 1984).

3. Generally regarded as the best statements of the instrumentalist perspective are V. I. Lenin's classic *State and Revolution* (many editions), and Ralph Milliband's *The State in Capitalist Society* (London: Weidenfield & Nicolson, 1968).

4. See, especially, Nicos Poulantzas, *Political Power and Social Classes* (London: New Left Books, 1974).

5. For discussion and critique of the structuralist approach, see Theda Skocpol, "Political Response to Capitalist Crisis: Neo-Marxist Theories of the State and the Case of the New Deal," *Politics and Society* 10 (1980): 155–201.

6. Joshua Cohen and Joel Rogers, *On Democracy* (Harmondsworth, England: Penguin, 1983), pp. 48–49.

7. Thomas Ferguson, "Party Realignment and American Industrial Structure: The Investment Theory of Political Parties in Historical Perspective" *Research in Political Economy* 6 (1983): 24.

8. Nicos Poulantzas, *State, Power, and Socialism* (London: Verso, 1980).

9. Jessop, *The Capitalist State,* p. 176.

10. Ferguson, "Party Realignment," p. 30.

11. For a survey of neostatism, see Peter Evans, Dietrich Rueschmeyer, and Theda Skocpol, eds., *Bringing the State Back In* (Cambridge: Cambridge University Press, 1985); for the agency of state elites, see Fred Block, "Beyond Relative Autonomy: State Managers as Historical Subjects," in Ralph Miliband and John Saville, eds., *The Socialist Register* (London: Merlin Press, 1980).

12. Ronald W. Cox, *Power and Profits: U.S. Policy in Central America* (Lexington: University Press of Kentucky, 1994).

13. Miliband, *The State in Capitalist Society.*

14. David Easton, *The Political System* (New York: Alfred A. Knopf, 1971), p. 108.

15. Ibid., p. 113.

16. Ibid.

17. Theda Skocpol, *States and Social Revolutions: A Comparative Analysis of France, Russia, and China* (Cambridge: Cambridge University Press, 1979).

18. David N. Gibbs, *The Political Economy of Third World Intervention: Mines, Money, and U.S. Policy in the Congo Crisis* (Chicago: University of Chicago Press, 1991).

19. Jessop, *State Theory,* pp. 248–272.

20. Robert Bianchi, *Unruly Corporatism* (New York: Oxford University Press, 1989), esp. p. 56.

21. Thomas Ferguson and Joel Rogers, *Right Turn: The Decline of the Democrats and the Future of American Politics* (New York: Hill & Wang, 1986), p. 44.

22. Fred Block, "The Ruling Class Does Not Rule," *Socialist Revolution* 7, no. 3 (1977): 6–28.

23. Mancur Olson Jr., *The Logic of Collective Action* (Cambridge, Mass.: Harvard University Press, 1965).

24. James O'Connor, *The Fiscal Crisis of the State* (New York: St. Martin's Press, 1973).

25. Antonio Gramsci, *Selections from the Prison Notebooks* (New York: International Publishers, 1971).

26. Ferguson, "Party Realignment," p. 24.

27. Adam Przeworski, "Material Interests, Class Compromise, and the Transition to Socialism," in John Roemer, ed., *Analytical Marxism* (Cambridge: Cambridge University Press, 1986).

28. Hans Georg Gadamer, *Truth and Method* (New York: Crossroads, 1992).

29. Jeffry Frieden, *Debt, Development, and Democracy* (Princeton, N.J.: Princeton University Press, 1991).

30. Ferguson and Rogers, *Right Turn,* op cit., p. 46.

31. Eric Devereaux, "The Partisan Press Revisited," Ph.D. diss., University of Texas at Austin, 1992.

Appendix to Chapter 10

1. David N. Gibbs, *The Political Economy of Third World Intervention: Mines, Money, and U.S. Policy in the Congo Crisis* (Chicago: University of Chicago Press, 1991). Note that the Congo is now called Zaire.

2. Ibid., p. 144.

3. See sources in Michael G. Schatzberg, *Mobutu or Chaos?* (Lanham, MD: University Press of America, 1991), pp. 72–74; and Elise Pachter, "Our Man in Kinshasa: U.S. Relations with Mobutu, 1970–1983, Patron-Client Relations in the International Sphere," Ph.D. diss., Johns Hopkins University, School of Advanced International Studies, 1987, pp. 161–163.

4. This argument is nicely summarized (and eviscerated) in Lars Schoultz, *National Security and United States Policy Toward Latin America* (Princeton, N.J.: Princeton University Press, 1987), chap. 4.

Select Bibliography

Abraham, David. *The Collapse of the Weimar Republic: Political Economy and Crisis.* 2nd ed. New York: Holmes & Meier, 1986.

Ake, Claude. *A Political Economy of Africa.* London: Longman, 1981.

Alexander, J. "The Mass Media in Systemic, Historical, and Comparative Perspective." In E. Katz and T. Szeskö, eds., *Mass Media and Social Change.* Beverly Hills, Calif.: Sage, 1981.

Allison, Graham. *Essence of Decision.* Boston: Little, Brown & Co., 1971.

Amin, Samir. *Accumulation on a World Scale: A Critique of the Theory of Underdevelopment.* Trans. Brian Pearce. New York: Monthly Review Press, 1974.

Amin, Samir, ed. *Dynamics of Global Crisis.* New York: Monthly Review Press, 1982.

Art, Robert. "Why We Overspend and Underaccomplish: Weapons Procurement and the Military-Industrial Complex." In Steven Rosen, ed., *Testing the Theory of the Military-Industrial Complex.* Lexington, Mass.: Lexington Books, 1973.

Ashley, Richard K. *The Political Economy of War and Peace: The Sino-Soviet-American Triangle and the Modern Security Problematique.* New York: Nichols Publishing Co., 1980.

Axelrod, Robert. *The Evolution of Cooperation.* New York: Basic Books, 1984.

Ayoob, Mohammed. "The Security Predicament of the Third World State: Reflections on State Making in a Comparative Perspective." In Brian Job, ed., *The Insecurity Dilemma,* pp. 63–80. Boulder, Colo.: Lynne Rienner Publishers.

Azarya, Victor. "Reordering State-Society Relations: Incorporation and Disengagement." In Donald Rothchild and Naomi Chazan, eds., *The Precarious Balance: State and Society in Africa.* Boulder, Colo.: Westview Press, 1988.

Baldwin, Robert E. *The Political Economy of U.S. Import Policy.* Cambridge, Mass.: MIT Press, 1985.

Baran, Paul A. *The Political Economy of Growth.* New York: Monthly Review Press, 1957.

Baran, Paul A., and Paul M. Sweezy. *Monopoly Capital.* New York: Monthly Review Press, 1966.

Barry, Tom, and Deb Preusch. *The Central America Fact Book.* New York: Grove Press, 1986.

Bates, Robert. *Beyond the Miracle of the Market: The Political Economy of Agrarian Development in Kenya.* Cambridge: Cambridge University Press, 1989.

Bergsten, C. Fred, Thomas Horst, and Theodore Moran. *American Multinationals and American Interests.* Washington, D.C.: Brookings Institute, 1978.

Bianchi, Robert. *Unruly Corporatism.* New York: Oxford University Press, 1989.

Block, Fred. "Beyond Relative Autonomy: State Managers as Historical Subjects." In Ralph Miliband and John Saville, eds., *The Socialist Register*. London: Merlin Press, 1980.

Block, Fred. *The Origins of International Economic Disorder*. Berkeley: University of California Press, 1973.

Block, Fred. "The Ruling Class Does Not Rule." *Socialist Revolution* 7, no. 3 (1977): 6–28.

Braestrup, P. *Big Story: How the American Press and Television Reported and Interpreted the Crisis of Tet 1968 in Vietnam and Washington*. Boulder: Westview Press, 1977.

Bodenheimer, Thomas, and Robert Gould. *Rollback: Right-Wing Power in U.S. Foreign Policy*. Boston: South End Press, 1989.

Brewer, Anthony. *Marxist Theories of Imperialism: A Critical Survey*. New York: Routledge, 1980.

Bukharin, Nikolay. *Imperialism and World Economy*. New York: International Publishers, 1929.

Business International Corporation (BIC). *Improving International Competitiveness Through Sourcing in Latin America*. New York: BIC, 1989.

Cameron, D. "The Politics and Economics of the Business Cycle." In Thomas Ferguson and Joel Rogers, eds. *The Political Economy: Readings in the Poltics and Economics of American Public Policy*. Armonk, N.Y.: M. E. Sharpe, 1984.

Canterbury, E. Ray. *Economics on a New Frontier*. Belmont, Calif.: Wadsworth Publishing Co., 1968.

Carnoy, Martin. *The State and Political Theory*. Princeton, N.J.: Princeton University Press, 1984.

Carr, Edward H. *The Twenty Years' Crisis, 1919–1939*. London: Macmillan, 1939.

Chester, Lewis, Godfrey Hodgson, and Bruce Page. *An American Melodrama: The Presidential Campaign of 1968*. London: Andre Deutsch, 1969.

Choucri, Nazli, and Robert C. North. *Nations in Conflict: National Growth and International Violence*. San Francisco: W. H. Freeman, 1975.

Choucri, Nazli, Robert C. North, and Susumu Yamakage. *The Challenge of Japan: Before World War II and After*. New York: Routledge, 1992.

Cline, W. Raymond. *The Future of World Trade in Textiles and Apparel*. Washington, D.C.: Institute for International Economics, 1987.

Cohen, B. *The Press and Foreign Policy*. Princeton, N.J.: Princeton University Press, 1963.

Cohen, Joshua, and Joel Rogers. *On Democracy*. Harmondsworth, England: Penguin, 1983.

Cohen, Steven. *The Making of U.S. International Economic Policy*. New York: Praeger Publishers, 1977.

Committee for Economic Development (CED). *East-West Trade: A Common Policy for the West*. New York: CED, 1965.

Committee for Economic Development. *A New Trade Policy Toward Communist Countries*. New York: CED, 1972.

Cooling, Benjamin Franklin, ed. *War, Business and American Society*. Port Washington, N.Y.: Kennnikat Press, 1977.

Corden, W. M. *The Theory of Protection*. London: Oxford University Press, 1974.

Cox, Robert. *Production, Power, and World Order: Social Forces in the Making of History*. New York: Columbia University Press, 1987.

Cox, Ronald W. *Power and Profits: U.S. Policy in Central America*. Lexington: University Press of Kentucky, 1994.

Cronin, Thomas E., and Sanford D. Greenberg, eds. *The Presidential Advisory System*. New York: Harper & Row, 1969.

Cummings, Bruce. "Chinatown: Foreign Policy and Elite Realignment." In Ferguson and Rogers, eds., *The Hidden Election*.

Cummins, Margaret. "Interest Group Competition and NAFTA." Unpublished manuscript, University of North Carolina, Chapel Hill, 1992.

Dale, Richard. *Anti-Dumping Law in a Liberal Trade Order*. London: Macmillan, 1980.

Davis, Mike. *Prisoners of the American Dream*. New York: Verso, 1986.

Destler, I. M. *American Trade Politics: System Under Stress*. New York: Twentieth Century Fund, 1986; and Washington, D.C.: Institute for International Economics, 1992.

Destler, I. M. "Executive-Congressional Conflict in Foreign Policy: Explaining It; Coping with It." In Lawrence C. Dodd and Bruce I. Oppenheimer, eds., *Congress Reconsidered*. 2nd ed. Washington, D.C.: Congressional Quarterly Press, 1981.

Destler, I. M., and John S. Odell. *Antiprotection: Changing Forces in United States Trade Policy*. Washington, D.C.: Institute for International Economics, 1987.

Devereux, Erik. "Media Coalitions in the 1964 Elections: A Political Investment Analysis." Working Paper 92–38, H. John Heinz III School of Public Policy and Management, Carnegie Mellon University, 1992.

Devereux, Erik. "The Partisan Press Revisited." Ph.D. diss., University of Texas, Austin, 1992.

Diamond, Larry. "Class Formation in the Swollen African State." *Journal of Modern African Studies* 25, no. 4 (1987): 567–596.

Diamond, Sara. *Spiritual Warfare: The Politics of the Christian Right*. Boston: South End Press, 1989.

DiBacco, T. "The Business Press and Vietnam: Ecstasy or Agony." *Journalism Quarterly* 45, no. 3 (1968): 426–435.

Dicken, Peter. *Global Shift*. New York: Guilford Press, 1992.

Domhoff, William. *The Powers That Be: Processes of Ruling Class Domination in America*. New York: Vintage Books, 1979.

Downs, Anthony. *Inside Bureaucracy*. Boston: Little, Brown & Co., 1967.

Dunlavy, Colleen. *Politics and Industrialization: Early Railroads in the United States and Prussia*. Princeton, N.J.: Princeton University Press, 1994.

Easton, David. *The Political System*. New York: Alfred A. Knopf, 1971.

Eckes, Alfred, Jr. *The United States and the Global Struggle for Minerals*. Austin: University of Texas Press, 1979.

Eden, Lorraine, and Maureen Appel Molot. "Continentalizing the North American Auto Industry." In Ricardo Grinspun and Maxwell Cameron, eds., *The Political Economy of North American Free Trade*. New York: St. Martin's Press, 1993.

Edsall, Thomas. *The New Politics of Inequality*. New York: W. W. Norton, 1984.

Entman, R. *Democracy Without Citizens: Media and the Decay of American Politics.* New York: Oxford University Press, 1989.

Ernst, D. "U.S.-Japanese Competition and Worldwide Restructuring of the Electronics Industry: A European View." In J. Henderson and M. Castells, eds., *Global Restructuring and Territorial Development*, chap. 3. London: Sage, 1987.

Ethier, W. J. "Dumping." *Journal of Political Economy* 90, no. 3 (1982): 487–506.

Evans, Peter, Dietrich Rueschemeyer, and Theda Skocpol, eds., *Bringing the State Back In.* New York: Cambridge University Press, 1985.

Feis, Herbert. *Europe: The World's Banker, 1870–1914.* New York: Council on Foreign Relations, 1964.

Ferguson, Thomas. "By Invitation Only: Party Competition and Industrial Structure in the 1988 Election." *Socialist Review* 19, no. 4 (1989): 73–103.

Ferguson, Thomas. "From Normalcy to New Deal: Industrial Structure, Party Competition and American Public Policy in the Great Depression." *International Organization* 38, no. 1 (winter 1984): 41–94.

Ferguson, Thomas. "Party Realignment and American Industrial Structure: The Investment Theory of Political Parties in Historical Perspective." *Research in Political Economy* 6 (1983): 1–82.

Ferguson, Thomas, and Joel Rogers. *Right Turn: The Decline of the Democrats and the Future of American Politics.* New York: Hill & Wang, 1986.

Ferguson, Thomas and Joel Rogers, eds., *The Hidden Election: Politics and Economics in the 1980 Presidential Campaign.* New York: Pantheon Press, 1981.

Frieden, Jeffry. *Banking on the World.* New York: Harper & Row, 1987.

Frieden, Jeffry. *Debt, Development, and Democracy.* Princeton, N.J.: Princeton University Press, 1991.

Frieden, Jeffry. "A Pax on Both Their Houses: State, Society, and Social Science," *Contention* 3, no. 3 (spring 1994): 171–182.

Frieden, Jeffry. "Sectoral Conflict and U.S. Foreign Economic Policy, 1914–1940." In Ikenberry, Lake, and Mastanduno, eds., *The State and American Foreign Economic Policy*, pp. 59–90; and *International Organization* 42, no. 1 (winter 1988).

Gadamer, Hans Georg. *Truth and Method.* New York: Crossroads, 1992.

Galbraith, J. "The Ammunition Boom: Procurement for the Vietnam War." Unpublished honors thesis, Harvard University; 1974.

Galbraith, John Kenneth. "How to Control the Military." In Carroll W. Pursell Jr., ed., *The Military-Industrial Complex.* New York: Harper & Row, 1972.

Garcia, Emilio Pantojas. "The United States Caribbean Basin Initiative and the Puerto Rican Experience." *Latin American Perspectives* 12 (fall 1985): 105–128.

Garthoff, Raymond. *Confrontation and Détente.* Washington, D.C.: Brookings Institute, 1986.

Gerschenkron, Alexander. *Economic Backwardness in Historical Perspective: A Book of Essays.* Cambridge, Mass.: Harvard University Press, 1962.

Gibbs, David N. "Does the USSR Have a 'Grand Strategy'? Reinterpreting the Invasion of Afghanistan." *Journal of Peace Research* 24, no. 4 (1987):367–369.

Gibbs, David N. "The Emperor's New Tautology: Reply to Krasner, Lake, Ikenberry, and also Skocpol." *Contention* 3, no. 3 (spring 1994): 163–170.

Gibbs, David N. *The Political Economy of Third World Intervention: Mines, Money, and U.S. Policy in the Congo Crisis.* Chicago: University of Chicago Press, 1991.

Gibbs, David N. "Taking the State Back Out: Reflections on a Tautology." *Contention* 3, no. 3 (spring 1994): 115–138.

Gill, Stephen. *American Hegemony and the Trilateral Commission.* Cambridge: Cambridge University Press, 1990.

Gilpin, Robert. *The Political Economy of International Relations.* Princeton, N.J.: Princeton University Press, 1987.

Gilpin, Robert. *War and Change in World Politics.* New York: Cambridge University Press, 1981.

Gold, David, Clarence Y. H. Lo, and Erik Olin Wright. "Recent Developments in Marxist Theories of the Capitalist State." *Monthly Review* (October 1975): 39.

Goldstein, Judith. "The Political Economy of Trade: Institutions of Protection." *American Political Science Review* 80, no. 1 (March 1986): 161–184.

Gramsci, Antonio. *Selections from the Prison Notebooks.* New York: International Publishers, 1971.

Grunwald, Joseph, and Kenneth Flamm. *The Global Factory.* Washington, D.C.: Brookings Institute, 1985.

Haendel, Daniel. *Corporate Strategic Planning: The Political Dimension.* Washington, D.C.: Center for Strategic and International Studies, 1981.

Haggard, Stephen. "The Institutional Foundations of Hegemony: Explaining the Reciprocal Trade Agreements Act of 1934." In Ikenberry, Lake, and Mastanduno, eds. *The State and American Foreign Economic Policy,* pp. 91–119.

Halliday, Fred. *The Making of the Second Cold War.* London: Verso, 1983.

Halliday, Fred. *Soviet Policy in the Arc of Crisis.* Washington, D.C.: Institute for Policy Studies, 1981.

Hallin, D. *The "Uncensored War": The Media and Vietnam.* New York: Oxford University Press, 1986.

Hammond W. *Public Affairs: The Military and the Media, 1962–1968.* Washington, D.C.: GPO, 1989.

Hanson, Betty C., and Bruce M. Russett. "Testing Some Economic Interpretations of American Intervention: Korea, Indochina, and the Stock Market." In Steven Rosen, ed., *Testing the Theory of the Military-Industrial Complex.* Lexington, Mass.: Lexington Books, 1973.

Hauner, Milan. *The Soviet War in Afghanistan.* Lanham, Md.: University Press of America, 1991.

Hayes, Michael. *Lobbyists and Legislators: A Theory of Political Markets.* New Brunswick, N.J.: Rutgers University Press, 1981.

Heatherly, Charles, ed. *Mandate for Leadership: Policy Management in a Conservative Administration.* Washington, D.C.: Heritage Foundation, 1981.

Heckscher, Eli F. *Mercantilism.* Trans. Mendel Shapiro. 2 vols. New York: Macmillan, 1935.

Heller, Walter W. "Economic Policy Advisers." In Cronin and Greenberg, eds., *The Presidential Advisory System,* pp. 29–39.

Herman, Edward, and Frank Brodhead. *Demonstration Elections: U.S.-Staged Elections in the Dominican Republic, Vietnam, and El Salvador.* Boston: South End Press, 1984.

Herman, Edward, and Noam Chomsky. *Manufacturing Consent: The Political Economy of the Mass Media.* New York: Pantheon Press, 1988.

Herring, G. *America's Longest War: The United States and Vietnam, 1950–1975.* New York: Alfred A. Knopf, 1986.

Hilferding, Rudolf. *Finance Capital: A Study of the Latest Phase of Capitalist Development.* Trans. by M. Watnick and S. Gordon. London: Routledge & Kegan Paul, 1981.

Hirschman, Albert O. *National Power and the Structure of Foreign Trade.* Berkeley: University of California Press, 1980.

Hobson, J. A. *Imperialism: A Study* London: James Nisbett, 1902.

Holmes, John. "The Globalization of Production and the Future of Canada's Mature Industries: The Case of the Automobile Industry." In D. Drache and M. S. Gertler, eds., *The New Era of Global Competition: State Policy and Market Power.* Montreal: McGill-Queens Press, 1990.

Hufbauer, Gary, and Jeffrey Schott. *The North American Free Trade Agreement.* Washington, D.C.: Institute for International Economics, 1992.

Huntington, Samuel. *The Crisis of Democracy.* New York: Trilateral Commission, 1975.

Hyden, Goran. *No Shortcuts to Progress.* Berkeley: University of California Press, 1981.

Ikenberry, G. John. "Conclusion: An Institutional Approach to American Foreign Economic Policy." In Ikenberry, Lake, and Mastanduno, eds., *The State and American Foreign Economic Policy.*

Ikenberry, G. John. "State, Society, and Everything in Between." *Contention* 3, no. 3 (spring 1994): 139–144.

Ikenberry, G. John, David Lake, and Michael Mastanduno, eds. *The State and American Foreign Economic Policy.* Ithaca, N.Y.: Cornell University Press, 1988.

Jackson, Robert. *Quasi-states.* New York: Cambridge University Press, 1990.

Jenkins, Rhys. *Transnational Corporations and the Latin American Automobile Industry.* London: Macmillan, 1987.

Jessop, Bob. *The Capitalist State.* New York: New York University Press, 1982.

Jessop, Bob. *State Theory.* University Park: Pennsylvania State University Press, 1990.

Joseph, Richard. *Democracy and Prebendal Politics in Nigeria.* New York: Cambridge University Press, 1990.

Karsten, Peter. *The Naval Aristocracy.* New York: Free Press, 1972.

Katzenstein, Peter. *Small States in World Markets.* Ithaca, N.Y.: Cornell University Press, 1985.

Kautsky, Karl. "Ultra-imperialism." *New Left Review* 50 (January–February 1970): 41–46.

Kehr, Eckart. *Economic Interest, Militarism, and Foreign Policy.* Berkeley: University of California Press, 1977.

Keohane, Robert. *After Hegemony: Cooperation and Discord in the World Political Economy.* Princeton, N.J.: Princeton University Press, 1984.

Keohane, Robert. "Realism, Neorealism, and the Study of World Politics." In Robert Keohane, ed., *Neorealism and Its Critics.* New York: Columbia University Press, 1986.

Keohane, Robert. "State Power and Industry Influence: American Foreign Oil Policy in the 1940s." *International Organization* 36, no. 1 (1982): 165–183.

Keohane, Robert, and Joseph Nye. *Power and Interdependence: World Politics in Transition.* Boston: Little, Brown & Co., 1977.

Key, V. O. *Politics, Parties, and Pressure Groups.* New York: Thomas Y. Crowell, 1942.

Kindleberger, Charles. *The World in Depression, 1929–1939.* New York: Penguin, 1987.

Kirkpatrick, Jeanne. *Dictatorships and Double Standards.* New York: Simon & Schuster, 1982.

Kissinger, Henry A.. *The White House Years.* London: Weidenfeld & Nicolson, 1979.

Knoke, David. *Organizing for Collective Action: The Political Economies of Associations.* New York: de Gruyter, 1990.

Kobrin, Stephen. "Political Risk: A Review and Reconsideration." *Journal of International Business Studies* 10, no. 1 (spring-summer 1979).

Koebner, Richard, and Helmut Dan Schmidt. *Imperialism: The Story and Significance of a Political Word, 1840–1960.* Cambridge: Cambridge University Press, 1964.

Koistinen, Paul A.C. *The Military-Industrial Complex: A Historical Perspective.* Lexington, Mass.: Lexington Books; and New York: Praeger Publishers, 1980.

Krasner, Stephen. *Defending the National Interest: Raw Materials Investments and U.S. Foreign Policy.* Princeton, N.J.: Princeton University Press, 1978.

Krasner, Stephen. "Regimes and the Limits of Realism: Regimes as Autonomous Variables." In Krasner, ed., *International Regimes.*

Krasner, Stephen, ed., *International Regimes.* Ithaca, N.Y.: Cornell University Press, 1983.

Kristol, Irving. *Reflections of a Neoconservative.* New York: Basic Books, 1983.

Krugman, Paul. *Rethinking International Trade.* Cambridge, Mass.: MIT Press, 1990.

Kruskal, J., and M. Wish. *Multidimensional Scaling.* Beverly Hills, Calif.: Sage, 1978.

Kurth, James. "Aerospace Production Lines and American Defense Spending." In Steven Rosen, ed., *Testing the Theory of the Military-Industrial Complex.* Lexington, Mass.: Lexington Books, 1975.

Kurth, James. "The Political Consequences of the Product Cycle: Industrial History and Political Outcomes." *International Organization* 33, no. 1 (winter 1979): 1–34.

Kurth, James. "The United States and Central America: Hegemony in Historical and Comparative Perspective." In Richard Feinberg, ed., *Central America: International Dimensions of the Crisis.* New York: Holmes & Meier, 1982.

Kurzer, Paulette. *Business and Banking: Political Change and Economic Integration in Western Europe.* Ithaca, N.Y.: Cornell University Press, 1993.

Lake, David. "In, Out, and Between: Reflections on Statist Theory." *Contention* 3, no. 3 (spring 1994): 155–162.

Lake, David, and G. John Ikenberry. "Toward a Realist Theory of State Action." *International Studies Quarterly* 33 (1989); 457–474.

Law, Christopher M., ed. *Restructuring the Global Automobile Industry.* London: Routledge, 1991.

Lenin, Vladimir I. *Imperialism: The Highest Stage of Capitalism.* Moscow: Progress Publishers, 1977.

Leys, Colin. "The 'Overdeveloped' Post-Colonial State," *Review of African Political Economy* 5 (1976): 39–48.

Lindblom, Charles. *Politics and Markets.* New York: Basic Books, 1977.

Lipson, Charles. "The Transformation of Trade." *International Organization* 36, no. 2 (spring 1982): 417–456.

List, Frederick. *The National System of Political Economy.* New York: Augustus M. Kelley, 1966.

Lowi, Theodore. "American Business, Public Policy, Case Studies, and Political Theory." *World Politics* 16 (July 1964): 677–693.

Lunch, W., and P. Sperlich. "American Public Opinion and the War in Vietnam." *Western Political Quarterly* 32, no. 1 (1979): 21–44.

Magaziner, Ira, and Robert Reich. *Minding America's Business.* New York: Harcourt Brace Javonovich, 1982.

Magdoff, Harry. *The Age of Imperialism.* New York: Monthly Review Press, 1969.

Markuson, Ann, Peter Hall, Scott Campbell, and Sabina Deitrick. *The Rise of the Gun Belt.* New York: Oxford University Press, 1991.

Mastanduno, Michael. "Trade as a Strategic Weapon: American and Alliance Export Control Policy in the Early Postwar Period." *International Organization* 42, no. 1 (winter 1988): 121–150.

McCarthy, Terrence. "American Dollar in Jeopardy: Can Flight to Gold Be Halted?" In Seymour Melman, ed., *The War Economy of the United States.* New York: St. Martin's Press, 1971.

Melman, Seymour. *Pentagon Capitalism.* New York: McGraw Hill, 1970.

Migdal, Joel. *Strong Societies and Weak States.* Princeton, N.J.: Princeton University Press, 1988.

Miliband, Ralph. *The State in Capitalist Society.* London: Weidenfield & Nicolson, 1968; and New York: Basic Books, 1969.

Mills, C. Wright. *The Power Elite.* New York: Oxford University Press, 1959.

Milner, Helen. *Resisting Protectionism: Global Industries and the Politics of International Trade.* Princeton, N.J.: Princeton University Press, 1988.

Mintz, Beth, and Michael Schwartz. *The Power Structure of American Business.* Chicago: University of Chicago Press, 1985.

Moody, Kim. "Reagan, the Business Agenda, and the Collapse of Labour." In Ralph Miliband, Leo Panitch, and John Saville, eds., *Socialist Register.* London: Merlin Press, 1987.

Moran, Theodore. *International Political Risk Assessment: The State of the Art.* Washington, D.C.: School of Foreign Service, Georgetown University, 1980.

Moran, Theodore. *Multinational Corporations and the Politics of Dependence: Copper in Chile.* Princeton, N.J.: Princeton University Press, 1974.

Morgenthau, Hans. *Politics Among Nations: The Struggle for Power and Peace.* New York: Alfred A. Knopf, 1973.

Mueller, J. "Trends in Popular Support for the Wars in Korea and Vietnam." *American Political Science Review* 65, no. 2 (1971): 358–375.

Nestor, William. *Japan's Growing Predominance Over the World Economy.* New York: St. Martin's Press, 1990.

Neumann, Franz. *Behemoth: The Structure and Practice of National Socialism, 1933–1944.* New York: Octagon Books, 1963.

Newman, Philip. *Cartel and Combine: Essays in Monopoly Production.* Ridgewood, N.J.: Foreign Studies Institute, 1964.

Nixon, Richard M. *The Memoirs.* New York: Grosset & Dunlap, 1978.

Nolt, James Herbert. "Business Conflict and the Origins of the Pacific War." 2 vols. Ph.D. diss., University of Chicago, 1994.

Nowell, Gregory P. *Mercantile States and the World Oil Cartel, 1900–1939.* Ithaca, N.Y.: Cornell University Press, 1994.

O'Connor, James. *The Fiscal Crisis of the State.* New York: St. Martin's Press, 1973.

Ohmae, Kenichi. *Triad Power: The Coming Shape of Global Competition.* New York: Free Press, 1985.

Olson, Mancur, Jr. *The Logic of Collective Action.* Cambridge, Mass.: Harvard University Press, 1971.

Oye, Kenneth, Robert Lieber, and Donald Rothchild, eds., *Eagle Resurgent? The Reagan Era in American Foreign Policy.* Boston: Little, Brown & Co., 1983.

Ozawa, T. "Japanese Multinationals and 1992." In B. Burgenmeier and J. L. Mucchielli, eds., *Multinationals and Europe, 1992,* pp. 135–154 London: Routledge, 1991.

Pastor, Robert. *Congress and the Politics of U.S. Foreign Economic Policy-Making: 1929–1976.* Berkeley: University of California Press, 1980.

Peele, Gillian. *Revival and Reaction: The Right in Contemporary America.* Oxford: Clarendon Press, 1984.

Peterson, Peter G. *U.S.-Soviet Commercial Relationships in a New Era.* Washington, D.C.: GPO, 1972.

Petras, James, and Morris Morley. "The U.S. Imperial State." In *Class, State, and Power in the Third World,* pp. 1–36. James Petras, et al., eds., London: Zed Books, 1981.

Pipes, Richard. *Survival Is Not Enough.* New York: Simon & Schuster, 1984.

Pollins, Brian. "Does Trade Still Follow the Flag?" *American Political Science Review* 83, no. 2 (1989).

Poulantzas, Nicos. *Political Power and Social Classes.* London: New Left Books, 1974.

Poulantzas, Nicos. *State, Power, and Socialism.* London: Verso, 1980.

Preeg, Ernest. "The Compatibility of Regional Economic Blocs and GATT." In Sidney Weintraub, ed., *Free Trade in the Western Hemisphere.* London: Sage Periodicals Press, 1993.

Przeworski, Adam. "Material Interests, Class Compromise, and the Transition to Socialism." In John Roemer, ed., *Analytical Marxism.* Cambridge: Cambridge University Press, 1986.

Robinson, Joan. *The Economics of Imperfect Competition.* London: Macmillan, 1965.

Rogowski, Ronald. *Commerce and Coalitions: How Trade Affects Domestic Political Alignments.* Princeton, N.J.: Princeton University Press, 1989.

Ross, Robert, and Kent Trachte. *Global Capitalism: The New Leviathan.* New York: City University of New York Press, 1991.

Rubenstein, James. "The Impact of Japanese Investment in the United States." In Law, ed., *Restructuring the Global Automobile Industry.*

Ruggie, John G. "International Responses to Technology: Concepts and Trends." *International Organization* 29 (summer 1975): 557–584.

Rupert, Mark Edward. "Producing Hegemony: State/Society Relations and the Politics of Productivity in the United States." *International Studies Quarterly* 34, no. 4 (December 1990): 427–456.

Russett, Bruce M. "A Countercombatant Deterrent? Feasibility, Morality, and Arms Control." In Sam Sarkesian, ed., *The Military-Industrial Complex: A Reassessment.* Beverly Hills, Calif.: Sage, 1972.

Samatar, A., and A. I. Samatar. "The Material Roots of the Suspended African State: Arguments from Somalia." *Journal of Modern African Studies* 25, no. 4 (1987): 669–690.

Sandbrook, Richard. *The Politics of Africa's Economic Recovery.* New York: Cambridge University Press, 1993.

Sandbrook, Richard. *The Politics of Africa's Economic Stagnation.* New York: Cambridge University Press, 1985.

Sandbrook, Richard. "Taming the African Leviathan." *World Policy Journal* 8, no. 3 (1990): 673–701.

Sanders, Jerry. *Peddlers of Crisis: The Committee on the Present Danger and the Politics of Containment.* Boston: South End Press, 1983.

Sassen, Saskia. *The Global City.* Princeton, N.J.: Princeton University Press, 1991.

Schattschneider, R. E. *Politics, Pressures, and the Tariff.* New York: Prentice-Hall, 1935.

Scheer, Robert. *With Enough Shovels: Reagan, Bush, and Nuclear War.* New York: Random House, 1982.

Schuknect, Ludger, and Joerg Stephan. "EC Trade Protection Law: Produmping or Antidumping?" *Public Choice* 80, nos. 1–2 (1994): 143–156.

Shoup, Lawrence, and William Minter. *Imperial Brain Trust: The Council on Foreign Relations and U.S. Foreign Policy.* New York: Monthly Review Press, 1977.

Skidmore, David. "The Carter Administration and Hegemonic Decline: Constraints on Policy Adjustment." Ph.D. diss., Stanford University, 1989.

Sklar, Holly. *Trilateralism: The Trilateral Commission and Elite Planning for World Management.* Boston: South End Press, 1980; and New York: Monthly Review Press, 1981.

Skocpol, Theda. "Bringing the State Back In: Strategies of Analysis in Current Research." In Evans, Rueschmeyer, and Skocpol, eds., *Bringing the State Back In,* introduction.

Skocpol, Theda. "The Limits of the New Deal System and the Roots of Contemporary Welfare Dilemmas." In Margaret Weir, Ann Shola Orloff, and Theda Skocpol, eds., *The Politics of Policy in the United States.* Princeton, N.J.: Princeton University Press, 1988.

Skocpol, Theda. "Political Response to Capitalist Crisis: Neo-Marxist Theories of the State and the Case of the New Deal." *Politics and Society* 10 (1980): 155–201.

Skocpol, Theda. *States and Social Revolutions: A Comparative Analysis of France, Russia, and China.* New York: Cambridge University Press, 1979.

Skocpol, Theda, and Margaret Weir. "State Structures and the Possibilities for 'Keynesian' Responses to the Great Depression in Sweden, Britain, and the United States." In Evans, Rueschemeyer, and Skocpol, eds., *Bringing the State Back In,* pp. 107–163.

Smith, Joan, Immmanuel Wallerstein, and Maria de Carmen Baerga. *Creating and Transforming Households: The Constraints of the World Economy.* Cambridge: Cambridge University Press, 1992.

Steinfels, Peter. *The Neoconservatives: The Men Who Are Changing America's Politics.* New York: Simon & Schuster, 1979.

Stern, Paula. *Water's Edge: Domestic Politics and the Making of American Foreign Policy.* Westport, Conn.: Greenwood Press, 1979.

Stockwell, John. *In Search of Enemies.* New York: W. W. Norton, 1978.

Strachey, John. *The End of Empire.* New York: Random House, 1959.

Strange, Susan and John Stopford. *Rival States, Rival Firms.* New York: Cambridge University Press, 1991.

Talbot, Strobe. *Deadly Gambits: The Reagan Administration and the Stalemate in Nuclear Arms Control.* London: Pan Books, 1985.

Tarbell, Ida M. *The Nationalizing of Business, 1878–1898.* New York: Macmillan, 1936.

Thurow, Lester. *Head to Head: The Coming Economic Battle Among Japan, Europe, and America.* New York: Morrow Press, 1992.

Tilly, Charles. *Coercion, Capital, and European States.* New York: Basil Blackwell, 1990.

Trubowitz, Peter, and Brian E. Roberts. "Regional Interests and the Reagan Military Buildup." *Regional Studies* 26, no. 6 (1992).

Tullock, Gordon. *The Economics of Special Privilege and Rent Seeking.* Boston: Kluwer Academic Publishers, 1989.

Vernon, Raymond. "International Investment and International Trade in the Product Cycle." *Quarterly Journal of Economics* (May 1966): 190–207.

Viner, Jacob. *Dumping: A Problem in International Trade.* New York: Augustus M. Kelley, 1966.

Vogel, David. *Fluctuating Fortunes: The Political Power of Business in America.* New York: Basic Books, 1989.

Wallerstein, Immanuel. *The Modern World System: Capitalist Agriculture and the Origins of the European Economy in the Sixteenth Century.* New York: Academic Press, 1976.

Wallerstein, Immanuel. *The Modern World System II: Mercantilism and the Consolidation of the European World Economy, 1600–1750.* New York: Academic Press, 1980.

Wallerstein, Immanuel. *The Modern World System III: The Second Era of Great Expansion of the Capitalist World Economy, 1730–1840s.* New York: Academic Press, 1989.

Wallerstein, Immanuel, and Terrence Hopkins, eds., *World Systems Analysis: Theory and Methodology.* Beverly Hills, Calif.: Sage, 1982.

Waltz, Kenneth. *Man, the State, and War: A Theoretical Analysis.* New York: Columbia University Press, 1959.

Waltz, Kenneth. "The Myth of National Interdependence." In Charles P. Kindleberger, ed., *The International Corporation*, pp. 205–226. Cambridge, Mass.: MIT Press.

Waltz, Kenneth. *Theory of International Politics.* Reading, Mass.: Addison-Wesley, 1979.

Wares, William A. *The Theory of Dumping and American Commercial Policy.* Lexington, Mass.: Lexington Books, 1977.

Weber, Max. *Economy and Society.* Trans. Guenther Roth and Claus Wittich. Berkeley: University of California Press, 1968.

Weber, Max. *The Methodology of the Social Sciences.* New York: Free Press, 1949.

Weidenbaum, Murray. "The Need for Reforming the Military-Industrial Relationship." In Morton H. Halperin, Jacob A. Stockfisch, and Murray Weidenbaum, eds., *The Political Economy of the Military-Industrial Complex.* Berkeley, Calif.: Institute of Business and Economic Research, 1973.

Weintraub, Sidney, Luis Rubio, and Alan Jones, eds., *U.S.-Mexican Industrial Integration.* Boulder, Colo.: Westview Press, 1991.

Wilczynski, J. *The Multinationals and East-West Relations: Towards Transideological Collaboration.* London: Macmillan, 1976.

Wilson, Graham. *Interest Groups in the United States.* Oxford: Clarendon Press, 1981.

Wolanin, Thomas R. *Presidential Advisory Commissions: Truman to Nixon.* Madison: University of Wisconsin Press, 1975.

Wolfe, Alan. *The Rise and Fall of the Soviet "Threat."* Washington, D.C.: Institute for Policy Studies, 1979.

Womack, James P., Daniel T. Jones and Daniel Roos. *The Machine That Changed the World.* New York: Macmillan, 1990.

Yarbrough, Beth V., and Robert M. Yarbrough. *The World Economy: Trade and Finance.* 2nd ed. Chicago: Dryden Press, 1991.

Young, Crawford, and Thomas Turner. *The Rise and Decline of the Zairian State.* Madison: University of Wisconsin Press, 1985.

Zumwalt, Elmo, "Heritage of Weakness: An Assessment of the 1970s." In Scott Thompson, ed., *National Security in the 1980s: From Weakness to Strength.* San Francisco: Institute for Contemporary Studies, 1980.

About the Book and Editor

Challenging the traditional notion that state officials act autonomously in formulating and implementing international policy, the contributors to this volume argue that the influence of organized business groups has been consistently underestimated in recent decades. Each uses a "business conflict" model of state-society relations as a new paradigm for understanding key policy conjunctures in U.S. trade and foreign policy. Applying this model to such concerns and crises as the Vietnam War, Afghanistan, the former Soviet Union, the North American Free Trade Agreement, the rise of the New Right, the Latin American debt crisis, and the political instability of West Africa, the contributors conclude that the political power of business groups in shaping policy is very real indeed. Their provocative conclusions advance our understanding of the relationship between business groups and policymakers in capitalist societies.

Ronald W. Cox is assistant professor of political science at Florida International University and is the author of *Power and Profits: U.S. Policy in Central America.* He has also published articles on the political economy of food production, international trade, and U.S. foreign policy.

About the Contributors

Amy Ansell is assistant professor of sociology at Bard College in New York, where she has authored *Race and Reaction: New Right Ideology in Britain and the United States,* forthcoming from New York University Press.

Erik A. Devereux is assistant professor of public policy at Carnegie Mellon University, where he has completed articles and working papers on the relationship between business firms and the media during the Vietnam War. He has also written extensively in the area of U.S. political economy.

Thomas Ferguson is professor of political science at the University of Massachusetts at Boston. His most recent work is *Golden Rule: The Investment Theory of Party Competition and the Logic of Money-Driven Political Systems* from University of Chicago Press.

Jeffry A. Frieden is professor of political science at the University of California at Los Angeles. He is the author of *Debt, Development, and Democracy* and numerous other works exploring the issues of sectoral and class interests in international political economy.

David N. Gibbs is assistant professor of political science at University of Arizona, where he has completed a book for the University Press of Chicago entitled *The Political Economy of Third World Intervention,* which explored the relationship between business sectors and the U.S. government in the making and implementation of foreign policy toward the Congo. Professor Gibbs has also written extensively on the history of U.S.-Soviet relations.

Gregory P. Nowell is assistant professor of political science at the State University of New York at Albany. His most recent work is *Mercantile States and the World Oil Cartel* from Cornell University Press.

William Reno is assistant professor of political science at Florida International University, where he has completed a book entitled *The Politics of Informal Markets and Reform in Africa,* from Cambridge University Press. He has also written extensively on the international political economy of African development.

Daniel Skidmore-Hess is assistant professor at Armstrong State College, where he is currently working on articles tracing the domestic determinants of U.S. trade policy and theories of globalization.

Jerri-Lynn Scofield is a Ph.D. candidate at Oxford University where she is working on a dissertation tracing the influence of U.S. business groups on trade policy toward the USSR.

William N. Stant is a Ph.D. candidate at Loyola University in Chicago. He is working on a dissertation which traces the influence of business groups on protectionist trade legislation in the late 1970s and early 1980s.